P9-EDQ-820

CONNECTIONISM: THEORY AND PRACTICE
Edited by Steven Davis

Vancouver Studies in Cognitive Science is a series of volumes in cognitive science. The volumes will appear annually and cover topics relevant to the nature of the higher cognitive faculties as they appear in cognitive systems, either human or machine. These will include such topics as natural language processing, modularity, the language faculty, perception, logical reasoning, scientific reasoning, and social interaction. The topics and authors are to be drawn from philosophy, linguistics, artificial intelligence, and psychology. Each volume will contain original articles by scholars from two or more of these disciplines. The core of the volumes will be articles and comments on these articles to be delivered at a conference held in Vancouver. The volumes will be supplemented by articles especially solicited for each volume which will undergo peer review. The volumes should be of interest to those in philosophy working in philosophy of mind and philosophy of language; to those in linguistics in psycholinguistics, syntax, language acquisition and semantics; to those in psychology in psycholinguistics, cognition, perception, and learning; and to those in computer science in artificial intelligence, computer vision, robotics, natural language processing, and scientific reasoning.

VANCOUVER STUDIES IN COGNITIVE SCIENCE
forthcoming volumes

VOLUME 4   *Foundations for Cognition*
Editors, John Macnamara, Psychology &
Gonzalo Reyes, Mathematics
McGill University & Université de Montréal

VOLUME 5   *Perception*
Editor, Kathleen Akins, Philosophy
University of Illinois - Champaign-Urbana

SERIES EDITOR

Steven Davis, Philosophy, Simon Fraser University

EDITORIAL ADVISORY BOARD

Susan Carey, Psychology, Massachusetts Institute of Technology
Elan Dresher, Linguistics, University of Toronto
Janet Fodor, Linguistics, Graduate Center,
    City University of New York
F. Jeffry Pelletier, Philosophy/Computing Science,
    University of Alberta
John Perry, Philosophy/Center for the Study of Language and
    Information, Stanford University
Zenon Pylyshyn, Psychology/Centre for Cognitive Science,
    University of Western Ontario
Len Schubert, Computing Science, University of Rochester
Brian Smith, System Sciences Lab, Xerox Palo Alto Research Center/
    Center for the Study of Language and Information,
    Stanford University

BOARD OF READERS

William Demopoulos, Philosophy, University of Western Ontario
Allison Gopnik, Psychology, University of California at Berkeley
Myrna Gopnik, Linguistics, McGill University
David Kirsh, Cognitive Science,
    University of California at San Diego
François Lepage, Philosophy, Université de Montréal
Robert Levine, Linguistics, Ohio State University
John MacNamara, Psychology, McGill University
Georges Rey, Philosophy, University of Maryland
Richard Rosenberg, Computing Science,
    University of British Columbia
Edward P. Stabler, Jr., Linguistics,
    University of California at Los Angeles
Susan Stucky, Center for the Study of Language and Information,
    Stanford University
Paul Thagard, Cognitive Science Lab, Princeton University

connectionism
theory
and
practice

edited by Steven Davis

New York   Oxford
OXFORD UNIVERSITY PRESS
1992

Oxford University Press

Oxford New York Toronto
Delhi Bombay Calcutta Madras Karachi
Kuala Lumpur Singapore Hong Kong Tokyo
Nairobi Dar es Salaam Cape Town
Melbourne Auckland

and associated companies in
Berlin Ibadan

Copyright 1992 by Oxford University Press, Inc.

Published by Oxford University Press, Inc.,
200 Madison Avenue, New York, NY 10016

Oxford is a registered trademark of Oxford University Press

All rights reserved. No part of this publication may be reproduced,
stored in a retrieval system, or transmitted, in any form or by any means,
electronic, mechanical, photocopying, recording or otherwise,
without the prior permission of the publisher.

Library of Congress Cataloging-in-Publication Data
Connectionism: Theory and Practice / edited by Steven Davis.
p. cm. ISBN 0-19-507665-06
1. Artificial Intelligence 2. Language and languages 3. Cognition
I. Davis, Steven, 1937-

9 8 7 6 5 4 3 2 1

Printed in the United States of America
on acid-free paper

Acknowledgments

I would like to thank the Social Sciences and Humanities Research Council of Canada and the Dean's Office and the Centre for Systems Science at Simon Fraser University for the generous support of the publication of the volume and of the conference at which many of the papers were delivered.

There are many people who helped in preparing the volume and the conference. Michael Hayward spent many long hours helping with the preparation of the camera ready copy and assisting with the art work; Joanne Richardson did a marvelous job copy editing the manuscript and Lindsey Martin and Anna Shishkov proof read various versions and helped enter the material into disk form. I would also like to thank Arifin Graham for the art work for the cover. Tom Perry and Tanya Beaulieu were enormous help with the conference.

I would also like to thank the authors of the volume for their patience with the delay in publication of the volume and with the number of telephone calls which they received from me about their papers.

Cambridge University Press was kind enough to allow me to reprint David Rumelhart's paper, "Towards a Microstructural Account of Human Reasoning," which appeared in *Similarity and Analogical Reasoning*, edited by S. Vosniadou and A. Ortony in 1989.

I would also like to thank my wife, Lysiane Gagnon, for her wonderful patience and encouragement.

AUGUSTANA UNIVERSITY COLLEGE
LIBRARY

Contents

Contents

connectionism
theory
and
practice

1

Using Coherence Assumptions to Discover the Underlying Causes of the Sensory Input

G.E. Hinton and S. Becker

This chapter is based on a conference talk given by the first author. In order to make the ideas as intelligible as possible we have attempted to preserve the informal style of the talk. Some of the more technical details can be found in Hinton and Becker (1990), and the full details are given in Becker and Hinton (1989).

Introduction to Neural Network Learning Procedures

During the last decade people have discovered new learning procedures for multi-layer networks of simple neuron-like units. Using these new procedures they have succeeded in getting neural networks to solve much more complicated tasks than was previously possible.

Supervised learning

The kind of learning procedure that has been most successful is called supervised learning. A multilayer network of the kind shown in Figure 1.1 is presented with an input vector at the bottom layer, which typically represents something like preprocessed sensory data. At the top layer, we want the network to produce an output vector that represents the correct response to the input vector. This response is often a classification in which one of the output units is active and the rest are silent, but other more complex kinds of response can also be learned. During training we tell the network the correct output vector for each input vector, and the aim of the learning is to reduce the difference between the actual output vector produced by the network and the desired output vector. This is achieved by gradually modifying all the weights in the network in the appropriate direction. For each training case an algorithm called back-propagation (Rumelhart, Hinton, and Williams 1986) can be used to determine how much a change in a weight will change the discrepancy between the actual and the desired output vectors. A simple learning procedure called 'steepest descent' is then used to update the weights. Each weight is modified in proportion to how rapidly a change in the weight reduces the squared difference between the actual and desired output vectors.

After learning, we hope that the network will do more than just give the correct outputs for the training cases. We hope that when we give it an input vector that it has never seen before it will generalize correctly and will therefore give the correct output vector. There has been a lot of progress, both empirical and theoretical (Baum and Haussler 1989), in achieving good generalization. So far, supervised learning has been much more successful than the methods described below. But it is not very plausible as a model of most human learning, because it requires a teacher and because the learning speed is much too slow in very large networks. Also, it is hard to see how to implement anything like the back-propagation process in real neural networks. The naive idea of using the same connections in the opposite direction is certainly wrong.

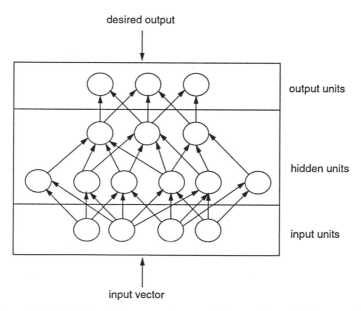

Figure 1.1: A typical multilayer neural network that can be trained to transform input vectors into the desired output vectors. The network learns by adjusting the weights on the connections.

Reinforcement learning

There is another kind of learning procedure, called reinforcement learning, where we do not tell the network the right answer. We just tell it how good its answer is. Typically, we interpret the output vector as a command to perform some action, and then we tell it how good that action was under these circumstances. Using this reinforcement signal, we try to train the network so that it learns weights that make it perform the actions with the highest payoffs. It is easier to see how this kind of learning could be implemented in a real neural network, but reinforcement learning has been less successful in practice than has supervised learning, and we will not say any more about it here.

Unsupervised learning

There is a third kind of learning procedure, called unsupervised learning, that is the subject of this chapter. In unsupervised learning a network just looks at the world, and, without any further instructions, it constructs an internal representation. Clearly, if we could get this kind of learning to work it would be fascinating. Some people believe that the whole idea is preposterous because it is impossible to know what is worth representing until we know what the task is. This objection is superficially reasonable but deeply wrong. It is wrong because it ignores the fact that if two representations capture the data equally well, but one representation has much lower complexity than does the other, then the lower complexity representation is objectively better. Naturally, it is possible to raise endless philosophical objections to this commonsense argument. We think that the simplest way to show that it is possible to construct sensible internal representations without any supervision or reinforcement is simply to build systems that do it.

If we think of learning as altering the weights in a network so as to achieve something, it is clear that the big problem with unsupervised learning is the question of what we are trying to achieve. This chapter proposes an answer to that question: The learning is trying to achieve significant agreement between the outputs of different modules that look at different parts of the input. We show that by reaching agreement the modules can internally reconstruct the real external causes of the input. This may be of some interest to philosophers (and even sociologists), because it can be viewed as the social construction of *objective* reality. Provided the members of the society operate on different inputs, the only things they can non-trivially agree upon are the common causes of their different inputs. The difficulties come in getting this idea to actually work.

Why supervised learning procedures are a dead end

In the long run, the supervised learning procedures, even though they have been very successful so far, are not going to explain how people form their internal representations of the world. The fatal flaw of a pure supervised learning procedure is the way in which the learning time scales with the sizes of the network and the task. Suppose we have a network, even a fairly loosely-coupled, tree-structured network, as shown in Figure 1.2, where there is apparently not much interaction between separate parts of the tree.

As we make bigger and bigger networks with more and more layers and more and more units per layer, the learning will get slower and slower. Even for networks of fixed depth, the learning time (in a serial simulation) is approximately proportional to the cube of the number of connections (Hinton 1989). So even if we use separate hardware for each connection, if we make the network a thousand times as big, it takes a million times as long to learn. The poor scaling is caused by the fact that the back-propagation process couples all the weights together, even in a loosely connected network. In Figure 1.2, for example, a change in w_1 causes a change in the output of the network. This causes a change in the difference between the actual and the desired output, so it changes the error-derivatives that are back-propagated to w_2. So changing w_1 changes the way in which modifications to w_2 affect the error. This means that when we modify all the other weights a little, the effect of a change in w_2 may be altered a lot, so a modification which would have reduced the error if the other weights had stayed the same

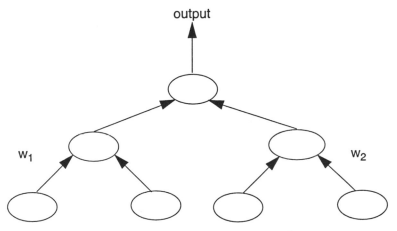

Figure 1.2: A sparsely connected network that illustrates how supervised learning couples all the weights together (see text).

may actually increase the error a lot. The only way around this is to make all the modifications very tiny, so learning becomes very slow.

To get good scaling, what we would really like is some way of knowing what one part of the network should be doing internally without any external teacher and without any dependence on what other parts of the network are doing. We need one piece of the network to arrive at a good internal representation of the data solely on the basis of its own input.

How much innate knowledge is required?

One of the main motivations of this chapter is to resolve, or at least illuminate, the following issue: How much innate knowledge does a system need to have in order to be able to figure out the causes of its sensory inputs? This is, of course, a question that philosophers have asked. We think that this is an empirical question which cannot be answered just by thinking about it. We have to try out particular learning techniques operating in particular worlds to get a reasonable feel for what works and what does not. It is important to take the speed of learning into account, since, if we allow evolutionary time, it is clear that a heap of inorganic mud (or something similar) can form complex internal representations, and few people would attribute much innate knowledge to a heap of mud.

There is a traditional 'empiricist' position that claims you can learn everything starting with no innate ideas. That type of armchair empiricism is quite different from the open-minded empiricist position that claims that questions like this should be settled by building systems and seeing what works. This chapter explores whether a particular type of innate goal is sufficient to allow the causes of the sensory input to be discovered in reasonable time. The innate goal might be called a 'transcendental aesthetic' because the system has it before it looks at the data, and it causes the system to prefer some representations to others.

Spatio-temporal Coherence as a Principle for Constructing Representations

We show that a single aesthetic principle, a principle for choosing between internal representations, allows a system to discover a lot. The principle is simply to find properties that are coherent across different parts of the sensory input. After a brief discussion of some of the many types of coherence, we describe one way of formalizing the idea of coherence and show what it can do in a few specific cases.

There are all sorts of coherence in the sensory input that organisms receive from the real world. For example, there is coherence between visual input and tactile input. People sometimes think that this can provide a quick solution to the mystery of how we figure out what the visual input represents. The proposed solution is that we just reach out and touch reality and use this 'direct' knowledge to calibrate vision. The problem is that it is just as difficult to know what tactile stimuli represent. As we shall see, both problems can be finessed by discovering what is common to the two modalities (and to different spatio-temporal parts of each modality).

Another type of coherence which some people think is very special is the coherence between the motor output and the sensory input. It is often claimed that only by acting in the world can we learn what the sensory input really represents. We suspect that many of the people who regard action as a *necessary* condition of objective knowledge arrive at this view because they cannot imagine any alternative possibility.

A very informative kind of coherence is the temporal coherence between the visual input at two adjacent times. In a world of translating and rotating rigid objects, temporally adjacent images will often contain different projections of the very same three-dimensional shape. So a mechanism that learns to extract the same underlying representation from adjacent images should discover true three-dimensional shape, because this underlying cause of the images is more coherent across time than is the raw sensory input itself. If the objects are in free motion, other temporal invariants include their linear and angular momenta. So the same type of mechanism should be able to extract these fundamental physical properties, although we suspect that it will be a long time before we can get simple learning mechanisms to make such profound discoveries.

There is another type of coherence that people in vision have thought about a lot – coherence between different sources of depth information. Stereo, texture, shading, motion, and contour all provide information about depth, so by searching for parameter values on which all these information sources can agree, it should be possible to discover depth.

In this chapter we focus on yet another type of coherence that exists *within* a modality such as vision – the coherence between the sensory input from nearby parts of space. In real images, nearby patches of the image are usually caused by nearby parts of the surface of the same object. So the patches of surface that give rise to nearby image patches usually have similar depths, surface orientations, reflectances, etc. As a result, one patch of an image typically contains a lot of information about what is in a neighbouring patch of an image. But this mutual information between neighbouring patches is in a very messy form – given all the intensity values in one patch, it is very hard to predict the particular combination of intensity values that will be found in the neighbouring patch. Intuitively, it would be much easier to make predictions if we first converted the raw intensities into underlying properties of surfaces, such as depth and surface orientation, and then predicted the depth and orientation of one patch from the depth and orientation of its neighbours. We can stand this argument on its head and say that depth, surface orientation, texture etc. can be *defined* as those properties which are coherent in a simple way and are, therefore, easy to predict from patch to patch. The learning procedure works by homing in on those locally extractable properties that are most coherent from patch to patch.

We can think about coherence in terms of probability distributions. Suppose we consider two nearby intensity patches in an image (like patch A and patch B in Figure 1.3). Let us suppose they are 4 x 4 patches, so the intensities in one patch correspond to a point in a sixteen-dimensional space, because they can be described by sixteen numbers. Similarly, the intensities of the neighbouring patch are a point in another sixteen-dimensional space. Now we can ask the following question: if I tell you where A is in its sixteen-dimensional space, what can you tell me about where B is in its sixteen-dimensional space? Obviously, you

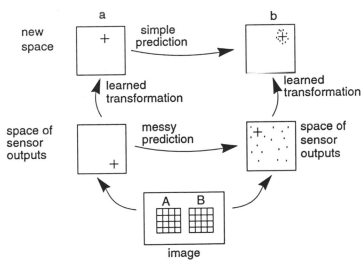

Figure 1.3: The intensities in an image patch can be represented as points in a high dimensional space. Using the obvious space in which each axis corresponds to the intensity of one pixel, it is hard to predict the representation of patch B from the representation of patch A. The representations are shown as + signs, and the distribution of predictions of B from A is shown as dots. If the network can transform the raw input to a new space that makes explicit the spatially coherent underlying causes of the input, it is much easier to predict the representation of B from the representation of A.

cannot tell me exactly where B is because it is not completely determined by A, but, after seeing A, you should be able to guess B better
than you could if you did not see A. The problem is that the information
that A provides about B is in a terrible form. Before you see A, the probability distribution for B will have high entropy – it will be very spread
out. After seeing A, this distribution has much less entropy – it is much
less spread out, because A contains a lot of information about B. Unfortunately, knowledge of A does not concentrate the distribution for B
around a single point – it concentrates it around a lot of different points,
as shown in Figure 1.4b. This makes it very hard to say anything sensible about B when given A, and it also makes it hard to represent what
A conveys about B without using an enormous sixteen-dimensional
table.

Things would be much simpler if knowledge of A caused the distribution for B to concentrate around a single point. The idea of the learning
procedure is that we can achieve this by working in a different space.
We transform the sixteen-dimensional space of the raw intensites into
some other space, in which knowledge of the representation of A has a
simple effect on the probability distribution of the representation of B.
There are many possible definitions of 'simple effect.' To begin with we
shall assume that we want the information to be in the following form:
A and B are each represented by single numbers, a and b. When a is unknown, b has high variance, but when a is known, b has more or less the
same value as a, with a little variance that is much smaller than the variance of b before a is known. In other words, we want to find a transformation from the raw input space into a one-dimensional space in which
a and b have approximately the same value.

 If we chose an arbitrary transformation, the distribution of b given a
would be no tighter than the distribution of b when a was unknown. So

B $\longrightarrow$

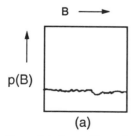
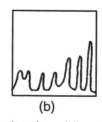
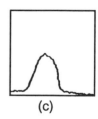

p(B)

(a)   (b)   (c)

Figure 1.4: A one-dimensional illustration of two different ways in which the entropy of
  a distribution can be reduced. (a) has high entropy because all the possibilities are
  more or less equally probable. (b) has much lower entropy because it is less uniform,
  but it has many peaks, so it is hard to describe. (c) has roughly the same entropy as (b)
  but is a much easier distribution to describe.

we can search for the transformation we want by changing the weights in a network so as to make the distribution of b given a as tight as possible relative to the distribution of b alone. In fact, to make things symmetrical, it is better to change the weights to optimize the following function:

$$I(a; b) = log[V(a + b)/V(a - b)] \qquad (1)$$

where V is the variance measured across the ensemble of different training cases. This information measure is clearly large when a and b vary a lot from image to image, but $a - b$ varies very little. In other words, a is approximately equal to b relative to how much a and b vary. One advantage of using this equation is that, given appropriate gaussian assumptions, it represents the information that a and b contain about the common causes of the inputs A and B (see Becker and Hinton 1989 for details).

So we start with a preconceived notion of how we would like the representation of patch A to convey information about the representation of patch B, and we then adjust the weights so as to capture as much of the mutual information between A and B as possible in this preconceived framework. Later, we will see how the framework can be relaxed to allow more complex types of mutual information to be captured.

An Example: Discovering Depth in Stereo-pairs

As an example of the power of the spatial coherence learning algorithm, we are going to see how it can discover the third dimension. Unfortunately, this example requires an understanding of how depth is encoded in stereo images, so this needs to be explained.

A stereo-pair is a pair of images of the same scene taken from slightly different viewpoints corresponding to the two eyes. Stereograms contain information about the depths of the surfaces in the scene, because a feature in one image is shifted sideways relative to the same feature in the other image, and the magnitude of this shift is determined by the depth of the feature. The shift is called the disparity of the feature and it does not directly specify the absolute depth, because the disparity can be altered just by moving one eye relative to the other. Simplifying the geometry a little, disparity specifies the depth of the feature relative to the fronto-parallel plane at which the optical axes of the two eyes converge. This is called the plane of fixation. In the rest of this chapter we use the word depth to mean depth relative to the plane of fixation, and we assume that all the depths are small and all the images are near the centre of the field of view, so that depth is simply proportional to disparity.

In a stereo-pair of a real scene, there are many other sources of information about depth in addition to disparity. These sources include all the various cues that allow us to perceive depth with one eye closed. To eliminate most of these other cues, we can use 'random-dot' stereograms in which we imagine that a 3-D surface is covered in random dots, which are then imaged from two slightly different viewpoints.

If we form a random-dot stereo-pair of a surface whose depth varies smoothly, nearby patches of the image-pair will have similar disparities. So it should be possible to discover that disparity is a property worth extracting by simply searching for properties that have similar values for nearby patches. Notice that the number of potential properties is huge, so to home in on disparity will probably take quite a lot of computation.

One more technical trick must be used before we can turn the learning algorithm loose on stereo-pairs. We could use binary images in which the dots on the surface project to white pixels and the remaining pixels are black. Unfortunately, this makes it very hard to represent continuous gradations of depth, because a dot in one image must be shifted by in integer number of pixels relative to a dot in the other image. So only a discrete set of depths can be represented. Figure 1.5 shows how we can overcome this difficulty by using real-valued intensities for the

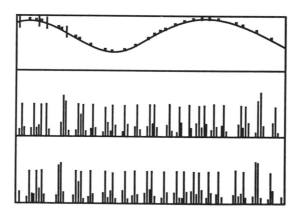

Figure 1.5: Part of a cubic spline fitted through seven randomly chosen control points with randomly located features scattered on it, and the 'intensity' values in the two images of the surface strip. The images are made by taking two slightly different parallel projections of the feature points, filtering the projections through a Gaussian, and sampling the filtered projections at equally spaced sample points. The sample values in corresponding patches of the two images are used as the inputs to a module. The boundaries of two neighbouring patches are shown on the spline.

pixels. After projecting a dot into an image, it is blurred through a gaussian, and the intensity of the blur is sampled at discrete points corresponding to the pixels. The intensities of several adjacent pixels then encode the exact location of the dot in the image. If it moves sideways slightly, the intensities change slightly, so disparities are represented exactly, provided we do not have too many dots right next to each other.

Using one-dimensional strips of stereo images like the ones shown in Figure 1.5, we tested out the learning procedure and discovered the various technical tricks that were necessary to get it to work in reasonable time (Becker and Hinton 1989). Figure 1.6 shows the type of network we used. Roughly corresponding patches of the two images are used as input to module A, and nearby patches are used as input to module B. The inputs are not directly connected to the 'outputs' of the two modules, because we know that hidden units are required to extract higher order properties like disparity. So each module is given a hidden layer. The hidden units are of the type most commonly used with back-propagation. They have a real valued output between zero and one, which is a logistic function of the total input they receive from the layer below. The output units, a and b, are linear. The modules start with small random weights.

A set of 1,000 training stereo-pairs is presented to the two modules, and they accumulate statistics, such as the mean and variance of $a - b$ and $a + b$. The 1,000 training cases are then presented again, and, for each training case, each module computes the derivative of the mutual information measure in equation 1 with respect to the activity of the output unit for that training case. This computation of the derivative is performed by a separate computer program. We are working on ways of performing an equivalent computation in a neural net, but for the research described here, this part is distinctly unneuronlike. Given the

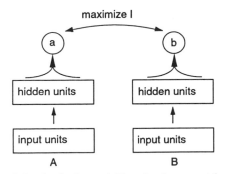

Figure 1.6: Two modules that look at neighbouring image patches and learn to transform their input vectors into scalar output values that have high mutual information.

derivative of the mutual information w.r.t. the output, it is then trivial to use the back-propagation algorithm to calculate the derivative of the mutual information w.r.t. each weight in a module. After accumulating these weight derivatives for all 1,000 training cases, the weights are updated in the direction that increases the mutual information (see Becker and Hinton 1989 for details). This whole procedure, involving two sweeps through all 1,000 training cases, is then repeated with the new set of weights. Many weight updates are required before the modules eventually learn to extract disparity.

After learning, we can get some idea of what the outputs of the modules represent by plotting the activity of an output unit against the depth of the surface strip that was used to generate the image. Figure 1.7 shows such a plot for a network that was trained on images of flat, fronto-parallel surfaces. The fact that the plot forms a diagonal band shows that the output unit represents depth. The procedure also works when applied to images of curved surfaces, but the representation of depth that it discovers is noisier. Remember that we did not give it any knowledge of the third dimension. It discovered depth because depth is what is coherent across the 2-D image space. Of course, there is a worrying sense in which it has no idea what the outputs of the modules mean, but that does not worry the network and does not stop it from extracting depth and making it explicit in the activity level of a single unit.

More Complex Kinds of Coherence

In the previous example, we assumed that the network should try to discover a property which was approximately equal for nearby patches of its input. This assumption is good for discovering depth in an ensemble of stereo images of fronto-parallel planes, but it is less good for

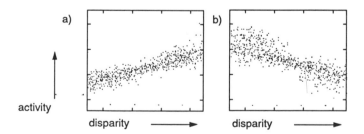

Figure 1.7: The activity of the linear output unit of a module (vertical axis) as a function of the disparity (horizontal axis) for all 1,000 test cases using planar surface strips. (a) shows the response for a network trained with ten adaptive nonlinear hidden units per module, and (b) shows the response for a network trained with 100 nonadaptive Gaussian hidden units per module.

slanted planes or curved surfaces. While it is true that nearby patches have similar depths even for these more complex surfaces, there are much stronger regularities. For a slanted plane, the depth at one point is exactly the average of the depth at two neighbouring points. For curved surfaces of the kind we used, the depth at a point can be computed almost exactly by linearly combining the depths of two neighbouring points on either side. If all five points are equally spaced on a straight line, the depth, d_3, of the middle point is almost exactly determined by the following linear equation:

$$d_3 = -0.2d_1 + 0.7d_2 + 0.7d_4 - 0.2d_5 \qquad (2)$$

So instead of building on the assumption that we should extract a property that has similar values for neighbouring patches, we can build on the far more general assumption that we should extract, from each patch of the image, a property that is a linear combination of the properties extracted from nearby patches. As we shall see, it is not necessary to assume that the linear function has the particular coefficients shown in equation 2. The learning procedure can discover the best coefficients at the same time as it discovers how to extract the property that is linearly predictable from the immediate context. There is a loose analogy here with a very successful methodology in physics: Try to find properties of the world (such as current and voltage or length and force) that are related together by linear equations.

Figure 1.8 shows the type of architecture that we used. The network does not know what it is meant to be extracting. Its aim in life is to

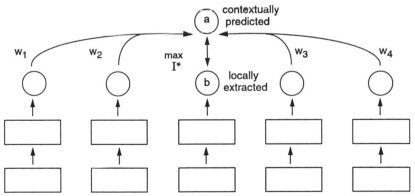

Figure 1.8: A network in which the goal of the learning is to maximize the information between the output of a local module and the contextually predicted output that is computed by using a linear function of the outputs of nearby modules. This network is used for curved surface interpolation.

extract something locally from each patch that agrees with some kind of average of the things that it is extracting from nearby patches. In trying to maximize the mutual information between the locally extracted property value and the contextually predicted value, the network computes how the mutual information would change if it changed the locally extracted value. Then it uses back-propagation to train up the weights that are doing the local extraction. It also computes the derivative of the mutual information w.r.t. the contextually predicted value. By back-propagating this derivative through the weighted connections coming from nearby patches, it can learn the weights that should be used in the linear prediction as well as the weights used for extracting property values in nearby modules.

More details of the actual learning are given in Becker and Hinton (1989). Several technical tricks were used to speed up the learning. After learning, the network can extract depth from curved surfaces, and it has also learned how to interpolate these surfaces. The actual coefficients it learned for the linear interpolating function were -0.04, 0.64, 0.65, -0.04. These differ slightly from the optimal coefficients shown in equation 2, but they actually work better, because the locally extracted depth estimates are noisy. With noisy depth estimates it is better to use smaller coefficients in the interpolating function, because the squares of the coefficients amplify the variance of the noise in the depth estimates. So the network learned an even better interpolating function than we had intended.

Discovering the Single Viewpoint Constraint

We have used random-dot stereo-pairs to illustrate the power of a learning algorithm that uses an assumption of spatial coherence. To dispel the idea that the algorithm only works for finding depth in stereo-pairs, we briefly describe a completely different example, in which the same basic learning procedure discovers a very significant underlying regularity in images of a rigid object.

Consider an ensemble of images of the same two-dimensional shape, but at different positions, orientations, and scales. To make life easy for ourselves, let us constrain the images so that one end of the object always falls in one half of the image and the other end in the other half, as shown in Figure 1.9. Now, what kind of mutual information exists between the two halves of the image? Since all the images are of the same object, there is no point in identifying the object from one half of the image and predicting that the other half contains another part of the same object. We already know this, so it conveys no information. All of the mutual information lies in the fact that the position, size, and

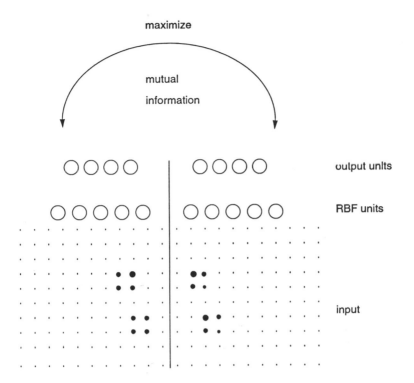

Figure 1.9: A module with two halves that try to agree on their predictions. The input to each half is 100 intensity values (indicated by the areas of the black circles). Each half has 200 gaussian radial basis hidden units (constrained to be the same for the two halves) connected to four linear output units via connections with modifiable weights.

orientation of one end of the object completely determine the position, size, and orientation of the other end. If you look at one half of the image you can predict the size, position, and orientation of the whole object. If you look at the other half you can predict the same four parameters. So these four parameters are invariant across space. They can be extracted locally from each half of the image, and the parameters extracted from adjacent patches will then agree perfectly.

Figure 1.9 shows a network, designed by Rich Zemel, that learns to extract these four parameters. The intensities in each half of the image are converted into the activity levels of 17200 'radial basis functions.' These radial basis functions (Moody and Darken 1989) are non-adaptive and are introduced to allow the network to extract properties that are nonlinear functions of the raw images. The only parts of the network that learn are the weights connecting the radial basis functions to the four linear output units of each module. These weights are modified to maximize the mutual information between the four output units of one module and the four output units of the other. Since the output of each module is a vector of four activities instead of a single scalar, we need to optimize a slightly more complex information measure than the one given in equation 1.

$$I(a; b) = log[Det(Cov(a+b))/Det(Cov(a-b))] \qquad (3)$$

where *Cov* means covariance matrix, *Det* means determinant, and *a* and *b* are vectors.

The network learns to extract four parameters that agree very significantly between the two modules. We hoped that these four parameters would be a simple linear transformation of the x-position, y-position, horizontal-extent, and vertical-extent of the object. Unfortunately, they are not (Zemel and Hinton 1990) – they are a nonlinear encoding of these four parameters.

One good thing about this kind of network is that, after learning, it is very good at recognizing the object. If we show it an image of the object it was trained on, the outputs of the two modules will agree fairly precisely. If, however, we deform the object, or we use an image of some other object, the outputs of the two modules will not agree, so the network can use this lack of agreement as evidence that its object is not present. This may seem like a curious way to recognize objects, but, in practice, the very best systems for recognizing three-dimensional objects from single grey-level images work on exactly this principle (Lowe 1985).

Conclusion

We have seen how the assumption of spatial coherence can be used to discover important underlying properties in two very different ensembles of images. Several different kinds of 'innate' knowledge were built into these networks:

(1) Innate knowledge about two-dimensional spatial proximity is built into the architecture of the network.
(2) The number and width of the hidden layers within each module encodes assumptions about the complexity of the process that extracts underlying parameters from an image patch.
(3) The way in which the outputs of modules interact encodes assumptions about whether the underlying parameters are invariant across space or just linearly predictable across space.

(4) The number of outputs of each module (and the form of the information measure being optimized) encode information about how many parameters should be extracted from each patch.

Nevertheless, the basic principle is the same in both the tasks described and can be applied to a very wide range of other tasks. By using other forms of coherence, particularly coherence across time, it should be possible to discover a great many of the underlying causes of the sensory input with no explicit instruction.

Of course this kind of learning procedure would not work if we lived in a pathological world in which underlying causes did not leave coherent footprints in the sensory data. Cryptographers spend their time trying to design schemes for encrypting underlying structure in such a pathological way. Fortunately, although nature may play dice, it is not a cryptographer. In the natural world the sensory data is not produced by an adversary – it is produced by physics. So although, in the worst case, a relatively simple technique would not stand a chance of working, in reality it can do a very good job of discovering the underlying causal structure.

Acknowledgments

We thank Peter Brown, Barak Pearlmutter, and the Connectionist Research Group at the University of Toronto for helpful discussions. This research was supported by grants from the Information Technology Research Centre of Ontario and the Natural Science and Engineering Research Council of Canada. Geoffrey Hinton is the Noranda fellow of the Canadian Institute for Advanced Research.

References

Baum, E.B. and Haussler, D.(1989). What size net gives valid generalization? *Neural Computation* 1: 151-60

Becker, S. and Hinton, G.E. (1989). Spatial coherence as an internal teacher for a neural network. University of Toronto Technical Report CRG-TR-89-7

Hinton, G.E. (1989). Connectionist learning procedures. *Artificial Intelligence* 40: 185-234

– and Becker, S. (1990). An unsupervised learning procedure that discovers surfaces in random-dot stereograms. *Proceedings of the International Joint Conference on Neural Networks*, Lawrence Erlbaum Associates, Hillsdale, NJ 1: 218-22

Lowe, D.G. (1985). *Perceptual Organization and Visual Recognition*. Kluwer Academic Publishers, Boston

Moody, J. and Darken, C. (1989). Fast learning in networks of locally-tuned processing units. *Neural Computation* 1: 281-94

Rumelhart, D.E., Hinton, G.E., and Williams, R.J. (1986). Learning representations by back--propagating errors. *Nature* 323: 533-36

Zemel, R.S. and Hinton, G.E. (1991). Discovering and using the single viewpoint constraint. To appear in *Neural Information Processing Systems 3*, Morgan Kaufmann: San Mateo, CA

COMMENT

Modularity, Unsupervised Learning, and Supervised Learning

Michael I. Jordan and Robert A. Jacobs

Hinton and Becker present a novel unsupervised learning algorithm for connectionist networks. The algorithm is one of the most interesting yet proposed in the literature on unsupervised learning. It has a number of features that distinguish it from classical algorithms in the unsupervised learning framework; most noteworthy among these are the interaction between two or more network modules and the use of the mutual information between module outputs as the criterion to drive the adaptive process. These aspects of the proposal have implications for a number of general issues in the study of learning systems – in particular, the relationship between modularity and learning, the role of competition and co-operation in learning, and the relationship between unsupervised learning and supervised learning. In this chapter, we discuss certain of these implications in the light of other recent work on connectionist learning. We also provide some critical commentary on technical aspects of the IMAX learning scheme.

Unsupervised Learning and Supervised Learning

We begin with a discussion of the distinction between unsupervised learning and supervised learning. First and foremost, we would like to temper the critique of supervised learning offered by Hinton and Becker. In particular, we do not subscribe to the view that supervised learning is 'not very plausible as a model of human learning because it requires a teacher.' To the contrary, we believe that much of human learning, human skill learning in particular, is supervised learning. To be sure, our conception of supervised learning goes beyond the classical paradigm in which a 'teacher' provides explicit targets for the output units of a network – we agree with Hinton and Becker that such a paradigm is limited as a model of human learning. Human learning, however, can often be characterized as a process of error correction in which an internal hypothesis or control strategy is formulated and

21

tested, errors are made, and the errors are used to improve the hypothesis. The notion of an error implies the notion of a goal, thus adaptive processes that are driven by errors have more of the character of supervised learning than unsupervised learning. The problem for the classical supervised learning paradigm is not that errors or goals are unavailable, but that they are not always provided in a format that is easily deciphered by the learner.

To develop this argument in more detail, consider the following example (cf. Jordan and Rumelhart 1990). When learning to throw a ball at a target the human learner does not typically have access to a 'teacher'; that is, there is no external agency to provide explicit instruction regarding the arm motions that are needed to propel the ball towards the target. As Jordan and Rumelhart point out, however, the ball-throwing task has the ingredients of a supervised learning task: There is a desired outcome, which is the image of the ball striking the target; there is an actual outcome, which is the image of the ball missing the target; and there is an error between the desired outcome and the actual outcome. Moreover, the directionality of the visual error vector clearly plays a role in the process by which humans correct the motor program that underlies throwing behaviour. Tosses too far to the left lead to an attempt to throw more to the right. The problem for classical supervised learning algorithms is that the errors that are needed to correct the arm motion are not provided explicitly in the visual data.

How can the ball-throwing task be treated within the supervised learning framework? Jordan and Rumelhart propose that the supervised learning paradigm must be modified to include a modelling phase that precedes the traditional error-correcting phase. During the modelling phase the learner gathers data that allow errors to be transformed appropriately. In particular, the learner acquires an internal model of the relationship between actions (e.g., the motion of the arm) and sensory outcomes (e.g., the trajectories of the ball). The acquisition of an internal model (a 'forward model' in Jordan and Rumelhart's terminology) makes it possible to relate errors between desired outcomes and actual outcomes to errors in the variables that the learner controls directly. In particular, the learner utilizes the forward model to compute estimates of the sensitivities of changes in ball trajectories with respect to changes in arm motion. These sensitivities are used in the error-correcting phase to convert errors in ball trajectories into errors in arm motion. The latter can then be used directly in changing the motor program. This two-phase approach is general enough to handle a variety of problems that arise in human skill learning (Jordan 1990; Jordan and Rumelhart 1990).

To summarize, the classical notion of 'learning with a teacher' can be misleading as a model of human learning if taken too literally. It is indeed unreasonable to assume that an external teacher provides an explicit target vector to the mental agent responsible for learning a particular task. This does not imply, however, that the supervised learning paradigm should be abandoned. Rather, learning systems must include mechanisms to induce desired outputs from information that is implicit in the training data. The two-phase approach of Jordan and Rumelhart is an example of such a mechanism in which errors in the outputs of a network are induced by making use of an internal model of an external transformation. We suspect that additional techniques such as this will be developed and that a more realistic conception of supervised learning will involve a variety of mechanisms to handle situations in which desired outputs are well-defined but not provided explicitly to the learner.

Similarly, it can be argued that unsupervised learning techniques that rely 'only on the input' are of limited utility and that realistic unsupervised learning algorithms must incorporate devices that compare the outputs of different subsystems. Indeed, the proposal by Hinton and Becker can be seen as an example of such an approach. Their algorithm can be thought of as a form of unsupervised learning that has elements of the comparative process normally associated with supervised learning. To see this, consider that the mutual information between random variables A and B can be written as:

$$I(A, B) = H(A) + H(B) - H(A,B) \tag{1}$$

where $H(A)$ is the entropy of A, $H(B)$ is the entropy of B, and $H(A,B)$ is the joint entropy of A and B. In the Gaussian case this equation leads directly to Equation 1 in Hinton and Becker. Mutual information can also be written in an asymmetric form:

$$I(A, B) = H(A) - H(A \mid B) \tag{2}$$

or alternatively:

$$I(A, B) = H(B) - H(B \mid A) \tag{3}$$

where $H(A)$ is the entropy of A and $H(A \mid B)$ is the conditional entropy of A given B (similarly for $H(B)$ and $H(B \mid A)$). From the point of view of A, the term $- H(A \mid B)$ is a sensible supervised cost function in which B is viewed as indirectly providing a target value for A. Indeed, closely related information-theoretic cost functions have been proposed in the context of supervised learning (Hinton 1989). Similarly, A can be viewed as indirectly providing a target value for B (cf. Equation 3). This perspective simply restates Hinton and Becker's desiderata that modules A and B should have 'consistent' outputs. The particular target value that is chosen for each module is determined by the additional requirement that $H(A)$ and $H(B)$ – the entropies of the respective distributions – be maximized. Requiring that the output of a module have maximum entropy given its input is a technique utilized in the classical unsupervised learning framework (Linsker 1988). Thus the IMAX learning algorithm has aspects of both traditional supervised learning and traditional unsupervised learning. The algorithm is clearly closer in spirit to the latter; however, we would be reluctant to classify IMAX as an algorithm that depends 'only on the input.' Rather, by using one view of an object to provide information about another view of an object, the algorithm takes a step towards the middle ground of algorithms that induce desired outputs from information that is implicit in the training data.

Finally, we would like to suggest that the theoretical assumptions underlying supervised learning and unsupervised learning are not as different as Hinton and Becker would have us believe. The distinction between supervised learning and unsupervised learning that underlies their discussion is a traditional distinction that has its origins in the literature on pattern recognition (Duda and Hart 1973). In this literature, each input vector is assumed to belong to one of a discrete set of categories. The problem is to process the data in the training set for the purposes of predicting the categories of novel inputs. If the correct categories of the vectors in the training set are known, the learning algorithm is said to be supervised, otherwise the learning algorithm is said to be unsupervised. In the classical literature, most unsupervised learning algorithms are essentially algorithms for performing on-line clustering of data. They are based on the assumption that clusters are likely to correspond to categories – an instance of the general epistemological assumption that 'nature is not a cryptographer.' This important assumption, which has extensive empirical support even if its philosophical status is not entirely clear (Wigner 1960), provides justification for the study of unsupervised learning algorithms. The need for such assumptions, however, is not restricted to the unsupervised learning paradigm – assumptions that nature is 'simple' are also necessary for the theory of supervised learning. The major problem in supervised learning is that of interpolating from the categories of the data in the training set to the categories of novel inputs. Such interpolation can only be based on assumptions about the simplicity of the natural process that generates the data.

Modularity

An interesting aspect of the learning algorithm proposed by Hinton and Becker is its reliance on a multi-network, or modular, architecture. The architecture is modular in at least two senses of the term: (1) by utilizing different networks for different input channels, the transduction of the data is channel-specific, and (2) by utilizing a cost function that depends only on the outputs of the networks involved, the learning process is modular with respect to adaptive processes further downstream. That is, the architecture as a whole can be embedded as an independent module in a larger architecture without introducing unwanted couplings among modules. In this section we discuss these relationships between modularity and learning and we contrast Hinton and Becker's architecture with another recently proposed modular connectionist architecture.

In situating the problem of modularity and learning in a larger context it is useful to distinguish between two kinds of computational processes: *convergent* processes and *divergent* processes. Convergent computation involves taking data in different channels or different formats and integrating them into a common channel or format. An example of a convergent computation is the integration of visual data and somatosensory data that is achieved when an object is simultaneously manipulated and perceived visually. Convergent computation is useful whenever a single external event leaves its trace in different channels or sensory modalities and it is desired to recover a single coherent description of the external event.

Divergent computation involves taking data from a single source and performing different computations on the data. Divergent computation is useful whenever the organism has multiple goals and must utilize the input data differently depending on the goal. For example, the percept of an arriving baseball yields different motor behaviour depending on whether the goal is that of catching the ball, hitting the ball, or dodging the ball. Examples of divergent computation often arise in motor control and are reflective of an organism's ability to overcome the limitations of simple fixed reflexive behaviour. They also arise in perception whenever there are specialized processes operating in parallel on a single piece of input data.

Convergent computation and divergent computation pose different kinds of problems for a learning system. To implement a convergent computation the learner must find a common format that is appropriate for two or more input channels and must discover how to map input data into the common format. To implement a divergent computation the learner must discover how to allocate different subsets of the training data to different modules and how to train each module separately. Different kinds of computational principles are needed for learning systems to realize these two types of computation.

The architecture proposed by Hinton and Becker is a particularly clear example of convergent computation. The modules in their architecture receive input from a set of non-overlapping sensory channels. For example, in the stereo vision problem, the channels correspond to different retinal patches (although there is nothing in the algorithm that restricts the input to a single sensory modality). The goal of the learning procedure is to yield modules that transform the data into a common output format. The algorithm is particularly interesting as a proposal for organizing convergent computation, because it does not require the output format to be known a priori.

Systems that implement convergent computation are useful for finding features that are invariant across the input channels. This is exemplified by Hinton and Becker's stereo vision simulation, in which the feature of disparity is invariant across different retinal patches. In the simulation, the modules share not only a common output format, but they also share a common input format and, therefore, ideally perform the same transformation of the input data. The mature system is composed of a set of modules that are essentially copies of each other, translated with respect to retinal position. Such replication of effort is the limiting case of convergent computation.

It is also possible to conceive of learning algorithms for modular networks in which the emphasis is on divergent computation. Jacobs, Jordan, Nowlan, and Hinton (1991) describe a supervised learning algorithm for multi-network architectures in which the modules learn to compute different functions of a single input vector. The assumptions on which the architecture is based are different from Hinton and Becker's proposal, reflecting the differing nature of divergent and convergent computation. Rather than assuming that the data are generated by a single underlying event, it is assumed that the environment can be modelled as a collection of idiosyncratic 'processes,' where a process is characterized by a particular probabilistic rule that maps input vectors to output vectors. The training data are assumed to be generated in the following way. On any given trial it is assumed that (1) an input vector is selected according to a prior probability distribution, and (2) a particular process is chosen according to a probability distribution that depends on the input vector. The selected process generates an output vector and the resulting input-output pair is treated as a basic datum for a supervised learning trial. Particular processes have higher probabilities of generating particular input-output pairs in different regions of the input space, thus the learner that wishes to produce the most probable output corresponding to a given input must attempt to (1) partition the input space appropriately and (2) estimate the mapping corresponding to the most probable process within each partition. Jacobs et al. describe a multi-network architecture that attempts to find partitions in the input space by utilizing a form of maximum a posteriori (MAP) estimation. The essential feature of the learning algorithm is that the modules compete between themselves to account for the data. The competition forces the modules to focus on different subsets of the training data and thereby learn to compute different functions. Jacobs et al. (1991) show that their learning algorithm is a maximum likelihood estimation procedure for modelling the probability distribution generated by a finite collection of probabilistic processes.

In complex environments it seems likely that the assumptions underlying the competitive architecture of Jacobs et al. and the co-operative architecture of Hinton and Becker are best viewed as complementary. Given that an 'environment' is an ensemble of data available at a particular site in the nervous system, it may be that modules at different sites are under different pressures to compete or co-operate. It is also important to emphasize that complex environments have structure at different levels of granularity, and that both convergent computation and divergent computation may be useful in the same data stream. For example, within each partition induced by the competitive modular architecture the computation may be either convergent or divergent. Thus different kinds of learning algorithms may be embedded within each other.[1] Convergent computation and divergent computation are best thought of as modular building blocks out of which more complex systems may be constructed.

Hinton and Becker also discuss a second aspect of modularity that has implications for the scaling behaviour of learning algorithms. Systems can be modular with respect to the credit assignment process; that is, it may be possible to combine modules without introducing unwanted couplings between the learning processes that assign credit within modules. Hinton and Becker argue that this form of modularity is related to the distinction between supervised learning and unsupervised learning. In particular, they argue that only unsupervised learning algorithms are modular in their credit assignment, and that supervised learning algorithms scale poorly because they necessarily introduce couplings between the weights in different modules. Although we agree that such coupling is an important problem in complex networks, we are not convinced that problems with coupling between modules are diagnostic of the unsupervised-supervised distinction. Many current supervised learning algorithms, such as backpropagation, suffer from unwanted couplings because the credit assignment process is a linear operator. It may be that there are nonlinear credit assignment procedures by which the error terms are orthogonalized as they pass backward in the network. To a limited degree, the competitive algorithm of Jacobs et al. is such a procedure. As the modules in the competitive architecture begin to specialize, the coupling between the modules decreases.

It also seems unlikely that unsupervised learning algorithms can avoid couplings in realistic problems. Consider, for example, the stereo vision problem discussed by Hinton and Becker. One of the reasons for the success of their simulations is that in random dot stereograms the only mutual information between the left patch and the right patch of the image is due to the disparity. In realistic images, however, there are many additional sources of mutual information. Suppose, for example, that a low pass filter is applied to the image. Most of the mutual information now inheres in the low pass characteristic of the filter rather than in the disparity. Thus the IMAX algorithm has to do considerable work to extract the relatively uninteresting sources of coherence in the image before it can find the interesting sources of coherence. Indeed, our major technical concern with the IMAX learning procedure is that it may fare poorly in the multi-dimensional case because of the high degree of nonlinear coupling that is introduced by the determinant operator. There are other examples of successful one-dimensional algorithms that fail when the extension to multiple dimensions involves the determinant (Safonov 1980). This is, of course, an empirical issue.

Conclusion

The development of a novel learning algorithm often forces a re-evaluation of the distinctions that underlie our understanding of adaptive systems. We have attempted to initiate such a re-evaluation in the light of the algorithm proposed by Hinton and Becker and other recent algorithms proposed in the connectionist literature. We have suggested that the classical distinctions between supervised learning and unsupervised learning are inadequate, and that realistic learning algorithms are neither entirely supervised nor entirely unsupervised. We have discussed the problem of modularity and learning and proposed a distinction between convergent computation and divergent computation. These two kinds of computation capture different aspects of the notion of modularity in an adaptive system and require different kinds of computational principles.

Note

1 This point was also made by Hinton in the discussion at the Vancouver workshop.

References

Duda, R.O. and Hart, P.E. (1973). *Pattern Classification and Scene Analysis*. New York: Wiley

Hinton, G.E. (1989). Connectionist learning procedures. *Artificial Intelligence* 40: 185-234

Jacobs, R.A., Jordan, M.I., Nowlan, S., and Hinton, G.E. (1991). Adaptive mixtures of local experts. *Neural Computation* 3: 1-12

Jordan, M.I. (1990). Motor learning and the degrees of freedom problem. InM.-Jeannerod (ed.), *Attention and Performance XIII*. Hillsdale, NJ: Erlbaum

– and Rumelhart, D.E. (1990). *Forward models: Supervised learning with a distal teacher*. Occasional Paper #40, Center for Cognitive Science, MIT, Cambridge, MA

Linsker, R. (1988). Self-organization in a perceptual network. *Computer* 21:105-17

Safonov, M.G. (1980). *Stability and Robustness of Multivariable Feedback Systems*. Cambridge, MA: MIT Press

Wigner, E.P. (1960). The unreasonable effectiveness of mathematics in the natural sciences. *Communications in Pure and Applied Mathematics* 13: 222-37.

2

A Deeper Unity: Some Feyerabendian Themes in Neurocomputational Form

Paul M. Churchland

Introduction

By the late sixties, every good materialist expected that epistemological theory would one day make explanatory contact, perhaps even a reductive contact, with a proper theory of brain function. Not even the most optimistic of us, however, expected this to happen in less than fifty years, and most would have guessed a great deal longer. And yet the time has arrived. Experimental neuroscience has revealed enough of the brain's microphysical organization, and mathematical analysis and computer simulation have revealed enough of its functional significance, that we can now address epistemological issues directly. Indeed, we are in a position to reconstruct, in neurocomputational terms, issues in the philosophy of science specifically. This is my aim in what follows.

A general accounting of the significance of neural network theory for the philosophy of science has been published elsewhere (Churchland 1989a, 1989b). My aim here is to focus more particularly on five theses central to the philosophy of Paul Feyerabend. Those five theses are as follows:

(1) Perceptual knowledge, without exception, is always an expression of some speculative framework, some *theory*: it is never ideologically neutral (Feyerabend 1958, 1962).

(2) The common sense (but still speculative) categorial framework with which we all understand our mental lives may not express the true nature of mind nor capture its causally important aspects. This common sense framework is in principle *displaceable* by a matured materialist framework, even as the vehicle of one's

spontaneous, first-person psychological judgments (Feyerabend 1963a).

(3) Competing theories can be, and occasionally are, *incommensurable*, in the double sense that a) the terms and doctrines of the one
theory find no adequate translation within the conceptual resources of the other theory, and b) they have no logical connections to a common observational vocabulary whose accepted
sentences might be used to make a reasoned empirical choice
between them (Feyerabend 1962).

(4) Scientific progress is at least occasionally contingent on the *proliferation* and exploration of mutually exclusive, large-scale conceptual alternatives to the dominant theory, and such
alternative avenues of exploration are most needed precisely
when the dominant theory has shown itself to be 'empirically
adequate' (Feyerabend 1963b).

(5) The long-term best interests of intellectual progress require that
we proliferate not only theories, but research *methodologies* as
well (Feyerabend 1970).

In my experience, most philosophers still find these claims to be individually repugnant and collectively confusing. This is not particularly surprising. Each claim is in conflict with common sense, and with a
respectable epistemological tradition as well. Taken in isolation, and
against that background, each one is bound to seem implausible, even
reckless. But taken together, they form the nucleus of an alternative conception of knowledge, a serious and far-reaching conception with major
virtues of its own. Those virtues have been explored by a number of
writers, most originally and most extensively by Feyerabend himself,
but it is not my purpose here to review the existing arguments in support of these five themes. My purpose is to outline an entirely new line
of argument – one drawn from computational neuroscience and connectionist AI. Research in these fields has recently made possible a novel conception of such notions as *mental representation, knowledge,
learning, conceptual framework, perceptual recognition,* and *explanatory understanding*. Its portrayal of the kinematics and dynamics of cognitive
activity differs sharply from the common sense conception that underlies orthodox approaches to epistemology. The mere existence of such
an alternative conception, one grounded in the brain's microanatomy,
is sufficient to capture one's general interest. But this novel conception
is of especial interest in the present context, because it strongly supports
all five of the Feyerabendian themes listed above. It provides a unitary
explanation of why all five of them are jointly correct.

The claim being made here is fairly strong. Just as Newtonian mechanics successfully reduced Keplerian astronomy, so does a connectionist account of cognition reduce a Feyerabendian philosophy of science. Not everything in Kepler's account survived its Newtonian reduction, and not everything in Feyerabend's account survives its neurocomputational reduction. But in both examples the parallel of principle is sufficiently striking to make the claim of intertheoretic reduction and explanatory unification appropriate. And, as with the case of Kepler and Newton, the cross-theoretic parallels serve to vindicate the principles reduced – at least in their rough outlines. I begin with a summary account of the kinematical and dynamical ideas that support this explanatory reduction.

Neural Nets: An Elementary Account

A primary feature of neuronal organization is schematically depicted in the 'neural network' of Figure 2.1a. The circles in the bottom row of the network represent a population of sensory neurons, such as might be found in the retina. Each of these units projects a proprietary axonal fibre towards a second population of neuron-like units, such as might be found in the lateral geniculate nucleus (LGN), a mid-brain structure that is the immediate target of the optic nerve. Each axon there divides into a fan of terminal branches so as to make a synaptic connection with every unit in the second population. Real brains are not quite so exhaustive in their connectivity, but a typical axon can make many thousands or even hundreds of thousands of connections.

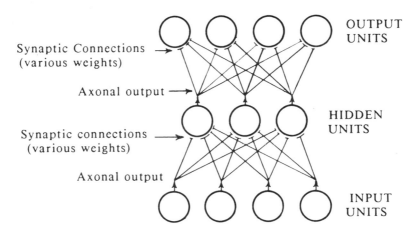

Figure 2.1a

This arrangement allows any unit at the input layer to have an impact on the activation levels of all, or a great many, of the units at the second or 'hidden' layer. An input stimulus such as light produces some activation level in a given input unit, which then conveys a signal of proportional strength along its axon and out the end branches to the many synaptic connections onto the hidden units. These connections stimulate or inhibit the hidden units, as a function of (a) the strength of the signal, (b) the size or 'weight' of each synaptic connection, and (c) its polarity. A given hidden unit simply sums the effects incident from its many input synapses. The global effect is that a *pattern of activations* across the set of input units produces a distinct *pattern of activations* across the set of hidden units. Which pattern gets produced, for a given input, is strictly determined by the configuration of synaptic weights meeting the hidden units.

The units in the second layer project in turn to a third population of units, such as might be found in the visual cortex at the back of the brain, there to make another set of synaptic connections. (In real brains this pattern typically branches and is iterated through many layers – roughly, $5 < n < 50$ – before the chain concludes in some population of motor or other 'output' neurons. Real brains also display recurrent or 'feedback' pathways not shown in Figure 2.1a. But for purposes of illustration, a nonbranching feed-forward network of just three layers will suffice.) In this upper half of the network also, the global effect is that an activation pattern across the hidden units produces a distinct activation pattern across the output units. As before, exactly what pattern- to-pattern transformation takes place is fixed by the configuration of synaptic weights meeting the output units.

All told, this network is a device for transforming any one of a great many possible input vectors (i.e., activation patterns) into a uniquely corresponding output vector. It is a device for computing a specific function, and exactly which function it computes is fixed by the global configuration of its synaptic weights.

Now for the payoff. There are various procedures for adjusting the weights so as to yield a network that computes almost any function – that is, any general vector- to- vector transformation – that we might desire. In fact, we can even impose on it a function we are *unable to specify*, so long as we can supply a modestly large set of *examples* of the desired input-output pairs. This process is called 'training up the network.'

In artificial networks, training typically proceeds by entering a sample input vector at the lowest layer, letting it propagate upwards through the network, noting the (usually erroneous) vector this produces at the topmost layer, calculating the difference between this actual output and this desired output, and then feeding the error measure into

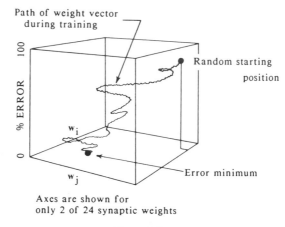

Figure 2.1b

a special rule called the generalized delta rule (Rumelhart et al., 1986a, 1986b). This rule then dictates a small adjustment in the antecedent configuration of all of the synaptic weights in the network. This particular learning procedure is the popular 'back-propagation' algorithm. Repeating this procedure many times, over the many input-output examples in the training set, forces the network to slide down an error gradient in the abstract space that represents its possible synaptic weights (Figure 2.1b). The adjustments continue until the network has finally assumed a configuration of weights that does yield the appropriate outputs for all of the inputs in the training set.

To illustrate this technique with a real example, suppose we want the network to discriminate sonar echoes of large metallic objects, such as explosive mines, from sonar echoes of large submarine rocks. The discrimination of such echoes poses a serious problem, because they are effectively indistinguishable by the human ear and vary widely in character even within each class. We begin by recording fifty different mine echoes and fifty different rock echoes – a fair sample of each. We then digitize the power profile of each echo with a frequency analyzer and feed the resulting vector into the bank of input units (Figure 2.2a). We want the output units to respond with appropriate activation levels (specifically, {1, 0} for a mine; {0, 1} for a rock) when fed an echo of either kind.

The network's initial verdicts are confused and meaningless, since its synaptic weights were set at random values. But under the pressure of the weight-nudging algorithm, it gradually learns to make the desired distinction among the initial examples. Its output behaviour progressively approximates the correct output vectors. Most gratifyingly, after

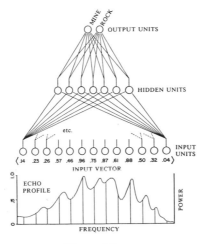

Figure 2.2a

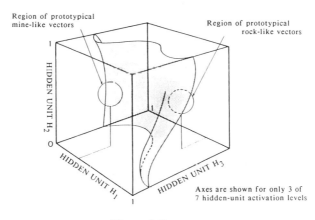

Figure 2.2b

it has mastered the echoes in the training set, it will generalize: it will reliably identify mine and rock echoes from outside its training set – echoes it has never heard before. Mine echoes, it turns out, are indeed united by some subtle weave of features, to which weave the network has become tuned during the training process. The same is true for rock echoes. (See Gorman and Sejnowski 1988.)

Here we have a binary discrimination between a pair of diffuse and very hard-to-define acoustic properties. Indeed, *we never did define them!* It is the network that has generated an appropriate internal characterization of each type of sound, fuelled only by examples. If we now examine the behaviour of the hidden units during discriminatory acts in

the trained network, we discover that the training process has partitioned the space of possible activation vectors across the hidden units
(Figure 2.2b). (Note that this space is not the space of Figure 2.1b. Figure
2.1b depicts the space of possible synaptic weights. Figure 2.2b depicts
the space of possible activation vectors across the middle layer.) The
training process has generated a *similarity gradient* that culminates in
two 'hot spots' – two rough regions that represent the range of hidden-
unit vector codings for a *prototypical* mine and a *prototypical* rock. The
job of the top half of the network is then just the relatively simple one
of discriminating these two subvolumes of that vector space.

Some salient features of such networks beg emphasis. First, the output verdict for any input is produced very swiftly, for the computation
occurs in parallel. The global computation at each layer of units is distributed among many simultaneously active processing elements: the
weighted synapses and the summative cell bodies. Hence the expression, 'parallel distributed processing.' Most strikingly, the speed of processing is entirely independent of both the number of units involved
and the complexity of the function executed. Each layer could have ten
units or a hundred million; and its configuration of synaptic weights
could be computing simple sums or second-order differential equations. It would make no difference. Speed is determined solely by the
number of distinct *layers* in the network. This makes for very swift processing indeed. In a living brain, where a typical information-processing pathway has something between five and fifty layers, and each pass
through that hierarchy takes something between ten and twenty milliseconds per layer, we are looking at overall processing times (even for
complex recognitional problems) of between one-twentieth of a second
and one second. As both experiment and common knowledge attest,
this is the right range for living creatures.

Second, such networks are functionally persistent. They degrade
gracefully under the scattered failure of synapses or even entire units.
Since each synapse contributes such a tiny part to any computation, its
demise makes an almost undetectable difference. In living creatures, the
computational activity at any layer is essentially a case of multiplying
an input vector by a very large matrix, where each synaptic weight represents one coefficient of that matrix (Figure 2.3). Since the matrix is so
large – typically in excess of $(10^5 \times 10^3)$ elements – it might have hundreds of thousands of positive and negative coefficients revert to zero,
and its transformational character would change only slightly. That loss
represents less than one tenth of one per cent of its functional coefficients. Additionally, since networks learn, they can compensate for such
minor losses by adjusting the weights of the surviving synapses.

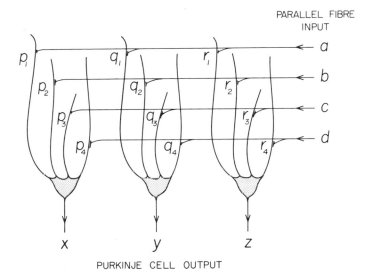

Figure 2.3

Third, the network will regularly render correct verdicts given only a degraded version or a smallish part of a familiar input vector. This is because the degraded or partial vector is relevantly *similar* to a prototypical input, and the internal coding strategy generated in the course of training is exquisitely sensitive to such similarities between possible inputs.

And exactly which similarities are those? They are whichever similarities meet the joint condition that (a) they unite some significant portion of the examples in the training set, and (b) the network managed to become tuned to them in the course of training. The point is that there are often many overlapping dimensions of similarity being individually monitored by the trained network: individually they may be modest in their effects, but if several are detected together their impact can be decisive. Here we may recall Ludwig Wittgenstein's famous description of how humans can learn, by ostension, to detect 'family resemblances' that defy easy definition. Artificial neural networks recreate exactly this phenomenon.

Finally, such networks can learn functions far more complex than the one illustrated and make discriminations far beyond the binary example portrayed. In the course of learning to produce correctly pronounced speech (as output) in response to printed English text (as input), Rosenberg and Sejnowski's NETtalk (1987) partitioned its hidden-unit vector space into fully seventy-nine subspaces, one for each of the seventy-nine letter- to- phoneme transformations that characterize the phonetic significance of English spelling. Since there are seventy-nine distinct phonemes in English speech but only twenty-six letters in the alphabet, each letter clearly admits of several different phonetic interpretations, the correct one being determined by context. Despite this ambiguity, the network learned to detect which of several possible transforms is the appropriate one by being sensitive to the contextual matter of which other letters flank the target letter inside the word. All of this is a notoriously irregular matter for English spelling, but, even so, the network learned a close approximation to the correct function.

As in the mine-rock network, an analysis of the behaviour of the hidden units during each of the seventy-nine learned transformations reveals an important organization. For each letter-to-phoneme transformation, of course, the hidden layer displays a unique activation vector: a total of seventy-nine vectors in all. If one examines the similarity relations between these vectors in the trained network, as judged by their Euclidean proximity in the abstract activation vector space (see again Figure 2.2b), one discovers that the learning process has produced a tree-like hierarchy of types (Figure 2.4). Similar sounds are grouped together and a global structure has emerged in which the deepest division is that between the consonants and the vowels. The network has spontaneously recovered, from the text on which it was trained, the phonetic structure of English speech!

Such revealing organization across the hidden-unit vector space is typical of trained networks in a great many contexts and is a provocative feature of these machines. They partition that space into useful and well-organized *categories* relative to the functional task that they are required to perform.

Other networks have learned to identify the three-dimensional configuration and orientation of curved surfaces, given only flat grey-scale pictures of those surfaces as input. That is, they solve a version of the classic shape-from-shading problem in visual psychology (Lehky and Sejnowski 1988a, 1988b). Still others learn to divine the grammatical elements of sentences fed as input, or to predict the molecular folding of proteins given amino acid sequences as input, or to categorize olfactory stimuli into a hierarchical taxonomy, or to guide a jointed limb to grasp perceived objects, or to predict payment behaviour from loan-application profiles. These networks perform their surprising feats of learned categorization and perceptual discrimination with only the smallest of 'neuronal' resources – usually much less than 10^3 units. This is less than one hundred millionth of the resources available in the human brain. With such powerful cognitive effects being displayed in such modest artificial models, it is plausible that they represent a major insight into the functional significance of our own brain's microstructure.

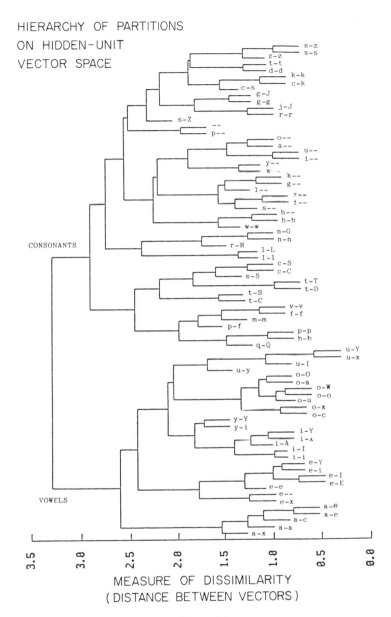

HIERARCHY OF PARTITIONS
ON HIDDEN-UNIT
VECTOR SPACE

CONSONANTS

VOWELS

MEASURE OF DISSIMILARITY
(DISTANCE BETWEEN VECTORS)

Figure 2.4

Let us briefly contrast this approach with the rule governed symbol-manipulation approach of classical artificial intelligence (AI). Unlike standard serial-processing programmable computers, neural nets typically have no representation of any rules, and they do not achieve their function-computing abilities by following any rules. They simply 'embody' the desired function as opposed to calculating it by recursive application of a set of rules listed in an externally imposed program. Moreover, since neural nets perform massively parallel processing, they can be many millions or even billions of times faster than serial machines on a wide range of problems, even though they are constructed of vastly slower physical components.

A further contrast concerns the manner of information storage. In neural networks, acquired knowledge is stored in a distributed fashion: specifically, in the intricate permutational structure of the global configuration of synaptic weights, which number at least 10^{14} in a human brain. The relevant aspects of that vast store are instantly accessed by the input vectors themselves, since the weights have been configured by the learning process precisely so as to produce the appropriate activation patterns in the layer receiving that input vector. This constitutes a form of 'content-addressable' memory. Given the very high-dimensional representations employed by neural nets (namely, activation vectors across large cell populations), even smallish nets can be exquisitely sensitive to subtle and hard-to-express similarities among their perceptual inputs, and to the intricate contextual features that they may contain.

This welcome feature allows a network to activate the appropriate prototype vector at the hidden layer even when the input vector is only a partial or degraded version of a typical input. The prototypical 'hot spots' in the activation space of the trained hidden layer function as 'attractors' into which a wide variety of partial or degraded inputs will 'fall.' This phenomenon allows a well-trained network to recognize instances of its categorial system even in novel or noisy circumstances and given only partial information. In the language of philosophical theory, this means that a trained network will regularly make an ampliative 'inference' to the best available 'explanation' of the input phenomena. And it will do so in milliseconds.

Finally, neural nets can learn a desired function and generate a categorial system adequate to compute it even where its makers and trainers are ignorant of both. All it needs is sufficient examples of the relevant function. These are some of the more striking rewards we gain from our modest attention to the brain's empirical architecture.

Epistemological Issues in Neurocomputational Guise

Let us now turn away from smallish artificial networks and refocus our attention on a large-scale biological network: the human brain. The suggestion to be explored below is that cognitive activity in the brain follows the same pattern displayed in the artificial networks. Knowledge is stored in the global configuration of the brain's synaptic weights. Learning consists in the modification of those synaptic weights according to some adjustment procedure that is somehow sensitive to successful or erroneous performance by the network. Successful configuration of the weights yields a complex and hierarchically organized set of partitions across the various subpopulations of 'hidden units' scattered throughout the brain. That is, it yields one of many possible categorial or conceptual frameworks. Conceptual change consists in reconfiguring the synaptic weights so as to produce a new set of partitions across the relevant population(s) of neurons.

In humans, such categorial frameworks can be of remarkable complexity, since the human brain boasts something like 10^3 neural subpopulations ('layers of hidden units') at a minimum, each of which has something like 10^8 distinct neurons. A coding vector with 10^8 elements in it can code the contents of a very large book, so we may expect the prototypes involved to characterize intricate things such as 'stellar collapse' and 'economic depression,' as well as simple things like 'raven' and 'black.'

Perceptual recognition consists in the activation of an appropriate prototype vector across some appropriate population of post-sensory neurons. The achievement of explanatory understanding consists in exactly the same thing, although here the occasion that activates the vector need not always be sensory in character. Perceptual recognition is thus just a special case of explanatory understanding.

The preceding begins to evoke the range of epistemological material we can reconstruct in neurocomputational terms. (A more detailed and far reaching account can be found in Churchland 1989b.) We are now prepared to address the claim that motivated this paper, the claim that five salient themes of Paul Feyerabend's philosophy of science are a natural consequence of the neurocomputational perspective.

(1) On the theory ladenness of all perception

The argument here is about as brief and as decisive as it could be. Perception is, of course, more than mere peripheral transduction: it is a cognitive achievement. But on the model of cognition outlined above, no cognitive activity whatever takes place without the relevant input vectors passing through the complex filter of a large set of synaptic weights (see again Figure 2.1a). Most importantly, any configuration of synaptic weights dictates a specific set of partitions on the activation space of the post-sensory neurons to which they connect. And that set of partitions constitutes a specific conceptual framework or theory – one of many millions of possible alternative frameworks.

Any activation pattern produced across the relevant population of hidden units is thus a point in an antecedently existing space, a space with antecedently prepared similarity gradients and antecedently prepared partitions having an antecedently prepared significance for subsequent populations of neurons in the processing hierarchy. That antecedent framework and the configuration of weights that dictates it represent whatever 'knowledge' the network has accumulated during past training. That framework may be well trained and finely tuned, or it may be uninstructed and inchoate. But whichever it is, no cognitive activity takes place save as the input vectors pass through that *speculative* configuration of synaptic connections, that *theory*. Theory-ladenness thus emerges not as an unwelcome and accidental blight on what would otherwise be a neutral cognitive achievement but, rather, as that which makes processing activity genuinely *cognitive* in the first place.

From this perspective it is evident that the process of learning about the world is not just the process of learning which general beliefs to embrace, as guided by our neutral perceptual judgments. It is also a process of learning how most usefully and penetratingly to *perceive* the world, for there is just as much room for conceptual variation and conceptual exploration at the perceptual level as there is at any other level of knowledge.

The basic point to emphasize is that, since there are almost endlessly many different possible observational frameworks (that is, hidden-layer weight configurations), where the choice between *them* is *also* an epistemic decision, there can be no question of grounding all epistemic decisions in some neutral observation framework. There is no such framework, and epistemic decisions are not made by reference to its contents in any case. One can certainly regard the unprocessed activation vectors at the sensory input layer as theoretically neutral, but those epithelial activation vectors are not themselves propositional attitudes, they are not truth-valuable, and they stand in no logical relations to anything. Their impact on subsequent activity is causal, not logical. Human knowledge thus has *causal* 'foundations,' but it has no *epistemic* foundations.

(2) On displacing folk psychology

Given the model of cognition outlined above, any conceptual framework whatever is a speculative attempt to process incoming vectors in a way that is useful to the network, and it is subject to modification or replacement as a function of whatever pressures are exerted by the network's learning algorithm. The system of partitions that constitutes one's 'folk' conception of mental reality is no exception. It is a learned framework whose purpose is to render intelligible both the intro-spectible reality of one's own case and the continuing behaviour of people in general. A suitable regime of training should be able to produce any one of a large variety of alternative conceptions (indeed, even the 'folk' conception is nonuniform across cultures and across individuals).

The idea of embracing an alternative to folk psychology was never very compelling so long as we could not even point towards a plausible alternative conception. But now we can. The neurocomputational framework of the preceding pages portrays cognitive representations as high-dimensional activation vectors rather than as sentential or propositional attitudes. And it portrays cognitive activity as the synapse-driven transformation of vectors into other vectors rather than as the rule-governed drawing of inferences from one proposition to another. It presents a fundamentally novel kinematics and dynamics of cognitive activity. Although it is not yet sufficiently developed for a general transfer of allegiance to take place, it does hold promise of being descriptively and explanatorily superior to current folk psychology, and it already presents real opportunities for first-person use.

One class of such opportunities concerns the various subjective sensory qualia which have so often been held up as paradigm examples of what materialism can never hope to explicate. A specific colour quale emerges as a specific activation vector in a three (or four) dimensional space whose axes correspond to the three types of retinal cones (and perhaps also the rods). A taste quale emerges as a four-element activation vector in a four dimensional space whose axes correspond to the four types of taste sensors in the mouth. Auditory qualia emerge as more variable vectors whose elements correspond to the places on the cochlea whose natural frequency corresponds to one element in the complex incoming sound. The dimensionality of these qualia is relatively low, and thus their internal structure is potentially learnable and reportable in detail, just as the structure of musical chords is learnable and reportable. As in the musical case, there is also an increased insight into the structure of and the relations within the apprehended domain. One has therefore mastered more than just an esoteric set of labels: one has increased one's understanding of the phenomena.

Qualia are peripheral phenomena, to be sure, and complexity goes up as we ascend the processing hierarchy. It remains to be seen how the story will go in the case of cognitive processing at the level of systematic linguistic activity. Perhaps the familiar propositional attitudes will be smoothly reduced by the computational structures we find there, and perhaps they will simply be eliminated from our scientific ontology because nothing of dynamical importance in the brain answers to them. But whichever is their fate – reduction by something superior or elimination by something superior – the categories of folk psychology remain displaceable in favour of some more penetrating categorial framework. The only real question is how large the doctrinal and ontological gap will turn out to be between the triumphant new framework and its poorly-informed historical predecessor.

(3) On incommensurable alternatives

Consider a typical brain subpopulation of something like 10^8 neurons. Its abstract activation space will have 10^8 dimensions. Clearly a space of such high dimensionality can support an extraordinarily intricate hierarchical system of similarity gradients and partitions across that space. Equally clear is the commensurately great *variety* of such partitional configurations possible with such generous resources. Now the demand that all possible conceptual frameworks must be somehow translatable into our current conceptual framework is just the demand that each and every one of the billions of possible configurations just alluded to must stand in some equivalence relation to our current configuration. But there is not a reason in the world to think that there is any such relation that unites this vast diversity of frameworks: not in their internal structure, nor in their relations to the external world, nor in the input-output functions they sustain. On the contrary, they are all in competition with one another, in the sense that they are mutually incompatible configurations of the same activation vector space.

The prospect of widespread incommensurability is unsettling to many philosophers, because it threatens to make a reasoned empirical choice between competing theoretical frameworks impossible. The real threat, however, is not to the possibility of rational empirical choice but to a deeply-entrenched *theory* of what rational empirical choice consists in. That superannuated theory requires a relevantly neutral observation vocabulary among whose sentences the competing theories at issue have different logical consequences. So long as one embraces that superannuated theory, one will perceive incommensurability as a threat to reason and objectivity. But once one puts that theory aside, one can get down to the serious business of exploring how empirical data *really* steer our theoretical commitments.

On the model of cognition here being explored, ongoing learning consists in the continual readjustment of the value-configuration of one's myriad synaptic weights. Exactly what factors drive such readjustments in the human brain is currently the focus of much research, but the familiar philosopher's stories about sets of sentences being accepted or rejected as a function of their logical relations with other sentences plays no detectable role in that research, and no detectable role in the brain's activity, either. Instead, synaptic change appears to be driven by such factors as local increases in presynaptic or postsynaptic activity (posttetanic potentiation), by temporal correlations or anticorrelations between the activity reaching a given synapse and the activity reaching other synaptic connections onto the same postsynaptic neuron (Hebbean learning), by the mutual accommodation of synaptic values under specific global constraints (Boltzmann learning), perhaps by the return distribution of conflict messages (back-propagation), and by other decidedly preconceptual or subconceptual processes.

None of this precludes the possible relevance of sentential and logical factors for some cases of learning at some high level of processing, but it does undermine the parochial view that all or even most of human learning must be captured in those terms. And it therefore frees us forever from the short-sighted objection that incommensurable alternatives would make objective learning impossible. Learning then proceeds, as it *usually* does, by other than 'classical' means. This is good, because incommensurable alternatives are both possible and actual. They are also welcome, since 'commensurability' is just a measure of the similarity between alternative frameworks, and sometimes what the epistemic situation requires is a profoundly different perspective on the world. Which brings us to the next theme.

(4) On proliferating theories

Feyerabend's argument (1963) for the wisdom of proliferating theories is very striking. He points out that important empirical facts can often be quite properly dismissed as unrevealing noise or intractable chaos when they are viewed from within one conceptual framework, while those 'same' empirical facts appear as tractable, revealing, and as decisively incompatible with the first framework when viewed from within a second conceptual framework. His illustrative example is the empirical phenomenon of Brownian motion, which constitutes a perpetual motion machine of the second kind and is thus incompatible with the second law of classical thermodynamics. However, its status as such was not appreciated, and could not be fully appreciated, until the relevant details of Brownian motion were brought into clear focus by the new and very different kinetic theory of heat. What had been an exceedingly minor and opaque curiosity then emerged as a major and unusually revealing experimental phenomenon – one that refuted the classical second law.

Feyerabend has been criticized for overstating the case here. Lamon (1977) insists that Brownian motion could have been, and to some extent actually was, recognized as a problem for classical thermodynamics in advance of its successful analysis by the kinetic theory. Lamon may have a point, but I think his resistance here is a quibble (see also Couvalis 1988). Whatever minor worries might have been brewing in a few isolated breasts, the fact remains that the kinetic theory transformed our conception of Brownian motion and made salient certain of its experimentally accessible features that otherwise might never have risen to consciousness. It is not true that all empirical facts are equally accessible, nor that their significance is equally evident independently of the conceptual framework one brings to the experimental situation. This is all one needs to justify the proliferation of theories, and the case of Brownian motion remains a striking example of this important lesson.

From a neurocomputational perspective, this lesson is doubly clear. Anyone who has spent idle time watching a Hinton diagram evolve during the training of a neural network will have noticed that networks often persist in ignoring or in outright misinterpreting salient data until they have escaped the early and relatively benighted conceptual configuration into which the learning algorithm initially pushed them. They persist in such behaviour until they have assumed a more penetrating conceptual configuration – one that responds properly to the ambiguous data. (A Hinton diagram is a raster-like display of all of the synaptic-weight values of the network being trained. These displayed values are updated after each presentation of a training example and consequent modification of the weights. Accordingly, one can watch the weights evolve under the steady pressure of the training examples.) If the proper final configuration of weights happens already to be known from prior training runs, one can even watch the 'progress' of the weights as they collectively inch towards their optimal configuration.

What is striking is that for some problems (the exclusive OR function, for example) some specific weights regularly start off by evolving in exactly the *wrong* direction – they become more and more strongly negative, for example, when their proper final value should be strongly positive. One may find oneself yelling at the screen 'No! This way! Over this way!', as the early network persists in giving erroneous outputs, and the wayward weights persist in evolving in the wrong direction. These frustrations abate only when the other weights in the network have evolved to a configuration that finally allows the network's learning algorithm to appreciate the various examples it has been 'mishandling' and to pull the miscreant weights towards more useful values. The proper appreciation of some of the training data, to summarize the point, is sometimes impossible without a move to a different conceptual configuration.

This example illustrates that the moving point in weight-error space (see again Figure 2.1b) is often obliged to take a highly circuitous path in following the local error gradient downwards in hopes of finding a global error minimum. That path may well go through points that preclude both a decent output from the network and a proper lesson from the learning algorithm for at least some of the student weights. Only when the network reaches a subsequent point can these defects be repaired.

A more dramatic example of this empirical blindness occurs when, as occasionally happens, the evolving weight-space point gets caught in a purely 'local minimum,' that is, in a cul-de-sac in weight-error space in which the network is still producing somewhat erroneous outputs, but where every relatively small change in the synaptic weights produces an *increase* in the error measured at the network's output layer. For any learning algorithm that moves the weight-space point in small increments only, the network will be permanently stuck at that point. So far as it is concerned, it has achieved the 'best possible' theory.

In order to escape such an epistemic predicament (and occasional entrapments are inevitable), we need a learning algorithm that at least occasionally requires the network to make a relatively *large* jump: a jump to a significantly different portion of synaptic weight space, to a significantly different conceptual configuration. From that new weight-space point, the network may then evolve quickly towards new achievements in error reduction.

It is evident that, for some global minima and some starting points, *you can't get there from here*, at least not by small increments of instruction. This is a clear argument for the wisdom of a learning strategy that at least occasionally exploits multiple starting points, or discontinuous shifts, in the attempt to find a descending path towards a genuinely global error minimum. It may be difficult to achieve such diversity in a single individual (but it is certainly not impossible: see Churchland 1989b, Chapter 11). But it can be achieved with different individuals in the same scientific community. And of course it *is* achieved. That is the point of different 'schools.'

These considerations do not resolve the essentially political conflict between Feyerabend and Thomas Kuhn concerning how *much* of our resources to put into proliferation and how much into pursuing a single but highly progressive 'paradigm.' But it does mean that a wise research policy must recognize the need for striking, and endlessly restriking, a useful balance between these two opposing tensions. Proliferation is a desideratum that will never go away, because the prospect of a false but compelling local error minimum is a threat that will never go away, and because complacency is endemic to the human soul.

(5) On proliferating methodologies

The Feyerabend I have in mind here is of course the Feyerabend of *Against Method* (1970), in which he recommends an opportunistic anarchism, constrained only by the innate organization of the human nervous system, as a more promising policy in guiding our scientific behaviour than is any of the methodological straitjackets so far articulated by scientists and philosophers of science. In a climate of methodological stories benighted by their formulation in logico-linguistic terms, this is certainly good advice. But it need not always be good advice: someday, perhaps, our acquired methodological wisdom may equal or surpass the innate wisdom of a healthy nervous system, because we have figured out how the nervous system works and can see how to make it work even better.

This is not a vain hope. Guided by a variety of nonclassical learning algorithms, artificial neural networks have recently proved capable of some astonishing feats of knowledge acquisition – feats that represent a quantum leap over any of the classical logico-linguistic achievements. A new door has opened in normative epistemology, and it concerns the comparative virtues and capabilities of alternative learning algorithms– algorithms aimed not at adjusting sets of propositions so as to meet certain criteria of consistency or coherence, but at adjusting iterated populations of synaptic weights so as to approximate certain input-output functions or certain dynamical behaviors. What is striking, even at this early stage of exploration, is that the *space of possible learning algorithms is enormous.* In the newly developed research program called 'connectionist AI,' almost as much research time is spent on critically exploring the diverse properties of various existing learning algorithms and on devising and exploring new ones as is spent on the properties of trained networks themselves (see Hinton 1989).

This is a healthy situation, and such proliferation should be encouraged. There are at least two major reasons for this. The first concerns the relatively limited aim of trying to understand how the human brain conducts its epistemic affairs. We need to explore the space of possible learning algorithms until we discover which specific place in it corresponds to the brain's mode of operation.

The second reason is deeper. Even supposing we succeed in identifying the brain's place in that space, there is no reason to suppose that our biologically innate learning algorithm is the best possible algorithm, or even that there *exists* a uniquely best learning algorithm. Perhaps they just get better and better, ad infinitum, which means that we must explore them indefinitely. Or perhaps they radiate along diverse dimensions of distinct virtue, to be explored as our changing needs dictate. The proliferation of learning algorithms is a virtuous policy of long-term science for much the same reasons that proliferation is a virtue in the case of theories. The alternatives are certainly there, and we will not appreciate their virtues unless we explore them.

This may place unreasonable demands on the human nervous system, since presumably it is insufficiently plastic to participate directly in this exploration. Its learning algorithms may be hopelessly hardwired into its structure. Methodological proliferation may therefore show itself only in artificially constructed brains designed specifically to do novel kinds of scientific exploration on our behalf. But this changes the philosophical point not at all.

The preceding defence of the proliferation of methodologies does not justify exactly the position that Feyerabend outlined in *Against Method*. He is there reacting to the shortcomings of an old tradition in methodological research rather than anticipating the possible virtues of a new tradition. But that is all right. The bottom line is that proliferating methodologies is still a very good idea, and for reasons beyond those urged by Feyerabend.

Conclusion

Philosophers are not always so fortunate as Feyerabend appears to be, in respect to finding a systematic vindication of their ideas through an intertheoretic reduction by a later and more penetrating theoretical framework. One must be intrigued by the convergence of principle here, and one must be impressed by the insight that motivated Feyerabend's original articulation and defence of the five theses listed. It seems likely that each one of these important theses will live on, and grow, in a neurocomputational guise.

References

Churchland, P. M. (1989a). On the nature of theories: a neurocomputational perspective. In W. Savage, (ed.), *Minnesota Studies in the Philosophy of Science:14*. Minneapolis: University of Minnesota Press

– (1989b). *A Neurocomputational Perspective: The Nature of Mind and the Structure of Science*. Cambridge: MIT Press

Couvalis, S. G. (1988). Feyerabend and Laymon on Brownian motion. *Philosophy of Science* 55: 415-21

Feyerabend, P. K. (1958). An attempt at a realistic interpretation of experience. *Proceedings of the Aristotelian Society, new series*. Reprinted in Feyerabend, P. K., *Realism, Rationalism, and Scientific Method: Philosophical Papers* 1. Cambridge: Cambridge University Press, 1981

– (1962). Explanation, reduction, and empiricism. In Feigl, H. and Maxwell, G., (eds.), *Minnesota Studies in the Philosophy of Science*. Minneapolis: University of Minnesota Press

– (1963a). Materialism and the mind-body problem. *Review of Metaphysics* 17: 49-66. Reprinted in *The Mind-Brain Identity Theory*, C. V. Borst, (ed.) Toronto: Macmillan, 1970 142-156. Also reprinted in Feyerabend, P. K., *Realism, Rationalism, and Scientific Method: Philosophical Papers* 1. Cambridge: Cambridge University Press, 1981

– (1963b). How to be a good empiricist. In B. Baumrin, (Ed.), *Philosophy of Science: The Delaware Seminar* 2. New York, NY: Interscience Publications 3-19. Reprinted in H. Morick, (ed.), *Challenges to Empiricism*. Belmont, California: Wadsworth 1972

– (1970) *Against Method: outline of an anarchistic theory of knowledge*. In Radner and Winokur, (eds.), *Minnesota Studies in the Philosophy of Science* 4. Minneapolis: University of Minnesota Press

Gorman, R. P. and Sejnowski, T. J. (1988). Learned classification of sonar targets using a massively-parallel network. *IEEE Transactions: Acoustics, Speech, and Signal Processing* 36: 1135-40

Hinton, G. E. (1990). Connectionist learning procedures. *Artificial Intelligence* (forthcoming).

Laymon, R. (1977). Feyerabend, Brownian motion, and the hiddenness of refuting facts. *Philosophy of Science* 44: 225-247

Lehky, S. and Sejnowski, T. J. (1988a). Computing shape from shading with a neural network model. In Schwartz, E., (ed.), *Computational Neuroscience*. Cambridge: MIT Press

– (1988b). Network model of shape-from-shading: neural function arises from both receptive and projective fields. *Nature* 333: 452-4

Rosenberg, C. R., and Sejnowski, T. J. (1987). Parallel networks that learn to pronounce english text. *Complex Systems* 1: 145-68

Rumelhart, D. E., Hinton, G. E. and Williams, R. J. (1986a). Learning representations by back-propagating errors. *Nature* 323

– (1986b). Learning internal representations by error propagation. In Rumelhart, D. E., and McClelland, J. L., (eds.), *Parallel Distributed Processing: Explorations in the Microstructure of Cognition* 1. Cambridge: MIT Press, 1986, 318-62

COMMENT
Waarheden als Koeien[1]

Charles Travis

Like Professor Churchland, I think neural network theory (NNT) has philosophical promise. But perhaps that is not that much like Professor Churchland. What he thinks, I take it, is that NNT has already delivered. Specifically, he cites five theses of Paul Feyerabend which he thinks NNT demonstrates to be correct. This raises two issues. First, *are* the theses correct? Second, are they shown to be by NNT? Or, if NNT provides less than apodictic proof, how, if at all, does it support them?

On one point I disagree with Churchland. He says of the theses that 'most philosophers ... find these claims to be individually repugnant and collectively confusing,' and that they are 'in conflict with common sense. 'I find that, with one exception, these theses range from platitudinous to intriguing. I think that, when they are stated carefully, most philosophers would agree. One of Churchland's biggest contributions in the present paper is to show us how to make something interesting and suggestive out of some of the more platitudinous theses. As I feel some discomfort with the first two theses, it is these I propose to discuss.

Languages and Theories

Churchland's first thesis is: 'perceptual knowledge, without exception, is always an expression of some speculative framework, some the *theory*. What could this mean? Suppose I say that there is, or that I see, a dun cow in that field, or that the cow in that field is dun. What I say is mistaken if there is no cow in that field, or if that is not a cow, or, in the second case, if that cow is not dun. That is not enough, by normal lights, for what I said to be an expression of a *theory*. On the contrary: I *may* simply have reported what I saw: a dun cow, or that there was one there. Or, if I was mistaken, then I *misrepresented* what I saw, and did so in saying how things looked to me rather than how I *concluded* that they were. Similarly, it is not a dun cow in the field if it is a mere mechanical mock cow. But again, it does not follow that I hold a theory to the effect that what I saw was not a mock cow, or that I *assume* this or am inferring it

51

from anything. Thus far, I see no reason to flout the obvious. Nor, I think, does Churchland.

Where someone says or thinks, *blah*, it is natural to call it an expression of a theory where he holds some theory, or set of beliefs, and takes what he thus believes as partial reason for saying *blah*. A colleague says of a job candidate: 'He will never amount to much,' which *may* be an expression of the theory, held by him, that nice guys finish last, or that crypto-urban-quasi-sophisticate realism has seen its day; but which is not *inevitably* an expression of any theory at all. Perhaps Churchland sees reason to obliterate the distinction marked here. Perhaps he thinks that, in this sense, we inevitably express theories whenever we talk. If so, he has produced no reason for thinking so and is, I think, wrong. But I do not think that this is what Churchland has in mind.

There is another sense in which what we say might be thought to express a theory – one highly relevant to Feyerabend's thought. One might think: the terms in which we express what we say would have no coherent application – would mark no distinction between two types of situations the world actually presents us with (situation in which one of those terms are true), if not for given facts as to the sorts of properties situations might (coherently) have. Making sense in speaking as we do would thus presuppose those facts. Our so speaking/thinking might then be said to express a theory incorporating them.

I will show why this is untrue. True, any particular way of separating one sort of case from others presupposes certain principles, in the sense that it would not identify cases as of one sort or another unless those principles held. Any *procedure* for classifying would, if certain things were true, come up empty handed. What is supposed to identify a case as of a given sort may always turn out to be something that could not be a feature of any actual case. The mistake is to think that given words are wedded to some particular *way* of drawing a distinction – of identifying cases where they apply and cases where they do not – or that they are wedded by what they mean to some particular view of how that distinction is to be drawn. In fact, words are more resilient – more polymorphous than that. As a rule, they, and their correct applications, will mesh with whatever reasonably drawn distinctions turn out to be in the general area they are reasonably taken to have aimed at. So merely supposing that there is some sort of thing or situation that words would correctly describe does not (as Churchland and Feyerabend seem to think) commit us to any further views on what in fact distinguishes some ways for the world to be from others.

Some history will help. In the wake of the problems that beset some analytic/synthetic distinctions, it is not surprising that, between the mid-fifties and the early sixties cogent attacks were mounted on a range of related supposed distinctions between, on the one hand, observation, and, on the other, theory, or inference, or prediction. (Think of Putnam here, not Quine.) The two most important attacks, to my mind, were mounted by Putnam[2] and Austin.[3] On the observation side, the main point was that one cannot identify some class of predicates or properties they might express nor, correspondingly, some class of sentences (each with meaning fully fixed) nor thoughts (things to be said) as observational *as such* in any interesting sense. In other words, any sensible observation/theory distinction cannot be a distinction between one kind of predicate, or property, or proposition, and another. Rather, observational status, insofar as this makes sense at all, is very much an occasion-variable affair. What is more, choose an occasion for expressing, or supporting, a thought, and the role observation counts as having played on it will be an occasion-variable affair, varying across occasions for describing what happened on that one particular occasion. This is partly because what a predicate *says* of something is an occasion-variable. But even fixing a given contribution for a predicate to make, observation plays various roles on various occasions in establishing whether what the predicate thus says of something is so.

Choose a candidate observational property– being dun, or a cow, say. Then sometimes one may just *see* that something is a dun cow. What one sees settles the matter, with no residual issue left open. Sometimes, though, one must *deduce* that something is a dun cow from other facts and/or by appeal to some theory. One must, for example, collect evidence for its being dun, or a cow. So that something is a dun cow is sometimes something one just observes, and sometimes it is something that observation alone cannot settle. Even whether on some given occasion it *was* just observable that there was a dun cow in the field may be an occasion-variable matter – epistemic positions are not in general enjoyed tout court. All of the above could be said of virtually any putative *theoretical* predicate or property. So much the worse for the idea of a distinction on these lines.

As Putnam emphasizes, both observational and theoretical considerations will play a role, in general, in determining how given situations classify with respect to being thus and so.[4] So, in this sense, considerations of both kinds enter into the conditions for the truth of an assertion that this is dun or a dun cow. To say all this is not to deny the importance or coherence of the notion of observation. As Austin argued, that notion, with its occasion-sensitivities properly understood, is crucial to the description of epistemic positions we must recognize ourselves as capable of being in.

Paul Feyerabend stood at the centre of this critique of observation/theory contrasts from an early date. His contribution, like Putnam's, was to show how the correct specification of what is said to be so in given words – whether supposedly 'observational' or 'theoretical' – and of the conditions for *that's* being so may be conditioned by both observational and theoretical factors. Feyerabend's concern, that is, was with the conditions under which things said, whether in 'ordinary' or 'technical' language, would be true.

Feyerabend did not put things quite this way. His exposition is marred by one crucial error. That error is the idea that a language has something which he calls an 'interpretation.' Although he does not explain what an interpretation is, it is clear that he sees a tight connection between what words *mean* and the conditions for them to apply truly – much tighter than is in fact the case. With respect to his idea of an interpretation, what a predicate means must determine, once and for all, precisely how states of affairs would sort out into ones in which it was true of an item, and ones in which it was not. But, as Feyerabend notes, anything which determined that much would presuppose (at least) the coherence, or applicability to the world, of a certain method for classifying that with which the world in fact confronts us. Any such method would provide no coherent principles of classification for some things with which the world conceivably could have confronted us. As Feyerabend might put it, any such way of classifying would be incoherent if some possible theories were true; some intuitively plausible methods *are* incoherent given the actual world. So, given what words do mean, they apply to phenomena (either truly or falsely) only if certain ways of classifying what the world presents us with *are* coherent – on Feyerabend's view, only if some specific set of principles is true. Those principles, entailed by the assumption that a given vocabulary is thus applicable, Feyerabend calls the 'ontological consequences' of that vocabulary. On this view, it is not stretching a point to think of the semantics of a language – the properties conferred on it by its expressions meaning what they do – as entailing some sketchy theory of the world.

The above endorses an all too common conflation of languages with theories. As I have argued elsewhere, there is a radical and deep gulf between meaning and truth conditions. The above position underlines *part* of the point of that gulf: it allows words, while their meaning is fixed, to vary what they require for correct application and thus to exhibit much more resilience in the face of what the world presents than Feyerabend's position allows. The compatibility of fixed meaning with various ways of determining in which situations a word was applied truly permits scientific discoveries to be incorporated into what then counts as the right way of determining the presence or absence of that of which words were always speaking. Just this gulf between meaning and what decides applications was always at the heart of Putnam's way with the analytic/synthetic.

Take one of Feyerabend's examples. We first think that whether or not a cow is dun is an issue to be settled *simply* by looking, with a certain insouciance about how the looking is done. We then see the light: there is a Doppler effect. If the cow is moving (rapidly) relative to the observer, there is more than one way to speak of its colour. For some purposes the colour of the cow is what it would be with the Doppler effect reckoned in. That then turns out to be the right way of settling the colour of the cow – whether it is what 'is dun' says it to be (and always did). We may have supposed initially that the colour of a cow is something you can just see. We now see that, for some purposes, the way it looks is a matter of its colour *and* its motion. Nothing about the meanings of colour words ruled on that point in advance of what the optical facts turned out to be. What those words' meaning did do in advance is to leave room for discoveries about optics, as they are made, to matter.

It is on just this point that Austin and Putnam differ from Feyerabend. The data are: whales are not really fish, gold need not be yellow, and so on. What they show is that, for different theories that might prevail, different semantics would count as that which our terms and concepts have and had. So, in advance of the facts as to which theory is right, our concepts are committed to none of them.

Now for Churchland's demonstration. It is suspicious that he does not cite any particular *result* of NNT. Rather, he appeals only to the general fact that visual stimulus processing can be described in NNT terms. Actually, he does not even appeal to that fact. His argument proceeds from the mere fact that processing of visual stimuli occurs. It would proceed as well on any other model – a computational one, say. This is a sure sign that what we are going to get is *not* a scientific demonstration but a philosophical argument. (Not that there is any harm in that.)

The 'demonstration' appeals to NNT for this premise: an NNT visual processor, like any other, classifies stimuli as belonging to one or another of some range of categories; it is in virtue of its so doing that what we see are, for example, dun cows. (An NNT explanation of the processor so working would typically appeal to the fact that there are dun cows 'out there' acting on it; a significant part of what distinguishes NNT from other approaches. An NNT device 'learns' to retrieve (some of) whatever information is actually *present* in the stimulus. This undermines Churchland's Feyerabendian point as to these categories, or some conceptual scheme they support, carrying 'ontological commitments' that are in any sense *speculative*. Insofar as NNT is special, it thus seems to work against Churchland. Let us, though, bracket that point.)

Aside from the fact that Churchland appeals to no *special* property of NNT, it is a long hard journey from this premise to the conclusion: 'perceptual knowledge ... is always an expression of some speculative framework'– that is, commitments presupposed by its way of being put. Churchland attempts to span the gaping expanse here with an argument that appeals to two principles. The first is that the processor, in virtue of categorizing as it does, determines a particular set of concepts by which we see the world: *what* we see, and may take ourselves to see, is always something fitting one or more of these concepts. The second principle is that any set of concepts has 'ontological commitments'(to use Feyerabend's term): it coherently distinguishes between different ways there actually are for the world to be given the truth of some (well-defined?) set of principles, which, to use Churchland's term, it thus 'expresses.'

NNT, of course, lends no support to either of these principles. How *could* NNT do that? The second, in fact, merely repeats the contentious point distinguishing Putnam and Austin from Feyerabend; a point on which philosophers may differ while recognizing the thorough-going intermingling of observation and theory. (What are in conflict here are background philosophies of language.)

Churchland's argument is broken-backed at both steps. His first claim is false for reasons well stated by Feyerabend, with whom he is at odds. His second claim agrees with Feyerabend but is mistaken for reasons already indicated. On the first point, Feyerabend says,

> It is quite obvious that, however well behaved and useful a physical instrument may be, the fact that in certain situations it consistently reacts in a well defined way does not allow us to infer (logically!) what those reactions mean. First, because the existence of a certain observational ability ... is compatible with the most diverse interpretations of the things observed ... It should then be equally obvious that, however well behaved and useful a human observer may be, the fact that in certain situations he (consistently) produces a certain noise, does not allow us to infer what this noise means.[5]

The point, crudely put, is that a concept is not identified simply by some mechanism or procedure for classifying items as falling under it or not, much less for classifying stimuli as produced by such items or not. There is, inter alia, the question of when, if ever, the mechanism is to be seen as having gone wrong, or even to be such as to go wrong systematically. (For any such mechanism and any one of *our* concepts, the answer will not be 'never'; which is related to the reason why language does not saddle us with *commitments* in the way both Churchland and Feyerabend take it to.)

A simple illustration is furnished by a problem posed by Leibniz (a problem which exercised Russell). Suppose I have a friend, Jane. I know who Jane is so, on one criterion, have a concept of her; a concept of her being such and such a person. I am also equipped with certain devices for recognizing her when I confront her. These are *very* reliable. But, Leibniz demonstrated,[6] being Jane cannot be equivalent to being so classified by any such device. There is more to being Jane than meets the eye or any other organ; more in what it is to be her than in any set of cues to which such a device might be sensitive. Conversely, the concept of being Jane is not exhausted, if even touched on, by a full account of what any such device is doing. The factors which constitute a state of affairs of something fitting that concept– what is required for such a fit – are quite different from any factors that would make a recognition device yield one or another result. The same gap between recognition and the actual structure of a concept exists, as Feyerabend recognizes, for any concept. What makes something look (to be) flurg and what makes something flurg may be related in any of indefinitely many ways. The former alone, thus, could not fix the concept of *flurg*.[7]

Churchland has, I think, roughly this idea. Suppose Martians are rather like us, but their visual processors are a bit different: whatever in us classifies stimuli as to colour, those same stimuli are classified on different principles for Martians. Where we see dun, Martians see (if 'see' is the mot juste) something else. If Martians have colour concepts at all, they then have a different range of them than we do. I do not dispute this. It is no reason to obliterate the distinction between concepts and particular procedures or devices for classifying things as falling under them.

Moreover, it is not yet demonstrated that, merely in thus having different concepts, we and Martians disagree on any substantive issue. If I call a cow dun, and a Martian, lacking that concept, calls it *blarth*, applying to it some concept we cannot grasp, why should we not both be right, our perceptual equipment allowing us to capture different aspects of reality? Why should a cow's being dun bar it from fitting the Martian's concept as well?

Turn, now, to Churchland's final step, on which he and Feyerabend agree. The mistake here is to miss what I have called language's resilience, which might be pictured like this: we begin with a concept, or term, *flurg*, about which, in our state of prelapsarian innocence, we take certain things to be true – e.g., that, as a rule, you can just see whether it is flurg; there is no more to it than the way it looks; and, perhaps, if it looks flurg at all then it looks flurg tout court. We also take the concept flurg to apply in a variety of cases and so apply it for a variety of purposes. It then emerges that what we *thought* it was to be flurg, together with our practice and the way the world has shown itself to be, forms an inconsistent triad. We may then ask: given all this, what is it most reasonable to take the semantics of the concept flurg to be – given what we *thought* it was to be flurg, and the troubles those thoughts have delivered, what is it *really* to be flurg? It is a *nearly* invariable rule, I claim, that the *right* answer to the question thus posed will not be one that makes *flurg* a useless concept – one with no coherent application to the actual world. The semantics of a concept – in particular, its requirements for correct application – is an occasion-variable affair: a concept may count as having different semantics on different occasions for considering that question as well as for different ways the world may have turned out to be. That being so, there is so far no argument that concepts 'express theories' in the sense of Churchland and Feyerabend. Concepts adapt themselves to the world much better than that.

Seeing Attitudes

My second cause for concern is Churchland's claim that 'the common sense (but still speculative) framework with which we all understand our mental lives may not express the true nature of the mind, nor capture its causally important aspects. This common sense framework is in principle *displaceable.*'My worry is about the idea that, for example, in reporting what people believe, desire, or expect, we are expressing, perhaps even deploying, a speculative framework – a theory about how the mind works.

I hear Jane say, triumphantly, that, even though it would be bizarre to say that I am now wearing socks, I am, for all that, now wearing socks. I take it she thinks she has thus refuted my view on Moore's misuse of 'know.' There are, of course, ways I could be wrong about this. Conceivably, Jane mistook our conversation for one about shoes and socks and believes she has refuted my view of footwear. Thus far, I stick my neck out. Though it would be odd so to deploy terminology, one just *might* say that I have a theory about Jane – one that would, in conceivable circumstances, be refuted.

I do not think that this is what Churchland has in mind. His idea is that talk about beliefs, desires, and the other usual suspects contains within it a theory, or definite presuppositions, about the etiology of behaviour – those mechanisms whose actions have our doings as results. The very idea that people believe and desire things entails a definite theory of such etiologies. A particular description of Jane – say, as believing that she has refuted me – entails, or presupposes, a particular account of the causal histories of some of her doings or other features – the gloating look, say.

If this *is* what Churchland thinks, then he and I disagree. In my view, our ordinary talk about beliefs, desires, and so on, expresses and presupposes no theory whatever as to 'how the mind works.' There is nothing in our wielding of such concepts (either the way we do it or the fact that we do) for science to refute, no matter what it discovers about the mind. We are not in an area where there is a say for science at all. It may, exceptionally, show that certain cases should be classified differently than we have done with respect, say, to believing X or wishing for Y. (Psychoanalysis springs to mind here.) But it will never show either 'at last and for the first time' what it really is to believe something or that no one really does. From the way 'believe' works, no claims are extractable as to the way the mind works (or none that mesh with scientific enterprises). I do not think that this disagreement can be resolved within present confines. I can, though, present a few considerations.

In my comments on the first point above, I noted that concepts are, as a rule, quite prepared to take the deliveries of science on board, incorporating them in the most expeditious way into conditions for their correct application. Such was the basis of Putnam's critique of the analytic/synthetic. I now note the obvious point that different concepts behave differently. In particular, they may be sensitive in quite different ways and to quite different degrees (including zero) to what science might show. It all depends on the business they are in.

Contrast the concept of a heart (the organ) ($heart_O$) with that of a heart (the suit) ($heart_S$). Science might show what it really is for something to be a $heart_O$. In doing so, it may show that the criteria we always *thought* to be what identifies something as a $heart_O$ are not what really do so, and, in fact, even sometimes lead us to misidentify things. Perhaps some things we always *thought* were $heart_O$s are really kidneys.

We may be confident that similar discoveries are not in the cards when it comes to $heart_S$s. It would be futile, for example, to study the sort of ink with which they are usually printed. The full story of what makes something a $heart_S$ is no doubt long, not to mention tedious. (Filling in on a deck with a missing queen of hearts, for example, we may designate a certain joker to fill that role. It is then, pro tem, at least, a $heart_S$.) Despite the nuances, we may correctly take ourselves to know all one could ever reasonably want to know about $heart_S$s. Science has nothing further to tell. It is part of the concept of a $heart_S$ that what you see is, nuances aside, what you get. All this is quite consistent with the notion of being a $heart_S$ playing explanatory, and even causal-explanatory, roles. A card's being a $heart_S$ may explain why it is likely to be discarded. There being many $heart_S$s in a given hand may explain why it is a winning hand and even why it will win. Such does not bring science further into the picture.

AUGUSTANA UNIVERSITY COLLEGE
LIBRARY

I do not think that beliefs (nor desires) are 'just like suits of cards,' whatever that may mean. Nor do I think them much like organs. In present respects, I think they are *more* like cards than like organs. But that tells us little. What I *do* think is that it is an open question as to what sorts of concepts believing and desiring are and just how they are supposed to be taken to function. Surprising as it may seem so late in the twentieth century, a really thorough investigation of their behaviour is yet to be undertaken. (As Wittgenstein noted, 'what is in question here are similarities and differences of concepts, not phenomena.'[8]) In advance of that investigation, it is premature, I think, to appeal to science to try to settle what beliefs are, much less whether there are any.

Belief, desire, and the rest figure in our ordinary explanations of what people do or are like. Jane is gloating because she thinks she refuted me. That makes her happy. Sometimes, too, such things merit the title *cause*: Jane's loathing for Hugo caused her to take a detour. I suspect it is just this that misleads Churchland into supposing that 'believe,' 'want,' and so forth refer to (elements in) causal *mechanisms*. But again, not all causes are mechanisms, nor do all causal explanations refer to such. The toy on the carpet caused Bill to sprain his ankle. The obstruction in the road caused motorists to drive around it. Your having left Sam's present on the table in the open caused him to see what he was getting before it was his birthday. Losing the ace caused Pia to lose the hand. Why not also: Sara's latest paper caused Jane to lower her opinion of her?

There are in the literature models of what is said in ascribing beliefs and the rest to people on which there is no reference to, or implication of, specific causal mechanisms. While I do not quite subscribe to these models, they have not to my knowledge ever been refuted. Nor are they noticeably inferior to any others in the literature. The model I have in mind for purposes of illustration is a popular version of Ryle.[9] The rough idea is this. When I say that Jane believes she has refuted me, I classify her as belonging to certain ranges of cases by virtue of sufficient similarity to other members of those ranges. For example, I classify her with cases of people believing they have refuted someone. To so classify someone is to identify his life as fitting a certain (roughly delineated) pattern. (Roughly as one might do in calling someone miserly, irascible, or a roué.) The pattern, while difficult to characterize in other terms, is constituted by what a person (whose life fits it) does or would do. It is observable, not hidden. Not all of the pattern is observable at once, of course – it is a life that is in question here. But when it is settled what the observable patterns of doings etc. *are*, nothing further could be relevant to the question as to whether the pattern was this one or that.

The Rylean model concedes to science a role in showing how correct ascriptions of belief etc. really go. But it also sets definite limits to what that role might be. At no time do we see every bit of that which, in a given person, instantiates a pattern he fits. What we see of him (typically) leads us to expect more; thwart enough such expectations and you cut away the grounds for the belief attributions we make. Science may show, in particular cases, that we are wrong in expecting thus given so; so that the instantiation we took to be present really was not. Or it may give reason for assimilating certain specifics to an instantiation of one pattern rather than another. (Psychoanalysis again.) Given the patterns and their instantiations, though, there is nothing further to be shown by empirical discovery as to which ascriptions fit. We *may* believe that it takes mechanisms to fit a person to a pattern. Whether that belief is right or wrong, our ascriptions speak of no such mechanism nor, hence, does their correctness depend on which causal processes, in which devices, bring the patterns about.

The model assigns an explanatory and causal role to beliefs. But it does this without viewing beliefs as any specific 'cog' in some works whose workings yield behavior. That Jane's is, at the moment, the sort of life of one who believes she has refuted me explains why she would do thus and so – gloat, for example. It is the sort of life in which one *would* gloat. Further, the model supports *causal* explanations of a quite interesting sort. That Jane was in some way[10] such as to fit the pattern of a loather of Hugo caused her to take a detour. Perhaps some particular mechanism made her that way. The above *causal* explanation refers to none and supposes nothing about what, specifically, such might be like. It does, for all that, explain by specifying a cause.

Being such as to exhibit a pattern in one's life is enough to cause some things. Although we may believe that one could not be so without a mechanism churning the pattern out, the above causal story mentions, and commits itself to, none. On Ryle's model, that is the way beliefs and so on may cause our doings.

I failed to endorse the above 'Rylean' view, although it shows how Churchland could be wrong about the theoretical commitments of belief and desire talk. It would thus be nice to give some reasons I believe in for thinking that I, and not Churchland, am right on that issue. What I can say here, while immensely less than apodictic, is something.

One consideration is brought out by Moore's paradox. Half the paradox is the fact that to say, for example, 'I believe this is the way to the beach' is, on its most standard use, to say *roughly* the same as, 'This is the way to the beach.' The two forms of expression stand on *nearly* equal footing in a number of respects. In the first, I may be taken to have told you something about 'my state of mind'; but not in any way in which I have not told you the same in the second form. In that respect, the same conclusions (roughly) may be drawn from either. Further, the same facts, in both cases, would show what I said to be mistaken. The natural refutation in the first case, just as much as in the second, would run something like, 'No it's not; it's the way to the top of the cliff' and *not* 'No you don't. You believe that lilacs are blue/nothing at all.' This indicates that both forms say at least roughly, and apparently exactly, the same thing to be so. Both are ways of speaking of the way to the beach and saying such and such to be that. Both, that is, speak of extradermal states of affairs. Neither is a *description* of my state of mind (in any sense in which the other is not). That both state the same explains why one cannot consistently assert the one and deny the other.

To be sure, there are *some* differences in the circumstances in which each form would supply the mot juste. One (only) of the outstanding uses for the first form is to lessen one's responsibility for what is asserted by explicitly recognizing, or making clear, that there is some doubt about it: 'I *think* this is the way to the beach, but I'm not entirely sure.' What this, seen together with the above facts, suggests is that 'I believe' – in the use now being considered – is a sort of illocutionary force operator: what it changes is not what is said to be so but the *way* in which it is said to be so – that is, with some reservation – and hence the terms of assessment appropriate to that saying of it.

The rough equivalence has both positive and negative implications in present matters. On the positive side, it suggests a view of what is said (and done) in saying 'believe'; that is, it suggests in what *some* correct applications of such words would consist. *What* it suggests leaves no room for future surprises as to whether there are such applications. On the negative side, it suggests that what such talk is doing could not be what it would have to be if Churchland's sort of scientific discovery were really relevant to the question as to whether in speaking of people as believing this or that we are really speaking of anything at all. Here I can but scratch the surface of each side.

On the positive side, the equivalence supports the following strong, though presently rough, intuition. Suppose Pia is in a position to say, 'This is the way to the beach,' so that in doing so she would speak correctly in every respect; she would be entirely free from criticism for misusing words – using them other than as (and for) what they are to be – in any way whatever. Then she is, ipso facto, in a position to say, with equal correctness and right, 'I believe that this is the way to the beach.'

To this intuition I append a condensed argument. If the latter is entirely correct, she *does* believe that that is the way to the beach.[11] So if there are cases of people being in a position for saying anything at all, which is like Pia's, above, for 'This is the way to the beach,' then there are cases of people having some beliefs. Moreover, there are cases where it is pertinent to say so, since this may be a way of (at least partially) classifying someone as being in such a position. So, in supposing (at least some) belief talk to be sensible and to fit coherently with some ways for things to be, we suppose no more than that people may sometimes use words, or be able to, from the sort of position described for Pia.

The argument might be bolstered as follows. If we are right in supposing there to be a coherent distinction to be drawn between cases of using words as they are meant to be (cases they are fit for) and cases of not so doing, then there *are* positions such as Pia's; we sometimes, in fact often, enjoy them. All the more so if drawing such a distinction is pertinent. But give up *this* premise, and we thereby give up any reason we might have had either for talking or for listening – certainly on any occasion like the present one.

I will briefly indicate a line along which the above thought might be refined. It is commonly thought that whether words are used (on an occasion) as they are meant to be (or may properly be) depends, in general, on two factors. First, speaking very roughly, there is what the words mean or say, and thereby require for correct use. Second, there is the nature of the circumstances to which, on that use, the words would be fitted. Criticism of someone's use of words might be directed at either half of this distinction: someone may have erred in taking words to mean or say what fits them to (use in/of) such and such (sort of) circumstances and so exhibit a deficient perception or appreciation of how those words are to be used, or what their correct use would be. Or, while free from error of that sort, someone may mistakenly take given circumstances to be of such and such a sort, where that is a sort for which the words are fit.

If Pia says, 'I believe this is the way to the beach,' she may be subject to criticism of either of the above sorts if what she actually said is mistaken (that is, the way she pointed to is not the way to the beach). Suppose, though, *we* say, 'Pia believed that was the way to the beach.' Our remark directs criticism of Pia along certain lines: thus far, the first sort of criticism is not in order; her mastery of that bit of language is not deficient. Pertinent criticism, if any, is to be directed to her appreciation of how things stood (relevantly) in the world. This exhibits one point in seeing people as believers of this or that. We *may* think Pia's performances need mechanisms whose actions cause them. But in assessing her as above we suppose nothing about that. Nor might the brain's dynamics, when revealed, give us cause to cease doing so.

Wittgenstein noted the negative implications of Moore's paradox for a view like Churchland's: on such a view, the paradox should not arise. In Wittgenstein's words,

The difficulty becomes insurmountable if you think the sentence (*Satz*) 'I believe ...' states something about the state of my mind. If it were so, then
Moore's paradox would have to be reproducible if, instead of saying something about the state of one's mind, one were making some statement about
the state of one's own brain. But the point is that no assertion about the state
of my (or anyone's) brain is equivalent to the assertion which I believe – for
example, 'He will come.'[12]

Suppose for a moment that in saying 'X believes that P,' one is referring
to some specific cog in the etiology of X's doings; one with workings,
with those doings as effects. Then it is mysterious why there should be
a *paradox* where Moore finds one: I say that this is the way to the beach;
and I also say that the relevant cog is not in the right position. There is
no contradiction in that. There may, as Wittgenstein notes, be the kind
of 'paradox' involved in saying, 'I can't speak a word of English.' But
that is *not* Moore's paradox.

The above is both unfinished and contentious. It points, though, both
to fruitful questions for understanding belief, talk, etc. and to questions
one must assume settled before saying, with Churchland, that talk of
what people believe and want involves a 'speculative framework.'

A second consideration is a set of reasons for believing in the
nonopacity of belief ascriptions. The general slogan here is: when using
words to say what it is that so and so believes, one is responsible for
those words in *very* nearly the way one is normally responsible for his
own words. Start with a trivial case. Yesterday, Jane thought, what she
might have put in saying, 'Today is the day I refuted Travis,' or 'Today
there is a dun cow in the field. Yesterday it was a pied one. What will
tomorrow bring?' If I now want to say what she then believed, as Frege
noted, I must say something like, 'Jane believed that yesterday was the
day she refuted me.' I cannot use the word 'today'; to do so would be to
refer to the day on which I spoke. Mutatis mutandis for the other case.
Similarly for predicates. For most purposes, though not for all, if I say,
pointing at a cow, 'Jane believes that that cow is dun,' what I thus say is
true only if the way Jane believes the cow to be is what counts *from the
perspective of my words* as being dun. It is not enough if, on some other
occasion, Jane could have used the word 'dun' correctly in saying how
she took the cow to be.

Names provide a vivid case in point. First, I am normally obliged
only to use names that have been properly introduced to my audience
or with which I may suppose them to be familiar. Suppose I am a secret
admirer of an obscure amateur philosopher from Alice Springs named
Ned. In my circles, Ned is as obscure as another human being could be.
Then in the middle of a debate over whether, say, knowledge might be

a hybrid concept, it would be bizarre for me to say, with no preparation, 'Ned has said some interesting things about this.' Whatever the source of this bizarreness, it is fully preserved if I say, 'Jane believes that Ned has said some interesting things about this' even if Jane knows Ned and thinks of the matter in just those terms. (I might, of course, say, 'There's this amateur in Alice Springs, and *he* has said ...' Mutatis mutandis for 'Jane believes that he has said ...')

Second, if I use a 'name' that names nothing, I have misspoken; doubly so if I *know* the 'name' to name nothing; trebly so if it is *generally* known to name nothing. 'Palmerston,' it emerges, is a myth; pure invention by Saatchi and Saatchi (Victorian virtue). Then if I say, 'Palmerston drank Port,' although purporting to say something about someone, I unwittingly say nothing about anyone; hence I fail to say anything to be so. Once the myth is thoroughly exploded, I cannot (in normal contexts) even *purport* to say anything to be so in so speaking. So that if I do so speak, I have simply behaved bizarrely; nothing can be made of my words – specifically, nothing can be taken to have been said to be so in them.

The point to note is that all of this remains intact when I speak of what Jane believes. If I say, 'Jane believes ...,' my filling of that blank purports to provide something that one *might* take to be so, that is, believe. To provide that is to provide what *might* be so or not. I do this only where there is something my filling would have said; not where there is nothing it could have. Where my filling is 'Palmerston drank Port,' I have failed to do it. Where the myth about 'Palmerston' has been thoroughly exploded, my words, in so speaking, will be no more interpretable and no less bizarre than they would with the 'Jane believes' left off. I have failed to indulge in an even putative way of saying what someone believes, for I have not even putatively produced anything one might believe. If Jane still believes in Palmerston's existence, and that the man she thus takes there to have been drank Port, then something like that, and not the ingenuous 'Jane believes that Palmerston ...,' is the correct way of putting the point (and the way we normally would put it).

Third, if Hugo is also called Bill, and we all know that, then for most purposes, either name will do as well for saying what Jane believes if she believes, say, that Hugo is deceiving Pia. Even if Jane does not know that Hugo is called Bill, what we *cannot* say correctly is: 'Jane believes that *Hugo* is deceiving Pia, but she does not believe that *Bill* is.' To say this is just to contradict ourselves, and, given what everyone here knows, to make no good sense at all. (There may be a point to be made in this vicinity; but the right way to make it is by circumlocution.)

The general upshot is this. When we say what Jane believes, using a simple locution like 'Jane believes that she has refuted me,' we state one fact, and exactly one fact, about the way Jane represents the world: she represents it as being in a state in which she has refuted me. No doubt, for Jane to do that she must think of me and of her refutation, in particular ways. She associates me, for example, with a particular face or with particular occasions on which I aroused such and such passions in her. But those aspects of the way she represents the world are little or no part of the state of affairs I said to obtain when I said, 'Jane believes she has refuted me.' In so speaking, I say nothing to identify the particular ways in which Jane represents these other matters. The indications are that I *could* not do this, so that those factors could not play such a role. For to make my words responsible to *those* aspects of Pia's mental life would be incompatible with my responsibilities to use *all* of my words as those particular words *are* to be used from my own perspective on the world.

If Jane's believing she has refuted me corresponded to a *mechanism* or cog in the etiology of her behaviour, then which mechanism that is would presumably depend on the *whole* story of the way she represents relevant features of the world, such as me and her 'refutation.' But the belief ascription just made refers to, and presupposes, no such specifics. It is committed, at most, to there being *some* such story or other to tell – so, insofar as we believe that such a story requires some suitable etiological mechanism, to there being some such mechanism or other. One thing, anyway, that a 'Rylean' account got right: the way in which reference to beliefs is reference to *causes* of what we do and to just what sort of causation is involved.

Again, the full story must be much longer than the above. Inter alia, it will be noticed that some of what I have just said is contentious. Let us then contend. But let us also once again note, with Wittgenstein, that the issue is how certain *concepts* behave; not of what phenomena there are.

Churchland's 'demonstration' of his second thesis consists in two remarks. The first repeats the 'proof' of thesis 1. To see people as having beliefs, desires, etc., we must posses, and implicate in our so seeing things, stimulus – or data – processing mechanisms of some sort or another. Or so Churchland supposes. Martians might have different mechanisms and, thus, process the same stimuli differently. That is, Martians could be the sorts of organisms that did not see people as believers and desirers. Churchland concludes from this, illegitimately and almost certainly erroneously, that we *learn* to see people as believers and desirers and might learn to see them otherwise. NNT, of course, entails no such thing. It is compatible with there being limits to learning as well as with there being ways we are *constructed* to see the world, and do not learn to see it. It is, after all, a plan for doing psychology, not a dogma about what the result of doing psychology must be. But, so far, NNT has played no role in the argument. It could hardly have done so; there has *been* no argument.

Churchland's second remark appeals to the fact that NNT describes what *mechanisms* do in terms of 'high-dimensional activation vectors.' He concludes that, taking NNT on board, we might describe Jane in terms of her activation vectors and give some such descriptions in place of saying she believes she has refuted me. Nothing has been said about what such descriptions might look like; how the right vectors are to be specified; or by what properties one is to be distinguished from another. Nothing has been said about what such descriptions would be identifying. The correct response, then, is: we *might*, of course, do lots of things.

To which I append a suspicion. If such vector-ascriptions are to do what belief ascriptions in fact do for us, they must have at least two properties. First, those things about Jane that tell me that a certain belief ascription applies (that gloating look, produced as it was in those circumstances, for example) must similarly tell one equipped with the right vocabulary that such and such vector-ascriptions apply. Or at least the way she is when I see her to believe such and such must be equally informative to a wielder of vector-ascriptions. One must be able to read her vectors in her face. This means, I think, that suitable vector ascriptions could be no more responsible for the way Jane represents the world than are belief ascriptions. Second, one must be able to infer (with right, and the same right) from suitable vector ascriptions what can be inferred from the belief ascriptions they displace – for example, that it is now time for me to start pointing out to Jane the holes in her argument. The suspicion is: vector ascriptions with those properties would turn out to be no more than arcane and recherché ways of saying what people believe and want.

Churchland comments, 'perhaps the familiar propositional attitudes ... will simply be eliminated from our scientific ontology because nothing of dynamical importance in the brain answers to them.' I have tried to show that propositional attitude ascriptions in no way purport to say anything 'of dynamical importance'about the brain or anything else. They are in a quite different line of work; the question of their failing in *that* way just does not arise. They tell *no* story about the brain nor any story about *mechanisms* by which our doings are produced. If I am right, then the sort of scientific discovery Churchland awaits is just not in the cards.

Notes

1 Literally, *truths like cows*; used to mean *truisms*. (Dutch).
2 In 'What Theories Are Not,' in *Mathematics Matter and Method*, Philosophical Papers, Vol. I, Cambridge University Press, Cambridge, 1975. (Originally published in 1962).
3 In *Sense and Sensibilia*, Oxford University Press, Oxford, 1962, lecture 10.
4 I have developed this thought further in my 'Vagueness, Observation and Sorites,'in *Mind*, Vol. 93 (May-June) 1985.
5 P.K. Feyerabend, 'An Attempt At A Realistic Interpretation Of Experience,'*Proceedings of the Aristotelian Society*, Vol. 59 (1958/9), 150.
6 See *Discourse on Metaphysics*, section 8.
7 A related point: people may share a concept (know who Jane is, what a cow is, or etc.) while failing to share recognition abilities or devices.
8 *Remarks on the Philosophy of Psychology*, Vol. 1, §472.
9 What Ryle himself actually thought is, to my mind, a vexed question.
10 Or the way she was, whatever that may have been.
11 More precisely: for at least some purposes she so counts.
12 *Remarks on the Philosophy of Psychology*, Vol. 1, §501.

References

Austin, J.L. (1962). *Sense and Sensibilia*. Oxford, Oxford University Press
Feyerabend, P.K. (1958). An attempt at a realistic interpretation of experience. *Proceedings of the Aristotelian Society* 59: 143-70
Leibniz, G. (1988). *Discourse on Metaphysics*. New York, St. Martin's Press
Putnam, H. (1975). What theories are not. *Mathematics, Matter and Method*. Cambridge, Cambridge University Press
Travis, Charles. (1985).Vagueness, observation and sorites. *Mind*. 93: 345-66
Wittgenstein, Ludwig. (1980). *Remarks on the Philosophy of Psychology*. Oxford, Basil Blackwell

3

Towards a Microstructural Account of Human Reasoning

David E. Rumelhart

For the past several years my colleagues and I have been analyzing what we call parallel distributed processing (PDP) systems and looking at what we call the microstructure of cognition (cf. McClelland, Rumelhart, and the PDP Research Group 1986; Rumelhart, McClelland, and the PDP Research Group 1986). In this work we developed computational models of cognitive processes based on principles of 'brain-style' processing. The major focus of this work has been in perception, memory retrieval, and learning. The question remains as to how this work extends to the domains of 'higher mental processes.' We have made one attempt to show how our PDP models can be used to account for schemalike effects (Rumelhart, Smolensky, McClelland, and Hinton 1986). This chapter is designed to push those ideas further and to sketch an account of reasoning from a PDP perspective. I will proceed by first describing the basic theoretical structure of the PDP approach. I will then give a brief account of the reasoning process and finally show how it can be seen as resulting from a parallel distributed processing system.

Parallel Distributed Processing

Cognitive psychology/information processing has become the dominant approach to the understanding of higher mental processes over the past twenty-five years or so. The computer has provided, among other things, the primary conceptual tools that have allowed cognitive psychology to succeed. These tools have been powerful and have offered a conceptualization of mind that has proven both more rigorous and more powerful than any that have preceded it. There have, however, been some drawbacks. Because we have, by and large, worked with serial, digital, stored-program, symbol-processing Von Neumann-type computers, we have (perhaps inadvertently) carried much of the baggage of the Von Neumann computer into the 'computer metaphor' and thence into our formal theories and into our intuitions. The argument is not that we should abandon the computational approach to the study of cognitive processes. Viewing the human cognitive system as a computational system is surely valuable, but, I believe, we have been drawing our insights from the wrong kind of computer. It is clear that brains are very different kinds of computers from the Von Neumann systems, with which we have gained so much experience. The PDP approach suggests that we should ask the question directly about what kind of computer the brain might be, experiment with 'brainlike' computers, and then draw our inspiration from these computational systems. In short, we want to replace the computer metaphor with the brain metaphor for cognitive systems.

Our work builds on the classical work on neural networks (cf. Grossberg 1976), associative memories (cf. Anderson 1977; Kohonen 1977, 1984), and the work on perceptions and other self-organizing machines from the artificial intelligence literature from the late 1950s and early 1960s (cf. Minsky and Papert 1969; Rosenblatt 1962). We have tried to take these developments, understand their import for the nature of mental processing, develop our own variations on these ideas, evaluate the formal characteristics of such systems, build concrete models of specific psychological processes, and develop new kinds of networks for application to the particular problems that have seemed most important.

PDP models, like brains, consist of very large networks of very simple processing units, which communicate through the passing of excitatory and inhibitory messages to one another. All units work in parallel without a specific executive. The results emerge from a relaxationlike interaction between the relatively homogeneous processing units. Knowledge resides only in the connections, and all learning involves a modification of the connections.

Thinking and reasoning

One of the areas that has been least touched by our work on PDP models is that of reasoning and problem solving. Some believe that the existence of inferences implies a kind of logical system similar to that employed in conventional symbol-processing models. I have become increasingly convinced that much of what we call reasoning can better be accounted for by processes, such as pattern matching and generalization, which are well carried out by PDP models.

If the human information-processing system carries out its computations by 'settling' into solutions as the PDP perspective suggests rather than applying logical, symbolic operations as we might have thought, why are humans so intelligent? How *do* we make inferences? How do we know how to respond to new situations? How can we do science, mathematics, logic, and so on? In short, how can we do logic if our basic operations are not logical at all? We can begin to see an answer to these questions, I believe, with a careful look at reasoning tasks and the cognitive processes involved in them.

There are, it seems to me, three common processes for reasoning about novel situations.

(1) *Reasoning by similarity*, in which a problem is solved by seeing the current situation as similar to a previous one, to which the solution is known (generalization and analogical reasoning fall in this category).

(2) *Reasoning by mental simulation*, in which a problem is solved by imagining the consequence of an action and making the knowledge that is implicit in our ability to imagine an event explicit.

(3) *Formal reasoning*, in which a formal symbolic system, such as mathematics, is employed in the solution of a problem.

The major point of this chapter will be to make these types of processes explicit and to show how PDP systems can naturally account for these three types of behaviour.

The basic idea is that we succeed in thinking and logical problem solving by making the problems we wish to solve conform to problems we are good at solving. People seem to have three essential abilities, which together allow them to come to logical conclusions without being logical. It is these three abilities that underlie the three reasoning strategies mentioned above. These abilities are:

(1) *Pattern matching*: We seem to be able to 'settle' quickly on an interpretation of an input pattern. This is an ability that is central to perceiving, remembering, comprehending, and reasoning by similarity. Our ability to pattern-match is probably not something that sets humans apart from other animals but is probably *the* essential component to most cognitive behaviour.

(2) We are good at modelling our world. That is, we are good at anticipating the new state of affairs resulting from our actions or from an event we might observe. This ability to build up expectations by 'internalizing' our experiences is probably crucial to the survival of all organisms in which learning plays a key role. This is the fundamental ability that underlies our ability to imagine and to perform mental simulations.

(3) We are good at manipulating our environment. This is another version of man-the-tool-user, and I believe that this is perhaps

the crucial skill that allows us to think logically, do mathematics and science, and, in general, build a culture. Especially important here is our ability to manipulate the environment, so that it comes to represent something. This is what sets humans and their intellectual accomplishments apart from other animals.

In the following sections I will outline the PDP mechanisms that allow for these abilities and show how they may result in the reasoning categories postulated above.

Reasoning by Similarity

Most everyday reasoning probably does not involve much in the way of manipulating mental models. It probably involves even less in the way of formal reasoning. Rather, it probably involves assimilating the novel situation to other situations that are in some way similar – that is, reasoning by similarity. Now, it is possible to see a continuum of possible situations for reasoning by similarity involving, at one pole, what might be called *remembering* and, at the other, what might be called *analogical reasoning*. In between, we have such processes as *generalizing, being reminded*, and *reasoning by example*.

There are, within the framework of PDP models, ideal mechanisms for accounting for a large portion of these phenomena. To see this, it is useful to conceptualize a PDP system as a content-addressable memory system (cf. McClelland and Rumelhart 1985). The simplest way to do this is to imagine a memory system consisting of a very large number of processing units. These units are rather densely interconnected, and for simplicity we imagine that each unit has a potential connection to each other unit in the memory. Each unit receives input from outside the memory system (either from the external world or from other modules in the information-processing system itself). The memory system, in turn, sends outputs to other modules. The units themselves can be seen as microfeatures. A particular situation is represented by turning on those microfeatures that constitute a description of the represented situation. Certain collections of microfeatures might represent the physical characteristics of the situation, such as the colour or size of an object being viewed, whether some particular object is present, and so on. Other microfeatures represent more abstract relational aspects of a situation, such as whether or not two objects are the same shape. An experience is assumed to result in a particular pattern of activation impinging on the memory units. Retrieval is assumed to occur when this previously active pattern is reinstated over the set of memory units. Information is stored in the memory by strengthening the connections between those units that co-occur and weakening the connections between pairs of units in which one is on and the other is off.[1] Although the exact values of the weights connecting any two units in the memory system will differ, depending on the rule employed for changing the weights, to a first-order of approximation, the connection strengths will be a function of the correlation between the two units. If they are positively correlated, their connection strengths will be positive. If they are negatively correlated, the connection strengths will be negative. If they are uncorrelated, the connection strengths will be near zero. Retrieval involves pattern completion. The memory is given a probe in which the activation of a subset of the units of the memory systems is set and the system is allowed to settle into a stable state of activation. Such a memory system can be shown to have the following characteristics.

(1) When a previously stored (i.e., familiar) pattern enters the memory system, it is amplified, and the system responds with a stronger version of the input pattern. This is a kind of recognition response.

(2) When an unfamiliar pattern enters the memory system, it is dampened, and the activity of the memory system is shut down. This is a kind of unfamiliarity response.

(3) When part of a familiar pattern is presented, the system responds by 'filling in' the missing parts. This is a kind of recall paradigm in which the part constitutes the retrieval cue and the filling in is a kind of memory reconstruction process. This is a content-addressable memory system.

(4) When a pattern similar to a stored pattern is presented, the system responds by distorting the input towards the stored pattern. This is a kind of assimilation response in which similar inputs are assimilated to similar stored events.

(5) Finally, if a number of similar patterns have been stored, the system will respond strongly to the central tendency of the stored patterns – even though the central tendency itself was never stored. Thus this sort of memory system automatically responds to prototypes, even when no prototype has been seen.

McClelland and I have studied this sort of memory system in some detail (McClelland and Rumelhart 1985) and have shown how this model can be applied to a range of memory phenomena. It should be noted that this is a substantially different view of memory than that suggested by the traditional *place* metaphor for memory. In this model an experience corresponds to a pattern of activation over the memory units. A memory trace corresponds to the specific set of weight changes that occur in response to a particular experience. A distributed model of this sort leads naturally to the suggestion that semantic memory may be just the residue of the superposition of episodic traces. Consider, for example, the representation of a pattern encountered in several different contexts, and assume for the moment that context and content are represented by different units. Over repeated experience with the same pattern in different contexts, the pattern will remain in the interconnections of the units relevant to the content subpattern, but the particular associations to particular contexts will wash out. However, material that is encountered only in one particular context will tend to be somewhat contextually bound. So we may not be able to retrieve what we learn in one context when we need it in other situations.

The heart of this proposal, which makes it so useful for our present purposes, is that the memory access is determined by the similarity between the input patterns and the stored patterns. At the same time that it is considered a content-addressable store, the memory can be seen as a device for making generalizations to novel situations. Note that what is really being stored is the degree to which one microfeature predicts another. Thus, if there are regularities in the stored patterns, such that whenever a certain configuration of microfeatures is present a certain other set of microfeatures is present, these regularities are as much stored as is the particular instance. In this way, the system can respond correctly in the face of novel situations. Consider, for example, a memory system in which we store patterns one part of which represents the pronunciation of the root form of a verb and another part of which represents the past-tense form of the verb. Since there are regularities between the present-tense and the past-tense forms of the verb, these regularities are stored. Subsequently, when a probe is given consisting of a representation of a completely novel root form of a verb, the system will construct the correct form of the past tense (cf. Rumelhart, McClelland, and the PDP Research Group 1986). This generalization is stored just as much as the patterns that were actually observed (unless, of course, the novel verb is irregular – in which case the memory will 'over-regularize').

Similarly, reminding 'falls out' of the structure of this system. If the current situation is similar to a previously encountered situation, it is then possible that the previous situation will be evoked in the face of the current situation. It should be noted that the dimension of similarity on which the match occurs may be of any sort. It may be primarily on the basis of object similarity, in which case the situation of which you are reminded would bear a good deal of surface similarity to the current situation, or it could depend primarily on more abstract relational microfeatures. In this case, the system could well settle into a state that constituted a memory for a situation that was quite different on the surface but that had a similar abstract structure. Generally, of course, reminding would depend on a mix of relational and more concrete microfeatures.

Analogical reasoning is a small step from being reminded of a situation primarily on the basis of relational microfeatures. Essentially, I imagine the following situation. The microfeatures are ordered somehow in terms of abstractness from most concrete to most abstract and relational. I imagine that upon encountering a novel situation certain aspects of the situation come to attention and serve as the 'retrieval cue' for the system. There are now a number of possible situations. It might happen that we had encountered a very similar situation in the past. In this case, the system would settle on an 'interpretation' of the present situation that would amount to remembering a similar situation and filling in the missing microfeatures based on this situation. It might also happen that there is no close match wholly consistent with the input features. In this case, I imagine that the input 'constraints' would gradually be weakened. Normally, in these systems we 'clamp' the inputs, requiring that the final state of the system be consistent with the retrieval cue. Now consider a case in which the retrieval cue itself is gradually weakened. Suppose that, first, the most concrete inputs are released. Progressively more abstract microfeatures are released until an acceptable match is reached on the subspace, containing as many as possible of the more relational features. The system could then generalize based on this subspace and, in that way, come to conclusions about the present situation based on another set of stored patterns that have the same basic relational structure as the current situation. In short, the system would do analogical reasoning.

Figure 3.1 gives a more concrete illustration of the process. We assume that we have a set of microfeatures ordered, in some way, according to their 'abstractness.' The most concrete features are indicated on the left and the most abstract on the right. A reasoning situation begins with the observation of some set of features. These features are 'clamped.' Some of the clamped features are concrete surface features and others are more abstract relational aspects of the novel situation. Once these features are clamped, the system begins the process of filling in the missing features. The filling in is done in such a way as to maximize a 'goodness' function (see Rumelhart, Smolensky, McClelland, and Hinton 1986). The system will always find a maximum of this goodness-of-fit function (that is, a function that measures the degree to which the reconstructed information is consistent with the stored information). Normally, when retrieval occurs, the overall fit will be good. The system will be able to find a minimum that corresponds to some

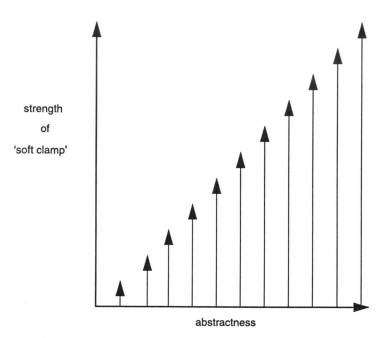

strength

of

'soft clamp'

abstractness

Figure 3.1: Memory features organized from most concrete to most abstract from left to
right. The inputs may either clamp certain features on or simply provide a constant input to certain of the units.

stored experiences, and the result will be retrieval. Other times, however, the overall goodness will be not as great but still adequate. This case
may correspond to a case of generalization or, perhaps, the memory of
an unusual situation. Finally, it can sometimes happen that the resulting
goodness measure is very low indeed. This corresponds to a situation
in which the memory contains no close matches to the probe situation.
In this case, we can 'release' the clamp on the leftmost microfeature and
see if a good fit will occur after ignoring this input feature. If not, the
next feature can be released, and so on. This process can continue until
a satisfactory fit is discovered. When such a fit is discovered, it will constitute the discovery of a situation that shares the same abstract structural features as the current situation – namely, an analogous situation.
    Ideally, one would like to find a state that matched as many of the in-
put features as possible, giving greater weight to the relational features
but generally preferring more matches to fewer. Moreover, it would be
nice if we did not need an explicit mechanism for monitoring the level
of the goodness function and deciding that it was time to release a feature. Fortunately, it is possible to solve both problems simultaneously

by introducing the idea of a 'soft clamp.' Rather than clamp inputs on, we can simply have an input line deliver a constant amount of activation to an input unit. The lower that constant, the more easily the system can override the input constraint. The size of the smallest input determines the goodness threshold before it overrides *any* of the input features. This system can find the overall best fit, overriding input features only when doing so will lead to a sufficiently good fit to make it worthwhile to give up the goodness contribution given by conforming to the input. Under this scheme of soft clamps, we would make the weight of the concrete features the least and the abstract features the most, and the system will 'automatically' go from merely retrieving, to generalizing, to analogizing, as is required by the problem. This will occur without any specific control process determining which to do when.

Mental Models and Mental Simulation

Reasoning by similarity is the most common method of reaching conclusions, but it is not the only one. Much of reasoning seems to involve imagination. It seems that to some degree we can solve problems by imagining situations and 'seeing' what would happen. Broadly, I take it that the term *mental model* refers to our knowledge of some domain that allows us to reason about it by stepping through a sequence of operations and imagining what would happen. Thus, for example, when we answer the question of how many windows our home has by imagining ourselves walking through it and counting the windows, I take this to be the application of a mental model of our home. Similarly, when we imagine what would happen as a result of some action, say, throwing a cup of water on a desk or sitting on a salt shaker, we are employing mental models to reason about the consequences of our actions. How can we account for such phenomena in the context of PDP models? When discussing the normal PDP interpretation system above, I suggested that the system simply received a set of inputs and then settled to a state that amounted to the best account of the input, a standard 'comprehension' assumption. When we reason through the application of mental models, however, we carry out a sequence of mental activities – not a single settling. How can that sequence be represented and controlled in a PDP model?

Suppose, for argument's sake, that the system is broken into two pieces, two sets of units. One piece is the one that we have been discussing – it receives inputs and relaxes to an appropriate state that includes a specification of an appropriate action, which will, in turn, change the inputs to the system. The other piece of the system is similar in nature, except it is a 'model' of the world on which we are acting. This consists of a relaxation network that takes as input some specification of the actions we intend to carry out and produces an interpretation of 'what would happen if we did that.' Part of this specification would be expected to be a specification of what the new stimulus conditions would be like. Thus one network takes inputs from the world and produces actions; the other takes actions and predicts how the input would change in response. This second piece of the system could be considered a mental model of the world events. This second portion, the mental model of the world, would be expected to be operating in any case, inasmuch as it is generating expectations about the state of the world and thereby 'predicting' the outcomes of actions.

Now, suppose that the world events did not happen. It would be possible to take the output of the mental model and replace the stimulus inputs from the world with inputs from our model of the world. In this case, we would expect that we could 'run a mental simulation' and imagine the events that would take place in the world when we performed a particular action. This mental model would allow us to perform actions entirely internally and to judge the consequences of our actions, interpret them, and draw conclusions based on them. In other words, we can, it would seem, build an internal control system based on the interaction between these two modules of the system. Indeed, we have built a simple two-module model of tic-tac-toe that carries out exactly this process and can thereby 'imagine' playing tic-tac-toe (cf. Rumelhart et al. 1986). Figure 3.2 shows the relationships between the interpretation networks, the inputs, the outputs, and the network, representing a model of the world and the process of mental simulation in PDP models. For example, it should be possible to have the system carry out 'mental rotations' by applying a rotation model to some perceptual inputs. It also should be possible to build a system capable of doing mental arithmetic by imagining doing arithmetic with pencil and paper (see discussion of formal reasoning in the next section).

Formal Reasoning

Roughly speaking, the view is this: We are good at 'perceiving' answers to problems. Unfortunately, this is not a universal mechanism for solving problems and thinking, but, as we become more expert, we become better at reducing problem domains to pattern-matching tasks (of the kind best accomplished by PDP models). Thus, chess experts can look at a chess board and 'see' the correct move. This, I assume, is a problem strictly analogous to the problem of perceiving anything. It is not an easy problem, but it is one that humans are especially good at. It has proven to be extraordinarily difficult to duplicate this ability with a

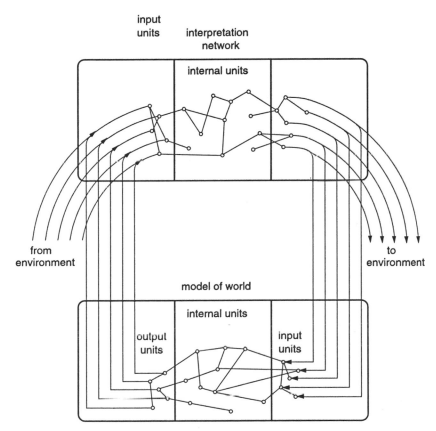

Figure 3.2: The relationships between the model of the world, the interpretation network, the inputs, and the outputs for the purpose of mental simulations.

conventional symbol-processing machine. However, not all problems can be solved by immediately 'seeing' the answer. Thus, few (if any) of us can look at a three-digit multiplication problem (such as 343 times 822) and see the answer. Solving such problems cannot be done by our pattern-matching apparatus; parallel processing alone will not do the trick; we need a kind of serial processing mechanism to solve such a problem. Here is where our ability to manipulate our environment becomes critical. We can, quite readily, learn to write down the two numbers in a certain format when given such a problem:

343
822

Moreover, we can learn to see the first step of such a multiplication problem (viz., that we should enter a 6 below the 3 and 2):

```
343
822
───
  6
```

We can then use our ability to pattern-match again to see what to do next. Each cycle of this operation involves first creating a representation through manipulation of the environment, then processing this (physical) representation by means of our well-tuned perceptual apparatus, which leads to a further modification of this representation. By doing this we reduce an abstract conceptual problem to a series of concrete operations at which we can become very good. Now, not only does this apply to solving multiplication problems, it applies to solving problems in logic (e.g., syllogisms), in science, in engineering, and so on. These dual skills of manipulating the environment and processing the environment that we have created allow us to reduce very complex problems to a series of very simple ones. This ability allows us to deal with problems that are otherwise impossible. This is *real* symbol processing and, I am beginning to think, the primary symbol processing that we are able to do. Indeed, on this view, the external environment becomes a key extension to our minds.

There is one more piece to the story. This is the tricky part and, I think, the part that fools us. Not only can we manipulate the physical environment and then process it, we can also learn to internalize the representations we create, 'imagine' them, and then process these imagined representations – just as if they were external. As I said before, I believe that we are good at building models of our environment so that we can anticipate what the world would be like after some action or event takes place. As we gain experience with the world created by our (and others') actions, we develop internal models of these external representations. We can thus imagine writing down a multiplication problem and imagine multiplying the numbers together. If the problem is simple enough, we can actually solve the problem in our imagination; similarly for syllogisms. Consider, for example, a simply syllogism: All *A* are *B* and no *C* are *B*. We could solve this by drawing a circle for *A*, a larger circle including all of the *A*'s around the first circle to represent the *B*'s, and a third disjoint circle standing for the *C*'s. We could then 'see' that no *A*'s are *C*. Alternatively, we need not actually draw the circles; we can merely imagine them. I believe that this ability to do the problem in our imagination is derived from our ability to do it physically, just as out ability to do mental multiplication is derived from our ability to do multiplication with pencil and paper. The argument that external

representations play a crucial role in thought (or, say, in solving syllogisms) is sometimes challenged on the grounds that we do not really
have to draw Venn diagrams (or whatever) to solve them since we *can*
solve them in our head. I suspect that the major way we can do that is
to imagine doing it externally. Since this imagination is dependent on
our experience with such representations externally, the argument that
we *can* solve them mentally loses its force against the view that external
symbols are important for thought processes.

It is interesting that it is apparently difficult to invent new external
representations for problems we might wish to solve. The invention of
a new representation would seem to involve some basic insight into the
nature of the problem to be solved. It may be that the process of invent-
ing such representations is the highest human intellectual ability. Perhaps simply creating an external representation sufficient to support
problem solving of a particular kind is evidence of a kind of abstract
thinking outside of the simpleminded view sketched here. That may be,
but it seems that such representational systems are not very easy to develop. Usually they are provided by our culture. Usually they have
evolved out of other, simpler such systems and over long periods of
time. Newer ones, when they are developed, usually involve taking an
older system and modifying it to suit new needs. One of the critical aspects of our school system would seem to be teaching such representational schemes. The insights into the nature of the problem become
embedded in the representations we learn to use to solve the problems.

Language plays an especially interesting role in all of this. Perhaps
the internal/external issue is not too important with language. The notion here is one of 'self-instruction.' This follows Vygotsky's (1934/
1962) view, I believe. We can be instructed to behave in a particular way.
Responding to instructions in this way can be viewed simply as responding to some environmental event. We can also remember such an
instruction and 'tell ourselves' what to do. We have, in this way, inter-
nalized the instruction. I believe that the process of following instructions is essentially the same whether we have told ourselves or have
been told what to do. Thus, even here, we have a kind of internalization
of an external stimulus (i.e., language). I do not want to make too much
of this point because I recognize that the distinction between external
and internal when we ourselves produce the external representation is
subtle at best, but I do not really think it differs too much from the case
in which we write something down and therefore create a real, physically viewable representation. Saying something aloud creates a hear-
able representation. Imagining saying something aloud creates a
representation that can be processed just as if someone else had said it.

Before leaving this topic, we should note one more important aspect of external representations (as opposed to internal representations). External representations allow us to employ our considerable perceptual/motor abilities in solving abstract problems. This allows us to break problems into a sequence of relatively simple problems. Importantly, once an external representation is created, it can be reinterpreted without regard to its initial interpretation. This freedom allows us to discover solutions to problems without 'seeing' our way to the end. We can inspect intermediate steps and find alternative solutions that might, in some ways, be better. In this way, we can discover new features of our representations and slowly extend them and make them more powerful.

Conclusion

I have tried to show that three of the most common aspects of reasoning can be naturally and simply produced by distributed memory systems. I have argued that the memory system naturally supports reasoning by similarity. I have argued that such a memory system coupled with a prediction system offers an account of reasoning by mental simulation. Finally, I have argued that formal reasoning is essentially the product of carrying out a sequence of perceptual/motor operations on external representations. I have suggested that these external representations may only be imagined on any particular occasion. It should be noted that these are all methods of coming to valid conclusions without the need of an internal logic – natural or otherwise.

Note

1 There are actually a number of important details to the memory storage procedures that determine the detailed behaviour of such systems. The rule described in the text is a variant of the so-called Hebbian learning rule. Although this rule is simple, in many cases it is not adequate. A more complex version of the rule for learning, which I call the generalized delta rule or sometimes the back-propagation rule, would be required in a realistic situation. For present purposes it is sufficient to think of the Hebbian learning rule.

References

Anderson, J.A. (1977). Neural models with cognitive implications. D LaBerge and S.J. Samuels (eds.), *Basic Processes in Reading: Perception and Comprehension*: Hillsdale, NJ: Erlbaum, 27-90.

Grossberg, S. (1976). Adaptive pattern classification and universal recoding: 1. Parallel development and coding of neural feature detectors. *Biological Cybernetics* 23: 121-34

Kohonen, T. (1977). *Associative Memory: A System Theoretical Approach.* New York: Springer

Kohonen, T. (1984). *Self-organization and Associative Memory.* Berlin: Springer Verlag

McClelland, J.L., and Rumelhart, D.E. (1985). Distributed memory and the representation of general and specific information. *Journal of Experimental Psychology: General* 114: 159-88

–, Rumelhart, D.E., and the PDP Research Group. (1986). *Parallel Distributed Processing: Explorations in the Microstructure of Cognition, Vol. 2. Psychological and Biological Models.* Cambridge, MA: MIT Press (Bradford Books)

Minsky, R.L. and Papert, S. (1969). *Perceptions.* Cambridge, MA: MIT Press

Rosenblatt, F. (1962). *Principles of Neurodynamics.* New York: Spartan

Rumelhart, D.E., and McClelland, J.L. (1986). On learning the past tenses of English verbs. In J.L. McClelland, D.E. Rumelhart, and the PDP Research Group. *Parallel Distributed Processing: Explorations in the Microstructure of Cognition: Vol. 2. Psychological and Biological Models.* (Cambridge, MA: MIT Press (Bradford Books) 216-71

–, McClelland, J.L., and the PDP Research Group. (1986). *Parallel Distributed Processing: Explorations in the Microstructure of Cognition Vol 1. Foundations.* Cambridge, MA: MIT Press (Bradford Books)

–, Smolensky, P., McClelland, J.L., and Hinton, G.E. (1986). Schemata and sequential thought processes in PDP models. In J.L. McClelland, D.R. Rumelhart, and the PDP Research Group, *Parallel Distributed Processing: Explorations in the Microstructure of Cognition: Vol 2. Psychological and Biological Models.* Cambridge, MA: MIT Press (Bradford Books) 7-57

Vygotsky, L.S. (1962). *Thought and Language* (E. Hanfmann and G. Vakar, eds. and Trans.). Cambridge, MA: MIT Press. (Original work published in 1934)

4

Connectionism without Tears

Mark S. Seidenberg

What accounts for the cool reaction to the emergence of connectionism in the 1980s on the part of people who study language for a living? Most of the critical assessments of connectionism that followed the initial explosion of interest in the approach came from people such as Bever, Fodor, Pinker, and Prince, whose works are firmly situated within the mainstream of linguistics and psycholinguistics. It will be an interesting project for a future student of the history of ideas or the sociology of science to investigate why, as Prince and Smolensky recently observed, connectionism was seen as 'at best orthogonal and at worst antithetical to the goals of linguistic theory.'[1] This issue is of particular interest to me as someone who was trained in the standard linguistic-psycholinguistic school of thought but has utilized connectionist modelling techniques in studies of language processing. My own work has been grounded in the belief that connectionism and linguistics have more in common than some of the more polemical critiques of the approach would suggest. In this paper I will discuss some of the issues that have tended to separate the two approaches and describe some potentially interesting points of contact.

Nativism and Empiricism

It is clear that many linguists view connectionism as a revival of the radical empiricist approach that dominated the dark ages in psychology–the behaviourist era. Pinker, in particular, equates connectionism with 'associationism,' a move that has the effect of eliciting, almost by reflex, the intellectual and emotional antipathy that most linguists feel towards the behaviourist account of language (establishing a kind of guilt by association(ism)).[2] Rumelhart and McClelland's (1986) claims as to what their model of past tense learning showed about the acquisition of language must surely have elicited widespread feelings of deja vu all over again. I think that the attempt to equate connectionism with radical empiricism is a mistake. The correct point of contact is not with the learning theories developed by the animal behaviourists of the 1950s but, rather, with the learnability approach developed by the linguists and psycholinguists of the 1970s and 1980s (for example, Wexler and Culicover 1980; Pinker 1979; Baker and McCarthy 1981).[3] Learnability theory attempts to explain language acquisition in terms of several factors: the initial state of the organism (i.e., innate capacities that are probably species- and domain-specific), the steady state to be achieved (i.e., grammar), the input to the child ('Motherese' and other aspects of the environment; Newport et al. 1977), and the child's capacity to learn. The same factors govern the operation of connectionist models. The initial state of the organism can be equated with the initial configuration or architecture of the model. Steady-state behaviour represents the target to which the model should converge. The model's behaviour changes in response to experience – the 'input to the child.' What connectionism adds to the learnability approach is a novel way of representing knowledge and a substantive theory of learning. The novel way of representing knowledge is in terms of weights on connections between units. The substantive theory of learning is given by the many learning algorithms that operate over networks employing these distributed representations. The main implication I draw from explorations of learning algorithms such as back-propagation (Rumelhart, Hinton, and Williams 1986) is that far richer underlying structures can be recovered from far noisier data than anyone ever imagined. (Indeed, the reinforcement learning techniques of the behaviourists occupy a small and undistinguished corner in a very large space of learning algorithms.) Applications of such learning principles to human behaviour (for example, Gluck and Bower 1988; Elman 1990; Hare 1990) suggest that they capture important aspects of at least some ways in which people learn.

At the same time, it is obvious that the behaviour of connectionist systems is highly dependent on their initial configuration. To the extent that there is evidence that innate capacities govern the acquisition of language (and I think there is), they can be straightforwardly incorporated in connectionist models. McClelland and I provided a simple illustration of this point with our model of word recognition and pronunciation (Seidenberg and McClelland 1989). We described a simple multi-layer backprop net that was trained on a large corpus of monosyllabic words and which simulated numerous aspects of peoples' performance in behavioural experiments employing such stimuli (subjects in these experiments perform tasks such as reading words aloud or deciding whether or not strings of letters form words). The model that closely simulated many aspects of skilled performance was configured with 200 hidden units. We also replicated this simulation using an architecture that provided only 100 hidden units. The disabled model could master some aspects of word recognition and naming but made systematic errors. The interesting part of this exercise was that the pattern of performance exhibited by the disabled model resembled that of some children who are dyslexic (i.e., fail to acquire age-appropriate reading skills). Thus, whether the model performed like a skilled reader or a dyslexic reader depended on its initial configuration – specifically, whether it contained sufficient units and connections to encode all of the information that the task demanded. One way to view these results is that humans have an innate capacity to allocate different neural resources to different tasks, such as reading or speaking (subject to considerable plasticity; Neville 1988). For unknown reasons, dyslexic children may dedicate too little in the way of neural resources to the task of learning to read. Though speculative, this theory is suggestive in light of recent evidence concerning morphological anomalies in the brains of dyslexic children revealed by magnetic resonance imaging (Hynd and Semrud-Clikeman 1989). In sum, the model's performance is both consistent with and lends substance to the idea that tasks such as learning to read are subject to biological constraints.

I realize that when linguists talk about innate capacities for language they have in mind something more specific than a tendency for certain brain areas to be recruited for certain tasks. The inventory of hypothesized innate capacities includes language-specific knowledge structures, tendencies to analyse linguistic input in specific ways, and constraints on the range of hypotheses that are formed, among others. Connectionism is equally compatible with these ideas. Moreover, it provides a basis for exploring exactly how innate capacities of various sorts would affect the course of acquisition. For example, it should be possible to determine why only certain types of generalizations are formed given the starting configuration of the system, the input to the child, and a specific learning algorithm. Again, our model provides a simple illustration. The model addresses a certain range of phenomena concerning word recognition. Our principal focus was on the acquisition of knowledge concerning the correspondences between spelling and sound. The goal was to understand the kinds of generalizations concerning these correspondences that could be learned on the basis of experience. In its initial configuration the model was endowed with ways of representing orthography and phonology. Although the correspondences between the codes were learned, the codes themselves were not. Thus the model tacitly embodies the idea that children who are learning to read already possess considerable knowledge of the sound structure of the language (for example, its phonemic inventory and phonotactic constraints). Some of this knowledge is thought to derive from innate capacities to analyse speech in special ways (for example, Liberman and Mattingly 1985). In an admittedly oversimplified way (the phonological representation we used was, after all, Wickelphones), the model captures this idea. Our particular model did not address where these phonological representations come from because that was not its primary focus. Assume, for the sake of argument, that these aspects of phonology are entirely innate. The model could then be taken as having exemplified how biological constraints of a certain sort constrain what can be learned. The general point is that if, in fact, it is the case that knowledge of some kinds of phonological distinctions (or of other aspects of language) is innate, this can be represented in a net. It would certainly be a reasonable goal, for the future, to endow such models with exactly the innate capacities for which there is independent evidence.

These observations merely establish the simple point that connectionism is compatible with nativism. More important, however, I think that rather than being merely compatible with the nativist view, connectionism is likely to provide what is needed in order to establish the essential correctness of this view with regard to language. The learnability equation I gave above seems to be the proper way to decompose the language acquisition problem but, unfortunately, it yields an equation with more than one unknown. Rather more attention has been focused on characterizing the steady state than on understanding the learning component or the input to the child. Nonetheless, very strong inferences about the initial state of the organism have been drawn. This neglect of the role of learning is perhaps understandable given the meager kinds of learning principles available during much of the history of generative grammar. Lack of interest in learning may also have contributed to a lack of attention to many aspects of the child's experience. Connectionism now provides an interesting theory of learning, motivating empirical studies of whether children utilize such principles, and closer assessments of the behavioural input relevant to the acquisition process. The important implication is that, with a serious theory of human learning nearly in hand, a better understanding of the nature of the input to the child (for example, Fernald 1984; Hirsch-Pasek, Treiman, and Schneiderman 1984), and a rigorous theory of the structure of language (for example, Chomsky 1981), it may be possible at last to solve for the final unknown in the equation – the biological endowment of the child relevant to language. That there is such an endowment seems obvious to me (see Seidenberg 1985a; Seidenberg and Petitto 1987) but it is hard to be specific about exactly what is innate without at the same time knowing what can be learned.

It is an empirical question, of course, but studies of connectionist learning suggest the possibility (in my view, the likelihood) that more of the task of acquiring a language is accomplished by means of learning principles operating on relatively fragmentary, noisy input than was previously assumed. Although the same learnability equation is involved, the division of labour among the various components may turn out to be somewhat different than standard accounts suggest. It would be a serious error to underestimate the power and importance of these learning principles. They will force the reassessment of 'poverty of the stimulus' arguments; puzzles that currently occupy child language researchers, such as how the child escapes from incorrect generalizations working only from positive exemplars, will disappear (connectionist models already learn without direct negative evidence). One of the regrettable consequences of the contentious way in which connectionism was presented to linguists (for example, Rumelhart and McClelland 1986) and the strenuous way in which it was attacked (for example, Pinker and Prince 1988) is that these points of contact between connectionism and learnability theory were obscured. It would be incorrect to conclude that the views expressed by Rumelhart and McClelland in their 1986 paper exhaust the range of possibilities afforded by the broader connectionist framework, though I think that is what in fact happened. Fortunately – in my view, it was inevitable – we are beginning to see the appearance of research that exhibits an appreciation of both the value of connectionism and of the facts about child language that need to be explained (for example, Punkett and Marchman 1991). I believe that as the polemics recede into the background, insights from connectionism are likely to be absorbed by more of the people who study language acquisition, with profound impact on our understanding of the phenomenon.

Connectionism and Linguistic Explanation

As Prince and Smolensky suggest, the initial work that emerged from the connectionist framework could be seen as largely orthogonal to the interests of theoretical linguists. One influential perspective was articulated by Pinker and Prince (1988). They take the view that knowledge of a language consists of knowledge of different kinds of systems of rules. According to this view, the task of the linguist is to identify the rules; the task of the child, to acquire them. Pinker and Prince observed that connectionist models such as the one proposed by Rumelhart and McClelland (1986) fail to capture the rule-governed character of human languages. The inadequacies of the Rumelhart and McClelland proposal about the English past tense led them to question whether connectionist models could contribute to understanding other linguistic phenomena. At best, they suggested, connectionist models might implement the kinds of rule systems posited within linguistic theory. Implementing rule systems in connectionist hardware might be a useful thing to do – it might contribute to understanding how the rules are re-alized in the brain, for example – but in their view the important gener-alizations are captured at the level of the rules themselves.

In light of the recent history of syntactic theory, it is ironic that the de-bate about connectionism and symbolic systems in general, and about connectionism and language in particular, was framed in terms of the issue of rules. Whereas earlier theories (for example, Chomsky 1965) in-corporated numerous structure-specific rules, current theories (for ex-ample, Chomsky 1981) do not. Government-binding theory is principle-based, not rule-based; a sentence is well-formed if it satisfies the constraints imposed by the several modules in the grammar. In a sense, well-formedness is treated as a constraint satisfaction problem (Stabler 1991), which is certainly congenial to the connectionist ap-proach. Similarly, in current theories, language acquisition is not seen as the process of acquiring rules but, rather, of setting parameters govern-ing the range of possibilities afforded by universal grammar. The irony, then, is that Pinker and Prince based their critique of connectionist ac-counts of language on a notion of rule that has little relevance to the dominant theory in syntax, which has provided the intellectual core of theoretical linguistics.

I am not prepared to speculate about the potential for convergence between connectionism and syntactic theory; for some interesting, though preliminary, work that is relevant to this issue see Berg (1991), who describes a recurrent net that learns aspects of X-bar syntax. Leav-ing syntax aside, the view of linguistic theory offered by Pinker and Prince is still widely held in areas such as phonology and morphology, and it is to these areas that I now turn. The fact that current syntactic theory largely eschews the notion of rule (and especially rule-ordering) compelled Bromberger and Halle (1989) to defend the proposition that phonology is really different (insofar as it demands the use of these for-mal mechanisms). Every phonological theory of which I am aware (au-tosegmental phonology; metrical phonology; lexical phonology) follows the Bromberger-Halle (Pinker-Prince) line about rules, though they differ, of course, in terms of the types of rules allowed as well as in other respects. Morphological theories typically embrace this approach as well (but see Bybee 1985, for a somewhat different view).

The picture that Pinker and Prince draw is a tidy one. Linguists have developed theories (for example, of phonology and morphology) em-ploying certain kinds of rules; these theories are demonstrably correct insofar as they capture important generalizations that would otherwise be unexplained. This leaves connectionism with a dilemma: either con-nectionist theories are wrong, insofar as they behave in ways that are in-consistent with the notion of rule relevant to linguistic theory, or they exhibit rule-governed behaviour, in which case they are mere implementations.

I think that connectionism has more to contribute to understanding language than the circumscribed role that Pinker and Prince assign to it, and in the material that follows I attempt to establish why. Since I cannot address all aspects of phonology and morphology for both practical and intellectual reasons, I will follow Pinker and Prince's lead and focus on a narrow but interesting set of phenomena: the past tense of verbs in English – the same phenomena that were at the center of their celebrated critique. It might first be observed, however, that morphological theory in its current state is nowhere near as tidy as Pinker and Prince imply. Morphology is probably the least developed of all the major subareas of linguistic theory. Aside from the fact that there is no unifying theoretical framework, there is debate about the range of phenomena that constitute the subject matter of the field. Some aspects of traditional morphology have been absorbed by phonology (for example, Kiparsky 1982), others by syntax (Selkirk 1984), leaving undecided whether morphology has a subject matter of its own and what its boundaries are (Anderson 1982). The disagreements here run very deep, and there are several competing theoretical frameworks.

English inflectional morphology (which includes past tense formation) is a rather simple system, and it might therefore be thought that, whatever the theoretical debates about, for example, triliteral roots in Arabic, there would be broad agreement about it. Such is not the case. There is a general commitment to generating at least some past tense forms by rule but exactly how many and what types of rules are involved varies across theories. A common (though by no means universal) assumption is that the lexical component of the grammar contains only a listing of idiosyncratic forms, such as irregular past tenses (so-called strong alternations such as BRING-BROUGHT or SING-SANG). However, which past tenses are irregular, and whether the irregularities are morphological or phonological, are unclear. The problem is illustrated by the fact that whereas Pinker and Prince consider alternations such as THINK-THOUGHT and SING-SANG to be idiosyncracies to be listed in the lexicon, Halle and Mohanan (1985) derive them by rule (THINK-THOUGHT, for example, is derived by a phonological rule the only other application of which is to BRING to form BROUGHT). In fact, Halle and Mohanan (1985) derive almost all strong verbs in English by rule. And theirs is not the only product in the marketplace. There have been several theoretical analyses of inflection, including past tense morphology, in the recent past and no one of them has come to predominate. Even the basic nature of the phenomenon is undecided: there are fundamental disputes as to whether the past tense and other aspects of inflection should be treated as part of an autonomous morphological component, as phonological phenomena, or as part of syntax (Anderson 1982; Spencer 1991).

In short, current treatments of inflectional morphology admit many possibilities other than the view promoted by Pinker and Prince. The lack of consensus about foundational issues, such as scope of morphological theory, calls into question their contention that existing linguistic theories provide adequate accounts of the phenomena, which connectionists could only aspire to implement.

Can a single mechanism accommodate both rules and exceptions?

Ignoring the technical disputes that animate current discussions of inflectional morphology, Pinker and Prince (1988) present an appealingly simple view: regular past tense forms are generated by rule; irregular forms are listed in the lexicon. The fact that identifying which forms are irregular is itself a theoretical problem, and the fact that at least some theories hold that even regular, rule-governed forms (for example, familiar ones) are listed (Halle 1973) does not figure in their discussion. They present a generic framework much like the one developed by Aronoff (1976). Aronoff's model takes the word as the primary unit of morphological analysis, in contrast to theories based on other units, for example, morphemes (Halle 1973). Words that are formed by entirely regular, productive processes are not listed in the lexicon. Pinker and Prince discuss a range of facts which they take to support the general distinction between past tense forms that are generated by rule and those that must be listed as exceptions. For example, the irregular pasts include neighbourhoods of phonologically-similar pairs such as SING-SANG and RING-RANG; the regular forms do not exhibit this clustering, because the rules can apply to any present tense form without regard for its phonological composition. The McClelland and Rumelhart model does not enforce this distinction and therefore, it is argued, cannot capture these systematic differences between regular and irregular forms. This raises questions as to whether any connectionist system could do better.

The general approach that Pinker and Prince present is not limited to the past tense; there have been many attempts to characterize various aspects of linguistic knowledge in terms of rules. The problem for such theories is what to do with cases in which the rules fail. These cases seem endemic to human language. Consider some examples. The written form of English is alphabetic; hence there are systematic correspondences between spelling and pronunciation. It is often assumed that these correspondences can be formulated as rules; see Hanna, Hanna,

Hodges, and Rudortf (1966), Wijk (1966) and Venezky (1970) for attempts to list them. That the system is rule-governed seems to be indicated by patterns such as MINT-LINT-SPLINT-HINT; that people know such rules seems indicated by the fact that they can pronounce novel strings such as BINT. On this view, then, one of the child's first tasks in learning to read is to master these rules. Although (as in morphology) there is no generally agreed-upon list of rules, it is clear that there will be numerous exceptions to them, however they are formulated. What kind of rules would accommodate minimal pairs such as MINT/PINT, GAVE/HAVE, PAID/SAID, LEAF/DEAF and triples such as POSE/DOSE/LOSE or COUGH/DOUGH/PLOUGH? Presumably items such as COLONEL, CORPS, and ONCE will be treated as exceptions to any felicitous set of rules. Thus, the spelling-sound correspondences of English are apparently rule-governed, but the system admits many exceptions. As in the case of past tense inflectional morphology, there are disagreements about the exact content of the rules, yielding uncertainty as to which items are exceptions. For example, should DONE be listed as an exception or generated by a minor rule that also applies to NONE (analogous to Halle and Mohanan's rule that only applies to BRING-BROUGHT and THINK-THOUGHT)?

The mapping between spelling and syllabification is another domain that has received a rules plus exceptions analysis. Hansen and Rodgers (1968) developed a set of rules for syllabifying written English words on a strictly orthographic basis; these rules were later incorporated by Spoehr and Smith (1973) into a theory of visual word recognition. The rules work correctly in many cases, and the Spoehr and Smith research suggests that they capture something about the way people process words in reading. There again are cases where the rules fail, however, illustrated by minimal pairs such as BAKED-NAKED, DIES-DIET, and WAIVE-NAIVE.

Similar phenomena occur in other areas. As I have noted, the standard approach is to treat inflectional morphology as rule-governed but, as Spencer (1991) notes, 'Inflectional morphology is notorious for being morphologically idiosyncratic.' In English, of course, there is the past tense, typically formed by adding /d/. This system is overwhelmingly regular: there are about 4400 verbs in the Francis and Kucera (1982) count, of which perhaps five percent are irregular forms such as RUN-RAN or TAKE-TOOK. The irregular cases tend to cluster among the higher frequency words in the language (see Seidenberg 1989, for a discussion of why they do); hence, on a token-wise basis, the percentage of irregular forms is somewhat greater, though still less than for the regular forms. In short, there are both rule-governed cases and exceptions, with the former greatly outnumbering the latter. The situation is similar with respect to forming the plural. There is a rule, add -s, as in PAN-PANS or FAN-FANS; there are exceptions such MAN-MEN and SHEEP-SHEEP (I am suppressing irrelevant details here concerning, for example, the conditions that determine whether the -s is realized as /s /, /z/, or /iz/).

Whereas inflectional morphology is relatively impoverished in English, derivational morphology is not. Many morphologists take as their goal the formulation of rules that will account for facts such as the following. A HEADACHE is a kind of ache in your head; a HEAD-COLD is a kind of cold in your head; a HEADLINE, however, is not a line in your head (that is a wrinkle). A DEADHEAD (in one sense) is a person who likes the Grateful Dead; a POTHEAD is a person who likes marijuana (and often Potheads and Deadheads are the same people). An EGGHEAD, however, is not a person who likes eggs, a BEACH-HEAD is not a surfer, and a BLACKHEAD is a kind of facial blemish. Although it is possible to formulate rules governing the formation of compounds in English (see Selkirk 1982 for discussion), it is doubtful whether they could be formulated in such a way as to cover all cases without admitting any exceptions.

Pinker and Prince's (1988) response to these sorts of phenomena is to suggest that the goal of a proper theory (for example, of verb morphology) should be the formulation of a set of rules that captures significant generalizations. Properties of language such as the ones sketched in the examples above seem to ensure that the kind of rules to which they are committed will necessarily fail in many cases (the only way to avoid this would be to have rules that apply to individual items, which would trivialize the notion of rule). The proposal for what to do with these anomalies is simply to list them separately. These are the items that will have to be learned 'by rote.' Thus, the idea that language is rule-governed at various levels of structure (exemplified in the Pinker and Prince paper by the treatment of past tense morphology) is preserved by introducing a second descriptive mechanism – a list – to deal with cases in which the rules fail.

It seems to me that any system can be described by a set of rules if the rules do not have to apply to all cases. Pinker and Prince claim as a major discovery of linguistic theory that languages are rule-governed at different levels; however, it is hard to see how any other outcome would have been possible, given their notion of rule and the existence of a second means of accommodating all of the cases where the rules fail. This is like saying that all of the observations in my experiment fit a particular hypothesis except for the ones that I have decided to exclude. Aside from the fact that it seems a logical necessity that any set of phenomena can be partitioned in this way, Pinker and Prince assert that this rules-

and-exceptions approach accounts for facts about verb morphology that would otherwise be unexplained. For example, it is thought to explain why clusters of phonologically-similar past tenses (RING-RANG, SING-SANG, etc.) only occur among the exceptions. Again, however, it is hard to see how any other outcome could obtain. That such similarity clusters as RING-RANG/SING-SANG exist is an interesting fact (one that is itself in need of explanation, since it is easy to imagine a system in which this patterning does not occur) but, given their definition of the rule, it seems tautological that if such patterning does occur it must be confined to the exceptions.

These logical considerations aside, it could be the case that the assertion that knowledge consists of a set of rules and a list of exceptions is merely true. Here it is worth returning to the area in which this idea has been investigated most thoroughly, the mapping between spelling and pronunciation. In so-called dual-route models of reading aloud, there are two types of knowledge representation: a set of rules governing spelling-sound correspondences (sometimes termed grapheme-phoneme correspondence rules) and a lexicon in which the irregular cases must be listed (Coltheart 1978). There are also two pronunciation mechanisms: the pronunciations of rule-governed items are generated by applying the rules; the pronunciations of the words that violate the rules are looked up in the list.

Dual-route models have been justified on a number of grounds (see Carr and Pollatsek 1985 and Seidenberg 1985b for reviews). They developed in response to a variety of empirical phenomena concerning reading aloud and the acquisition of this skill; they have also provided a useful framework for studying some kinds of reading impairment that occur as a consequence of brain injury (Patterson, Marshall, and Coltheart 1985). These models have also been justified on the basis of the intuition that no single type of knowledge representation or process could simultaneously account for the ability to read rule-governed items such as GAVE, irregular items such as HAVE, and novel, nonword items such as MAVE. Elsewhere I have termed this the 'central dogma' of dual-route models (Seidenberg 1988). This view was put forward with admirable clarity by Coltheart (1987):

> A crucial implication of this distinction [between the two pronunciation mechanisms], an implication around which much work on normal and abnormal reading has been organized, is that the two procedures are not capable of producing correct responses for every type of orthographic input ... The word-level procedure allows correct reading aloud only when the orthographic stimulus is a word .... In contrast the subword level procedure guarantees correct reading aloud only when the orthographic stimulus is a

regularly spelled word or a nonword. According to this general approach to modelling oral reading, then, correct reading of nonwords requires a procedure for subword-level translation from orthography to phonology, whereas correct reading of words irregular in spelling-sound correspondences requires a procedure for word-level translation (xvi).

There are now two connectionist models that directly contradict this central dogma. Both the Sejnowski and Rosenberg (1986) NETtalk model and the Seidenberg and McClelland model generate phonological codes for words on the basis of orthographic input. The models generate correct output for both 'rule-governed' cases such as LIKE and TAKE and irregular cases such as HAVE and GIVE. The important point is that within the limited domains in which these models operate (for example, in the Seidenberg and McClelland model, the domain is monosyllabic words), they illustrate the claim that connectionist nets can generate both rule-governed cases and exceptions by means of a single mechanism. These models appear to refute the central dogma as it applies to spelling-sound knowledge.

The next question is whether a similar model could successfully accommodate the past tense. One of the central claims of McClelland and Rumelhart (1986) is that both rule-governed instances and exceptions can be derived from a single underlying system of units and connections in learning the past tense. Pinker and Prince are correct in suggesting that the McClelland and Rumelhart model of the acquisition of the past tense does not substantiate this claim. As an account of an aspect of child language (as opposed to a demonstration of some interesting properties of connectionist networks), the model is fatally flawed. Leaving aside this particularly unhappy case, it could be asked whether other attempts might be more successful in refuting the central dogma as it applies to past tense acquisition.

The answer to this question is as yet unknown and will not be known until someone develops a model that addresses the many important empirical phenomena described in the Pinker and Prince paper and other phenomena as well (see below). The many similarities between the system of spelling-sound correspondences and the past tense in English are certainly suggestive, however. Both systems are 'rule-governed' but admit many exceptions; in both cases the exceptions tend to cluster among the higher frequency words in the language and thus are overrepresented among the words to which the child is first exposed. In fact, the spelling-sound system exhibits all of the differences between rule-governed cases and exceptions that Pinker and Prince (1989:188) ascribe to verbs:

(a) Irregular verbs cluster into "family resemblance groups" that are phonologically similar: BLOW/BLEW; GROW/GREW; THROW/ THREW.' Irregularly pronounced words also cluster: DONE/NONE; PUSH/BUSH; BREAK/STEAK.

(b) Irregular pasts can be fuzzy in their naturalness of acceptability ... In contrast, regular verbs, unless they are similar to an irregular cluster, have no gradient of acceptability based on their phonology.' The spelling-sound correspondences of COLONEL, ACHE, and BREAST seem less natural than those of KERNEL, TAKE, and BEAST.

(c) There are no sufficient conditions for a verb to be in any irregular class: though BLOW becomes BLEW in the past, FLOW becomes FLOWED; though RING becomes RANG, STRING becomes STRUNG and BRING becomes BROUGHT. In contrast, a sufficient condition for a verb to be regular is that it not be irregular.' HAVE-GAVE; SAID-PAID; BONE-DONE-GONE.

(d) Most of the irregular alternations can only apply to verbs with a certain structure: the pattern in 'send/sent,' namely to change a d to a t, requires that there be a d in the stem to being with. The regular rule, which adds a -d to the stem, regardless of what the stem is, can cover all possible cases by its very nature.' I am not clear what is being claimed here, other than that the exceptions are idiosyncratic patterns. However, the pattern -AVE requires the letter H in the initial position in order to change to /av/and similarly for other cases.

In summary, I hope to have established that, inadequacies of the Rumelhart and McClelland verb learning model aside, the idea that a single system might be responsible for both rule-governed items and exceptions is quite viable; in at least one domain there are existing models that implement the idea. It remains to be determined whether a similar account will apply to the past tense. However, the kinds of phenomena that Pinker and Prince take to implicate very different types of knowledge representations and processing mechanisms for rule-governed items and exceptions, and to be incompatible with connectionist models, also occur in the domain of spelling-sound correspondences, for which plausible models already exist. A number of people who attended closely to Pinker and Prince's critique of the Rumelhart and McClelland model have begun developing successors to it (for example, Plunkett and Marchman 1991; MacWhinney in press;

Cottrell and Plunkett 1991). It therefore seems likely that we will soon have a clearer picture of the relevance of connectionist models to verb learning. Although none of the existing models as yet achieves descriptive adequacy, a number of interesting results have been achieved. Both the models of MacWhinney (in press) and Cottrell and Plunkett (1991) use a single network to generate both regular and exceptional past tenses. It will be interesting to determine whether extensions of these models or others like them will be able to accommodate the entire range of facts.

Are rules and exceptions sufficient?

To this point I have argued that systems of knowledge that have the character of past tense morphology in English are compatible with known properties of simple connectionist networks. In light of the controversy that followed the Rumelhart and McClelland (1986) model I should stress that in the absence of an adequate, implemented model these observations are merely suggestive. For the sake of argument, let us assume that an adequate a model could be constructed. Two related questions then arise. One concerns whether such a net would merely implement the two mechanisms that Pinker and Prince envision. For example, the network might partition itself so that some units and connections are dedicated to implementing the rules and others to implementing the list of exceptions. The second question concerns whether there would be any way to determine which is the correct account. In this section I will present evidence suggesting that peoples' behaviour departs from that which would be expected if their knowledge of the past tense were represented in terms of rules. Moreover, I will argue that these departures from orderly rule-governed behaviour can be understood in terms of simple properties of connectionist networks. Therefore, the connectionist approach is to be preferred because it captures generalizations that the rules-and-exceptions approache misses. These considerations also suggest a somewhat different relationship between connectionism and linguistic theory than Pinker and Prince's 'implementational' view.

As noted above, Pinker and Prince's view of the past tense is that it involves two types of knowledge: a set of rules and a list of exceptions. These, in turn, involve two types of learning: inducing a set of rules and learning the exceptions 'by rote.' Prasada, Pinker, and Snyder (1990) further assume that these types of knowledge entail different processing mechanisms: the rule-governed cases are generated; the exceptions are looked-up from storage in memory. They present the results of reaction time experiments in which subjects generated past tense forms aloud. The data were seen as supporting the distinction between generating output by rule versus lexical lookup, and they offer logical arguments suggesting that the phenomena cannot be properly understood without making this distinction. This is the central dogma that I questioned previously, that is, that no single type of knowledge representation or process can simultaneously handle both the rule-governed cases and exceptions.

Models such as Seidenberg and McClelland's (1989) inspire the following alternative account. Knowledge of the past tense is encoded by weights on connections between units representing different types of knowledge (orthographic, phonological, grammatical, etc.). Learning involves adjusting the weights on the basis of experience. All forms are generated by a single process (for example, taking the present tense stem as input, along with other relevant information such as meaning, and computing the past tense as output). There are no rules in this type of model and no listing of irregular forms. The idea of a list of lexical entries is especially incongruent with this approach; in models of the lexicon employing distributed representations, there are no units or pools of units dedicated to individual words (see also Hinton 1986). Each word form is represented by a pattern of activation over one or more sets of units; each unit participates in the representation of many words.

As I have noted, the same theoretical alternatives arose in connection with spelling-sound knowledge. In the latter domain, however, there have been many studies of subjects' use of this knowledge under various conditions. There is a large body of data that is quite revealing about how this knowledge is represented and used, and it is sufficient to strongly call into question the dual-route account. In reading, the adequacy of the dual-route model began to be questioned because of the discovery of some unexpected phenomena that have come to be called consistency effects. The seminal study was by Glushko (1979). In the dual-route model, a word such as MUST is rule-governed and HAVE is an exception. Glushko asked a deceptively simple question: what about words such as GAVE? Under any plausible construal of the notion, GAVE is rule-governed. The rule presumably applies productively to SAVE, PAVE, RAVE and other words and can be used to pronounce nonsense words such as MAVE. However, the pronunciation of the -AVE pattern is inconsistent, owing to the irregular neighbour HAVE. In Glushko's experiments, subjects read such words aloud and their responses were timed. Subjects who are skilled, college-student readers perform this task at a high level of accuracy. Glushko replicated the earlier finding that irregular words (such as HAVE or SAID) take longer to pronounce than do regular words (such as MUST or LAKE). Unexpectedly, however, he found that so-called inconsistent words such as

GAVE or PAID also took significantly longer to read aloud than did entirely regular words. These results are important because both the regular and inconsistent words are rule-governed according to the standard dual-route approach. If such items were pronounced by applying rules, the two classes should have behaved alike. However, the inconsistent words yielded longer latencies due to the irregular neighbours.

Subsequent studies replicated the basic consistency effect but clarified it in a number of respects (see Jared, McRae, and Seidenberg 1991 for review). First, the effect is correlated with frequency: lower frequency words show larger effects, and among the highest frequency words in the language the effects are small or nonexistent. Second, the effects depend on reading skill: faster, more skilled readers show smaller effects. Third, the magnitude of the effect depends on the ratio of a word's friends and enemies. The friends of GAVE, for example, are all the rhyming -AVE words. Its only enemy is HAVE. Thus, regular words have many friends but no enemies; exception words have few friends and many enemies; and inconsistent words fall in-between. Jared et al. (1990) showed that the ratio of friends and enemies accounts for the results of about fifteen studies of consistency effects in the literature.

The important conclusion to be drawn from this research is that the generalization that accounts for word naming latencies is not whether they are rule-governed or exceptional. Rather, the correct generalization concerns the degree of consistency exhibited across a neighbourhood of similarly spelled items. The standard dual-route account suggests that the latency to pronounce a word should only depend on properties of the word itself: its frequency, length, and whether it is rule-governed or irregular. The empirical studies show that this assumption is false. Latencies systematically depend not only on the properties of the word itself but also on their neighbours. Thus, mechanisms for generating the pronunciations of words must take into account these relations among words.

The Seidenberg and McClelland (1989) model simulates these effects quite closely. The model was trained on a corpus of 2897 monosyllabic words, including almost all of the words used in studies of consistency effects. Hence it is possible to simulate each experiment using the same items as in the study. The naming latencies of the subjects are compared to an error score that is a quantitative measure of the model's performance. The fit between mean naming latencies and error scores for the same items is typically very good. Figure 4.1 provides a summary of the results of a study by Jared et al. (1990). The stimuli in the experiment were lower frequency inconsistent words (such as TINT, which is inconsistent because of PINT) and two control groups of matched regular words. All of the stimuli would be considered rule-governed in the

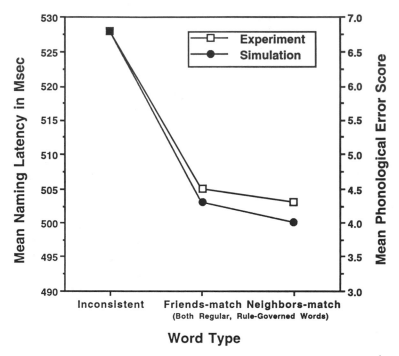

Figure 4.1: Results of an experiment on consistency effects (Jared et al. 1990). The 'friends match' and 'neighbours match' are two groups of entirely regular, rule-governed items.

dual-route account; however, the inconsistent items, which have enemies, yielded significantly longer naming latencies than did the regular words. As the figure indicates, the model produced very similar results. Many other simulations of this type are reported in Seidenberg and McClelland (1989) and Jared et al. (1990).

The explanation for why the model performs this way is simple. The weights mediating the computation from orthography to phonology encode facts about the frequency and consistency of spelling-sound correspondences in the lexicon. The model accounts for effects of lexical frequency (for example, McRae, Jared, and Seidenberg 1990) because frequency determines how often a word is presented during the training phase; words that are presented more often have a bigger impact on the weights. For the same reason, the model performs better on words containing sublexical spelling patterns that occur in many words. Thus, the model performs better on words containing spelling patterns that are consistently associated with a single pronunciation (for example, -UST in MUST, -IKE in LIKE) compared to inconsistent patterns associated with more than one pronunciation (for example, -OWN in TOWN,

BLOWN). These outcomes are simply a consequence of how the learning algorithm operates given a significant fragment of the English lexicon with which to work. Multiple exposures to consistent patterns such as -UST push the weights towards values that are optimal for producing the correct phonological output. Performance on inconsistent patterns such as -OWN is somewhat poorer because training on a word such as TOWN has a negative effect on the weights from the point of view of BLOWN and vice versa. In such cases, given sufficient training on the words, the model produces output that is closer to the correct pronunciation than to the alternative pronunciation of the inconsistent spelling pattern; however, error scores (the discrepancy between computed and veridical phonological codes) are larger than in the case of entirely consistent words.

The model's behaviour closely corresponds to that of human subjects asked to read words aloud; its performance is better on the words that subjects find easier and worse on the words they find more difficult. The accuracy of the model is such that it correctly simulates latency differences on the order of 15-25 msec. Many earlier studies of how subjects name different types of words aloud employed taxonomies of word types based on different assumptions about the nature of pronunciation rules and the perceptual units relevant to pronunciation (see Patterson and Coltheart 1987 for review). The model shows that the correct generalizations about naming performance derive from a deeper principle concerning the learning process.

These results have important theoretical implications. The inconsistency effects, which are exhibited by people and correctly simulated by the model, are not predicted by standard dual-route models, in which the fundamental distinction is between rule-governed words and exceptions. This dichotomy is not rich enough to capture facts about human performance. Highly regular words such as MUST and highly exceptional words such as CORPS represent different extremes on a continuum of spelling-sound consistency. Inconsistent words such as TINT or LEAF represent intermediate cases; they appear to be regular, 'rule-governed' items, but the naming of these items is in fact affected by knowledge of exception-word neighbours such as PINT and DEAF. Consistency effects are somewhat smaller than suggested by Glushko's (1979) original work but they can be detected with careful experimentation (see Jared et al. 1990), and they are theoretically important. Any number of theories can explain why a word with an irregular pronunciation might be more difficult to name than a regular word. However, the data indicate that differences among word types in terms of naming difficulty depend on the degree of consistency in the mapping between spelling and pronunciation. These differences in degree are realized in the model by the weights on connections, which reflect the aggregate effects of training on a large corpus of words.

Consistency of the past tense. With this background in hand, we can return now to the past tense. I previously argued that past tense inflection is analogous to spelling-sound correspondences in important respects and suggested that the two sets of phenomena might be explained by similar sorts of computational mechanisms. If this analysis is correct, it predicts that we should be able to observe analogous behavioural phenomena in the two domains. In particular, there should be consistency effects in the generation of the past tense. According to Pinker and Prince, WALK-WALKED is rule-governed and TAKE-TOOK is 'listed.' The 'Glushko question' for verbs, then, is what about BAKE-BAKED which, like TINT in the domain of spelling-sound correspondences, is rule-governed but inconsistent; its enemies are TAKE-TOOK and MAKE-MADE. Other examples are MIND-MINDED (inconsistent because of FIND-FOUND) and PUN-PUNNED (the enemy is RUN-RAN).[4]

Maggie Bruck and I (Seidenberg and Bruck 1990) examined these types of words in an on-line production task. On each trial subjects were shown a verb in the present tense, such as BAKE. Their task was either to name the word aloud or to generate its past tense. Subjects performed the tasks in two sessions separated by at least a week. Each subject performed both tasks; order of tasks was counterbalanced across subjects. The stimuli included fifty 'rule-governed' verbs with entirely regular past tenses, and fifty verbs with regular past tenses but one or more irregular neighbours (the 'inconsistent' items). There were also fifty-eight verbs with irregular past tenses included as filler items to keep subjects attending closely to the task. The regular and inconsistent items were closely matched in terms of properties of both the present and past tenses. We also chose the items so that, on average, the items in the two conditions had the same number of regular past tense neighbours. In this way we attempted to ensure that both the regular and inconsistent items involve 'rules' that are used about equally often in the language. The only systematic difference between the conditions was that the inconsistent items have enemies. The principal goal was to examine how past tense generation latencies relate to consistency. The present tense naming task was included in order to be certain that any differences in past tense generation times were not due to differences in the processing of the base words. The predictions should be clear: If the regular past tense is generated by rule, inconsistent past tenses such as BAKE-BAKED should yield the same results as entirely regular pasts such as WALK-WALKED. However, if the pattern of consistency across

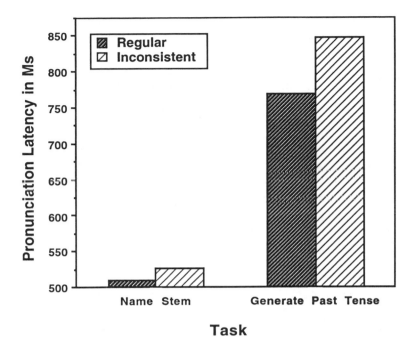

Figure 4.2: Results of the Seidenberg and Bruck (1990) study on past tense generation. Stimuli in both conditions were 'rule-governed'; however, the inconsistent items have enemies.

a neighbourhood of similarly-spelled forms is relevant, it should be harder to generate the past tenses of the inconsistent words.

The results, summarized in Figure 4.2, exhibit a strong, statistically reliable consistency effect. There were also 2 percent more errors in the inconsistent condition. In contrast, naming latencies for the present tense bases did not differ reliably in either latency or errors. One other interesting result was that for the inconsistent words, the latency to generate the past tense was related to the number of enemies, r (48) = .38, p < .01. The inconsistent words varied in terms of the number of enemies. Thus, items such as PICK-PICKED, whose only enemy is STICK-STUCK, were easier than items such as BLINK-BLINKED (whose enemies include SINK-SANK, THINK-THOUGHT, etc.).

The simplest interpretation of these results is that the regular past tense is not generated by rule. Rather, there is a computation over a neighbourhood of similarly-spelled patterns. As in the case of spelling-sound correspondences, it is the degree of consistency that captures the relevant generalization, not whether the item is 'rule-governed' or 'listed.'

As it happens, Prasada et al. (1990) also reported an experiment in which subjects generated the past tenses of verbs. They arrived at a somewhat different conclusion, however. Their experiment involved regular, rule-governed items and exceptions. In one case, they varied the frequencies of the present tense stems (as measured by the Francis and Kucera 1982 norms); thus, there were separate groups of high and low frequency regular and irregular items. The groups were equated, however, in terms of the frequencies of their past tenses. Hence, base word frequencies varied but past tense frequencies were the same. In a second condition, the stimuli in the two groups were equated in terms of base word frequencies but varied in terms of past tense frequencies (high versus low). As in our experiment, subjects saw the base word and generated the past tense. Prasada et al.'s results indicate that whereas the frequency of the base form affects the generation of both regular and irregular past tenses, the frequency of the past tense form itself was only relevant for irregular pasts. That is, the difference in frequency between TOOK (high frequency irregular) and BENT (low frequency irregular) affected response latencies, but the difference between LOOKED (high frequency regular) and BASKED (low frequency regular) did not.

Prasada et al. interpreted these results as support for the dual-route model. According to this account, regular past tenses are generated by rule. Overall latencies therefore consist of two components: the latency to identify the present tense stem (i.e., lexical access for LOOK) and a constant reflecting the time needed to apply the rule. Latencies to generate irregular past tenses also consist of two components: lexical access for the stem (for example, TAKE) and the amount of time it takes to find the irregular past tense listed in the mental lexicon. Importantly, the latter component is not a constant; it depends on the frequency of the word, under the assumption that the search process is frequency-ordered. It follows that the frequency of the base word affects both regular and irregular past tense generation, but the frequency of the past tense only affects the irregulars. Insofar as the data were in accord with these predictions, they were seen as confirming the dual-route account.

Bruck and I obtained very similar results using a slightly different design. The stimuli in our study were forty verbs with regular past tenses and forty with irregular past tenses. The present tense stems in the two conditions were equated in terms of Kucera and Francis (1967) frequency, length, and initial phoneme. Thirty subjects performed the two tasks described previously: naming the present tense base words aloud and generating the past tense forms. The tasks were again performed in separate sessions several days apart, with the order of tasks counterbalanced across subjects. The results are summarized in Figure 4.3. As in our previous experiment, naming latencies for the two types of present tense stems did not differ and they both yielded less than 1

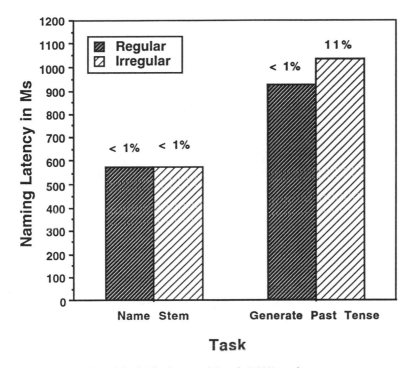

Figure 4.3: Results of the Seidenberg and Bruck (1990) study on past tense generation. Stimuli were either regular, rule-governed items or irregular, exception items.

percent errors. However, it took longer to generate the irregular past tense, and these words produced about 10 per cent more errors. Subtracting the stem naming latency from the past tense generation latency yields a net generation effect of 349 msec for the regular past and 456 msec for the irregular past. Thus, familiar irregular past tenses take about 100 msec longer to generate, even for skilled college student readers.

We also addressed the role of frequency by performing a median split on the lemma frequencies of the present tense stems. This yielded groups of high and low frequency stems for regular and irregular past tenses. Figure 4.4 presents the net past tense generation effects in these groups. Two findings should be noted: First, the difference between the regular and irregular conditions is larger for lower frequency words than high; second, there is a frequency effect for irregular past tenses but not for regular past tenses. This pattern is consistent with Prasada et al.'s results, which they took as evidence for the dual-route model.

Note, however, that the same pattern of results has repeatedly been observed in studies of spelling-sound correspondences. In these studies, the regularity effect (the difference in latency for exception

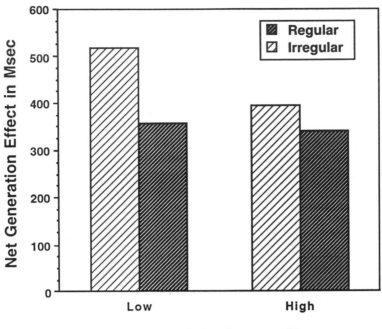

Figure 4.4: Data from the same experiment as in Figure 4.3, broken down by frequency.

words such as HAVE and regular words such as MUST) is larger for lower frequency words (Seidenberg 1985c). At the same time, frequency effects are smaller for regular words than they are for exceptions. The absolute size of the frequency effect for regular words depends on the range of frequencies sampled, but the effects are clearly smaller than for exceptions. Figure 4.5 presents the results of one representative study, by Waters and Seidenberg (1985), illustrating these effects. Data concerning the model's performance on the same words are also presented.

The Seidenberg and McClelland model simulates this frequency by regularity interaction quite closely. Hence, it exhibits the pattern of behaviour that Prasada et al. took as evidence for the dual-route model – even though it only has a single route. Specifically, it exhibits both the effect they interpreted as evidence for rule-use (minuscule frequency effects for regular items) and the effect that provided evidence for lexical-lookup (larger frequency effects for irregular items). However, it shows that these effects derive from the same source, namely, the effects of repeated changes to the weights during the training phase. Seidenberg and McClelland provided a detailed explanation of the factors that govern the model's behaviour. Performance on any given word is a

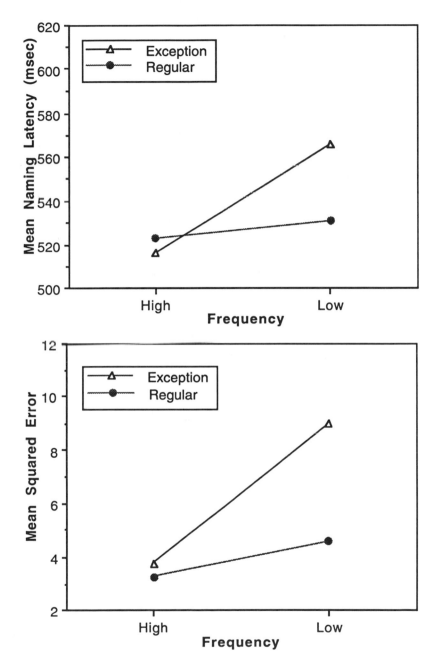

Figure 4.5: Data from an experiment by Waters and Seidenberg (1985) illustrating the frequency by regularity interaction in the naming of monosyllabic words.

function of the entire ensemble of training experiences. This is because all the changes to the weights that occur during learning are superimposed on each other. Hence, the weights reflect the aggregate effects of training on the entire corpus. For a given word, the factor that has the biggest impact on performance is the number of times the model was trained on the word itself. In this way lexical frequency has an impact on performance. However, performance is also affected by exposure to similarly-spelled neighbours; thus, performance on GAVE is affected by exposure to GAVE but also by neighbours such as SAVE and HAVE. There are also small effects due to more remote neighbours such as GIVE or MATE. The effects of these neighbours modulate effects of lexical frequency. As the number of neighbours (specifically, friends) goes up, the effects of number of exposures to the word itself decrease. Intuitively, mastering the pronunciation of GAVE is not highly dependent on exposure to GAVE because the model also benefits from SAVE, PAVE, and RAVE. In contrast, mastering the irregular pronunciation of HAVE is highly dependent on sufficient exposure to the word itself. Thus, frequency of exposure has a bigger impact on irregular patterns than on regular ones. For highly regular patterns with many friendly neighbours, effects of lexical frequency may be washed out entirely.

The claim here is that exactly the same factors govern latencies to generate the past tense. The regular, rule-governed patterns are highly productive. Hence, learning the past tense of words such as LOOK or LIKE is not highly dependent on the frequency of exposure to them. The correct past tenses can also be inferred on the basis of exposure to other regular, rule-governed forms. In contrast, learning the correct past tense of TAKE requires exposure to TOOK; therefore, performance is highly dependent on frequency. It follows from this view that frequency of the past tense should be a salient factor for irregular pasts but not for regular pasts, as in the data.

In summary, both Prasada et al. and Seidenberg and Bruck observed for past tense generation a frequency by regularity interaction like the one that has been observed for spelling-sound correspondences. The Seidenberg and McClelland model provides a simple account of the latter effect in terms of changes to the weights during learning. This single-process model obviates the need for a set of rules and a list of exceptions and suggests that a similar account should apply to past tense generation. Moreover, the Seidenberg and McClelland model also correctly predicts the effects of spelling-sound consistency observed in studies such as Glushko's (1979) and Jared et al.'s (1990), whereas the dual-route model did not. These consistency effects have now also been observed in past tense generation as well.

Error data. Subjects' errors on the past tense generation task also provide information that helps to differentiate between the theoretical alternatives. It is necessary to consider for a moment how errors might be generated within a dual-route model. The proposal is that regular past tenses are generated by rule rather than by being listed in the lexicon; irregular past tenses are produced by finding the forms in a memory list rather than by rule-application. A problem that arose with regard to the earlier, dual-route model of pronunciation was how the reader would know which route to use for any given input word. That is, if words are not labelled as 'regular' or 'irregular,' how does the reader know whether to pronounce by rule or to search for the irregular form? The usual answer to this is that both routes are tried in parallel, with a race between them (Meyer et al. 1974; Paap and Noel 1989). This proposal introduces other problems (for example, what happens when the routes yield different pronunciations), although I would say that they are unresolved rather than necessarily wholly intractable. In any case, Prasada et al. (1990) did not present a detailed process model addressing these issues. It would have to be assumed, however, that somehow the subject knows whether to apply a rule or to search the lexicon in generating the past tense for a given word. For example, words could carry tags indicating whether their past tenses are regular or irregular. An error would then result from reading the tag incorrectly; words with regular past tenses might be treated as irregular and vice versa. If a verb with an irregular past tense were mistakenly treated as though it were regular, the subject should produce a regularization error (for example, RUN-RUNNED). If a verb with a regular past tense were mistakenly treated as though it were irregular, however, it is not clear what kind of error should result. The subject would presumably initiate an unsuccessful search through the mental lexicon. Under these conditions, the subject might respond with another irregular past tense found in the list, apply the regular rule as a default, or make no response at all.

Subjects' actual errors suggest a somewhat different picture. Errors seem to result from drawing incorrect analogies to neighbours. Table 1 presents the errors that occurred in generating past tenses for inconsistent verbs such as SIGHT in the first Seidenberg and Bruck (1990) experiment. Recall that the correct responses to these verbs always involve the regular, -ED pattern. Some of the errors (such as STREAK-STRUCK) are congruent with the dual-route model's suggestion that errors in generating the regular past tense would come about by mistakenly searching the list of irregular past tenses stored in memory and producing one of them as output. Thus, STRUCK is the correct irregular past tense of STRIKE not STREAK. However, most of the errors were not of this sort. The most frequent error was one in which the subject produced an incorrect past tense that was analogous to an irregular past tense in a nearby neighbourhood. Thus, SIGHT was pronounced SOUGHT by analogy to FIGHT-FOUGHT; THRIVE-THROVE by analogy to DIVE-DOVE, and GLIDE-GLID by analogy to HIDE-HID. Another interesting set of errors occurred when subjects incorrectly produced past tenses that were identical to the present tense forms. These are analogous to rare items such as HIT and BEAT, which have identical present and past tense forms. Thus, the subjects responded with BLIND as the past tense of BLIND (instead of BLINDED) and SKID as the past tense of SKID (instead of SKIDDED).

Errors such as GLIDE-GLID suggest that subjects were generating the past tenses by analogy to other forms. GLIDE sounds like HIDE,

Table 4.1: Errors on the Regular But Inconsistent Verbs Used in Seidenberg and Bruck's Experiment 1

Vowel changes:	
sight-sought	(13)
thrive-throve	(5)
weave-wave	(3)
glide-glid	(2)
squeeze-squoze	(2)
streak-struck	(2)
streak-stroke	(1)
No change errors:	
blind	(2)
brand	(1)
free	(2)
skid	(1)
slow	(2)
thread	(2)
wing	(1)
Other errors:	
sight-saw	(4)
lean-leant	(4)
smell-smelt	(7)
trust-thrusted	(1)
rig-ringed	(1)
streak-shrieked	(1)
No response:	(7)

Note: Number of errors given in parentheses.

therefore the past tense should sound like HID. The same process would also produce errors such as SIGHT-SOUGHT and 'no change' errors as well. Thus, the errors that occurred for the regular but inconsistent verbs seem to reflect the effects of similarly spelled or pronounced neighbours. This is congruent with the hypothesis that the past tense is generated by means of a computation that reflects relationships among a neighbourhood of words rather than by simply applying a rule. The 'analogy' process is realized in the weights, which reflect the degree of consistency in the mapping between input (for example, present tense) and output (for example, past tense) forms.

For verbs with irregular past tenses, the only error that is expected on the dual-route account would be a regularization such as RUN-RUNNED. Some of these errors did occur (Table 4.2): KNOWED, HURTED, and FIGHTED are examples. However, subjects also produced a variety of other errors. Some were no-change errors; thus, in the case where the subject generated KNOW as the past tense of KNOW, he produced an irregular, no-change past tense but not one that would be 'listed' in the lexicon as the past tense of some other verb. Subjects also produced analogies that formed nonwords, such as SEEK-SOOK. These errors are especially important because they could not result from either mistakenly applying a rule or accessing the incorrect entry in the mental lexicon. Subjects also incorrectly produced some past participles such as SEE-SEEN. Again, the errors seem to reflect relationships between the stimulus verb and similarly spelled or pronounced neighbouring words rather than mere application of a rule. The very similar types of errors produced for both regular and irregular past tenses strongly suggest that these forms are generated by means of a common process. I should add that subjects produce similar errors in studies of naming monosyllabic words aloud. In reading familiar irregular words such as HAVE or DEAF, subjects sometimes produce regularizations (/hAv/, /dEf/), but they also produce other types of errors (HAVE-/hIv, DEAF-/det/). Conversely, regular but inconsistent words are sometimes incorrectly read by analogy to exceptions, for example, GAVE-/gav/ or TOWN-/tOn/.

In summary, three phenomena have been observed in these studies of past tense generation. First, subjects exhibit consistency effects for entirely regular, rule-governed past tenses such as BAKE-BAKED; second, frequency effects are bigger for the irregular past tense than for the regular past tense; third, errors reflect relationships between a word and its neighbours. These effects also occur in the domain of spelling-sound correspondences, and the Seidenberg and McClelland model simulates them closely. These observations strongly suggest that it

Table 4.2: Errors on the Irregular Verbs Used in Seidenberg and Bruck's Experiment 2

Regularizations

knowed	(1)
hurted	(2)
kneeled	(2)
fleed	(3)
holded	(1)
fighted	(1)
ridded	(3)

No change errors:

know	(1)
fly	(1)
flee	(3)
fall	(1)
run	(1)
draw	(1)
slide	(1)
stand	(1)
mean	(4)
stick	(1)

Past tenses of other words:

flee-flew	(8)
rid-rode	(3)
run-rung	(1)

Past participles:

seen	(1)
given	(1)
ridden	(3)
eaten	(2)
driven	(2)
broken	(1)
frozen	(1)
beaten	(2)
stolen	(1)

Other errors:

seek-sook	(1)
dig-dag	(1)
strike-stroke	(2)
lose-loose	(1)
swim-swum	(2)
fall-fail	(1)
mean-meent	(1)
give-gaved	(1)
steal-stoled	(2)

Note: Number of errors given in parentheses.

would be worth pursuing the single-route, connectionist approach to modelling the past tense.

Generalization. Before closing this discussion the important issue of generalization must be considered. Perhaps the quintessential property of a rule is that it can account for both known instances and the ability to generalize to novel instances. Thus, in the classic Berko (1958) study of children's knowledge of morphology, the inference that they had formulated a rule for the plural was based on the production of novel forms such as WUGS. It is obvious that people can generalize the past tense rule as well; what is the past tense of GLORP if not GLORPED? The single-route, connectionist interpretation of such behaviour is that novel forms are produced by the same mechanism as known forms, namely, the net. Thus, a model might be trained on a variety of verbs, resulting in changes to the weights that reflect facts about the past tense. The same weights would then be used in generating a novel past tense such as GLORPED. One of the important tests for future models of the past tense will be to determine if they generalize in appropriate ways. I myself doubt whether this will be a serious problem, assuming the model is trained in a way that faithfully reflects facts about the distribution of regular and irregular past tenses in the language. The system is overwhelmingly regular; and the weights will come to reflect this fact, making it likely that the regular past tense will be attached to almost any novel input. The only exceptions would be cases where the novel input happens to fall within one of the clusters of irregular pasts, for example, TING might be given the past tense TANG on the basis of neighbours such as RING-RANG and SING-SANG. There is some evidence that children produce such forms (Bybee and Moder 1983). I think it is likely to be more of a challenge to get a model to correctly produce irregular past tenses given the overwhelming degree of regularity in the system.

Although the Seidenberg and McClelland (1989) model illustrates how generalization occurs within a simple network, it also raises questions as to whether such networks can achieve performance that is as good as peoples'. The model was trained on monosyllabic words, and correctly generalizes when presented with simple nonwords such as NUST or RIKE. Glushko (1979) had observed that nonword naming latencies also exhibit consistency effects; thus nonwords such as NUST, from the entirely consistent -UST neighbourhood, are named more rapidly than are nonwords such as MAVE, from the inconsistent -AVE neighbourhood. Although the standard view is that novel forms are generated by applying the regular rules, these results suggest that generation involves a network that encodes similarity and consistency relationships among pools of neighbours, as in the case of words. The

Seidenberg and McClelland model also produces consistency effects for simple nonwords. The model does not perform as well as people in naming nonwords, however; it produces a larger percentage of errors on more difficult items such as JINJE or KEAD (Besner et al. 1990). As Seidenberg and McClelland (1990) noted, however, this behaviour of the model is closely related to the fact that whereas peoples' vocabularies are on the order of tens of thousands of words, the model was trained on only 2897. Thus, the model does well on nonwords that resemble items in the training corpus (for example, NUST) but poorly on unusual items such as JINJE. One way to view these results is that the model performs about as well as one might expect of a person who only knows 2900 monosyllabic words. Other aspects of the implementation, particularly the phonological representation that was used, also limit the model's performance on nonwords (see Seidenberg and McClelland 1990 for discussion). These observations suggest that the limitations that have been observed may not be insuperable. Still, given the concerns that have been raised regarding the capacities of simple backprop nets to generalize (McCloskey and Cohen 1989), it will be important to investigate this issue further – and considerable caution is in order. In the case of the past tense of verbs, it will be important to determine whether a network can both generate correct past tenses for known verbs and generalize even in the case of odd nonwords such as XPLK; even though XPLK has no close neighbours (or perhaps because of it?), we can agree that its past tense must be XPLKED. As I have noted, I think this is likely to be a tractable problem given the extreme regularity of the system but, this is a critical empirical question that must be addressed.

Conclusion

One of the most important contributions of the Pinker and Prince (1988) paper is that it provided a description of a broad range of phenomena that any adequate theory of the past tense must explain. I have suggested that it is by no means obvious that the phenomena they highlighted lie outside the scope of simple connectionist models, the failures of the McClelland and Rumelhart (1986) model notwithstanding.[5] To their list of phenomena should be added those that were uncovered in the Seidenberg and Bruck (1990) and Prasada et al. (1990) studies. These data are strongly reminiscent of that which were observed earlier in connection with spelling-sound correspondences.

If I am correct in suggesting that phenomena such as the past tense in English can be accommodated by a simple connectionist architecture, this would suggest a somewhat different relationship between linguistic theory and connectionist modelling than that implied by Pinker and Prince's 'implementational' view. The Seidenberg and Mc-Clelland (1989) model does not merely 'implement' the dual-route model of naming. Our analyses of the model indicate that it cannot be decomposed into components corresponding to a set of rules and a list of exceptions; thus, the two mechanisms of the dual-route model are not directly implemented. Moreover, the model behaves in ways that would not be predicted on the simple rules-and-exceptions view. The ways in which frequency and consistency of spelling-sound correspondences affect processing follow from an understanding of how learning works in a simple network employing distributed representations, not from the properties of the rule and lookup mechanisms proposed in earlier theories. It is a strong argument in the model's favour that people exhibit analogous behaviours. In the case of the past tense, there is as yet no implemented model that addresses all (or even most) of the relevant phenomena, but thinking about the generation of past tense forms in connectionist terms has already led to predictions that have been confirmed in behavioural studies. I suggest that these phenomena would not have been discovered without an understanding of how learning works in connectionist networks. To the extent that the connectionist framework both accounts for various facts and generates novel, correct predictions, it cannot be said to be simply 'implementing' the rules.

Is it the case that phenomena of the sort I have described (for example, consistency effects) are wholly incompatible with the rules-and-exceptions approach? Certainly not. One response to data of this sort would be to modify the dual-route model in order to accommodate them. That is what happened in the case of spelling-sound correspondences, and it could as well occur with respect to verbs. Thus, Patterson and Coltehart (1987) describe various modifications of the dual-route model intended to cope with the Glushko consistency effects. Similarly, Pinker (1991) has recently described a modified dual-route model in which some forms are generated by means of an associative net, and others are generated by rule. In response to the Seidenberg and Bruck (1990) results, Pinker now suggests that the associative net applies to inconsistent words, such as BAKE or MIND, previously thought to fall within the purview of the rule-component. Whether or not this move will be successful is unclear. It certainly introduces some important questions as to how such a system would ever be learned. The child would have to learn that BAKE-BAKED and TAKE-TOOK are processed by one mechanism, even though they are superficially quite different, whereas BAKE-BAKED and LIKE-LIKED are processed by separate mechanisms, even though they are superficially quite similar.

Still, it is not inconceivable that such problems could be resolved. Certainly, in the absence of an implemented connectionist model of the past tense that is at least descriptively adequate, Pinker's alternative is equally viable.

Note, however, that this discussion involves a very different relationship between connectionism and linguistic theory than Pinker and Prince (1988) envisioned. Their idea was that connectionist models could only 'implement' the types of knowledge structures and processing mechanisms uncovered by linguistic theory. That would involve investing the connectionist network with properties independently established within linguistic theory. What Pinker (1991) seems to have in mind is the exact opposite: investing a rule-based system with properties independently discovered on the basis of connectionist modelling. If it turns out that rules apply to words from consistent neighbours but not to words from inconsistent neighbourhoods, change the notion of rule so that it obeys this principle. If it turns out that facility in producing the past tense depends on how often a pattern occurs in the language, assign frequencies to the rules. In general, there is sufficient elasticity in the notion of 'rule' to permit a rule-based account to accommodate nearly any pattern of data. Unless there are constraints on the properties of rules, there would not seem to be any limits to their range of applicability.

What is important, of course, is not whether one theory can mimic another but, rather, from where the correct generalizations are derived. In this regard, the approach that I have advocated is profoundly different from Pinker and Prince's. I began this paper by suggesting that connectionist models can be properly understood with reference to the learnability notion that has been central to studies of language acquisition. The models I have been describing are systems that learn under certain specifiable constraints. From this point of view, it is critical to understand such things as the initial state of the system, the input to the system, and the capacity of the system to learn. The generalizations that govern performance derive from the interaction of these factors. It is because they are so critical to a model's performance that Pinker and Prince's criticisms of the Rumelhart and McClelland (1986) model (for example, of the training regime and the phonological representation) were so telling. The central, defining feature of this approach is that it is centred on the question of how a particular task is mastered (for example, learning a language). In a much simpler fashion, our models are also task-centred: they ask how a system can come to perform a task such as pronouncing words or generating the past tense.

Pinker and Prince's approach starts with a characterization of the knowledge of the adult – competence – and asks how this is achieved.

Thus, they assume a theory of inflectional morphology that distinguishes between rules and exceptions. This theory is primarily derived from distributional analyses of adult utterances rather than from the analysis of a task. The rules and lists of exceptions are attempts to rationalize the regularities implicit in this large set of observational data. As I have noted, the view that knowledge consists of rules and lists of exceptions is by no means universal among theoretical linguists. I would argue that this view is plausible only if one considers relatively simple systems such as inflectional morphology in English, and even in this simple domain there are phenomena suggesting that it is an oversimplification. Nonetheless, when Pinker and Prince turn to considering the acquisition process, they assume that a proper theory will necessarily respect the rule/list distinction. They are able to amass a large amount of data that are consistent with the distinction and attempt to sketch learning mechanisms that are compatible with it. Among the other approaches afforded by theoretical linguistics, however, is learnability. Ideally, what has to be independently motivated are the initial state of the system, the way in which knowledge is represented (for example, in terms of weights on connections), the input to the child, and the way in which learning occurs. From the interaction of these factors a certain type of competence necessarily follows. Thus, knowledge representations develop in the service of mastering a task. This contrasts with theories in which knowledge representations reflect generalizations derived from comparisons across adult utterances or across languages.

According to Rumelhart et al. (1986), the rules and the list of exceptions can be taken as simply an imprecise, higher level characterization of the behaviour of a complex system. Abstracting from the details of the Seidenberg and McClelland model, for example, one could say that it behaves as though it had induced the rules governing most words in the language but also represented the exceptions and not be wholly inaccurate. With the model in hand, however, one can see that it does not, in fact, implement anything like the rules or the list of exceptions previously envisioned. In fact, its behaviour departs systematically from what was expected on the rules-and-exceptions view. Thus, the fact that the model's behaviour can be summarized in a certain way should not blind us to how it actually works. And the virtue of having an implemented simulation model is that one can actually see.

Of course, there are very few models that achieve any kind of descriptive adequacy; even our model is severely limited in scope. It is absurdly ambitious to attempt to develop systems that mimic human behaviour in detail, and certainly very little has been achieved in this regard so far. Moreover, the difficulty of this task – and the limitations of scope that this imposes – ensures that any given model will simply be false insofar as it fails to be faithful to all of the phenomena of interest. These observations certainly justify Pinker and Prince's robust skepticism and suggest that theories of the sort they described will continue to play an important role and, in many domains, will continue to be the best accounts that can be achieved.

In my view, the great divide is not between linguistic theory and connectionism; it is between theories that are centred on the learnability question and those that treat it as secondary to characterizations of adult competence. I myself do not believe that the non-learnability approaches that are common in many areas of theoretical linguistics (for example, morphology) are powerful enough to converge on the correct characterizations of linguistic knowledge. Learnability questions are often acknowledged but in some domains they do not play a central role in theory development. I see connectionism as contributing in an essential way to achieving explanatory theories of a sort to which many linguists aspire.

Notes

1 I am quoting here from their description of a course they jointly offered at the Summer Institute of the Linguistic Society of America (Santa Cruz 1991).

2 I am quoting here from the title of a talk, 'Rules and Associations,' given at several locations. I heard it at a meeting convened by the McDonnell-Pew Foundation in San Diego 1990.

3 I include here the 'principles and parameters' approach to acquisition, even though it differs somewhat from the earlier learnability work.

4 Pinker and Prince (1989) appear to have sensed that the inconsistent items would behave differently than would entirely regular words: 'In contrast [to irregular verbs], regular verbs, *unless they are similar to an irregular cluster*, have no gradient of acceptability based on their phonology' (188; italics added).

5 Though I would not want the 'simple models' to be limited to feedforward nets trained using backprop.

References

Anderson, S.R. (1982). Where's morphology? *Linguistic Inquiry* 13:571-612

Aronoff, M. (1976). *Word Formation in Generative Grammar*. Cambridge, MA: MIT Press

Berg, G. (1991). Learning recursive phrase structure: Combining the strengths of PDP and X-bar syntax. TR 91-5, Department of Computer Science, SUNY Albany

Berko, J. (1958). The child's learning of English morphology. *Word* 14:150-77

Besner, D., Twilley, L., McCann, R., and Seergobin, K. (1990). On the connection between connectionism and data: Are a few words necessary? *Psychological Review* 97:432-46

Bromberger, S., and Halle, M. (1989). Why phonology is different. *Linguistic Inquiry* 20:51-70

Bybee, J.L. (1985). *Morphology: A Study of the Relation Between Meaning and Form.* Amsterdam/Philadelphia: John Benjamins

– and Moder, C. (1983). Morphological classes as natural categories. *Language* 59:251-70

Carr, T.H., and Pollatsek, A. (1985). Recognition of printed words: A look at current models. In D. Besner, T.G. Waller, and G.E. MacKinnon (eds.), *Reading Research: Advances in Theory and Practice* 5. New York: Academic Press

Chomsky, N. *Aspects of the Theory of Syntax.* Cambridge, MA: MIT Press

– (1981). *Lectures on Government and Binding.* Dordrecht, The Netherlands: Foris Publications

Coltheart, M. (1978). Lexical access in simple reading tasks. In G. Underwood (ed.), *Strategies of Information Processing.* New York: Academic Press

– (1987). Introduction. In M. Coltheart, G. Sartori, and R. Job (eds.), *Cognitive Neuropsychology of Language.* London: Erlbaum

Cottrell, G., and Plunkett, K. (1991). Using a recurrent net to learn the past tense. In *Proceedings of the Thirteenth Annual Meeting of the Cognitive Science Society.* Hillsdale, NJ: Erlbaum

Elman, J. (1990). Finding structure in time. *Cognitive Science* 14:179-211

Fernald, A. (1984). The perceptual and affective salience of mothers' speech to infants. In L. Feagans, C. Garvey, and R. Golinkoff (eds.), *The Origins and Growth of Communication.* New Brunswick, N.J.: Ablex

Francis, W. N. and Kucera, H. (1982). *Frequency Analysis of English Usage: Lexicon and Grammar.* Boston: Houghton-Mifflin

Gluck, M., and Bower, G. (1988). Evaluating an adaptive network model of human learning. *Journal of Memory and Language* 27:166-95

Glushko, R.(1979). The organization and activation of orthographic knowledge in reading aloud. *Journal of Experimental Psychology: Human Perception and Performance* 5:674-91

Halle, M. (1973). Prolegomena to a theory of word-formation. *Linguistic Inquiry* 4:3-16

– and Mohanan, K.P. (1985). Segmental phonology and modern English. *Linguistic Inquiry* 16:57-116

Hanna, P.R., Hanna, J.S., Hodges, R.E., and Rudorf, E.H. (1966). *Phoneme-Grapheme Correspondences as Cues to Spelling Improvement.* Washington: US Department of Health, Education, and Welfare

Hansen, D., and Rodgers, T.S. (1968). An exploration of psycholinguistic units in initial reading. In K.S. Goodman (ed.), *The Psycholinguistic Nature of the Reading Process.* Detroit: Wayne State University Press

Hare, M. (1990). The role of similarity in Hungarian vowel harmony: A connectionist account. *Connection Science* 2:123-50

Hinton, G.E. (1986). Learning distributed representations of concepts. *Proceedings of the Eighth Annual Conference of the Cognitive Science Society* 1-12. Hillsdale, NJ: Erlbaum

Hirsh-Pasek, K., Treiman, R., and Schneiderman, M. (1984). Brown and Hanlon revised: Mothers' sensitivity to ungrammatical forms. *Journal of Child Language* 11:81-88

Hynd, G., and Semrud-Clikeman, M. (1989). Dyslexia and brain morphology. *Psychological Bulletin* 106:447-82

Jared, D., McRae, K., and Seidenberg, M.S. (1990). The basis of consistency effects in word naming. *Journal of Memory and Language*, 29:687-715

Kiparsky, P. (1982). Lexical morphology and phonology. In I.-S. Yang (Ed.), *Linguistics in the Morning Calm*. Seoul: Hanshin, 3-91

Kucera, H., and Francis, W.N. (1967). *Computational Analysis of Present-day American English*. Providence, RI: Brown University Press

Liberman, A.M., and Mattingly, A.G. (1985). The motor theory of speech perception revisited. *Cognition* 21:1-36

MacWhinney, B. (in press). Paper to appear in *Cognition*

McCloskey, M., and Cohen, N.J. (1989). Catastrophic interference in connectionist networks: The sequential learning problem. In G.H. Bower (ed.), *The Psychology of Learning and Motivation*, 23. New York: Academic Press

McRae, K., Jared, D., and Seidenberg, M.S. (1990). On the roles of frequency and lexical access in word naming. *Journal of Memory and Language* 29:43-65

Meyer, D.E., Schvaneveldt, R.W., and Ruddy, M.G. (1974). Functions of graphemic and phonemic codes in visual word recognition. *Memory and Cognition* 2:309-21

Newport, E., Gleitman, L., and Gleitman, H. (1977). Mother, I'd rather do it myself: Some effects and non-effects of maternal speech style. In C.E. Snow and C.A. Ferguson (eds.), *Talking to Children: Language Input and Acquisition*. New York: Cambridge University Press

Paap, K., and Noel, R.W. (1989) Dual-route models of print to sound: Still a good horse race. Paper presented at the annual meeting of the Psychonomic Society

Patterson, K. E., Marshall, J. C., and Coltheart, M. (1985). *Surface Dyslexia: Neuropsychological and Cognitive Studies of Phonological Reading*. London: Erlbaum

– and Coltheart, V. (1987). Phonological processes in reading: A tutorial review. In M. Coltheart (ed.), *Attention and Performance XII: Reading*. London: Erlbaum

Pinker, S. (1991). *Rules of Language*. Unpublished ms., MIT

– and Prince, A. (1988). On language and connectionism: Analysis of a parallel distributed processing model of language acquisition. *Cognition* 28, 73-194

– and Prince, A. (1989). Rules and connections in human language. In R.G.M. Morris (ed.), *Parallel Distributed Processing: Implications for Psychology and Neurobiology*. Oxford, UK: Oxford University Press

Plunkett, K., and Marchman, V. (1991). U-shaped learning and frequency effects in a multilayered perceptron: Implications for child language acquisition. *Cognition* 38:43-102

Prasada, S., Pinker, S., and Snyder, W. (1990). Some evidence that irregular forms are retrieved from memory but regular forms are rule generated. Paper presented at the thirty-first annual meeting of the Psychonomic Society (November: New Orleans)

Rumelhart, D., Hinton, G., and Williams, R. (1986). Learning internal representations by error propagation. In Rumelhart, D.E., and McClelland, J.L., eds. (1986a), *Parallel Distributed Processing: Explorations in the Microstructure of Cognition* 1. Cambridge, MA: MIT Press

– and McClelland, J.L. (1986). On learning the past tenses of English verbs. In J. McClelland, and D. Rumelhart (eds.) *Parallel Distributed Processing* 2. Cambridge, MA: MIT Press

Seidenberg, M.S. (1985a). Evidence from great apes concerning the biological bases of language. In A. Marras and W. Demopoulos (Eds.), *Language Learnability and Concept Acquisition*. Norwood, NJ: Ablex

– (1985b). The time course of information activation and utilization in visual word recognition. In D. Besner, T. Waller, and G.E. MacKinnon (eds.), *Reading Research: Advances in Theory and Practice* 5. New York: Academic Press

– (1985c). The time course of phonological code activation in two writing systems. *Cognition* 19:1-30

– (1988). Cognitive neuropsychology and language: The state of the art. *Cognitive Neuropsychology* 5:403-26

– (1989). Reading complex words. In G. Carlson and M.K. Tanenhaus (eds.), *Linguistic Structure in Language Processing*. Dordrecht: Kluwer Academic Publishers

– and Bruck, M. (1990). Consistency effects in the generation of past tense morphology. Paper presented at the thirty-first meeting of the Psychonomic Society (November: New Orleans)

– and McClelland, J.L. (1989). A distributed, developmental model of word recognition and naming. *Psychological Review* 96, 523-68

– and McClelland, J.L. (1990). More words but still no lexicon: Reply to Besner et al. *Psychological Review* 97: 447-52

– and Petitto, L.A. (1987). Communication, symbolic communication, and language. *Journal of Experimental Psychology: General* 116:279-87

Sejnowski, T.J., and Rosenberg, C.R. (1986). NETtalk: A parallel network that learns to read aloud. Baltimore, MD: Johns Hopkins University EE and CS Technical Report JHU/EECS-86/01

Selkirk, E. (1982). *The Syntax of Words*. Cambridge, MA: MIT Press

– (1984). *Phonology and Syntax: The Relation Between Sound and Structure*. Cambridge, MA: MIT Press

Spencer, A. (1991). *Morphological Theory*. Oxford, UK: Blackwell

Spoehr, K.T., and Smith, E.E. (1973). The role of syllables in perceptual processing. *Cognitive Psychology* 5:71-89

Stabler, E. (1991). Book to be published by MIT press

Venezky, R. (1970). *The Structure of English Orthography.* The Hague: Mouton

Waters, G.S., and Seidenberg, M.S. (1985). Spelling-sound effects in reading: Time course and decision criteria. *Memory and Cognition* 13:557-72

Wijk, A. (1966). *Rules of Pronunciation for the English Language.* Oxford University Press

Connectionist Models in the Information Processing Paradigm

Michael E. J. Masson

In developing these comments on Seidenberg's chapter I have established three objectives. The first is to characterize the theoretical context within which connectionist models are emerging in psychology and, in particular, the information processing paradigm. The second objective is to provide an evaluation of the Seidenberg and McClelland (1989) model of word recognition within this context. The third objective is to explore some interesting extensions and implications of the model.

The Theoretical Context of Connectionist Models

There is a firm tradition within the information processing paradigm that places the emphasis of theoretical models on the notion of symbolic representation and manipulation (e.g., Anderson 1983; Kintsch 1974; Newell and Simon 1972). Two examples of this are shown in Table 4.1.

Table 4.1: Examples from Symbolic Representation Models

Production systems
IF the quantities v, v_0, and t are known
THEN assert that the acceleration a is known
Text propositions
KNOW[LINGUISTS, SOLUTION]

The first is an example of a production, or a condition-action pair, from a production system. When the conditions of the production are met, the action is executed. The second example is based on a propositional representation of a text. In these representational schemes symbols that stand for rich concepts, perceptual events, and ideas are directly manipulated. Connectionist systems are founded upon a very different

123

representational format. The format is based on highly interconnected processing units with concepts depicted as ephemeral patterns of activation across an entire set of units rather than as individuated elements or symbols. The lack of symbolic representation and manipulation in connectionist models has created debate about how connectionist models should be viewed within the established framework.

It has been claimed, for example, that connectionist models simulate events that occur at a level (e.g., physiological) that is different from that inhabited by events simulated in symbolic models (Broadbent 1985; Fodor and Pylyshyn 1988). The argument is that connectionist models should be construed as theories about the way in which cognitive algorithms are implemented, not as theories of the very character of those algorithms. The counter claim is that connectionist models actually do serve as models of mechanisms of thought (as models of the real cognitive algorithms), not just as implementations at a physiological level (McClelland and Rumelhart 1986; Rumelhart and McClelland 1986, 1985). Moreover, a means of testing this proposition has been put forward in the form of the claim that connectionist models are able to accomplish three important tasks (McClelland 1988). First, they provide new classes of explanations for basic findings. Second, the interaction between groups of processing units produces emergent properties of behaviour (e.g., schemas, prototypes, and rules) without any need to directly code those properties into the model. Third, connectionist models are capable of stimulating new research into cognitive phenomena. These are important criteria to adopt when evaluating the contribution of specific connectionist models.

Another issue within the information processing context concerns the standards that modelling schemes should live up to. Some classes of information processing models include a set of free parameters that may be adjusted to provide the best possible *quantitative* fit to data from specific experiments. For example, in the Kintsch and van Dijk (1978) model of text comprehension, one free parameter was the number of propositions maintained in short-term memory during sentence processing. By a quantitative fit, I mean that the model should provide predictions in the same dependent variables that are expressed in human behaviour. For example, the model should provide information about response times in milliseconds, error rates, and so on. The benefit of determining the number of free parameters in a model and measuring the accuracy of its quantitative fit is that it enables one to distinguish between correct and incorrect models or, at least, between models that are doing relatively good or poor jobs of accounting for data. In many cases different models can make roughly the same predictions, but the winner is the one that has the closest quantitative fit, according to measures such as root mean squared error based on the deviation between model predictions and observed behaviour. The testing of alternative models is a very important part of this set of standards.

Connectionist modelling appears to operate in a very different way, as is shown in the next section, and this has drawn strong criticism from some quarters (e.g., Massaro 1988). On the other hand, Estes (1988) has proposed a different strategy for addressing the testability of connectionist systems. The goal is to establish theoretically motivated constraints on the general architecture of a model and to adhere to those constraints as particular instantiations of that architecture are applied to specific domains. When testing implementations against sets of empirical data, it is possible to determine whether the constraints dictated by the general architecture contribute to the model's success or produce serious failures. At the same time, the domain-specific versions of the model are put to the test as well. This approach to evaluating connectionist models ensures sustained interaction with cognitive research and, arguably, constitutes a valuable heuristic for exploring this new enterprise. In Table 4.2 I have summarized some of the criteria for evaluating connectionist models within the information processing framework.

Table 4.2: Some Criteria for Evaluating Connectionist Models

---

(1) Provide new classes of explanations for basic findings
(2) Interaction among processing units has implications for cognitive operations
(3) Stimulate new research
(4) Provide good qualitative and quantitative fits to data, relative to alternative models
(5) Adhere to constraints imposed by a general architecture

The Seidenberg and McClelland Model

General criteria

To frame the Seidenberg and McClelland (1989) model within the context of the evaluative criteria reviewed above, consider first the overall architecture of the model. This architecture can be used to guide our understanding of how important aspects of reading go forward. For example, the architecture provides a way to understand the role phonological recoding plays during reading. Currently, there is a controversy in the literature regarding whether it is necessary for one to phonologically recode a visually presented word in order to gain access to its meaning (McCusker, Hillinger, and Bias 1981; Van Orden, Johnston, and Hale 1988). It is quite clear from the Seidenberg and Mc-Clelland architecture how that issue should be resolved. According to the model, access to meaning can follow two parallel routes. One route goes from the orthographic code to the meaning module without accessing phonology at all. The other route involves passing through the phonological module on the way to the meaning module and, in most instances, would be expected to take longer. In this sense the computation of the phonological representation during reading often does not directly contribute to identifying a word. On the other hand, the computation might be very useful when reading complicated text. Having a phonological code available for manipulation in working memory could be very important.

In their initial implementation of this architecture Seidenberg and McClelland have chosen to focus on the orthographic and phonological modules and their role in the identification of isolated words. With just these two modules the model provides a new and provocative account for important aspects of human behaviour. For example, the variables of word frequency and orthographic regularity interact when word naming time is measured. Specifically, orthographically regular words are named in less time than are exception words, but this effect is weak or absent when high frequency words are involved (Seidenberg, Waters, Barnes, and Tanenhaus 1984). The classic, dual-route account of this finding is that pronunciation can be achieved through the earlier finishing of two parallel processes: (a) assembly of a phonological code using spelling-sound correspondence rules and (b) activation of a word's lexical entry and looking up the pronunciation stored in association with that entry (e.g., Paap, McDonald, Schvaneveldt, and Noel 1987; Patterson and Coltheart 1987).

The account of the frequency by regularity interaction proposed by Seidenberg and McClelland is driven by the consequences of the distributed representation used in their model. This approach rejects the notion that each concept is represented as a single entry in a lexicon. In connectionist systems the code for a concept typically lies in the connections between an entire collection of processing units. There is no special representation for well known words. Orthographic and phonological knowledge about words is represented in the same scheme that we use to pronounce letter strings that we have never before encountered. The frequency by regularity interaction is an emergent property of the model's distributed scheme for representing orthographic and phonological knowledge. This approach is a significant departure from the way that knowledge of words has been characterized in the past. Moreover, the Seidenberg and McClelland explanation of the frequency by regularity interaction, word naming, and lexical decision tasks in general works without recourse to the meaning module. This is a striking accomplishment in light of the fact that word identification tasks, such as word naming and lexical decision, have been used extensively in psychological research because of the assumption that they tap aspects of access to the meaning of words.

The Seidenberg and McClelland model's simulation of the orthographic regularity effect provides an interesting example of an emergent property of its processing units. The model does not encode rules of pronunciation in any explicit way, but it does produce a regularity effect that could be construed as rule based. Although this result should be scored as a success, there is a problem. If asked, people can articulate some of their knowledge about rules of pronunciation and explain their application. It is unclear how a connectionist system can account for that kind of behaviour. Do we suggest that it is an epiphenomenon that comes about as a result of the regularity that is learned by the connectionist system? Or are these rules *not* applied during the actual production of a pronunciation? These important questions remain unanswered and are not addressed by the Seidenberg and McClelland model.

Another evaluative issue concerns the testability of a model and its comparative success at fitting observed data. One aspect of testability that highlights the contrast between the connectionist approach and the approach to modelling in the information processing tradition is that of free parameters. Seidenberg and McClelland (1989) claim that their model has seven free parameters that could be explicitly adjusted in an effort to improve fits to data. But this claim depends on the definition of free parameters. For instance, Massaro (1988) has argued that in a connectionist system one has as many free parameters as there are connections between nodes. The freedom of connection weights to take on any value within certain ranges as a result of training qualifies them as free parameters. In this view, the Seidenberg and McClelland model is charged with having not seven, but over 250,000 free parameters. Although I know of no resolution to the issue of counting free parameters, connectionist models are testable in the sense that they can be compared against other models with respect to the accuracy of their predictions. The falsifiability of connectionist models is demonstrated by the fact that they do not always come out on top in such comparisons (e.g., Massaro 1989).

Contrasts between the predictive success of models can be sharpened by requiring models to make quantitative predictions. Although Seidenberg and McClelland occasionally refer to their model's predictions as quantitative, within the context of classical psychological modelling the predictions they describe are actually classified as quali-tative. For example, their simulation of reaction time data is expressed in terms of error scores. There is no mechanism in the model to translate error scores into reaction time values, so the model is unable to provide quantitative fits. On the other hand, the model is able to make accurate qualitative predictions that capture important aspects of behavioural data. For current purposes dependence on qualitative predictions may be adequate, but it places limits on the degree to which we can make comparisons between models in terms of how well they fit observed data.

Specific criticisms

Although the Seidenberg and McClelland model measures up rather well against the general evaluative criteria for connectionist models, it has been criticized on a number of specific issues, two of which will be raised here. The first involves the model's performance on non-words. Besner, Twilley, McCann, and Seergobin (1990) have pointed out that the Seidenberg and McClelland model has difficulty in producing cor-rect pronunciations for certain non-words. In these instances, when giv-en a non-word pattern the phonological code produced by the model is better fit by a pronunciation that is different from the pronunciation that a human would generate. Besner et al. claim that this difficulty re-flects a fundamental problem with the architecture of the model; specif-ically, the lack of explicitly instantiated pronunciation rules. They point to the difficulty inherent in any attempt to capture both generalizability and specific instances in a single representational scheme.

Alternatively, it could be the case that there is not a problem with the model's architecture, but, rather, that there is a constraint on how real-istic a computer simulation can be. The model's behaviour is based on learning a corpus of 3,000 words, whereas human subjects' pronuncia-tions are based on a corpus of tens of thousands of words. The model's behaviour might be very different if trained on different numbers of words. Training with a larger corpus, for example, should produce a stronger generalization to non-words. Seidenberg and McClelland's claim that generalizable, rule governed behaviour can be captured in the same scheme as that which encodes information about frequently occurring words depends on the model's ability to produce correct pro-nunciations of novel letter strings. Failure of the model to produce reasonable performance on non-words would raise serious doubts about some of its basic architectural features.

A second criticism concerns the claim that the Seidenberg and McClelland model is capable of simulating performance in a word naming task without access to a lexical representation that is specific to the target word. This claim is in direct opposition to the dual-route views that assume pronunciation may either be built using orthographic-phonological correspondence rules or by accessing an item's entry in the lexicon (e.g., Paap et al. 1987; Patterson and Coltheart 1987). According to dual-route theories low frequency exception words (e.g., *deaf*) take longer to pronounce, because the results of assembling a pronunciation and the output of lexical access yield conflicting candidate pronunciations. In the Seidenberg and McClelland model the long response latency is simulated by an elevated phonological error score. Because of the word's low frequency of occurrence the system has not adequately adjusted the pattern of connection weights to allow the correct pronunciation to override the influence on the weights from many orthographically similar words (e.g., *dear, leaf, sheaf*).

In an attempt to demonstrate the validity of the dual-route model, Paap and Noel (1989) tested subjects under conditions of high and low memory load. The rationale was that assembly of a pronunciation would demand more attentional resources, and that, when under high memory load, this route would be inhibited. This reasoning produced the counterintuitive prediction, confirmed by the Paap and Noel experiments, that the advantage for regular over exception words would decrease under conditions of high memory load. In particular, the time taken to name low frequency exception words was reduced under high relative to low memory load conditions. It is clear that the implemented version of the Seidenberg and McClelland model cannot replicate this pattern of data.

It is conceivable, however, that another version of the model, one incorporating the proposed meaning module, would be able to reproduce the result. One could assume that the memory load requirement, either high or low, induced a strategy whereby subjects pursued the orthographic-meaning-phonological route proposed in the general architecture of the Seidenberg and McClelland model. For example, subjects may have taken extra time to encode the meaning of the word so they could cope with the demands of two simultaneous tasks. In keeping with this possibility, response latencies in the Paap and Noel data were as much as fifty per cent higher than is typically found in pronunciation studies. By following the route through the meaning module subjects could avoid the source of the exception effect, that is, the orthographic-phonological route. This account closely resembles the original dual-route explanation, but there are two important differences. First, in the Seidenberg and McClelland model the orthographic-phonological route typically dominates the pronunciation task. Dual task conditions were necessary in order to increase the role played by the meaning module. Second, no look-up of stored pronunciations (as opposed to assembly) is involved in the Seidenberg and McClelland model when the meaning module is invoked. The meaning module influences activation in the phonological nodes through the same computational function as do the orthographic nodes. The difficulty with this account is that the meaning module has not yet been implemented. Until that is accomplished critical tests of the model's architecture will not be possible.

Extensions of the Model

Dyslexia

A very important extension of the model, described in some detail in the Seidenberg chapter, has to do with dyslexia. Exploring a topic such as this in the context of a connectionist model provides the potential for some very important advancement, especially regarding sources of deficits. Seidenberg has suggested that dyslexia may be simulated by reducing the number of hidden units, and the resulting behaviour of the model is strikingly similar to observed word recognition deficits among dyslexics. There are, of course, other possible means of simulating dysfunction in connectionist models, such as altering the learning algorithm (as Seidenberg suggested).

Another possibility that deserves attention is the potential for problems with computations that are performed within the units themselves. For example, a computation must be performed on the activation that comes into a unit, and the result of that computation is then transmitted to other units. In the Seidenberg and McClelland model, part of that computation involves application of a *squashing function* that takes the incoming activation from neighbouring units, which can be a very large number, and reduces it to a value ranging between +1 and -1. This prevents the output of any single unit from reaching extremely large values that can exert an unduly strong influence on the system's behaviour. It might be that this mechanism is implicated in dyslexia.

Although I am not familiar with connectionist simulations that explore disabled computational functions as a means of simulating dysfunction, there is an analog to this concept in a different kind of distributed memory system. Metcalfe Eich (1982) has developed a model that uses a distributed representational scheme based on a large list of features, each of which can take on a real value. The knowledge about all the concepts the system knows is embedded across an entire vector of nodes or features. As the system acquires new knowledge, variability in the values of the features begin to increase. For instance, some features have large positive values, others are near zero, and so on. As new concepts are added there is a growth in variability of feature values, particularly with the addition of similar concepts, because their patterns of feature values are similar. Those nodes representing features with large positive values in many of the concepts will take on very large positive weights, those near zero will remain there, and so on. This situation leads to great difficulty in recovering memory for any one of the concepts that has been embedded in the system.

Metcalfe's (1990) approach to handling the problem is to normalize the vector, keeping values from going beyond some limit. This is analogous to the task performed by the squashing function in connectionist systems. Metcalfe has simulated problems that are observed in various amnesic syndromes by disabling the normalization routine. For example, she produced some very interesting effects simulating Korsakoff amnesia, in which there is failure to release from proactive interference. Given the suggested analogy between Metcalfe's normalization routine and the squashing function in connectionist systems, manipulation of the squashing function may be another fruitful means of exploring human dysfunction.

A final point on the topic of dyslexia concerns the potential for remediation. It is possible, for instance, to consider how the Seidenberg and McClelland model might be used to test ideas concerning remedial training programs. The model might be trained on different word corpora in an effort to produce improvement in specific aspects of word recognition performance. Corpora that yield promising results with the model might then be used in remedial programs with appropriately selected dyslexic readers.

Spelling

A natural extension of the Seidenberg and McClelland model is to the task of spelling. One might characterize the task of spelling a word as running the Seidenberg and McClelland model in reverse, going from a phonological pattern to an orthographic pattern. There are striking parallels, both in the empirical results and in the theoretical explanations, that have emerged from work on spelling and word identification tasks. With respect to behavioural data, in word naming there is an interaction between word frequency and orthographic regularity, such that regularity matters only for low frequency words. In spelling there is a similar effect regarding high and low frequency words that conform to or violate a regular spelling rule. There are more spelling errors for words that violate the rule, but the effect is found almost exclusively with low frequency words.

Interestingly, in the context of work on spelling, this interaction has led to a dual-route explanation in which one route is based on phoneme-to-grapheme correspondence rules, and the other depends on word-specific memory (Kreiner and Gough 1990). Knowledge about the specific words allows us to handle rule violators. The Kreiner and Gough proposal is a parallel to the dual-route models that have influenced the word identification literature, so it appears we have a familiar dragon for the Seidenberg and McClelland model to slay. The simulation of spelling behaviour, therefore, is an important extension for the Seidenberg and McClelland model.

Meaning

A crucial, but as yet unimplemented, part of the Seidenberg and McClelland architecture is the meaning module. Earlier I suggested a way in which that module might be used to simulate some results that are troublesome for the model. It will be essential to incorporate this module into an implemented version of the model if Seidenberg and McClelland hope to simulate a significant range of reading tasks and to conduct critical tests of the model. In addition to the empirical work already discussed, we can consider research involving the identification of words presented in a meaningful context. The model as it is currently instantiated would not be capable of reproducing the effects of context on word identification, because the meaning module has not been implemented.

Other connectionist models, however, have proven successful in their attempts to simulate context effects. I have been working on a Hopfield network model, for example, that is somewhat different from the architecture of the Seidenberg and McClelland model in that it does not have hidden units (Masson 1989, 1991). Sharkey (1989) has been independently using a similar model. The emphasis in these models is on a distributed memory representation. One of the most striking results of this simulation work is that certain behavioural results, which standard semantic network models (e.g., Collins and Loftus 1975) have failed to explain, fall naturally out of these models. For example, consider a task in which a target word is preceded by a semantically related *prime* word, and the delay between the onset of the prime and target is varied. It has been shown that facilitation produced by strong and by weak semantic associates of a target word have the same onset and reach asymptote at the same time (Lorch 1982; Ratcliff and McKoon 1981). Whereas semantic network models predict that strong associates should have an earlier onset and should reach asymptote sooner, the Hopfield network model accurately simulates the observed result (Masson 1991). These are very encouraging results, and they may be representative of effects that could come out of the Seidenberg and McClelland model by implementing the meaning module that is part of the proposed architecture.

Episodic effects

The final extension I would like to consider is the issue of the representation of episodic events. An important example is the finding that an episode consisting of a single presentation of a well-known word, even after one has mastered a vocabulary, can have a persistent beneficial effect on the fluency with which one can identify the word on a later occasion (Jacoby 1983; Jacoby and Dallas 1981). This result has proven to be a very difficult problem for certain classes of models, especially semantic memory models that propose that word identification consists of the activation of an appropriate entry in a stable lexicon (Forster 1976; Morton 1969). In these models each word is represented as a single node, and its identification depends on accessing and activating its entry. The problem is; if these representations are stable, how could a single presentation have such a powerful impact?

Episodic effects may pose a problem for some connectionist models as well (but see Rueckl 1990). Seidenberg and McClelland (1989) touched on this issue and provided a simulation of episodic effects, in which they presented a single word to their system after it had been fully trained on their corpus of monosyllabic words. The presentation of the word produced a reliable reduction in the model's error score on that word, but the problem is that in order to produce that effect Seidenberg and McClelland presented the item to the model ten times in succession. They may have tried other techniques that were not reported, but a single presentation of the item probably would not yield a noticeable effect. This shortcoming suggests that a change in the model is required that goes beyond the currently implemented architecture.

One possibility is that persistent episodic effects could be a result of constructing an interpretation of a stimulus (e.g., processing meaning in the case of word targets). Some of the work I have been doing on this phenomenon in the context of the word naming task involves pseudohomophones (Masson and Freedman 1990). A pseudohomophone is a letter string that does not spell a word but that sounds like a valid word when pronounced (e.g., *kruze*). In these studies subjects were initially asked to name a series of words and pseudohomophones mixed together. Later in the experiment subjects were presented with the real word that corresponded to a previously read pseudohomophone (e.g., *cruise*), and it was found that their pronunciation latency for that word was significantly reduced, virtually by the same amount as was found when the correct word was shown on both occasions. This result implies that we have to consider something beyond the orthographic-phonological connections when trying to account for episodic phenomena.

Conclusion

The connectionist model proposed by Seidenberg and McClelland (1989) and discussed by Seidenberg (this volume) represents a well articulated theory of word identification. Its implementation has produced successful simulations of a wide range of important behavioural data and, at the same time, permitted close scrutiny and comparison with other models (e.g., Besner et al. 1990). It is noteworthy that the model is capable of simulating various word identification paradigms without implementing a meaning module, and that there is no special representation for words that the model 'knows.' These facts have placed the model in strong contrast with a number of other models of word identification and set the stage for some interesting and useful debate. Moreover, the implementation of the Seidenberg and McClelland model is guided by an architecture that holds the promise for the development of even more compelling versions of the model.

Despite this promising start, Seidenberg and McClelland have left some high-priced promisory notes regarding the model's fundamental architectural assumptions. It remains to be seen, for example, whether the model's commitment to a representation with no special provision for known words can withstand continued empirical test. It is also unclear whether the model will be able to provide adequate *quantitative* fits of data from a variety of word identification tasks, such as lexical decision. Quantitative predictions may soon be necessary if the model is to be directly compared with other classes of competing models. The implementation of the meaning module will be a crucial next step in the model's evolution, and at this stage it is very difficult to predict how that will alter the model's behaviour. Without the meaning module, however, I suspect the model's utility will be severely limited. At least some of the arcane laboratory tasks that have been devised to study word identification processes call upon an observer to construct a meaningful interpretation of a printed pattern. When the ultimate challenge of exploring word identification as part of the task of reading for comprehension is accepted, we may see a major shift of emphasis in the model's development.

Acknowledgment

Preparation of this article was supported by an operating grant from the Natural Sciences and Engineering Research Council of Canada.

References

Anderson, J.R. (1983). *The architecture of cognition*. Cambridge, MA: Harvard University Press

Besner, D., Twilley, L., McCann, R. S., and Seergobin, K. (1990). On the association between connectionism and data: Are a few words necessary? *Psychological Review* 97: 432-46

Broadbent, D. (1985). A question of levels: Comment on McClelland and Rumelhart. *Journal of Experimental Psychology: General* 114:189-92

Collins, A.M., and Loftus, E.F. (1975). A spreading activation theory of semantic processing. *Psychological Review* 82: 407-28

Estes, W.K. (1988). Toward a framework for combining connectionist and symbol-processing models. *Journal of Memory and Language* 27:196-212

Fodor, J.A., and Pylyshyn, Z.W. (1988). Connectionism and cognitive architecture: A critical analysis. *Cognition* 28:3-71

Forster, K.I. (1976). Accessing the mental lexicon. In R.J. Wales and E. Walker (eds.), *New Approaches to Language Comprehension*. Amsterdam: North-Holland, 257-87

Jacoby, L.L. (1983). Perceptual enhancement: Persistent effects of an experience. *Journal of Experimental Psychology: Learning, Memory, and Cognition* 9:21-38

– and Dallas, M. (1981). On the relationship between autobiographical memory and perceptual learning. *Journal of Experimental Psychology: General* 110:306-40

Kintsch, W. (1974). *The Representation of Meaning in Memory*. Hillsdale, NJ: Erlbaum

– and van Dijk, T.A. (1978). Toward a model of text comprehension and production. *Psychological Review* 85:363-94

Kreiner, D.S., and Gough P.B. (1990). Two ideas about spelling: Rules and word-specific memory. *Journal of Memory and Language* 29:103-18

Lorch, R.F., Jr. (1982). Priming and search processes in semantic memory: A test of three models of spreading activation. *Journal of Verbal Learning and Verbal behaviour* 21:468-92

Massaro, D.W. (1988). Some criticisms of connectionist models of human performance. *Journal of Memory and Language* 27:213-34

– (1989). Testing between the TRACE model and the fuzzy logical model of speech perception. *Cognitive Psychology* 21:398-421

Masson, M.E.J. (1991). A distributed memory model of context effects in word identification. In D. Besner and G. W. Humphreys (eds.), *Basic processes in reading: Visual word recognition*. Hillsdale, NJ: Erlbaum, 233-63

8136   Connectionism: Theory and Practice

- (1989). Lexical ambiguity resolution in a constraint satisfaction network. *Proceedings of the Eleventh Annual Conference of the Cognitive Science Society.* Hillsdale, NJ: Erlbaum, 757-64
- and Freedman, L. (1990). Fluent identification of repeated words. *Journal of Experimental Psychology: Learning, Memory, and Cognition* 16: 355-73
McClelland, J.L. (1988). Connectionist models and psychological evidence. *Journal of Memory and Language* 27:107-23
- and Rumelhart, D.E. (1985). Distributed memory and the representation of general and specific information. *Journal of Experimental Psychology: General* 114:159-88
- and Rumelhart, D.E. (1986). *Parallel Dstributed Processing* 2. Cambridge, MA: MIT Press
McCusker, L.X., Hillinger, M.L., and Bias, R. G. (1981). Phonological recoding and reading. *Psychological Bulletin* 89:217-45
Metcalfe, J. (1990). Simulation model of aspects of metacognition. Paper presented at the Annual Interdisciplinary Conference, Jackson, WY
Metcalfe Eich, J. (1982). A composite holographic associative recall model. *Psychological Review* 89:627-61
Morton, J. (1969). Interaction of information in word recognition. *Psychological Review* 76:165-78
Newell, A., and Simon, H.A. (1972). *Human problem solving.* Englewood Cliffs, NJ: Prentice-Hall
Paap, K.R., McDonald, J.E., Schvaneveldt, R. W., and Noel, R. W. (1987). Frequency and pronounceability in visually presented naming and lexical-decision tasks. In M. Coltheart (ed.), *Attention and Performance XII.* Hillsdale, NJ: Erlbaum 221-44
- and Noel, R.W. (1989). Dual-route models of print to sound: Still a good horse race. Paper presented at the meeting of the Psychonomic Society, Atlanta, GA
Patterson, K.E., and Coltheart, M. (1987). Phonological processes in reading: A tutorial review. In M. Coltheart (ed.), *Attention and Performance XII.* Hillsdale, NJ: Erlbaum 421-77
Ratcliff, R., and McKoon, G. (1981). Does activation really spread? *Psychological Review* 88:454-62
Rueckl, J.G. (1990). Similarity effects in word and pseudoword repetition priming. *Journal of Experimental Psychology: Learning, Memory, and Cognition* 16: 374-91
Rumelhart, D.E., and McClelland, J.L. (1986). *Parallel Distributed Processing* 1. Cambridge, MA: MIT Press
Seidenberg, M.S., and McClelland, J.L. (1989). A distributed, developmental model of word recognition and naming. *Psychological Review,* 96:523-68
- Waters, G.S., Barnes, M.A., and Tanenhaus, M.K. (1984). When does irregular spelling or pronunciation influence word recognition? *Journal of Verbal Learning and Verbal Behavior* 23:383-404

Sharkey, N.E. (1989). The lexical distance model and word priming. *Proceedings of the Eleventh Annual Conference of the Cognitive Science Society.* Hillsdale, NJ: Erlbaum 860-67

Van Orden, G.C., Johnston, J.C., and Hale, B.L. (1988). Word identification in reading proceeds from spelling to sound to meaning. *Journal of Experimental Psychology: Learning, Memory, and Cognition* 14:371-85

5

Grammatical Structure and Distributed Representations

Jeffrey L. Elman

Introduction

Neural networks have a number of properties which make them attractive computational systems for modelling cognitive behaviour (McClelland, Rumelhart, and Hinton 1986; Rumelhart and McClelland 1986). One of the useful characteristics is their sensitivity to contextual factors, and another is their ability to seek a solution which satisfies multiple constraints.

For example, work by Kawamoto and McClelland (1986) and by St. John and McClelland (in press) has shown how grammatical cues can be combined with context information to make inferences about events. Elman (1990) demonstrated that sequential context can provide the basis for adducing the category structure of internal representations of lexical items. Mikkulainen and Dyer (in press) showed how a similar effect could be achieved for external representations (i.e., forms which could then be used by other processing modules).

In these studies, *distributed representations* (Hinton 1988; Hinton, McClelland, and Rumelhart 1986; van Gelder, in press) play a key role. Distributed representations provide a high-dimensional, continuously valued space which can support finely graded, multidimensional distinctions. This is clearly useful for language. However, there are other requirements for language processing, and it is not self-evident that distributed representations can meet these requirements.

Consider the problem of how to represent complex grammatical structure and, in particular, hierarchical constituent structure. In Elman (1990), for instance, a network developed an internal representation for the lexical item 'rock,' which captured the fact that this item (as used in the language environment to which the network was exposed) was a *noun, inanimate*, and of the class of things which may be used to break other things. This representation was induced solely from the behaviour of this word across many contexts; the input form itself was a basis

138

vector (i.e., a vector with a single randomly assigned bit turned on and orthogonal to all other vectors used to represent lexical items).

Although this is a useful result, other issues arise as we consider what sort of lexical representations might be required in sentences such as the following.

(1a) The boy threw the <u>rock</u>.
(1b) The boy broke the window with the <u>rock</u>.
(1c) The <u>rock</u> broke the window.
(1d) The boy who threw the <u>rock</u> later had to fix the window.

In a simple sense, the word 'rock' has, in all of these sentences, the same meaning. One would, therefore, want a model to reflect this by having representations which are more or less the same across the four sentences. At the same time, the usage of the word differs across contexts. In (1a) 'rock' is the direct object (patient, or theme). In (1b) 'rock' is used as the instrument of an action. In (1c) the word is still the instrument but also functions as the grammatical subject. Finally, 'rock' is used in (1d) in a context which is very similar to that in (1a); however, (1d) is a complex sentence and the representation of rock qua object must include the fact that this role occurs in the subordinate clause (in order to distinguish it from the object role in the main clause). Thus, while there is some aspect to the meaning of the word 'rock' which is fixed across usage, the way in which the word is construed is also dependent on its context.

One way of dealing with such phenomena would be to posit sharp distinctions between the various types of information which might be relevant to sentence interpretation and to assign information to different levels of representation. Thus, one might posit levels for phonological, morphological, lexical, syntactic, semantic, discourse, and pragmatic information (and possibly others).

Although this approach, which emphasizes the autonomy of levels, has enjoyed great popularity in the generative linguistic tradition, it is not without its shortcomings (cf. Langacker 1987, Chapter 1). At the very least, this approach leaves unanswered the question of how – lacking a shared vocabulary – information is to be exchanged between different levels. The problem is non-trivial. Furthermore, although many phenomena can be described superficially in purely syntactic or lexical (or semantic, morphological, phonological, etc.) terms, such encapsulation often requires glossing over important details or ignoring troublesome exceptions. For instance, morphology is usually defined as the level of representation at which minimal sound/meaning correspondences are encoded. There are, however, sound/meaning relationships ('sound symbolism') which are neither fully productive nor easily described and which occur at what might seem to be sub-morphological levels. And although one might think that the existence of a lexical level should not be controversial (certainly all languages have words?), in reality it turns out to be difficult, and perhaps impossible, to define the concept *word* in any way which is consistent within a language (let alone across languages). The distinction between words, compounds, and phrases (e.g., 'tooth,' 'teeth-mark,' 'man-in-the-street'), can be very tenuous.

Nonetheless, although there may be controversy regarding the appropriate way of representing the context-dependent role of the word 'rock' in the above sentences, it is clear that the representations in the different contexts must somehow be different. The representations must reflect facts about rocks in general as well as their usage in the specific contexts. These usage distinctions include the various roles filled by the rock and also the part of the sentence of which 'rock' is a constituent (e.g., the difference between 'rock' in (1a) and (1d)). This latter issue has been raised forcefully by Fodor and Pylyshyn (1988). They argued that the ability to represent compositional relations is fundamental to a theory of cognition, but they also claimed that such representations can only be supported by the so-called classical theories (more precisely, the language of thought, Fodor 1976).

I take Fodor and Pylyshyn's first claim (regarding the importance of compositionality) as relatively uncontroversial. What is less clear is that compositional relationships can only be achieved by the so-called classical theories or by connectionist models which implement those theories. Fodor and Pylyshyn present a regrettably simplistic picture of current linguistic theory. What they call the classical theory actually encompasses a heterogeneous set of theories, not all of which are obviously compatible with the language of thought. Furthermore, there have, in recent years, been well-articulated linguistic theories in which composition figures prominently but which do not share the basic premises of the language of thought (e.g., Chafe 1970; Fauconnier 1985; Fillmore 1982; Givon 1984; Hopper and Thompson 1980; Kuno 1987; Lakoff 1987; Langacker 1987). Thus the two alternatives presented by Fodor and Pylyshyn, that connectionism must either implement the language of thought or fail as a cognitive model, are unnecessarily bleak and do not exhaust the range of possibilities.

In what follows, I ask whether connectionist models can in fact encode compositional relationships between linguistic elements. The investigation proceeds in two parts. First, the question is raised indirectly by seeing whether it is possible to produce in a network behaviours which may plausibly be thought to require representations that reflect compositional relationships.[1] This is similar to the strategy employed by linguists, who infer abstract mental representations based on observable behaviour. The second approach is more direct. Because networks are artificial systems, one can inspect them directly and examine the mechanisms being used to produce the behaviour. Having done this, we may then be in a position to raise the more interesting question, which is how such representations differ (or are similar to) the available alternatives.

Although I cannot at present give a definitive answer to this question, I will suggest some ways in which connectionist representations (at least, of the sort described here) differ from the so-called classical representations. Two characteristics in particular stand out. First, the connectionist representation of composition seems to be inherently more efficient at encoding contextual dependencies and at handling interactions among constituents (what Langacker 1987 calls accommodation) than are classical alternatives. Secondly, the connectionist state representation of hierarchical relations involves what might be called 'leaky recursion.' This differs from the 'true recursion' afforded by stack machines. Leaky recursion allows information to spread more easily between levels of organization; this makes it unnecessary to assume movement of constituents, traces, etc. It also raises the possibility that when information-co-ordination (i.e., long-distance dependencies) is blocked in certain situations, it is, for processing reasons, very different than in a stack machine, which relies on percolation and subjacency constraints. These issues will be explored in the Discussion section.

I should emphasize that the work described below, whatever its merits, should not to be taken as a *theory* of language. A theory of language will require certain properties of a processing mechanism which implements it, and I wish to know whether or not connectionist models are viable candidates. The current work thus should be seen as an exploration in the representational characteristics of a class of connectionist models in order to determine their relevancy for language. But for various reasons (in part having to do with the artificiality of the task they are taught), the models here do not provide a complete account of natural language use.

The remainder of this paper is organized in two sections, the first of which reports empirical results. After reviewing a related simulation from Elman (1990), I describe a task in which a network has to construct abstract representations which encode grammatical relations, including embedding relations. The trained network is studied in terms of performance. Then the internal representations are analysed in order to understand how the network has solved the task. These results are discussed at greater length in the second section and are related to the broader question of the usefulness of the connectionist framework for modelling cognitive phenomena. Finally, I compare a connectionist model with classical representations.

Simulations

Language is structured in a number of ways. One important kind of structure has to do with the structure of the categories of language elements (e.g., words). The first simulation addressed the question of whether a connectionist model can induce the lexical category structure underlying a set of stimuli. A second way in which language is structured has to do with the possible ways in which strings can be combined (e.g., the grammatical structure). The second simulation addresses that issue.

Lexical category structure

Words may be categorized with respect to many factors. These include traditional notions such as *noun, verb*, etc., the argument structure they are associated with, and their semantic features. One of the consequences of lexical category structure is word order. Not all classes of words may appear in any position. Furthermore, certain classes of words, e.g., transitive verbs, tend to co-occur with other words. (As we shall see in the next simulation, these co-occurrence facts can be quite complex.)

The goal of the first simulation was to see if a network could learn the lexical category structure which was implicit in a language corpus. The overt form of the language items was arbitrary in the sense that the form of the lexical items contained no information about their lexical category. However, the behaviour of the lexical items – defined in terms of co-occurrence restrictions – reflected their membership in implicit classes and subclasses. The question was whether or not the network could induce these classes.

Network architecture. Time is an important element in language, and so the question of how to represent serially ordered inputs is crucial. Various proposal have been advanced (for reviews, see Elman in press; Mozer 1988). The approach taken here involves treating the network as a simple dynamical system in which previous states are made available as an additional input (Jordan 1986). In Jordan's work the prior state was derived from the output units on the previous time cycle. In the work here, the prior state comes from the hidden unit patterns on the previous cycle. Because the hidden units are not taught to assume specific values in the course of learning a task, they can develop

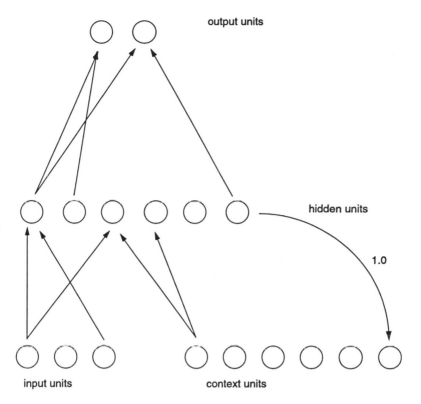

output units

hidden units

1.0

input units   context units

Figure 5.1: Network used in first simulation. Hidden unit activations are copied along
fixed weights (of 1.0) into linear context units on a one-to-one basis; on the next time
step the context units feed into hidden units on a distributed basis.

representations which encode the temporal structure of that task. In
other words, the hidden units learn to become a kind of memory which
is very task-specific.

The type of network used in the first simulation is shown in Figure
5.1. This network is basically a three-layer network with the customary
feed-forward connections from **input units** to **hidden units** and from
hidden units to **output units**. There are an additional set of units, called
context units, which provide for limited recurrence (and so this may be
called a **simple recurrent network**). These context units are activated
on a one-for-one basis by the hidden units, with a fixed weight of 1.0.

The result is that at each time cycle the hidden unit activations are
copied into the context units; on the next time cycle, the contexts combine with the new input to activate the hidden units. The hidden units
therefore take on the job of mapping new inputs and prior states to the
output; and because they themselves constitute the prior state, they

must develop representations which facilitate the input/output mapping.

The result is that at each time cycle the hidden unit activations are copied into the context units; on the next time cycle, the context combines with the new input to activate the hidden units. The hidden units therefore take on the job of mapping new inputs and prior states to the output. Because they themselves constitute the prior state, they must develop representations which facilitate this input/output mapping. The simple recurrent network has been studied in a number of tasks (Elman, in press; Hare, Corina, and Cottrell 1988; Servan-Schreiber, Cleeremans, and McClelland 1988). In this first simulation, there were thirty-one input units, one hundred and fifty hidden and context units, and thirty-one output units.

Stimuli and task. A lexicon of twenty-nine nouns and verbs was chosen. Words were represented as thirty-one bit binary vectors (two extra bits were reserved for another purpose). Each word was randomly assigned a unique vector in which only one bit was turned on. A sentence generating program was then used to create a corpus of 10,000 two- and three-word sentences. The sentences reflected certain properties of the words. For example, only animate nouns occurred as the subject of the verb **eat**, and this verb was only followed by edible substances. Finally, the words in successive sentences were concatenated so that a stream of 27,354 vectors was created. This formed the input set.

The task was simply for the network to take successive words from the input stream and to predict the subsequent word (by producing it on the output layer). After each word was input, the output was compared with the actual next word, and the back-propagation of error learning algorithm (Rumelhart, Hinton, and Williams 1986) was used to adjust the network weights. Words were presented in order, with no breaks between sentences. The network was trained on six passes through the corpus.

The prediction task was chosen for several reasons. First, it makes minimal assumptions about special knowledge required for training. The teacher function is simple and the information provided is available in the world at any moment. Thus, there are no a priori theoretical commitments which might bias the outcome. Second, although the task is simple and should not be taken as a model of comprehension, it does seem to be the case that much of what listeners do involves anticipation of future input (Grosjean 1980; Marslen Wilson and Tyler 1980; Salasoo and Pisoni 1985).

Results. Because the sequence is non-deterministic, short of memorizing the sequence, the network cannot succeed in exact predictions. That is, the underlying grammar and lexical category structure provides a set of constraints on the form of sentences, but the sentences themselves involve a high degree of optionality. Thus, measuring the performance of the network in this simulation is not straightforward. Root mean squared (rms) error at the conclusion of training had dropped to 0.88, but this result is not particularly positive in and of itself. In simulations where output vectors are sparse, as were those used in this simulation (only one bit out of thirty-one output bits is turned on for any particular pattern), the network quickly learns to reduce error dramatically by turning all the output units off. This drops error from the initial random value of ~15.5 to 1.0, which is close to the final rms error value of 0.88.

Although the prediction task is non-deterministic, it is also true that word order is not random or unconstrained. For any given sequence of words there are a limited number of possible successors. Under these circumstances, it would seem more appropriate to ask whether or not the network has learned what the class of valid successors is at each point in time. We therefore might expect that the network should learn to activate the output nodes to some value proportional to the probability of occurrence of each word in that context.

Therefore, rather than evaluating final network performance using the rms error calculated by comparing the network's output with the actual next word, we can compare the output with the probability of occurrence of possible successors. These values can be derived empirically from the training data base (for details see Elman 1989); such calculation yields a 'likelihood output vector' which is appropriate for each input and which reflects the context-dependent expectations given the training base (where context is defined as extending from the beginning of the sentence to the input). Note that it is appropriate to use these likelihood vectors only for the evaluation phase. Training must be performed on the actual successor words, because the point is to force the network to learn the context dependent probabilities for itself.

Evaluated in this manner, the error on the training set is 0.053 (sd: 0.100). The cosine of the angle between output vectors and likelihood vectors provides another measure of performance (which normalizes for length differences in the vectors); the mean cosine is 0.916 (sd: 0.123), indicating that the two vectors on average have very similar shapes. Objectively, the performance appears to be quite good.

Lexical categories

The question to be asked now is how this performance has been achieved. One way to answer this is to see what sorts of internal representations the network develops in order to carry out the prediction task. This is particularly relevant, given the focus of the current paper. The internal representations are instantiated as activation patterns across the hidden units which are evoked in response to each word in its context. These patterns were saved at a testing phase, during which no learning took place. For each of the twenty-nine unique words, a mean vector was computed and averaged across all occurrences of the word in various contexts. These mean vectors were then subjected to hierarchical clustering analysis. Figure 5.2 shows the tree constructed from the hidden unit patterns for the twenty-nine lexical items.The tree in Figure 5.2 shows the similarity structure of the internal representations of the twenty-nine lexical items. The form of each item is randomly assigned (and orthogonal to all other items), and so the basis for the similarity in the internal representations is the way in which these words 'behave' with regard to the task.

The network has discovered that there are several major categories of words. One large category corresponds to *verbs*; another category corresponds to nouns. The verb category is broken down into groups which require a direct object; which are intransitive; and for which a direct object is optional. The noun category is divided into major groups for *animates* and *inanimates*. Animates are divided into *human* and *non-human*; the *non-humans* are subdivided into *large animals* and *small animals*. Inanimates are divided into *breakables, edibles,* and *miscellaneous*.

This category structure reflects facts about the possible sequential ordering of the inputs. The network is not able to predict the precise order of specific words, but it recognizes that (in this corpus) there is a class of inputs (viz., verbs) which typically follow other inputs (viz., nouns). This knowledge of class behaviour is quite detailed; from the fact that there is a class of items which always precedes **chase, break**, and **smash**, it infers a category of large animals (or, possibly, aggressors).

Several points should be emphasized. First, the category structure appears to be hierarchical. **Dragons** are large animals, but also members of the class [-human, +animate] nouns. The hierarchical interpretation is achieved through the way in which the spatial relations of the representations are organized. Representations which are near one another in representational space form classes, and higher level categories correspond to larger and more general regions of this space.

Second, it is also the case that the hierarchicality and category boundaries are 'soft.' This does not prevent categories from being qualitatively distinct by being far from each other in space with no overlap. But there may also be entities which share properties of otherwise distinct categories, so that in some cases category membership may be marginal or ambiguous.

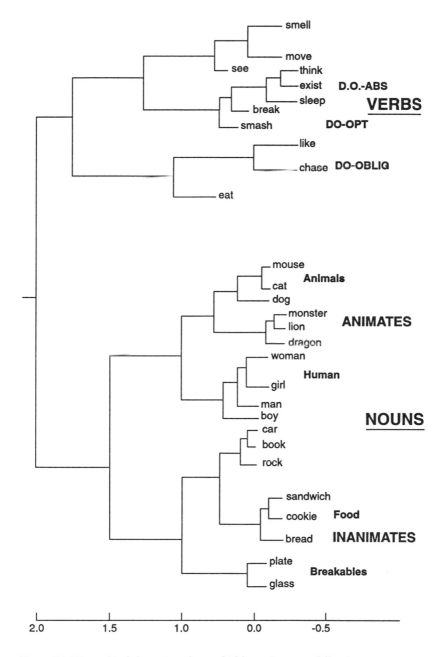

Figure 5.2: Hierarchical clustering of mean hidden unit vectors following presentation of each of the lexical items (in context). The similarity structure of the space reflects distributional properties of the lexical items.

Finally, the content of the categories is not known to the network. The network has no information available which would ground the structural information in the real world. This is both a plus and a minus. Obviously, a full account of language processing needs to provide such grounding. On the other hand, it is interesting that the evidence for category structure can be inferred so readily on the basis of language internal evidence alone.

Type-token distinctions

The tree shown in Figure 5.2 was constructed from activation patterns averaged across context. It is also possible to cluster activation patterns evoked in response to words in the various contexts in which they occur. When the context sensitive hidden units patterns are clustered, it is found that the large-scale structure of the tree is identical to that shown in Figure 5.2. However, each terminal leaf is now replaced with further arborization for all occurrences of the word. (There are no instances of lexical items appearing on inappropriate branches.)

This finding bears on the type/token problem in an important way. In this simulation, the context makes up an important part of the internal representation of a word. Indeed, it is somewhat misleading to speak of the hidden unit representations as word representations in the conventional sense, since these patterns also reflect the prior context. As a result, it is literally the case that every occurrence of a lexical item has a separate internal representation. We cannot point to a canonical representation for **John**; instead there are representations for **John1, John2, ... John**. These are the tokens of **John**, and the fact that they are different is the way the system marks what may be subtle but important meaning differences associated with the specific token. The fact that these are all tokens of the same type is not lost, however. These tokens have representations which are extremely close in space – closer to each other by far than to any other entity. Even more interesting is that the spatial organization within the token space is not random but reflects differences in context which are also found among tokens of other items. The tokens of **boy** which occur in subject position tend to cluster together as distinct from tokens of **boy** which occur in object position. This distinction is marked in the same way for tokens of other nouns. Thus, the network has learned not only about types and tokens, categories and category members; it has also learned a grammatical role distinction which cuts across lexical items.

This simulation has involved a task in which the category structure of inputs was an important determinant of their behaviour. The category structure was apparent only in their behaviour; their external form provided no useful information. We have seen that the network makes use of spatial organization in order to capture this category structure. We turn next to a problem in which the lexical category structure provides only one part of the solution, and in which the network must learn abstract grammatical structure.

Representation of grammatical structure

In the previous simulation there was little interesting structure of the sort that related words to one another. Most of the relevant information regarding sequential behaviour was encoded in terms of invariant properties of items. Although lexical information plays an important role in language, it actually accounts for only a small range of facts. Words are processed in the contexts of other words; they inherit properties from the specific grammatical structure in which they occur. This structure can be quite complex, and it is not clear that the kind of category structure supported by the spatial distribution of representations is sufficient to capture the structure which belongs, not to individual words, but to particular configurations of words.

As we consider this issue, we also note that till now we have neglected an important dimension along which structure may be manifest, that is, time. The clustering technique used in the previous simulation informs us of the similarity relations along spatial dimensions. The technique tells us nothing about the patterns of movement through space. This is unfortunate, since the networks we are using are dynamical systems whose states change over time. Clustering groups states according to the metric of Euclidean distance but, in so doing, discards the information about whatever temporal relations may hold between states. This information is clearly relevant if we are concerned about grammatical structure.

Consider the sentences

(1a) The man saw the **car.**
(1b) The man who saw the **car** called the cops.

On the basis of the results of the previous simulation, we would expect that the representations for the word **car** in these two sentences would be extremely similar. Not only are they the same lexical type, but they both appear in clause-final position as the object of the same verb. But we might also wish to have their representations capture an important structural difference between them. **Car** in sentence (1a) occurs at the end of the sentence; it brings us to a state from which we should move into another class of states that is associated with the onset of new sentences. In sentence (1b), **car** is also at the end of a clause but occurs in a matrix sentence which has not yet been completed. There are grammatical obligations which remain unfulfilled. We would like the state that is associated with **car** in this context to lead us to the class of states which might conclude the main clause. The issue of how to understand the temporal structure of state trajectories will thus figure importantly in our attempts to understand the representation of grammatical structure.

Stimuli and task. The stimuli in this simulation were based on a lexicon of twenty-three items. These included eight nouns twelve verbs, the relative pronoun **who**, and an end-of-sentence indicator, '.'. Each item was represented by a randomly assigned twenty-six bit vector in which a single bit was set to one (three bits were reserved for another purpose). A phrase structure grammar, shown in Table 5.1, was used to generate sentences. The resulting sentences possessed certain important properties, which include the following:

Table 5.1

S → NP VP '.'
NP → PropN I N I N RC
VP → V (NP)
RC → *who* NP VP I*who* VP (NP)
N → *boy* I *girl* I *cat* I*dog* I *boys* I *girls* I *cats* I *dogs*
PropN   → *John* I *Mary*
V → *chase* I *feed* I *see* I *hear* I *walk* I *live* I *chases* I
        feeds I*sees* I *hears* I *walks* I *lives*

Additional restrictions:
   • number agreement between N and V within clause and
   (where appropriate) between head N and subordinate V

   • verb arguments:
       hit, feed → require a direct object
       see, hear → optionally allow a direct object
       walk, live → preclude a direct object
       (observed also for head/verb relations in relative clauses)

Agreement

Subject nouns agree with their verbs. Thus, for example, (2a) is gram-matical but (2b) is not. (The training corpus consisted of positive exam-ples only; thus the starred examples below did not occur.)

(2a) John feeds dogs.
(2b) *Boys sees Mary.

Words are not marked for number (singular/plural), form class (verb/noun, etc.), or grammatical role (subject/object, etc.). The network must learn first that there are items which function as what we would call nouns, verbs, etc.; then it must learn which items are examples of sin-gular and plural; and then it must learn which nouns are subjects and which are objects (since agreement only holds between subject nouns and their verbs).

Verb argument structure

Verbs fall into three classes: those that require direct objects, those that permit an optional direct object, and those that preclude direct objects. As a result, sentences (3a-d) are grammatical, whereas sentences (3e, 3f) are ungrammatical.

(3a) Girls feed dogs. (*D.o. required*)
(3b) Girls see boys. (*D.o. optional*)
(3c) Girls see. (*D.o. optional*)
(3d) Girls live. (*D.o. precluded*)
(3e) *Girls feed.
(3f) *Girls live dogs.

Again, the type of verb is not overtly marked in the input, and so the class membership needs to be inferred at the same time as the co-occur-rence facts are learned.

Interactions with relative clauses

Both the agreement and the verb argument facts are complicated in rel-ative clauses. While direct objects normally follow the verb in simple sentences, some relative clauses have the direct object as the head of the clause, in which case the network must learn to recognize that the direct object has already been filled (even though it occurs before the verb). Thus, the normal pattern in simple sentences (3ad) appears also in (4a) but contrasts with (4b).

(4a) Dog who chases cat sees girl.
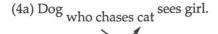

(4b) Dog who cat chases sees girl.
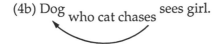

Sentence (4c), which seems to conform to the pattern established in (3), is ungrammatical.

(4c) *Dog who cat chases dog sees girl.

Similar complications arise for the agreements facts. In simple sentences agreement involves *N1-V1*. In complex sentences, such as (5a), that regularity is violated, and any straightforward attempt to generalize it to sentences with multiple clauses would lead to the ungrammatical (5b).

(5a) Dog who boys feed sees girl.

(5b) *Dog who boys feeds see girl.
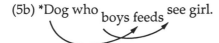

Recursion

The grammar permits recursion through the presence of relative clauses (which expand to noun phrases which may introduce yet other relative clauses, etc.). This leads to sentences such as (6) in which the grammatical phenomena noted in (a-c) may be extended over a considerable distance.

(6) Boys who girls who dogs chase see hear.

Viable sentences

One of the literals inserted by the grammar is '.' This mark occurs at the end of sentences and can, of course, potentially occur anywhere in a string where a sentence is viable (in the sense that it is grammatically well-formed and may at that point be terminated). Thus in sentence (7), the carets indicate positions where a '.' might legally occur.

(7) Boys see ∧ dogs ∧ who see ∧ girls ∧ who hear ∧.

*   *   *

The data in (4-7) are examples of the sorts of phenomena which linguists argue cannot be accounted for without abstract representations; it is these representations, rather than the surface strings, on which the correct grammatical generalizations are made.

A network of the form shown in Figure 5.3 was trained on the prediction task (layers are shown as rectangles; numbers indicate the number of nodes in each layer).The training data were generated from the phrase structure grammar given in Table 1. At any given point during training, the training set consisted of 10,000 sentences, which were

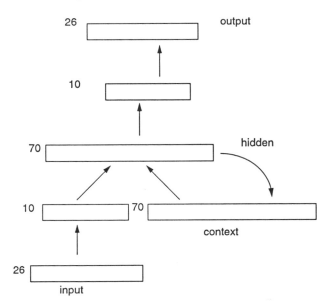

Figure 5.3: Hierarchical clustering of mean hidden unit vectors following presentation of each of the lexical items (in context). The similarity structure of the space reflects distributional properties of the lexical items.

presented to the network five times. (As before, sentences were concatenated so that the input stream proceeded smoothly, without breaks between sentences.) However, the composition of these sentences varied over time. The following training regimen was used in order to provide for incremental training. The network was trained on five passes through each of the following four corpora.

Phase 1: The first training set consisted exclusively of simple sentences. This was accomplished by eliminating all relative clauses. The result was a corpus of 34,605 words forming 10,000 sentences (each sentence includes the terminal '.'). Phase 2: The network was then exposed to a second corpus of 10,000 sentences which consisted of twenty-five per cent complex sentences and seventy-five per cent simple sentences (complex sentences were obtained by permitting relative clauses). Mean sentence length was 3.92 (minimum three words, maximum thirteen words). Phase 3: The third corpus increased the percentage of complex sentences to fifty per cent, with mean sentence length of 4.38 (minimum: three words, maximum: thirteen words). Phase 4: The fourth consisted of 10,000 sentences, seventy-five per cent complex, twenty-five per cent simple. Mean sentence length was 6.02 (minimum: three words, maximum: sixteen words).

This staged learning strategy was developed in response to results of earlier pilot work. In this work, it was found that the network was unable to learn the task when given the full range of complex data from the beginning of training. However, when the network was permitted to focus on the simpler data first, it was able to learn the task quickly and then move on successfully to more complex patterns. The important aspect to this was that the earlier training constrained later learning in a useful way; it forced the network to focus on canonical versions of the problems, which apparently created a good basis for then solving the more difficult forms of the same problems.

Results. At the conclusion of the fourth phase of training, the weights were frozen at their final values and network performance was tested on a novel set of data, which was generated in the same way as the last training corpus. The technique described in the previous simulation was used, and context-dependent likelihood vectors were generated for each word in every sentence. These vectors represented the empirically derived probabilities of occurrence for all possible predictions, given the sentence context up to that point. The rms error of network predictions, compared against the likelihood vectors, was 0.177 (sd: 0.463); the mean cosine of the angle between the vectors was 0.852 (sd: 0.259). Although this performance is not as good as in the previous simulation, it is still quite good. And the task is obviously much more difficult.

These gross measures of performance, however, do not tell us how well the network has done in each of the specific problem areas posed by the task. Let us look at each area in turn.

Agreement in simple sentences

Agreement in simple sentences is shown in Figures 4a and 4b. The network's predictions following the word **boy** are that either a singular verb will follow (words in all three singular verb categories are activated, since it has no basis for predicting the type of verb), or the next word may be the relative pronoun **who**. Conversely, when the input is the word **boys**, the expectation is that either a verb in the plural or a relative pronoun will follow. Similar expectations hold for the other nouns in the lexicon.

Verb argument structure in simple sentences

Figure 5.5 shows network predictions following an initial noun and then a verb from each of the three different verb types. When the verb is **lives**, the network's expectation is that the following item will be '.'

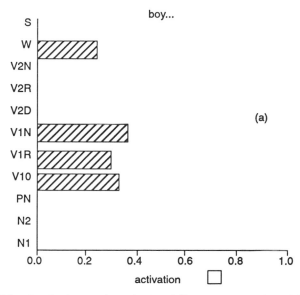

Figure 5.4 a: Graph of network predictions following presentation of the word **boy**. Predictions are shown as activations for words grouped by category. S stands for end-of-sentence ('.'); W stands for who; N and V represent nouns and verbs; 1 and 2 indicate singular or plural; and type of verb is indicated by **N, R, O** (direct object not possible, required, or optional).

(which is in fact the only successor permitted by the grammar in this context). The verb **sees**, on the other hand, may either be followed by a '.' or by a direct object (which may be a singular or plural noun, or proper noun). Finally, the verb **chases** requires a direct object, and the network learns to expect a noun following this and other verbs in the same class.

Interactions with relative clauses

The examples so far have all involved simple sentences. The agreement and verb argument facts are more complicated in complex sentences. Figure 5.6 shows the network predictions for each word in the sentence **boys who Mary chases feed cats**. If the network were generalizing the pattern for agreement found in the simple sentences, we might expect the network to predict a singular verb following **Mary chases** (insofar as it predicts a verb in this position at all; conversely, it might be confused by the pattern *N1 N2 V1*). But, in fact, the prediction (6d) is, correctly, that the next verb should be in the singular in order to agree with the first noun. In so doing, it has found some mechanism for representing the long-distance dependency between the main clause noun and

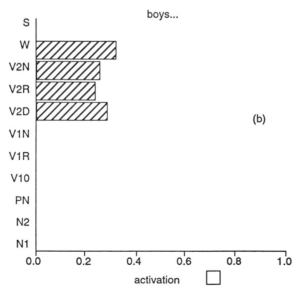

Figure 5.4 b: Graph of network predictions following presentation of the word **boys**.

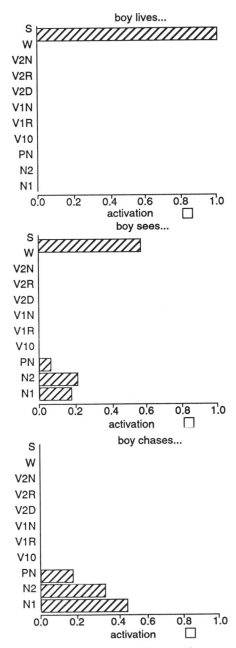

Figure 5.5: Graph of network predictions following the sequences **boy lives ...** ; **boy sees** **...** ; and **boy chases ...** (the first precludes a direct object, the second optional permits a direct object, and the third requires a direct object).

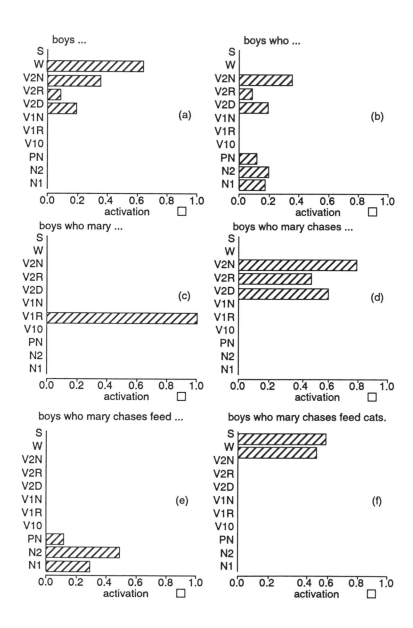

Figure 5.6: Graph of network predictions after each word in the sentence **boys who mary chases feed cats** is input.

main clause verb, despite the presence of an intervening noun and verb (with their own agreement relations) in the relative clause.

Note that this sentence also illustrates the sensitivity to an interaction between verb argument structure and relative clause structure. The verb **chases** takes an obligatory direct object. In simple sentences the direct object follows the verb immediately; this is also true in many complex sentences (e.g., **boys who chase Mary feed cats**). In the sentence displayed, however, the direct object (boys) is the head of the relative clause and appears before the verb. This requires that the network learn (a) there are items which function as nouns, verbs, etc.; (b) which items fall into which classes; (c) there are subclasses of verbs which have different co-occurrence relations with nouns, corresponding to verb direct object restrictions; (d) which verbs fall into which classes; and (e) when to expect that the direct object will follow the verb and when to know that it has already appeared. The network appears to have learned this, because in panel (d) we see that it expects that **chases** will be followed by a verb (the main clause verb, in this case) rather than a noun.

An even subtler point is demonstrated in (6c). The appearance of **boys** followed by a relative clause containing a different subject (**who Mary**) primes the network to expect that the verb which follows must be of the class that requires a direct object, precisely because a direct object filler has already appeared. In other words, the network correctly responds to the presence of a filler (**boys**) not only by knowing where to expect a gap (following **chases**); it also learns that when this filler corresponds to the object position in the relative clause, a verb is required which has the appropriate argument structure.

Network analysis. The natural question to ask at this point is how the network has learned to accomplish the task. It was initially assumed that success in this task would constitute prima facie evidence for the existence of internal representations which possessed abstract structure. That is, it seemed reasonable to believe that in order to handle agreement and argument structure facts in the presence of relative clauses, the network would be required to develop representations which reflected constituent structure, argument structure, grammatical category, grammatical relations, and number.

Having achieved success in the task, we would now like to test this assumption. In the previous simulation, hierarchical clustering was used to reveal the use of spatial organization at the hidden unit level for categorization purposes. However, the clustering technique makes it difficult to see patterns which exist over time. Some states may have significance not simply in terms of their similarity to other states but with regard to the ways in which they constrain movement into subsequent state space (recall the examples in (1)). Because clustering ignores the temporal information, it hides this information. It would be more useful to look at the trajectories, through state space over time, which correspond to the internal representations evoked at the hidden unit layer as a network processes a given sentence.

Phase-state portraits of this sort are commonly limited to displaying not more than a few state variables at once, simply because movement in more than three dimensions is difficult to graph. The hidden unit activation patterns in the current simulation take place over seventy variables. These patterns are distributed, in the sense that none of the hidden units alone provides useful information; the information instead lies along hyperplanes which cut across multiple units.

However, it is possible to identify these hyperplanes using principle component analysis. This involves passing the training set through the trained network (with weights frozen) and saving the hidden unit pattern produced in response to each new input. The covariance matrix of the set of hidden unit vectors is calculated, and then the eigen-vectors for the covariance matrix are found. The eigen-vectors are ordered by the magnitude of their eigen-values and are used as the new basis for describing the original hidden unit vectors. This new set of dimensions has the effect of giving a somewhat more localized description to the hidden unit patterns, because the new dimensions now correspond to the location of meaningful activity (defined in terms of variance) in hyperspace. Furthermore, since the dimensions are ordered in terms of variance accounted for, we can now look at phase state portraits of selected dimensions, starting with those with the largest eigen-values.

Agreement

The sentences in (8) were presented to the network, and the hidden unit patterns captured after each word were processed in sequence.

(8a) boys hear boys.
(8b) boy hears boys.
(8c) boy who boys chase chases boy.
(8d) boys who boys chase chase boy.

(These sentences were chosen to minimize differences due to lexical content and to make it possible to focus on differences to grammatical structure. (8a) and (8b) were contained in the training data; (8c) and (8d) were novel and had never been presented to the network during learning.) By examining the trajectories through state space along various dimensions, it was apparent that the second principal component played an important role in marking the number of the main clause subject.

Figure 5.7 shows the trajectories for (8a) and (8b); the trajectories are overlaid so that the differences are more readily seen. The paths are similar and diverge only during the first word, indicating the difference in the number of the initial noun. The difference is slight and is eliminated after the main (i.e., second chase) verb has been input. This is apparently because, for these two sentences (and for the grammar), number information does not have any relevance for this task once the main verb has been received.

It is not difficult to imagine sentences in which number information may have to be retained over an intervening constituent; sentences (8c) and (8d) are such examples. In both these sentences there is an identical relative clause which follows the initial noun (which differs with regard to number in the two sentences). This material, **who boys chase**, is irrelevant as far as the agreement requirements for the main clause verb are concerned. The trajectories through state space for these two sentences have been overlaid and are shown in Figure 5.8; as can be seen, the differences in the two trajectories are maintained until the main clause verb is reached, at which point the states converge.

Verb argument structure

The representation of verb argument structure was examined by probing sentences containing instances of the three different classes of verbs. Sample sentences are shown in (9).

(9a) boy walks.
(9b) boy sees boy.
(9c) boy chases boy.

The first of these contains a verb which may not take a direct object; the second takes an option direct object; and the third requires a direct object. The movement through state space as these three sentences are processed is shown in Figure 5.9, which illustrates how the network encodes several aspects of grammatical structure. Nouns are distinguished by role; subject nouns for all three sentences appear in the upper right portion of the space, and object nouns appear below them. (Principal component 4, not shown here, encodes the distinction between verbs and nouns, collapsing across case.) Verbs are differentiated with regard to their argument structure. **Chases** requires a direct object, **sees** takes an optional direct object, and **walks** precludes an object. The difference is reflected in a systematic displacement in the plane of principal components 1 and 3.

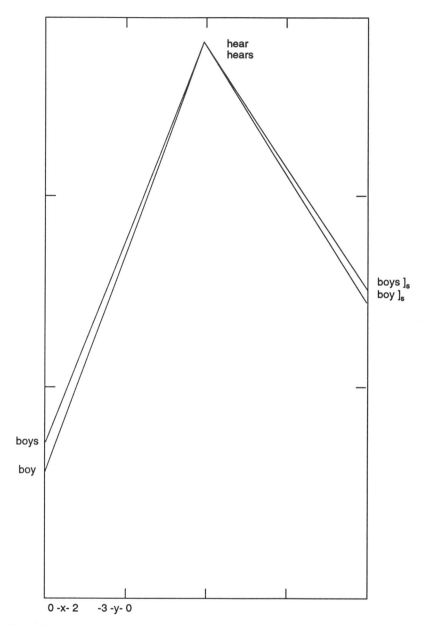

hear
hears

boys]ₛ
boy]ₛ

boys

boy

0 -x- 2   -3 -y- 0

Figure 5.7: Trajectories through state space for sentences (8a) and (8b). After the indicated word has been input, each point marks the position along the second principle component of hidden unit space. Magnitude of the second principle component is measured along the ordinate; time (i.e., order of words in sentence) is measured along the abscissa. In this and subsequent graphs the sentence-final word is marked with a]S.

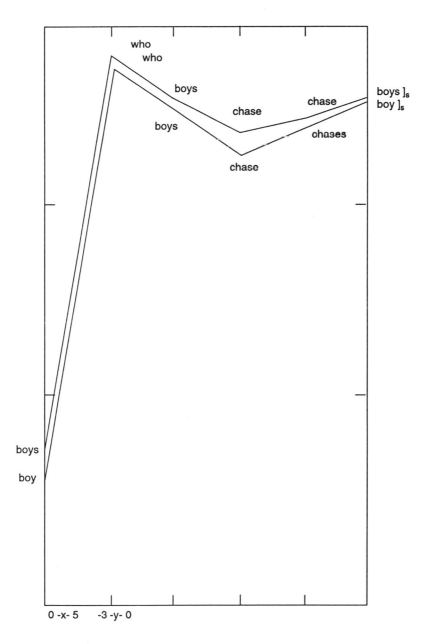

who
who

boys

chase   chase   boys]ₛ
        chase   boy]ₛ

boys   chases

        chase

boys

boy

0 -x- 5   -3 -y- 0

Figure 5.8: Trajectories through state space during processing of (8c) and (8d).

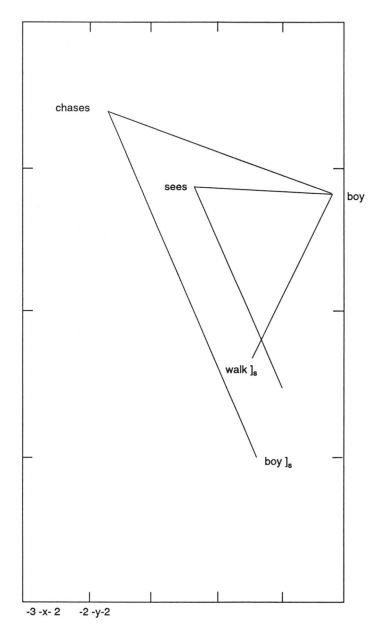

Figure 5.9: Trajectories through state space for sentences (9a), (9b), and (9c). Principal component 1 is plotted along the abscissa; principal component 3 is plotted along the ordinate.

Relative clauses

The presence of relative clauses introduces a complication into the grammar in that the representations of number and verb argument structure must be clause-specific. It would be useful for the network to have some way to represent the constituent structure of sentences. The trained network was given the following sentences.

(10a) boy chases boy.
(10b) boy chases boy who chases boy.
(10c) boy who chases boy chases boy.
(10d) boy chases boy who chases boy who chases boy.

The first sentence is simple; the other three are instances of embedded sentences. Sentence 10a was contained in the training data; sentences 10c, 10d, and 10e were novel and had not been presented to the network during the learning phase.

The trajectories through state space for these four sentences (principal components 1 and 11) are shown in Figure 5.10. Panel (10a) shows the basic pattern associated with what is in fact the matrix sentences for all four sentences. Comparison of this figure with panels (10b) and (10c) shows that the trajectory for the matrix sentence appears to be the same when; the matrix subject noun is in the lower left region of state space, the matrix verb appears above it and to the left, and the matrix object noun is near the upper middle region. (Recall that we are looking at only two of the seventy dimensions; along other dimensions the noun/verb distinction is preserved categorically.) The relative clause appears to involve a replication of this basic pattern but is displaced towards the left and moved slightly downward relative to the matrix constituents. Moreover, the exact position of the relative clause elements indicates which of the matrix nouns are modified Thus, the relative clause modifying the subject noun is closer to it, as is the relative clause modifying the object noun. This trajectory pattern was found for all sentences with the same grammatical form; the pattern is thus systematic.

Figure 5.10d shows what happens when there are multiple levels of embedding. Successive embeddings are represented in a manner which is similar to the way that the first embedded clause is distinguished from the main clause; the basic patter for the clause is replicated in the region of state space, which is displaced from the matrix material. This displacement provides a systematic way for the network to encode the depth of embedding in the current state. However, the reliability of the encoding is limited by the precision with which states are represented, which in turn depends on factors such as the number of hidden units

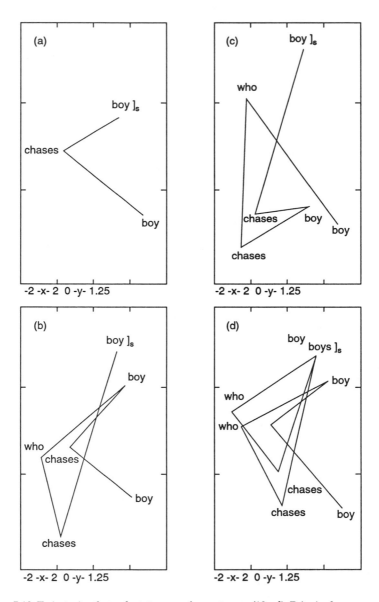

Figure 5.10: Trajectories through state space for sentences (10a-d). Principal component 1 is displayed along the abscissa; principal component 11 is plotted along the ordinate. It is interesting, although not a key point of this paper, that these abstract compositional relations are in fact learned by the network rather than innately specified. I assume that any theory of language must be learnable. How much is learned by individual language users in their lifetime, and how much is 'learned' through evolutionary mechanisms is an interesting question but orthogonal to the issues currently at hand.

and the precision of the numerical values. In the current simulation, the representation degraded after about three levels of embedding. The consequences of this degradation on performance (in the prediction task) are different for different types of sentences. Sentences involving centre embedding (e.g., 8c and 8d), in which the level of embedding is crucial for maintaining correct agreement, are more adversely affected than are sentences involving so-called tail recursion (e.g., 10d). In these latter sentences the syntactic structures, in principle, involve recursion, but in practice the level of embedding is not relevant for the task (i.e., does not affect agreement or verb argument structure in any way).

Figure 5.10d is interesting in another respect. Given the nature of the prediction task, it is actually not necessary for the network to carry forward any information from prior clauses. It would be sufficient for the network to represent each successive relative clause as an iteration of the previous pattern. Yet the two relative clauses are differentiated. Similarly, Servan-Schreiber, Cleeremans, and McClelland (in press) found that when a simple recurrent network was taught to predict inputs that had been generated by a finite state automaton, the network developed internal representations which corresponded to the FSA states; however, it also redundantly made finer-grained distinctions which encoded the path by which the state had been achieved, even though this information was not used for the task. It thus seems to be a property of these networks that while they are able to encode state in a way which minimizes context as far as behaviour is concerned, their nonlinear nature allows them to remain sensitive to context at the level of internal representation.

Discussion

I began by asking whether distributed representations could be used to encode grammatical relations, and, in particular, whether they could represent the embedding relationships in relative clauses. The results of the second simulation are encouraging and suggest that the networks of the sort studied here can support compositional relationships.

At this point it is reasonable to see if we can more precisely understand the nature of the mechanism that is used to represent the part/ whole hierarchies. Does the mechanism differ from the traditional approach? If so, are the differences desirable or not? These are difficult questions, and only tentative suggestions can be made at this time. However, two aspects stand out with particular salience. First, the representational apparatus used by these networks has definite limitations. The representations have a finite precision, and they degrade over time (since they are continually recycled and passed through a nonlinear squashing function). Second, the representations are highly context-sensitive. Even when contextual information is not needed, there is a tendency for the states of the system to reflect the path that was taken to get there.

The finite precision and tendency to degrade over time are, in fact, consistent with the observed abilities of language users. The representations, while continuously valued (in multidimensional space), have a finite precision. Locations in this space that are sufficiently close will be treated as identical. Furthermore, because these representations are repeatedly cycled through the nonlinear activation function of the hidden units (which tends to push them towards the centre of representational space), information cannot be held indefinitely. This limitation accounts for the difficulty the network has in processing centre embedded sentences compared with right-branching structures; compare (11a) with (11b):

(11a) The boy who the girl who the cat sees knows walks.
(11b) The boy likes the girl who knows the cat who walks.

Information in the network degrades equally over time in both sentences; but it is only in the centre-embedded sentence that early information is needed in later parts of the sentence; the right-branching structures can continue indefinitely, because the network does not need to refer back to earlier (lost) information. Note that this is not to say that the network cannot process centre-embedded sentences, only that its ability to do so is limited (and less than right-branching sentences).

This characteristic of the network – its finite state quality – is interesting in light of Chomsky's (1957) argument against the sufficiency of Finite State Markov processes (or automata; FSA) as models for natural language grammar. There were actually two arguments advanced.

The strong argument rested on the observation that natural languages (such as English) contain classes of sentences (such as relative clauses) which permit infinite recursion. Such infinite recursion is beyond the capacity of FSA's. Of course, in reality, sentences do not take advantage of infinite recursion. There are no English sentences which are infinitely long. If one is willing to arbitrarily fix an upper limit to the degree of recursion (or sentence length), choosing a limit sufficiently high that all sentences in the history of the language could be generated, then, in fact, it is possible to devise an FSA which could generate this set.

Consideration of this point leads to the second argument against the sufficiency of FSA's as models of natural language. This fall- back position is that although the construction of an FSA, given an arbitrary limit on sentence length, would not literally be impossible, it 'will be so complex that it will be of little use or interest' (Chomsky 1957: 23). An example of such a grammar would be a list of the sentences of the language. 'In general, the assumption that languages are infinite is made in order to simplify the description of the language. If a grammar does not have recursive devices it will be prohibitively complex. If it does have recursive devices of some sort, it will produce infinitely many sentences' (ibid, 24-5). Savitch (in press) has made a similar point and argued that there are classes of languages which are more perspicuously treated as 'essentially infinite,' even though they may have a finite number of sentences.

This second argument is, technically, the weaker of the two, since it depends on ill-defined and controversial notions of simplicity. But the intuitive appeal of this position should nonetheless be clear. Leaving aside the definition or even desirability of simplicity as a goal, I take it as at least desirable that grammars should provide insight into languages. Chomsky's claim was that FSA's – as understood at that time – can not in principle offer such insight. The current work provides an example of a machine which is a finite state device, yet which may well satisfy the desideratum for a mechanism whose form explicates the systematic properties of the language it produces. The machine is not literally recursive, both because of limited depth and, more importantly, because of leakage across levels (see below); but it allows structures to be combined hierarchically in what could be called (following Savitch's terminology) an 'essentially recursive' manner.

Let us now turn to the second way in which the networks appear to differ from conventional devices. This second characteristic may represent a more significant departure from the traditional approach. As noted earlier, Servan-Schreiber, Cleeremans, and McClelland (in press) found that, although their task only required that the network encode information in terms of a finite number of discrete states (in order to act like an FSA), the representations reflected the path information as well.

A similar effect can be found in the networks studied here. For example, the language learned by these networks contained classes of sentences such as (12):

(12) {boy, girl, cat, dog, John, Mary} chases ...

In this language, there were no meaningful consequences attendant upon the choice of subject, in fact the state of the network when it receives the verb chases is different from what it is as a function of the subject. The difference is systematic across verbs. The subject Mary, for example, perturbs the state of the network when it processes chases in a way that affects the representation of other verbs. In other words, the precise representation of the verb reflects not only properties of the verb but who the subject is as well.

At first, this seems odd, and it is certainly at variance with the classical approach to compositionality. In classical theories, complex representations are constructed following a building block metaphor. Each element is positioned in a larger structure and function is like a building block; that is to say, elements are not affected by their position nor do they interact in any way. The mechanism here, on the other hand, is highly interactive. Representational elements are subject to subtle adjustments as they combine. The resulting structure is not just the sum of the parts; it reflects interactions between those parts as well.

This sort of context-sensitivity appears to be very similar to the notion of *accommodation*, as developed by Langacker (1987), for cognitive grammar. Because this view of how composition works differs significantly from generative accounts, it is worth citing Langacker's comments at length.

> It must be emphasized that syntagmatic combination involves more than the simple addition of components. A composite structure is an integrated system formed by coordinating its components in a specific, often elaborate manner. In fact, it often has properties that go beyond what one might expect from its components alone. Two brief observations should make it clear why this is so. First, composite structures originate as targets in specific usage events. As such they are often characterized relative to particular contexts with properties not predictable from the specifications of their components as manifested in other environments. A related point is that one component may need to be adjusted in certain details when integrated with another to form a composite structure; I refer to this as **accommodation**. For example, the meaning of run as applied to humans must be adjusted in certain respects when extended to four legged animals such as horses, dogs, and cats (since the bodily motion observed in two legged running is not identical to that in four legged running); in a technical sense, this extension creates a new **semantic variant** of the lexical item. (Langacker 1987; 76-7)

It is true that current work does not take advantage of the network's propensity to combine elements in a highly context-sensitive manner; but it should not be difficult to imagine ways in which it could. If anything, the emergence of this property, despite not being utilized by the task that is taught, illustrates that it is central to the mechanism.

This sensitivity to context also occurs across levels of organization. Not only may the verb in the main clause be represented in a manner which reflects the main clause subject, but embedded material may also be coloured by elements in other clauses. Thus, the representation of

hierarchical structure does not use 'true' recursion, in which information at each level of processing is encapsulated and unaffected by information at other levels.

Again, one can ask whether this is good or bad. Certainly, there are
many situations in which one wants the informational encapsulation afforded by true recursion. Many programming languages, for instance,
depend crucially on the assumption that a procedure may be re-entered
without contamination from earlier invocations. But, for natural language, I think a strong argument can be made for the desirability of
what I will call the 'leaky recursion' provided by simple recurrent
networks.

The implicit claim of strict recursion – or more generally, of a machine
which uses a stack mechanism to construct hierarchically organized
structures – is that, normally, information at different levels of a complex structure should be processed autonomously, and that there will be
minimal interaction with information at other levels. But this is rarely
the case for linguistic structures. Relative clauses, for instance, typically
have an elaborative function; they provide information about a head
noun phrase (which is at a higher level of organization). Adverbial
clauses perform a similar function for main clause verbs. In general,
subordination involves *conceptual dependence* between clauses (Langacker in press; Chapter 10). Thus, it may be more important that a
language processing mechanism facilitate interactions across levels of
organization rather than impede the flow of information.

As one extreme example, consider the case of long-distance dependency relations. These are cases where one element in a sentence is in
some way dependant on another element in the sentence, but the two
are separated in linear order and also, possibly, across different levels of
organization. Information which in some sense coheres is broken; and
the problem for the listener, presumably, is to recognize the dependency
in spite of the (apparent) dislocation.

(12a) Who does Jeremy suspect Emily wanted me to invite to the
party?
(12b) It's the one on the left I want.
(12c) I saw the car that Mary said a thief had broken into.
(12d) Under which toadstool did you say there's a pot of gold?

In (12a) 'who' refers to the person whom Emily invited to the party;
in the clefted sentence (12b), the object phrase occurs at the beginning
of the sentence; in (12c) the head of the relative clause ('car') is also the
object of the verb at the end of the sentence; and in (12d), the preposi-
tional phrase has been topicalized and thus appears at the beginning of

the sentence. In many cases the dependency has a morphological reflex; thus in (12a) the form of the interrogative pronoun is determined by the fact that it is a person and not a thing, animal, concept, etc. that can be invited to a party. In some dialects, the pronoun would, additionally, be marked in the accusative.

The dependency may range over a considerable distance and may span multiple levels of organization. This raises an interesting and difficult problem for a system which utilizes a stack device to construct complex hierarchies, as do (at least implicitly) generative grammars. Stacks have an important limitation: Information is stored in them by pushing the current contents 'down' one level (like a stack of dishes) and storing new information on top; and information on the top may be pulled off, causing the contents below to pop up. In other implementations, information may be pulled off the bottom, according to the principle of 'first-in-first-out.' In either event, information in the middle (or at the wrong end) must percolate up or drip down one level at a time.

This limitation has curious consequences when one wants to account for long-distance dependencies of the sort illustrated in (12). As we have seen, the form of the pronoun is determined by information which occurs in a subordinate clause (two levels down). But in a stack, information is not normally available across levels. The implementation of this restriction in generative linguistics is subjacency, which constrains movement of constituents, as shown in (13) (Chomsky 1973f). A constituent in position Y may not move to position X, where X and Y are separated by more than one nesting level, as defined by a bounding node. (What constitutes a bounding node is a matter of some dispute.)

(13) **Constraint on Subjacency:**

$$\ldots X \ldots [_\alpha \ldots [_\beta \ldots Y \ldots {}_\beta] \ldots {}_\alpha] \ldots X \ldots$$

where $\alpha, \beta = [\,\overline{S}$ or NP$]$

The solution that is proposed to this dilemma is quite clever. Let us suppose that one has a sentence such as (14).

(14) Who do you think the fans believe the umpire should fine?

We might imagine that this sentence has the structural configuration shown in (15), and that 'who' originates in the position it would have as direct object of the verb 'fine.' Then we can account for the fact that it has the form appropriate to its grammatical usage. We derive the

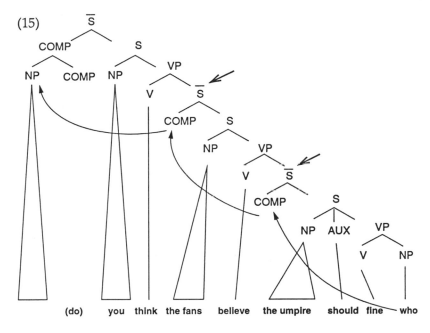

(15)

question by percolating the interrogative pronoun up successive layers of the hierarchy (i.e., letting it move up the stack) one level at a time.

Such analyses, in which constituents are moved around in the course of deriving a sentence, are common in many generative theories. Although this notion of deriving a sentence through (among other things) moving constituents around may strike us as contrived and unnatural, we can see that it is entirely consistent with – indeed, is strongly encouraged by – the stack machine which implicitly underlies much of generative linguistic theory.

In contrast, the network architecture described here uses a representational mechanism in which there is no movement of constituents. There is no notion of derivation of sentences through intermediate forms. Still, sentences may have a hierarchical structure, and there may be long-distance dependencies between distal elements in a sentence. Recall, for example, that the simulation reported here involved relative clauses, in which there is a long-distance conceptual dependency between the head noun and the embedded clause. The network learned this dependency, with the consequence that its expectations regarding noun/verb number agreement and location of arguments were correct (see Figure 5.6). But there is no movement of elements.

The key to the network's ability to encode a conceptual dependence between hierarchically disjoint elements is actually quite simple, but gets to the heart of the difference between the state representation of hierarchy and the stack representation. As we have already seen, information in a stack is encapsulated. In the state representation, on the other hand, all of the information about hierarchical structure is contained in a state vector (realized here as the context layer). This state vector is *entirely visible to the processor.* Thus, all the information is available simultaneously. (Simplistically, one can think of the state representation as a bit like what one would have if one took a traditional stack, replaced the walls with transparent material, and turned the entire device on its side; the result would be a kind of horizontal glass stack. This metaphor is not entirely accurate, since the state representation encodes information along many dimensions simultaneously; and the state representation facilitates interactions between dimensions in a way which is not conveyed by the image of the horizontal glass stack. But it conveys the idea that information from all levels of processing is available.) Because the information is visible in this manner, there is no need to move constituents around. They may all jointly participate in shaping the interpretation of the sentence.

I take this property to constitute perhaps the most striking difference from traditional language processing mechanisms. It suggests a conception of composition which emphasizes *integration* and *interaction.* These are, I believe, desirable traits for a language processor; they are also highly compatible with the theory of language that has been developed by Langacker (1988).

It is obvious that the current work raises many questions. For example, although the state vectors contain information that spans hierarchical structure (while respecting it), the relative accessibility of this information remains to be determined. The fact that the entire state is visible to the processing mechanism does not mean that all information is equally available. There are known constraints on what information can be co-ordinated in natural language; thus, certain grammatical forms seem to impede or block access to information (e.g., the infelicity of *'Who do you like the fact that she said no to?'*). A project is currently directed towards trying to understand whether the state representations developed in simple recurrent networks have consequences for processing which might explain such facts.

While much work remains to be done, the current work is encouraging. The networks studied here have properties which seem to be genuinely different from those of traditional processing mechanisms but which are very plausible for the processing of natural languages.

Acknowledgments

I am grateful for many useful discussions on this topic with Jay McClelland, Dave Rumelhart, Ron Langacker, Elizabeth Bates, Steve Stich, and members of the UCSD PDP/NLP Research Group.This research was supported by contracts N0001485K0076 from the Office of Naval Research and contract DAAB0787CH027 from Army Avionics, Ft. Monmouth. Requests for reprints should be sent to the Center for Research in Language, 0126; University of California, San Diego; La Jolla, CA920930126. The author can be reached via electronic mail at elman@amos.ucsd.edu.

References

Bates, E., and MacWhinney, B. (1982). Functionalist approaches to grammar. In E. Wanner, and L. Gleitman (eds.), *Language acquisition: The State of the Art*. New York: Cambridge University Press

Chafe, W. (1970). *Meaning and the Structure of Language*. Chicago: University of Chicago Press

Chomsky, N. (1973). Conditions on transformations. In S.R. Anderson and P.Kiparsky (eds.), *A Festschrift for Morris Halle*. New York: Holt, Rinehart and Winston

Dolan, C., and Dyer, M.G. (1987). Symbolic schemata in connectionist memories: Role binding and the evolution of structure. Technical Report UCLA AI8711. Artificial Intelligence Laboratory, University of California, Los Angeles

– and Smolensky, P. (1988). Implementing a connectionist production system using tensor products. Technical Report UCLAAI8815, Artificial Intelligence Laboratory, University of California, Los Angeles

Elman, J.L. (in press). Finding structure in time. *Cognitive Science*

Fauconnier, G. (1985). *Mental Spaces*. Cambridge, MA: MIT Press

Feldman, J.A. and Ballard, D.H. (1982). Connectionist models and their properties. *Cognitive Science* 6:205-54

Fillmore, C.J. (1982). Frame semantics. In *Linguistics in the Morning Calm*. Seoul: Hansin

Fodor, J. (1976). *The language of thought*. Harvester Press: Sussex

– and Pylyshyn, Z. (1988). Connectionism and cognitive architecture: A critical analysis. In S. Pinker and J. Mehler (eds.), *Connections and Symbols*. Cambridge, MA: MIT Press

Forster, K.I. (1979). Levels of processing and the structure of the language processor. In W.E. Cooper and E. Walker (eds.), *Sentence Processing: Psycholinguistic Studies Presented to Merrill Garrett*. Hillsdale, NJ: Lawrence Erlbaum Associates

Givon, T. (1984). *Syntax: A Functional-Typological Introduction.* Amsterdam: John Benjamins

Grosjean, F. (1980). Spoken word recognition processes and the gating paradigm. *Perception and Psychophysics* 28:267-83

Hanson, S.J., and Burr, D.J. (1987). Knowledge representation in connectionist networks. Bell Communications Research, Morristown, New Jersey

Hare, M., Corina, D., and Cottrell, G. (1988) Connectionist perspective on prosodic structure. CRL Newsletter 3:2. Center for Research in Language, University of California, San Diego

Hinton, G.E. (1988). Representing part-whole hierarchies in connectionist networks. Technical Report CRG TR882, Connectionist Research Group, University of Toronto

– McClelland, J.L., and Rumelhart, D.E. (1986). Distributed representations. In D.E. Rumelhart and J.L. McClelland (eds.), *Parallel Distributed Processing: Explorations in the Microstructure of Cognition* 1. Cambridge, MA: MIT Press

Hopper, P.J., and Thompson, S.A. (1980). Transitivity in grammar and discourse. *Language* 56: 251-99

Hornik, K., Stinchcombe, M., and White, H. (in press). Multilayer feedforward networks are universal approximators. *Neural Networks*

Jordan, M. I. (1986). Serial order: A parallel distributed processing approach. Institute for Cognitive Science Report 8604. University of California, San Diego

Kawamoto, A.H. (1988). Distributed representations of ambiguous words and their resolution in a connectionist network. In S.L. Small, G.W. Cottrell, and M.K. Tanenhaus (eds.), *Lexical Ambiguity Resolution: Perspectives from Psycholinguistics, Neuropsychology, and Artificial Intelligence.* San Mateo, CA: Morgan Kaufmann Publishers

Kuno, S. (1987). *Functional syntax: Anaphora, Discourse and Empathy.* Chicago: The University of Chicago Press

Lakoff, G. (1987). *Women, Fire, and Dangerous Things: What Categories Reveal about the Mind.* Chicago: University of Chicago Press

Langacker, R.W. (1987). *Foundations of Cognitive Grammar: Theoretical Perspectives.* Volume 1. Stanford: Stanford University Press

– (1988). A usage-based model. *Current Issues in Linguistic Theory* 50:127-61

Marslen-Wilson, W., and Tyler, L.K. (1980). The temporal structure of spoken language understanding. *Cognition* 8:1-71

McClelland, J.L. (1987). The case for interactionism in language processing. In M. Coltheart (Ed.), *Attention and Performance XII: The Psychology of Reading.* London: Erlbaum

– St. John, M., and Taraban, R. (1989). Sentence comprehension: A parallel distributed processing approach. Manuscript. Department of Psychology, Carnegie-Mellon University

McMillan, C., and Smolensky, P. (1988). Analyzing a connectionist model as a system of soft rules. Technical Report CUCS30388, Department of Computer Science, University of Colorado, Boulder

Mozer, M. (1988). A focused back-propagation algorithm for temporal pattern recognition. Technical Report CRGTR883, Departments of Psychology and Computer Science, University of Toronto

Mozer, M.C., and Smolensky, P. (1989). Skeletonization: A technique for trimming the fat from a network via relevance assessment. Technical Report CUCS42189, Department of Computer Science, University of Colorado, Boulder

Oden, G. (1978). Semantic constraints and judged preference for interpretations of ambiguous sentences. *Memory and Cognition* 6:26-37

Pollack, J.B. (1988). Recursive auto-associative memory: Decising compositional distributed representations. *Proceedings of the Tenth Annual Conference of the Cognitive Science Society.* Hillsdale, NJ: Lawrence Erlbaum

Ramsey, W. (1989). *The philosophical Implications of Connectionism.* Ph.D. thesis, University of California, San Diego

Rumelhart, D.E., Hinton, G.E., and Williams, R.J. (1986). Learning internal representations by error propagation. In D.E. Rumelhart and J.L. McClelland (eds.), *Parallel Distributed Processing: Explorations in the Microstructure of Cognition* 1. Cambridge, MA: MIT Press

Salasoo, A., and Pisoni, D.B. (1985). Interaction of knowledge sources in spoken word identification. *Journal of Memory and Language* 24:210-31

Sanger, D. (1989). Contribution analysis: A technique for assigning responsibilities to hidden units in connectionist networks. Technical Report CUCS43589, Department of Computer Science, University of Colorado, Boulder

Savitch, W.J. (in press). Infinity is in the eye of the beholder. In C. Georgopoulous and R. Ishihara (eds.), *Interdisciplinary Approaches to Language: Essays in Honor of S.Y. Kuroda.* Kluwer Academic Publisher

Sejnowski, T.J., and Rosenberg, C.R. (1987). Parallel networks that learn to pronounce English text. *Complex Systems* 1:145-68

Servan-Schreiber, D., Cleeremans, A., and McClelland, J.L. (1988). Encoding sequential structure in simple recurrent networks. CMU Technical Report CMUCS88183. Computer Science Department, Carnegie Mellon University

Shastri, L., and Ajjanagadde, V. (1989). A connectionist system for rule based reasoning with multi-place predicates and variables. Technical Report MSCIS8905, Computer and Information Science Department, University of Pennsylvania

Smolensky, P. (1987a). On variable binding and the representation of symbolic structures in connectionist systems. Technical Report CUCS35587, Department of Computer Science, University of Colorado, Boulder

– (1987b). On the proper treatment of connectionism. Technical Report CUCS 37787, Department of Computer Science, University of Colorado, Boulder

– (1987c). Putting together connectionism again. Technical Report CUCS37887, Department of Computer Science, University of Colorado, Boulder

– (1988). On the proper treatment of connectionism. *The Behavioral and Brain Sciences,*

St. John, M., and McClelland, J.L. (in press). Learning and applying contextual constraints in sentence comprehension. Technical Report. Department of Psychology. Carnegie-Mellon University

Stinchcombe, M., and White, H. (1989). Universal approximation using feedforward networks with non sigmoid hidden layer activation functions. *Proceedings of the International Joint Conference on Neural Networks.* Washington, DC

Touretzky, D.S. (1986). BoltzCONS: Reconciling connectionism with the recursive nature of stacks and trees. *Proceedings of the Eight Annual Conference of the Cognitive Science Society.* Hillsdale, NJ: Lawrence Erlbaum

– (1989). Rules and maps in connectionist symbol processing. Technical Report CMUCS89 158, Department of Computer Science,
    Carnegie-Mellon University

– and Hinton, G.E. (1985). Symbols among the neurons: Details of a connectionist inference architecture. *Proceedings of the Ninth International Joint Conference on Artificial Intelligence,* Los Angeles

Van Gelder, T.J. (in press). Compositionality: Variations on a classical theme. *Cognitive Science*

COMMENT

Making Conceptual Space

Tim van Gelder

When connectionists take up the task of modelling aspects of language processing using distributed networks, one of the most striking facts about the representations that are subsequently developed is also one of the most basic – namely, that they take the form of *vectors*, or, more accurately and revealingly, *points in the (partial) state space of a dynamical system*. The possibility that mental representation quite generally might take this form was, as far as I know, first articulated by Paul Churchland, who proposed, in a 1986 article in the philosophical journal *Mind*, that 'the brain represents various aspects of reality by a *position* in a suitable *state space*' (1986: 280). To avert the dumbfounded skepticism that this preposterous claim would inevitably provoke in philosophers and others safely removed from the conceptual frontiers of science, Churchland provided some plausible sketches of how the 'knowledge' involved in capacities such as sensorimotor coordination and sense perception could take the form of points in a state space. Moreover, aware of the seemingly vast difference between problems of sensorimotor coordination and what is normally thought of as cognitive performance – reasoning, language use, and the like – he went on to speculate that: 'One might try to find ... a way of representing "anglophone linguistic hyperspace" so that all grammatical sentences turn out to reside on a proprietary hypersurface within that hyperspace, with the logical relations between them reflected as spatial relations of some kind (305).' At the time this came across as an exciting but nevertheless hopelessly bold speculation. It seemed to belong to a category of empirical claims that, in Tom Nagel's terms, might turn out to be true but are such that we do not yet have even the slightest idea *how* they could be true.

Fortunately, a few years later, after an explosion of connectionist work and its application to an increasingly broad range of aspects of cognition, we are in a very different position. The aura of mystery surrounding this hypothesis is rapidly being dissolved by connectionist explorations of how language might be processed. Jeff Elman's work with simple recurrent network (SRN) models of sentence processing is a prime example of such research.[1] It can be understood as constituting

179

at least the beginnings of an explanation of how it might in fact be true that mental representations, even of complex linguistic structures, are points in the state space of a dynamical system; and, correspondingly, how the geometrical analysis of dynamical systems might be a more powerful conceptual framework than, say, rule-governed inference in predicate calculus, for understanding how mental representations are transformed.

In particular, Elman's work enables us to enrich the bold suggestion that 'all grammatical sentences turn out to reside on a proprietary hypersurface' in a variety of ways. Perhaps most obviously, we now have at least a qualitative sketch of the kind of shape that might be possessed by the 'hypersurface' formed in response to at least one language processing task – that of predicting the next word in simple English sentences. Once the network has been adequately trained, the hidden unit activation patterns formed after the partial or complete presentation of sentences fall, in a decidedly regular way, into *regions* of the overall 'hidden unit state space,' lending to that space a kind of intricate hierarchical structure.[2] Roughly speaking, the most generic partition of the space into regions is syntactically based: presenting sentence fragments culminating in nouns sends the hidden unit patterns into one broad region of the space, while presenting fragments culminating in verbs sends them to another. Within the noun region there are 'semantic' regions where the network ends up if the sentence fragment ends in a noun of a given semantic type, such as *animate* as opposed to *inanimate*; within the *animate* region, there are regions for *animal* and *human*; within the *human* region, there are further semantically based subdivisions for the *kind* of human. Remarkably, within these restricted 'semantic' domains, syntactically based divisions begin to emerge once again: thus the network ends up in a different portion of the 'boy' region if the sentence fragment is one in which 'boy' has appeared in object position than it does if the sentence is one in which it appeared as subject.

All these regions are formed, of course, in a high dimensional space, one that defies scrutiny by means of our native imaginative abilities. Cluster analysis is one reasonably effective way of gaining at least a glimpse of the internal structure of this space, although it only works by reducing all spatial relationships between representations to relationships of distance alone. To get a feel for how representations are actually *located* with respect to one another, it seems that the best we can do is to examine the projection of the various points and regions onto selected 2-D planes, or perhaps even 3-D volumes, which provide a kind of very narrow window onto high dimensional space. While techniques such as principal components analysis can help select an appropriate plane to use as a window, any such reduction of a high dimensional space that is itself intricately divided and subdivided into regions inevitably leaves much of the action lost from view.

Nevertheless, even at this stage a certain amount of progress can be made in trying to understand, in at least a qualitative way, the kind of structure the space of internal representations has, and indeed must have, if the network is to be able to carry out any reasonably complex language processing tasks. For example, we would be wrong if we supposed that the hierarchical partitioning of high dimensional space into regions is like the division of Europe into countries, countries into states or provinces, states into counties, and so on. There are many things wrong with this structural metaphor, but, most obviously, it mistakenly assumes that the regions at any level are *neighbouring*, in the sense of sharing a border with each other. This would imply that, just as there are Germans living only a few miles from Swiss, there would be points in, say, the noun region, which were very close to points in the verb region. The cluster analysis diagram itself shows this to be mistaken: the whole point is that noun-fragment representations cluster together in the diagram precisely because they are all similar to each other, and more similar to each other than they are to any verb-fragment representation. Thus there must be considerable open space between the clusters.

A more suitable spatial metaphor for this kind of structure is a cosmic one: the space as a whole corresponds to the universe, which contains individual *galaxies* separated by vast distances. Within a given galaxy, of course, there are further star clusters, but these are also separated by distances greater than the distances between the elements of the cluster; these clusters, in turn, contain solar systems in which individual planets are all closer to each other than they are to any of the planets of any other solar system. This nested clustering is a crucial feature of the connectionist system, for it is by this means that the system maintains, as far as possible, the *distinctness* of representations that is essential to effective processing. In a symbolic approach representations are kept clearly type-distinct by being systematically constructed from tokens of primitive symbols, which are themselves easily distinguished. In these connectionist systems, that role is filled by separation in the space, i.e., by leaving relatively large areas of 'no man's land' between clusters at any level of analysis.

To what do these galaxies and solar systems correspond? That is really just the question: what is the functional (and hence representational) significance of one region of the space as opposed to another? I have already mentioned how, in the space developed in Elman's SRN sentence prediction models, certain regions correspond to coarse syntactic features, while regions inside those correspond to semantic properties, and regions inside those correspond to more fine-grained syntactic distinctions. Thus, interestingly, the network is making no categorical distinction between syntactic and semantic features of the sentence fragment – or, putting the same point a slightly different way, there is no 'proprietary hypersurface' on which representations of purely syntactic structures are to be found independently of the representations of semantic features of those same structures. Both syntactic and semantic features tend to 'push' the point around in modelling space, and at some scales semantic features make the biggest difference, while at others – both above and below – syntax rules.

What underlies this relative indifference to the usual firm syntax versus semantics distinction? The particular character of the hidden unit representations results from at least two important general features of much connectionist modelling. The first is what Elman has described as an inherent *functionalism* – the idea that networks typically develop representations which encode just enough information to enable them to perform the particular task at hand, and that they encode that information in a *form* that is suited to performing that task. In this case the task is prediction of the next word of the sentence, and so the network is retaining as best it can, in the activity of the hidden units, just that information about the input sentence which is most relevant to predicting the next word. From our point of view, that information is regarded as a robust stew of syntactic and semantic considerations. However, from the network's point of view, that information is just a matter of the word order in the input thus far and how that compares with word order in all previously experienced sentences. Syntactic and semantic constraints are, as far as it is concerned, generically the same kind of thing, for both just amount to more or less coarse regularities in word order in the sets of sentences on which they were trained.

The second general feature is that these representations are genuinely *distributed* not merely in the obvious sense that they are *patterns* taking place over a large set of hidden units, but – primarily – because they encode the relevant information about the input in a *superimposed* fashion. Roughly speaking, information is stored in a superimposed fashion when one cannot find a more 'local' correspondence between various parts of the stored information and parts of the representation itself. In the classic example, a hologram is a genuinely distributed representation, because every part of the scene is represented over the whole surface of the hologram. In the current case, the hidden unit activation pattern which results from presentation of a sentence fragment is what has come to be described as a 'gestalt' of the relevant features of that whole fragment. The various aspects of the input sentence fragment that are effectively represented in the hidden unit activity pattern – such as the fact that a word of a given type was last presented, that a main verb is still required, that the subject was singular – are stored there in such a way that there is no discrete part of the activity pattern corresponding to each distinct component of the information. A partial explanation of this is to be found in the structure of the network itself. Since one layer is fully connected with the next, each hidden unit will vary its activity as a function of the whole of each input word; thus all features of the input tend to end up encoded over the whole set of hidden units.

Once we see that the representation of information can be effectively distributed in this way, it appears that there is no reason, in principle, to stop at the relatively modest stage of superimposing syntactic and semantic aspects of a single sentence. Thus, for example, a point in hidden unit activity space might correspond to two sentences, or to a whole paragraph, or perhaps even to the current stage in a conversation. In such cases just the information (concerning larger chunks of text) that is functionally relevant to performing some particular task would be encoded simultaneously and coextensively over the whole hidden unit pattern. Similarly, there is no apparent reason that a pattern should be restricted to storing just syntactic and semantic information together. An adequate prediction of what word will come next in a sentence depends in general on a host of further subtle contextual and pragmatic factors. For example, after hearing the sentence fragment, 'Get the,' you would make very different predictions about what the next word was likely to be if you knew the speaker was your grandmother than you would if it you knew it was Eddie Murphy (well known for his ribald embellishment of 'get out of here'). More traditional explanations of the difference here would combine a representation of the sentence with a separate representation of the fact that it was your grandmother who spoke it (together with some kind of further encoded knowledge about what kinds of things your grandmother does and does not usually say). But why could not knowledge of this contextually significant information simply correspond to another kind of shift of location in the space? Perhaps, in other words, grandmother-sayings will tend to be found in one area and Eddie Murphy-sayings in another; or perhaps these differences are encoded in shifts within broad regions already determined by more dominant factors. The general point is that if – as Elman's work indicates – the factors relevant to prediction or inference are represented by shifting the point which constitutes the representation of the current situation around in the space, then we should at least entertain the possibility that *all* factors relevant to the task – or at least a much wider range of such factors – correspond to some shift or other in some suitably expanded space.

Trying to peer way over the horizon, we eventually hope to see a network in which the task is not just prediction of the next word in the sentence but, rather, production of another sentence which is inferentially or pragmatically appropriate to the one(s) just encountered. Presumably, in such a system the relevant 'linguistic' units are still to be encoded as points in a space, and that space must make possible the encoding of all the functionally relevant distinctions. Clearly, any such space would require an extraordinarily intricate hierarchical structure of regions within regions. It is not merely that there is a diversity of functionally relevant factors that must correspond to shifts of location in the space. The problem is also that, even if we were encoding grammatical structure alone, we are confronted with the problem of the 'infinite' or 'productive' nature of our linguistic competence. Elman has convincingly shown how fine grammatical properties, such as the depth of embedding of a clause, correspond to subtle shifts of location of the representations. But what kind of structure would the space need to have if the network could represent and process *arbitrarily* complex grammatical structures – for example, sentences with no limit on the number of centre-embedded clauses? At this stage the galactic metaphor used above breaks down, because it implies strict lower limits on the scale at which one can see the hierarchical structure of regions (i.e., at the level of individual suns and planets). In theory, at least, we need a structure that is 'galaxies all the way down' – an infinite cascade of regions with differing functional significances, such that every possible grammatical structure finds an appropriate location in space.

Envisaging the structure of this kind of space is only possible on the basis of strange new metaphors drawn – as Jordan Pollack has stressed – from the domain of fractal mathematics. For example, one construct with an infinitely deep structure of nested regions (i.e., 'galaxies all the way down') is the classical Cantor Set. This is a set of points obtained in the following way. Begin with the set of all points on the unit interval (the segment of the real number line between 0 and 1) and delete the middle third open subinterval – that is, every point between 1/3 and 2/3, although being careful to not to delete these two points themselves. We are now left with two intervals, each 1/3 the length of the original. Now delete the middle third open subinterval of each of these, and the middle third open subinterval of the remaining intervals, and so on ad infinitum. What remains is usually termed a 'dust' – an infinite set of points, systematically arranged in an infinitely deep hierarchy of clusters, such that between any two clusters at the same level there is a gap as big as those clusters. Thus, paradoxically, in this dust the strict separation between clusters (and, eventually, points) is maintained at any level one cares to examine, even though, given any distance, no matter how small, one can find an unbounded number of clusters that are less than that distance apart.

The claim, then, is that the structure of the space of mental representations must be analogous, in a deep way, to that of the Cantor Set. Making sense of this claim requires seeing how there could be an appropriate mapping from what we might call 'linguistic manifolds' – that is, the totality of features of some linguistic situation that are relevant to some processing task – onto points in this kind of intricately subdivided space. Restricting attention once again to the problem of representing just grammatical aspects, what we need, in effect, is a mapping from an unbounded set of complex grammatical structures onto points of the Cantor Set – or, more generally, onto points of some analogue of the Cantor Set in some space with a suitably enlarged number of dimensions – such that the mapping preserves all relevant grammatical distinctions as spatial relationships. This kind of problem is clearly soluble *in principle*, as Pollack has elegantly shown with a simple example. He considered the relatively simple problem of assigning to all possible binary trees a distinct number between zero and one. Clearly, such a mapping has to be recursively specified – that is, the number assigned to a complex tree has to be obtained from the numbers assigned to its subtrees. The method he came up with, which involved interleaving the digits from the binary-fractional numerals for the two subtrees to obtain the numeral for the tree itself, results in a space with a 'devil's staircase' structure, which is graphically revealed when the number for a given tree is plotted against the numbers for its subtrees.[3] In this structure every point has a different height (i.e., every possible tree is assigned a unique number), yet the space is clearly divided into distinct plateaus, which themselves contain subplateaus, and so on. Note, however, that this mapping does *not* preserve at least one important feature of the galactic or Cantor Set metaphor, which is that clusters be separated by relatively wide regions of open space.

Is the problem soluble in practice? What we require is a network which performs a mapping from grammatical structures to points in, say, hidden unit activation space, such that the resulting space of representations has the kind of infinitely nested hierarchical structure that is needed in order that the system might be able to generate linguistic performance comparable to our own. Since connectionist networks (with sufficiently high connectivity) implement distributing transformations from input to hidden layers, the problem can be recast as one of searching the 'space' (here used in a slightly different sense) of possible distributing transformations to find one that results in an appropriately structured output. Alternatively, and equivalently, the problem concerns searching the 'space' of dynamical systems, systems which in this case happen to be implemented as neural networks, to find one whose behavioural topology effectively differentiates its own state space into a Cantor Set-like structure of regions.

How is this search conducted? Since the space of possible distributing transformations is so vast, and since we are not yet quite sure exactly what it is that we are looking for anyway, the practice so far has been to choose a relatively circumscribed task and to train a network to perform adequately on a series of instances of that task, known as a 'training corpus.' Thus, in Elman's models, the task was to predict the next word in a sentence, and he trained a network on a corpus of sentence instances. Linguistic competence, of course, is by its nature productive, so, paradoxically, the training corpus represents only a vanishing portion of the instances on which that task is defined, no matter how large the training corpus happens to be. The hope is that training on this particular set of instances will somehow *induce* the right structure in the space of internal representations (i.e., select the right distributing transformation, mould an appropriate dynamical system), such that any future input will find that a suitable niche in the space of internal representations has already been prepared for it. To throw out yet another metaphor, the training instances are supposed to act like the poles of a circus tent, strategically placed such that when the canvas is draped over them they define an appropriate overall shape for the tent. Likewise, the training instances are supposed to constrain the training process to come up with a network implementing a dynamical system whose behavioural topology is appropriate not just for the training instances themselves but also for all instances 'in between.' Clearly, the more tent poles one has the more precisely one can arrange the shape of the whole tent. If we wanted to give a real circus tent some kind of genuine 'devil's staircase' structure, nothing short of an infinite number of tent poles would suffice. Analogously, it would seem, developing a network with an internal representation space with the right kind of infinitely deep structure of nested regions would require an infinite training corpus. Since this is out of the question, it is worth asking how connectionists might ever hope to develop reasonably general language-processing abilities by training networks in strictly limited training environments.

One response begins by acknowledging that while language itself may well be best understood as truly productive in nature, our actual linguistic performance, while certainly very impressive, is limited. Thus, it is literally false to claim that we are capable of dealing appropriately with *arbitrarily* complex linguistic structures, and there are well-known examples illustrating how performance breaks down as grammatical complexity compounds: our inability to deal with very many centre-embeddings in one sentence is the classic case. One of the pivotal issues in thinking about the plausibility of various kinds of cognitive architectures is whether these kinds of performance limitations should be seen as somehow built into the architecture, or whether such limitations should be seen as resulting from (relatively uninteresting) resource restrictions on mechanisms which are themselves, in principle, truly productive in nature. The current connectionist response to the apparent need for an infinite training environment tends to side with the former approach. It takes seriously the actual limitations on our performance, regarding them as indicative of the actual shape of the internal mechanisms generating that performance rather than as indicative of contingent resource problems. Consequently, it doubts the need for an internal representation space with a genuine, *infinitely* deep fractal structure; rather, the nested hierarchy of functionally significant regions needs only to be deep enough to account for our actual linguistic capacities. Indeed, it sees any requirement of arbitrarily deep fractal structure as implausible in view of our knowledge of the noisiness and imprecision of actual neural activity.

The general hope, then, is that, just as careful placement of a limited number of poles imparts an appropriate shape to a tent, so careful training on a judicious sampling of instances will effectively induce an appropriate, albeit limited, nested structure on the space in internal representations. Using a finite training set we cannot expect to induce a genuinely Cantor Set-like structure with infinite layers of nested regions, but our actual linguistic capacities do not demand such infinite complexity, and the nature of the neural hardware available may even rule it out. The hope that this kind of pragmatic approach might work appears to be sustained when we examine the Elman models, for there we do in fact find a limited-depth version of cascading hierarchical structure. This entails limits on the ability of the network to handle certain kinds of intricate structures, but, interestingly, in at least some cases those limits appear to roughly coincide with limitations of our own.

There is, however, a more exciting possible response, which is that connectionist networks actually offer some quite special mechanisms for (a) providing a genuinely Cantor-Set like space or arbitrary depth, and (b) inducing the network which generates that space on the basis of an appropriate selection of training instances. In other words, perhaps it is not that fractal structures are something to be approximated by connectionist networks, but, rather, that *genuine*, arbitrarily deep fractal structures and corresponding dynamics will turn out to be a central feature of at least certain kinds of connectionist mechanisms (whether they are now available or yet to be developed). Thus, Pollack, for one, has claimed that 'It is my working hypothesis that alternative activation functions (i.e., other than the usual sigmoidal or threshold), based on fractal or chaotic mathematics, is the critical missing link between neural networks and infinite capacity systems' (Pollack 1989). Currently this general approach lies squarely in the realm of speculation; like so many other connectionist ideas, it is implemented only in neural 'hopeware.' I point to it here so as to acknowledge at least the possibility of a genuine reconciliation of distinctively connectionist mechanisms and productive linguistic capacities – a reconciliation that compromises neither. And while this scenario might come across as somewhat far-fetched, it is dangerous at such points to be too easily deterred by raw intuitions. After all, the idea that finite connectionist mechanisms could support a genuinely fractal space of mental representations is surely no more intuitively implausible than the now generally accepted thesis that there are certain machines which can mimic the operation of any other machine.

An unexpected bonus of the general kind of understanding of neural network approaches to language processing being endorsed here is that we can see both the grain of truth in the common claim that connectionism is a reincarnation of associationism *and* why such a claim might be less of an indictment than it is usually intended to be. 'Associationism' has meant many things to many people, but one of the most fundamental characteristics of associationist approaches is the idea that the behaviour of the system recapitulates the regularities found in experience; or that, put differently, the structure of the mind in a deep way amounts to a reflection of the structure of the world as it has been so far encountered. This basic idea has been cashed out in many forms; thus, for the British empiricist (or at least the cartoon version thereof) the order in which ideas succeed each other in the mind is determined by the order in which perceptions succeed each other in experience. In behaviourist research of this century it meant that the patterns of behaviour a system exhibits will, over time, come to reflect the connections between environmental conditions, behaviours, and rewards, connections that are themselves determined by the way the world is.

Now, much connectionist work is clearly associationist in this vague and general sense. The immediate goal of Elman's SRN models, for example, is to get the network to absorb the statistical regularities in the training set, and successful performance for the network is even defined as behaviour that is perfectly in accord with those regularities. The model is behaving correctly if its prediction of the next word in the sentence is in exact agreement with the statistics of the training set.

Nevertheless, connectionist approaches might turn out to be relatively immune to some of the deep criticisms that have traditionally been aimed at associationism. The standard attacks begin by taking the associationist position to be that the mind is a kind of recording device for listing discrete associative links between the basic or 'atomic' elements of mental functioning (whether 'ideas,' or stimuli and rewarded behaviours, etc.). Mental activity is then a matter of reproducing, in response to input, stimulus, or even just the current state of the system, the previously learned association. In more advanced versions of associationist theory, basic associative links could of course be chained together or otherwise concretely combined to produce more complex behaviours. Associationism of this form was claimed to be manifestly unable to account for our actual behaviour, which simultaneously exhibits flexibility, diversity and regularity. The basic difficulty can be brought out by considering the general problem of producing appropriate responses to novel situations. If the performance of an associative system is limited to reproducing the links it has previously encountered, it would seem that the system cannot – almost by definition – produce an appropriate response to an unencountered input. The classic example is our quite remarkable ability to respond in a sensible way to a sentence we have never seen before. Associationists traditionally responded to this challenge by gesturing in the direction of the *similarity* of the novel input to those previously experienced, but the measures of similarity, and the mechanisms by which an appropriately 'similar' response is produced, were ill-defined and implausible. The mind, it seemed, has to do much more than simply list the associative links found in previous experience. It has to recognize the basic associated items as themselves having a systematic internal structure in terms of which it can develop abstract rules for processing structures, rules which, once formulated, apply equally well to the potentially infinite range of novel situations. In short, the model of the mind as a mechanism for listing and reproducing discrete associative links between atomic elements had to be replaced with another model of the mind as processing systematically structured entities according to general rules.

Now, an obvious virtue of connectionist networks is an ability to generalize appropriately to novel inputs, and so they at least *seem* to be somehow overcoming, to some extent, this basic difficulty. It is important to understand how they could do this while remaining true to their associationist roots (i.e., without making the kind of fundamental architectural shift just mentioned). This is possible once we see connectionist networks as dynamical systems operating in a state space in which individual states occupying particular points count as representations of complex situations, and we see the representations in that space as falling into the kind of intricate cascading hierarchical structure described above. It is from this perspective that we can begin to see the connectionist middle road between a hopelessly simple-minded associationism on the one hand and a full-blown Chomskyan cognitivism on the other.

Sophisticated connectionist models overcome the limitations of the simplest associationist models in at least two ways. First, as Elman has stressed, their representations are structured, not only in the sense that they manage to represent complex structured entities such as sentences, but also because they themselves have an internal structure which determines how they are handled in the system. This internal structure is not, of course, *syntactic* structure (i.e., it is not the result of concatenatively combining primitive symbolic tokens according to grammatical rules). This structure is a particular configuration of activation values, which *locates* the representation in the state space and hence determines how the system will treat it. In other words, the internal structure of connectionist representations is significant not by virtue of instantiating syntactic structure directly but, rather, in how it fixes the location of the representation such that the system can *treat* it as *encoding* syntactic structure. The *systematicity* of connectionist representations is to be found in the wider structure of the space itself (i.e., in the dynamical 'shape' of the system which is instantiated by the network).[4]

Second, connectionist systems are not simply mechanisms for recording a set of discrete associative links between elements. The training process is, to be sure, one of getting the network to duplicate the specific regularities presented in the training environment. It does this, however, only by constructing a particular dynamical system, whose behaviour is defined not only over the set of instances ('associations') to which it has been exposed but rather over the full range of possible input (or hidden) states. That is, a connectionist system which can generate an appropriate response to a certain fixed range of inputs is automatically one that generates *some* response to the full range of possible inputs. It will generate the *correct* response to the full range of possible inputs if the training process succeeds in discovering a distributing transformation from input to internal representations which gives the space of internal representations the right kind of intricate hierarchical structure.

This point comes out more clearly if we compare the connectionist approach with the behavioural neuropsychology of the twenties and thirties. Pavlov and others had developed the specifically associationist hypothesis that all psychological activity is a matter of learned connections between stimuli and behaviour (i.e., conditioned reflexes) or chains of such connections. Each reflex was thought to be implemented via a proprietary 'engram' – that is, specific neural circuit travelling 'from sense organ to cerebral sensory area, thence through associative areas to the motor cortex and by way of the pyramidal paths to the final motor cells of the medulla and cord.'[5] The obvious task for neuropsy-chologists was simply to *locate* the engram – that is, to find the specific neural pathway for a given reflex. The assumption that *all* memory does is to record discrete conditioned reflexes was built into the whole approach, and virtually guaranteed an inability to explain the flexibility and diversity of behaviour. In the connectionist approach, by contrast, the instances that form the training set simply act as reference points in the process of constructing a dynamical system whose behavioural repertoire includes not only those reference points but also a vast range of points in between. Moreover, there are no distinct neural encodings of these initial points, for all associations the system performs are represented, in a thoroughly distributed fashion, in the one set of connection weights. Distribution and flexible generalization are in this way two sides of one coin.

In short, the internal representations used by more interesting kinds of connectionist networks to perform their 'associations' are complexly and systematically (though not syntactically) structured, and the associative operations the network performs take this structure into account; moreover, connectionist learning is not simply the recording of links found in prior experience but is essentially a matter of structure-based generalization. In these two ways, connectionism, though in a deep sense associationist, has resources enabling it to transcend the fatal limitations of earlier, simpler varieties of associationism. Consequently, when critics of connectionism claim that it is 'merely' associationist and will fail for the same reasons traditional associationism failed, they demonstrate not any inherent limitations of connectionism but, rather, limitations on their own understanding of what connectionism really amounts to.

My main concern in this commentary has been to emphasize the utility of certain kinds of geometrical metaphor for understanding the nature of connectionist representations. Combining, on the one hand, the basic connectionist thesis that representations are points in the (finite-dimensional) state space of a dynamical system on the one hand with, on the other, the complex, multi-faceted and productive nature of our linguistic capacities leads directly to the idea that mental representations must fall into the state space in some kind of regular, hierarchically organized structure of nested regions of differing functional significances. The claim has been that fractal metaphors, such as the Cantor Set and Pollack's 'devil's staircase,' are, at this stage, a natural and revealing way to conceptualize this kind of structure. Note that these metaphors, while playful, are not being advanced for their own sake but, rather, as a direct response to the situation in which we find ourselves if we accept certain very general basic commitments.

This line of thought has a natural, though highly speculative, extension which deserves brief mention insofar as the enterprise here is to make exploratory forays into strange new territory. It seems we are committed to the presence of fractal structures within the state space of neural networks, which are themselves dynamical systems. Together, these suggest that the behaviour of the network may well turn out to be chaotic in at least the following sense. An obvious property of the classical Cantor Set is that if one chooses any distance, no matter how small, there will be an infinite number of distinct points in the set that are less than that distance apart. We are, however, expecting the system to be able to distinguish clusters at arbitrarily deep levels (indeed, in the connectionist case the presence of clusters is only defined in terms of the ability of the system to treat small regions in a differential fashion). Two points in neighbouring clusters would, of course, have much in common, but they would also have differences in functional significance that could eventually be very important for the future direction of processing in the system. In short, these dynamical systems may well turn out to exhibit a kind of 'sensitive dependence' on small variations in the current state, which is one characteristic feature of chaotic dynamics.

In one sense this should not be at all surprising. Most connectionist networks are, after all, rather complex nonlinear dynamical systems, just the kind of environment in which chaotic behaviour tends to arise. There is already ample research demonstrating that actual chaotic behaviour (strictly defined) crops up in a variety of ways in neural network systems – in neurophysiological studies of brain activity, in artificial neural networks considered solely as dynamical systems, and even lurking suspiciously behind the scenes in applications of the backpropagation training algorithm. The current line of thought tentatively suggests that a form of chaotic behaviour may in fact turn out to have a *cognitive* significance *given* the kinds of basic assumptions we have been making about what information needs to be represented, the resources available for representing it, and (what amounts to virtually the same thing) the kinds of systems available for processing those representations.

Note that I am not here advocating any role for chaos in connectionist modelling; indeed, chaotic dynamics would seem to have some rather obvious disadvantages. The idea that small differences in spatial location of internal representations should make large differences to processing is precisely what connectionist systems strive to avoid. The whole idea is to develop a network whose internal representations are such as to maximally facilitate further processing, and this means trying to assign structures that should be processed in very different ways to points as far apart as possible. Further, the random nature of chaotic behaviour conflicts directly with the idea that even small differences of location are to make regular, systematic contributions to the direction of processing. The hierarchically nested space of representations discussed above is supposed to be capturing the order and regularity inherent in linguistic systems rather than saddling us with irregularity and unpredictability. My point is only that the current basic assumptions that are structuring connectionist investigations into language processing are forcing the development of systems where chaotic behaviour might naturally be expected. *If* we wish to represent linguistic structures as points in the state space of a complex nonlinear dynamical system, and *if* we want the system to be able to handle arbitrarily many such structures, then we must acknowledge that representations will have to be packed into that space with vanishingly small distances between them. Since small differences between linguistic structures can turn out to make large differences to, say, inferential significance, arbitrarily small variations in position in state space could direct processing in the system in widely diverging directions. This alone is not constitutive of chaos, but it is uncomfortably close.

On the other hand, there is a certain appeal in the notion that human thought might be in some deep sense chaotic. It accords well with our intuitive sense that thought processes are highly sensitive to extraordinarily subtle influences – that, for example, small changes in word order, intonation, or pragmatic context can make great differences to the responses that we will go on to regard as appropriate – and also with the more controversial theoretical claim that no set of formal rules could ever capture the fluidity, flexibility, and context-sensitivity of human thought (see Dreyfus 1972). As connectionists and others have often remarked, these features of human cognition seem so elusive from the strictly symbolic perspective, with its rigid representations and formal rules, yet they could be built into the very nature of certain connectionist systems. More generally still, a consequence would be that the same mathematical techniques that have been recognized as essential in describing so many other natural phenomena may describe the cognitive domain as well. 'The place of mind in nature' might turn out to have a mathematical answer framed in terms of sensitive dependence, bifurcations, and strange attractors. At the very least, we can say this much: importing this kind of framework at this stage is bound to have a liberating effect through revealing the relative poverty of those standard perspectives in terms of which philosophers have expected to explain mind and its relation to the physical world.

Notes

1 See, for example, Elman (1989) or Chapter 4 this volume.
2 For a depiction of these regions, see the cluster diagrams in Elman (this volume).
3 For Pollack's own description of this mapping, and a diagram, see Pollack (1989).
4 This perspective on the systematic encoding of syntactic structure in the structured state space of a connectionist network is elaborated in van Gelder (1990) and (forthcoming).
5 Lashley 1950: 455

References

Churchland P.M. (1986). Some reductive strategies in cognitive neurobiology. *Mind* 95:279-309

Dreyfus H.L. (1972). *What Computers Can't Do: A Critique of Artificial Reason.* New York: Harper and Row

Elman J. L. (1989). Representation and structure in connectionist models. CRL Technical Report 8903, Center for Research in Language, University of California, San Diego, La Jolla CA 92093

Pollack J.B.(1989). Towards a fractal basis for artificial intelligence. *Advances in Neural Information Processing Systems: Proceedings of the NIPS Conference*

Lashley K.S. (1950) In search of the engram. *In Symposia of the Society for Experimental Biology, No.4 Physiological Mechanisms in Animal Behavior;* Cambridge: Cambridge University Press

van Gelder T. (1990). Compositionality: aconnectionist variation on a classical theme. *Cognitive Science* 14:355-84

– (forthcoming) Connectionism and the structure of mental states. In Horgan T. and Tienson J. (eds.) *Connectionism and the Philosophy of Mind.* Kluwer

6

Structured Representations in Connectionist Systems?

Terence Horgan and John Tienson[1]

Fodor and Pylyshyn (1988, henceforth F&P) argued that connectionism must either be too weak to account for fundamental aspects of cognition or it must be a mere implementation of the 'classical' picture of cognition. Cognition is systematic, they argued, and systematicity can only be explained by syntactic structure. But if a connectionist system incorporates syntactically structured representations, they maintain, it will be nothing more than a novel implementation of the classical picture of cognition as rule governed symbol manipulation, in which case connectionism will not be able to live up to its advance billing as an alternative view of cognition.

Structure has become a hot topic in connectionism,[2] perhaps in part due to the prodding of F&P. Many recent papers purport to provide counter examples to their charge. But, as we think will become clear, none of them succeeds in avoiding the horns of the dilemma.[3] What this suggests is that the nature of F&P's charge against connectionism has not been clearly understood, and, perhaps, that its seriousness has not been appreciated.

We will try to make clear just what F&P's charge is and why and from what point of view it is serious. This will entail making clear why syntactic structure is needed (Section 2) and what is required to avoid the charge of being 'mere implementation' of the classical picture of cognition (Section 3).

One connectionist who has attempted to respond to F&P's *arguments* is Paul Smolensky (1987b, 1988b). Distributed representations, he argues, and, in particular, tensor product representations, allow connectionism to escape its dilemma. Now Fodor and Brian McLaughlin (1990, henceforth F&M) have replied to Smolensky. They say, 'tensor product representations fail to explain systematicity because they fail to exhibit the sort of constituents that can provide domains for structure sensitive mental processes' (183).

Tensor products and similar methods are the natural way of constructing representations in connectionist systems. So if F&M's claim is correct, this would be very serious indeed. We will argue, however, that they do not substantiate their claim (Section 4). On the other hand, it has not been shown that this claim is incorrect. We will try to say what would be a minimal system that would show that tensor products or the like are capable of supporting the kind of structure-sensitive processing that cognition requires (Section 5). This will make it clear, we think, that the alleged counter examples to Fodor and Pylyshyn have not demonstrated this kind of structure-sensitive processing.[4]

We will argue that, if, indeed, such structure sensitive processing is possible in connectionist systems, then connectionists can successfully explain why cognition is – and in complex cognizers must be – systematic (Section 6). And we will argue that a connectionism that incorporates effective syntax might very well embody a conception of cognition that is fundamentally incompatible with the classical conception (Section 7). Such a version of connectionism would escape F&P's dilemma, for it would not be an implementation of classicism and yet would not suffer the weaknesses and limitations of an approach that eschews syntactically structured representations.

The FPM/Smolensky Debate

F&P introduced, and F&M reiterate, what has come to be known as the systematicity argument. Cognitive systems are systematic in the sense that cognitive capacities come in structured bundles. 'You don't find organisms that can learn to prefer the green triangle to the red square but can't learn to prefer the red triangle to the green square. You don't find organisms that can think the thought that the girl loves John but can't think the thought that John loves the girl' (F&M 184). Thus, F&M argue (185):

(S) It is nomologically necessary that cognitive capacities are generally systematic, both in humans and in many infrahuman organisms.

Let us say that a cognitive system has *effective syntax* if it employs representations (with language-like structure) that are processed in structure sensitive ways. F&P's overall argument against connectionism can then be reformulated in the following way. Connectionism, as a putative new approach to the nature of cognition, is impaled on the horns of a fatal dilemma. On the one hand, if it does not incorporate effective syntax, then it will be inadequate because it will be incapable of explaining the systematicity of cognition; and it will be a version of associationism, with its well established inadequacies as a general approach to cognition. On the other hand, if it *does* incorporate effective syntax, then it will be a mere implementation of the classical conception of cognition, that is, cognition as rule-governed symbol manipulation; it will not be a new cognitive-level approach at all.

Smolensky accepts (S), but he claims that the F&P dilemma is false; there is a middle ground between inadequate associationism and mere implementation of classicism. And he has suggested that this middle ground is likely to involve representations of a certain sort – viz. tensor products – whose encoding of syntactic structure is distributed throughout the representation. Tensor product representation 'provides a formalization that is natural for connectionist computation of the non-formal notion of constituent structure, and is a likely candidate to play a role in connectionist cognitive science analogous to that played by constituent structure trees in symbolic cognitive science' (Smolensky 1987b, 156f). Others have recently produced similar arguments and have proposed alternative ways of introducing rich structure into distributed connectionist representations (Pollack 1988, 1989, forthcoming; Hinton 1988).

F&M reply that constituents of this sort cannot play the causal role required of them. They 'stipulate that, for a pair of expression types E1, E2, the first is a *Classical* constituent of the second *only if* the first is tokened whenever the second is tokened' (186). The obvious examples are constituents that are (spatially or temporally) *contained in* the representation of which they are constituents (although, as F&M remark in a footnote, the definition does not *imply* that expressions necessarily contain their classical constituents).

Constituent structure as formalized by tensor products is not classical in F&M's sense. Tokening a tensor product representation does not require tokening its constituents: this is the heart of F&M's reply to Smolensky.' We shall see presently that what Smolensky offers as the "constituents" of connectionist mental representations are non-Classical ... and that is why his theory provides no account of systematicity' (F&M 187). Thus F&M assume that to play an appropriate role in a cognitive system, constituents must be classical. Non-classical constituents cannot be causally efficacious, because they are not *there* in the system. Accordingly, F&M maintain, a connectionism that incorporated only non-classical constituents would have no apparent prospect of overcoming the first horn of the original dilemma. It would have no apparent way of explaining systematicity and (we take it) no way to overcome the limitations of mere associationism. (We will argue in Section 4 that this contention is quite dubious, and that there are some reasons for believing that Smolensky's tensor products or something like them have the potential to provide effective syntax despite their lack of classical constituents.)

We agree with Smolensky that the Fodor/Pylyshyn dilemma is false. We believe, however, that the area of logical space that Fodor and Pylyshyn have missed has to do more with mental *processes* than with mental representations.[5] But non-classical representations are natural in connectionism, and they are, we believe, the most promising way to realize non-classical mental processes. Therefore, the issue of whether there can be effective syntax based on non-classical constituents is quite important for connectionism.

The Need for Syntactic Structure

As Fodor et al. repeatedly emphasize, the classical picture is ideally suited to explain systematicity. The classical picture holds that cognition is symbol manipulation governed by rules which advert to the syntactic structure of the symbols. Classical representations necessarily have syntactic structure; they are made up of repeatable items of fixed syntactic types. So, for example, if a classical system contains a representation aRb, and a and b are of the same syntactic type, then that system is, by its very nature, capable of containing the representation bRa.

Syntactic structure explains systematicity. It seems plausible to us that no other explanation is possible for cognitive systems of any complexity. There is a *vast* number of potential, systematically related, cognitive states. There are on the order of 10^{20} English sentences of twenty words or less. For most of these there is a potential corresponding thought, and potential thoughts far outstrip sentences because of our ability to make relevant discriminations for which we lack linguistic resources. How could one explain the capacity to have so many systematically related thoughts except by the capacity to build them by repeatable components? One might, perhaps, provide ad hoc for systematicity in a simple system by wiring in all the potentially necessary states, but this is not possible for the complex cognitive systems we actually find in nature.

We agree with the conclusion that syntax is necessary, but we think there are somewhat more revealing arguments for this conclusion. We have argued elsewhere that cognitive systems require constituent structured representations to get on in the world (Horgan and Tienson 1987, 1988, 1989, forthcoming). Basketball is our favourite example of cognitive systems getting on in the world, because it presents such a range of features within such a small compass. But all of the features found in this example are common to the normal activities of the cognitive systems that we know and love.

To make a long and, we think, enjoyable story short, hundreds of times in the course of a basketball game a player is faced with a decision that must be made very rapidly: to pass or shoot on a fast break, to pass into the post or not, etc. Some of these decision situations are very complex; there may be several different teammates the player could pass to as well as several different things the player could choose to do with the ball himself. And, of course, the players without the ball make such decisions as well.

These decisions, obviously, are made in light of a certain goal – winning the game, which does not always mean scoring a basket as soon as possible. Various things have to be taken into account in coming to a decision: the position of the goal, the player's own position and motion relative to the goal, the position and motion of each of his teammates, and the position and potential activity of five aggressive, mobile obstacles – and not just their positions at the moment of decision or at the moment of release of the ball, but their predicted positions at the time the ball arrives at various points and for some time thereafter. So what is taken into account is the future positions of teammates and the positions and possible responses of opponents.

Thus the player must not only have a representation of the evolving scene, but various properties of the people in the scene have to be taken into account. These come in at least three general types. First, there are the basic properties that structure the game: who is in the game, and, of these, who is a teammate and who is an opponent. Second, at sophisticated levels of play it is imperative to take into account the specific skills of individual players: the height, jumping ability, and speed of each, their shooting ability, who has good hands, and so forth. These are relatively enduring properties of individuals. Third, more transient properties also must be taken into account: who is shooting well, who is having a good game and who is not, who is in foul trouble, who is guarding whom, and what position each player is playing

The upshot of these observations is that much of the information that goes into court decisions is of a sort that normally would be thought of as propositional. This information comes in repeatable chunks, and repeatable properties are attributed to different enduring individuals of different types. That it is the same individual or attribute makes a difference for what is to be done. And, therefore, something within the cognitive system must encode these identities. For a system of any size and complexity – and for real cognitive systems there is a vast number of identities of reference and predication to attend to – we see no way to do this unless identity of reference and of predication is recoverable from the representations themselves.

This means, roughly, that there must be representations that contain repeatable predicates applied to repeatable subjects, so that the relevant relations of co-reference and co-predication can get encoded and thus can get accommodated during processing. More precisely, it means that complex representations must be functions of representations of smaller chunks of content. That is, constituency relations – subject of, modifier of, etc. – must be definable for the system in appropriate mathematical or physical terms, so that they play a role in the processing of the system.[6] That is, real cognitive systems need effective syntax.

We call this the 'tracking' argument, because a fundamental part of the cognitive task that it refers to is keeping track of enduring but moving and changing individuals. As Fodor et al. insist, syntax explains systematicity. The tracking argument, however, is more basic. The systematicity argument says: Cognitive systems are observed to be systematic; the best explanation of this observed systematicity is effective syntax. We argue: To be a cognitive system beyond the most rudimentary, a system must have effective syntactic structure; effective syntactic structure implies systematicity; therefore, cognitive systems beyond the most rudimentary will exhibit systematicity.

Thus, as far as we can see, cognitive systems must have syntactic structure in the sense that cognitive states, beliefs, desires, etc. must be constructed in a systematic way from repeatable elements. Fodor and Pylyshyn assume that having effective syntactic structure makes a system classical. The burden of their argument against connectionism is that cognition requires effective syntactic structure. They take for granted that having established this they have refuted connectionism: 'if you need structure in mental representations anyway to account for the productivity and systematicity of minds, why not postulate mental processes that are structure sensitive to account for the coherence of mental processes? Why not be a Classicist, in short.' (F&P 67)?

However, neither the tracking argument nor the systematicity argument directly implies the need for *classical* syntax.[7] Nor, as we will explain shortly, do they imply that cognitive processes must conform to programmable representation level rules, as classicism requires. Postulating structure sensitive mental processes is not equivalent to being a classicist. What these arguments imply is that there must be a notion of constituency for a cognitive system according to which constituents play a causal role qua constituents. It may be that, as a matter of fact or law, the only way this is possible is for the constituents to be classical constituents. But that is a further question.

Thus, two closely related questions have emerged. Can there be a real connectionism – a genuine *alternative* to, and not merely an implementation of, classicism – that has effective syntax? And since classical constituents are not the natural way for connectionist systems, can you have effective syntax with non-classical constituents? One step in becoming clearer about these questions is to understand what it means to say that connectionism might constitute 'mere implementation' of the classical picture.

Mere Implementation

The classical AI conception of mentality, often dubbed the rules and representations conception (for short, the RR conception), asserts that cognition is a species of rule-governed symbol manipulation. Classicism makes three fundamental claims: First, human cognition employs structurally complex mental representations, many of which encode propositional information via language-like syntactic structure; second, cognitive processing is suitably sensitive to the structure of these complex representations and, thereby, is suitably sensitive to their content; third, cognitive processing conforms to programmable rules, statable over the representations themselves, that advert solely to the form or structure of the representations (rather than adverting to their content).[8]

It should be stressed that the third claim does not assert that the rules of cognitive processing must be represented by the cognitive system itself. Although rules, or sets of rules, are sometimes explicitly represented in classical systems as stored data structures, they need not be. Rather, a classical system can conform with representation-level rules simply because it is hard wired to do so. (Every classical system will be hard wired to obey some such rules – for instance, rules whereby it 'reads' and executes any explicitly represented rules it might contain. And some special-purpose classical systems do not represent any of the rules to which they conform.)

In classical AI, and in standard computers, language-like symbolic representations have 'classical constituents' in F&M's sense: Whenever a syntactically structured representation is tokened in a classical system, its constituents are also tokened. But this is best regarded, we suggest, as a de facto feature of classicism – not as one of its essential or defining features. What is essential is structure sensitive processing that is describable by programmable rules adverting to that structure.

Connectionism has been explicitly touted as a putative alternative to the classical conception of cognition. Unfortunately, it is far from clear what exactly the connectionist alternative to the RR view is supposed to be. This much does seem clear, however; insofar as connectionist systems engage in rule-governed manipulation of symbolic representations with classical constituents, these systems do not serve as a basis for an alternative conception of cognition. Hence the importance of the second horn of the FP dilemma: the threat of 'mere implementation.'

One thing often said in favour of connectionism is that connectionist networks are more brain-like than are von Neumann machines. Nodes are (somewhat) like neurons, and a structure consisting of many interconnected simple processors is more like the structure of the brain than is that of a conventional computer. But if one is looking for a new conception of cognition, rather than merely for a new way of implementing the classical RR conception, it is not clear that these brain-like features matter. When a classical computer is engaged in rule governed symbol manipulation (say, running a LISP program), it does so by performing mathematical computations that are causally but not conceptually related to its data processing. And it does this number crunching by transmitting electrical impulses. But these 'lower level' descriptions are not relevant to the cognitive level description of what is going on in the system. The numerical computations and electrical impulses constitute an implementation of the program – one possible implementation among many. For the same reason, if the brain-like features of connectionism – the individual nodes and their interactions – are far enough removed from the cognitive level, they might not figure in a cognitive level account of mental processing at all.

In some simple connectionist models, single nodes and single internode connection strengths are assigned their own representational contents. These tinker-toy models thereby avoid the 'mere implementation' charge but only at the price of falling prey to the other horn of the FP dilemma: they process representations in a purely associative way. Given the need for effective syntax in cognition, it seems likely that connectionist systems that deserve to be taken seriously as psychological models will have representations that are fully and broadly distributed over many nodes. No single node will represent anything by itself, just as there is no grandmother neuron or yellow Volkswagen neuron. But if all representations are distributed, then the nodes and their interaction are no more part of the cognitive level story than is the circuit diagram of a VAX part of the classical story about cognition. At least, so it would seem. It thus becomes very difficult to find anything in the connectionist literature that would count as an articulated connectionist conception of cognition.[9] And, to the extent that connectionism aspires to provide a new and different general conception of cognition, the mere implementation charge is very serious indeed.

A genuine alternative connectionist conception of *cognition* would have to do two things in order to avoid both associationism and mere implementation. On the one hand, it would have to include syntactically structured representations and structure sensitive processing, since these are required by cognition. On the other hand, it would have to eschew some central tenet or tenets of classicism. Thus, a viable cognitive connectionism would have to differ from the classical RR conception either about cognitive-level aspects of syntactically structured representations, about cognitive-level aspects of mental activity, or about both. That is, it must countenance either non-classical constituents, non-classical cognitive processing, or both.

There are a number of recent connectionist proposals for incorporating rich structure into connectionist representations, largely with an eye towards introducing effective syntax. Smolensky's tensor product representations are one notable example, but related approaches are being explored by other connectionists (Pollack 1988, 1989, forthcoming; Hinton 1988; Dyer in press). Each of these schemes involves, in one way or another, a notion of syntactic constituency that is non-classical. (We will discuss Smolensky's proposal, and F&M's skepticism about it, in sections 4 and 5.)

The other way to avoid implementing the classical RR conception of cognition is to eschew the kind of processing that is posited by classicism: viz., processing that conforms to programmable representation-level rules. That is, one might seek to develop a version of cognitive connectionism that repudiates the 'rules' component of the classicist package deal while still retaining representations with effective syntax. This general view of cognition we call 'representations without rules' (for short, RWR). Elsewhere we have argued that RR cognitive science is in Kuhnian crisis; that the root source of the crisis problems is classicism's methodological commitment to programmable representation-level rules; that the nature of these problems provides substantial evidence that human cognition does not conform to such rules; and that in light of this conclusion, plus the tracking argument, human cognition very likely conforms to the RWR conception (Horgan and Tienson 1987, 1989, 1990, forthcoming).

We maintain that connectionism ought to be striving to develop into an RWR paradigm, and that various features of connectionism make it look promising in this regard. Repudiating programmable representation-level rules does not mean claiming that cognition is anarchy, or that cognitive science is impossible. For it is likely that there are numerous true cognitive-level generalizations of a kind we call 'soft laws' – i.e., laws containing ineliminable ceteris paribus clauses adverting to an essentially unlimited range of potential same-level exceptions (exceptions statable in the language of psychology). Soft laws can be the basis of perfectly good psychological explanations and theories.[10] All this, too, we have argued elsewhere (see, especially, Horgan and Tienson 1990).

Given that non-classical syntax and non-classical processing are two avenues by which connectionists might seek to avoid merely implementing classical cognitive architecture, three potential non-implementational versions of cognitive connectionism can now be distinguished. Each would posit representations with effective syntax and would also assert at least one of the following claims:

(i) Cognitive representations with effective syntax have non-classical constituents.

(ii) Structure sensitive processing of syntactically complex representations does not conform to programmable representation level rules.

Type 1 connectionism would assert (i) but would retain the classicist assumption that cognitive processing is rule-describable at the representational level. Type 2 would assert (ii) but would retain the classicist assumption that the constituents of a syntactically complex representation must be tokened whenever the representation itself is tokened. Type 3 would assert both (i) and (ii) thereby, and repudiate both classical constituents and classical processing.

For reasons to be discussed below, the natural way to introduce structure into connectionist representations is with non-classical constituents. Suppose it should turn out that such representations are indeed susceptible to suitably structure-sensitive processing within connectionist systems, but that this processing conforms to programmable representation-level rules. That is, suppose we were to obtain a viable form of type 1 connectionism. This would, in a sense, avoid the charge that connectionism is no more than mere implementation of classical cognitive architecture, because classicists have traditionally assumed that effective syntax requires classical constituents. But in a deeper sense, it would not. For, as we remarked above, the commitment to classical syntax is not really an essential, or definitive, tenet of classicism. Rather, its essential tenets are the three we mentioned in the first paragraph of this section: syntactic structure, structure sensitive processing, and hard representation-level rules. But if human cognition really conforms to representation-level rules that advert to the purely formal or syntactic features of mental representations, then such processing can be carried out by means of traditional rule-governed symbol manipulation where the symbolic representations have classical constituents. Perhaps certain such rules would 'run' more easily – more quickly, say, or with fewer computational resources – on a connectionist network employing symbols that lack classical constituents. But these would be only implementational differences. So type 1 connectionism would really give us an implementation of classical cognitive architecture after all – if you like, a non-canonical implementation, involving non-classical syntactic constituents.

Admittedly, type 1 connectionism still could be extremely interesting and important. For one thing, the question of how cognition is implemented in humans is itself very important, even though it may not fall within the domain of cognitive psychology per se. Furthermore, an approach to cognition that emphasizes non-classical syntactic constituency and connectionist implementation might well lead to new cognitive-level rules of symbol manipulation. (Maybe certain rules are naturally and easily implemented connectionistically but are awkward to implement traditionally.) But these kinds of contributions, valuable though they might be, would really constitute new twists in the RR paradigm – they would not provide a fundamentally novel conception of cognition itself.

The real heart of the implementation issue, then, is the question as to whether cognitive processing conforms to programmable representation-level rules. The notion of implementation really only makes literal sense insofar as such rules are involved; for what gets 'implemented,' strictly speaking, is rule-conforming symbol processing. (For instance, processing conforming to the rules of LISP gets implemented in a standard computer via isomorphic numerical processing, which, in turn, gets implemented via isomorphic casual processes in the machine's electrical circuitry.) Type 1 connectionism would still be a way of implementing rules. But type 2 and type 3 cognitive connectionism would repudiate the classicist assumption that cognitive processing is describable, at the representational level, by programmable rules. So either of these versions of cognitive connectionism would be genuinely, deeply non-implementational.

As we said, we think there is good evidence that human cognition falls within the RWR region of logical space – not the RR region. This leaves open, however, whether or not a *connectionist* version of RWR can be developed; that remains to be seen. But given the evidence for RWR, and given the naturalness of non-classical constituency for connectionist representations, we suggest that the proper goal for connectionism should be developing a type 3 connectionist account of cognition. Successfully accomplishing this goal would certainly steer a safe course between the Scylla of associationism and the Charybdis of merely implementing the classical approach. Indeed, it would transform the current Kuhnian crisis into a scientific revolution.

Non-classical Constituents and Effective Syntax

In this section and the next we take up the question of whether non-classical syntax, of the kind proposed by Smolensky and others, can be effective syntax. We take this to be an open question; the answer is not known, and currently there is no strong or clear-cut epistemic presumption one way or the other. In the present section we will explain tensor product representations and what they do in enough detail to discuss the issues. We will also argue that many physical systems behave in a way that Fodor and McLaughlin appear to assume to be impossible, and, hence, that F&M are unconvincing in their attempt to argue that non-classical syntax cannot be effective. In the next section we consider what would be a minimum that would demonstrate non-classical effective syntax, and we discuss some considerations Smolensky offers for thinking that tensor product representations can deliver the goods. We repeat, however, that as far as the issue of 'mere implementation' is concerned, the question about the effectiveness of non-classical syntax is not fundamental – the fundamental question is whether processing conforms to programmable representation-level rules.

Within connectionism, representations are most naturally conceived as vectors. A tokened representation is a pattern of activation in certain nodes, with each node corresponding to a dimension of the vector and with that node's activation level being the numerical value of the corresponding dimension. So if one seeks to incorporate rich structure – including syntactic structure – into connectionist representation, then a natural approach is to construe the pre-theoretic notion of *constituency* in terms of some suitable relation, or relations, among vectors. Structured representations will be vectors that bear such relations to other vectorial representations.

In the first generation of connectionist models, this idea was pursued only rather crudely, if at all. Sometimes representation was completely local: single units were assigned fixed representational content, so that a given representation was tokened whenever its unit had above-threshold activity. Purely local representations are structurally atomic and, thus, lack representation-level constituents altogether. Sometimes, on the other hand, representation was modestly distributed: an entity was represented by a collection of active units, with each active unit in the collection locally representing some 'microfeature' instantiated by the represented entity. This approach does introduce a crude form of constituency, viz., the relation between a multiple-element vector and its various separate elements. But all this amounts to at the cognitive level is set theoretic membership or the part/whole relationship, not syntactic structure. Suppose, for instance, that three single nodes in a network, respectively, represent John, loving, and Mary. The simultaneous activation of these three nodes clearly will not do as a putative representation of the proposition that John loves Mary, for how, then, would the system represent the proposition that Mary loves John? Ways are needed to build richer kinds of constituency into vectorial representations – rich enough to accommodate syntactic constituency relations like subject-of, predicate-of, and the like.

In the current second generation of connectionist modelling and theorizing, the problem of structure is being approached in a more sophisticated way. This new attention to structure is motivated largely by an increasing appreciation of the need for language-like representation and for suitably structure sensitive processing. Particularly noteworthy are Smolensky's tensor product representations (henceforth, *TP representations*), Hinton's reduced descriptions, and Pollock's recursive distributed representations.[11] We will focus here on Smolensky, since his proposal is the specific target of F&M's discussion. But much of what we say is applicable, mutatis mutandis, to proposals like Hinton's and Pollock's.

Smolensky harnesses two mathematical operations on vectors: addition and tensor multiplication. For any two n-element vectors, **v** and **w**, their sum (**v** + **w**) is the n -element vector whose elements are the sum of the first element of **v** and the first element of **w**, the sum of the second elements of **v** and **w**, etc. For any n -element vector **v** and m - element vector **w**, their tensor product, **v** x **w**, is an (n x m)-element vector that is obtained by pairwise multiplication of each element of **v** with each element of **w**.

TP representations are characterized as follows: Suppose that F is a set of n-element vectors, each assigned to represent a 'filler' that can occupy various roles; and suppose that R is a set of m-element vectors, each assigned to represent a role that can be occupied by various fillers. If this is the case, then for any two vectors **f** and **r** (from F and R, respectively) the tensor product of **f** and **r** (i.e., the (n x m)-element vector **f** x **r**) represents a 'filler/role binding' (i.e., it is a representation of a particular filler occupying a particular role). So, for example, if v(John) is a vector representing the noun 'John,' and v(subj) is a vector representing the grammatical role, subject, then the tensor product v(John) x v(subj) is a vector that represents 'John' in the role of subject.

A TP representation of a structured object is the vector that results from adding together the vectors that represent the filler/role bindings for each of the constituents of the object. A TP representation of the sentence 'John loves Mary' might be the result of adding the vectors representing 'John' in the role of subject, 'loves' in the role of 'verb,' and

'Mary' as object. That is, [v(John) x v(subj)] + [v(loves) x v(verb)] + [v(Mary) x v(obj)].

This treatment of the sentence 'John loves Mary' is obviously unrealistically simple-minded as a general approach to sentence structure, and is meant only for illustration. For one thing, the sentence would standardly be thought of as having a (tree) structure that combines 'John' with the verb phrase 'loves Mary,' which, in turn, has constituents 'loves' and 'Mary.' Thus, a more realistic TP representation would be the vector that results from adding vectors representing 'John' in the role of subject and 'loves Mary' in the role of predicate. This latter vector would be constructed from TP vectors representing 'loves' in the role, say, 'head of verb phrase' and 'Mary' in the role 'object of verb phrase.'[12]

This illustrates one of the mathematical features of tensor products that makes them well suited for connectionist representation; they are recursive. Being vectors themselves, tensor product representations can serve as filler or role representations for higher-order tensor product representations.

Another important mathematical feature of tensor product representations is recoverability. When the filler representations are linearly independent of one another, and likewise the role representations, they are fully recoverable mathematically from the TP representation (i.e, the vector sum of the individual TP role/filler vectors). When the vectors are not linearly independent, a degree of recoverability may remain. In general, the greater the deviation from complete linear independence among filler representations or role representations, the less accurate will be the mathematical recoverability of the constituent filler- and role-representations.

TP representation can be implemented very naturally in a connectionist network. An n-element vector is represented by a pattern of activity, corresponding to the values of the elements of the vector, in a pool of n nodes. (n x m)-element tensor products can be implemented by an (n x m)- sized pool of 'binding units,' each capable of a continuous range of activation levels. Vector addition is implemented via superposition of one distributed TP representation 'on top of' another, summing activity in the units. Thus, when a particular TP representation is being tokened, the activation of each binding unit is typically the result of summing activation from several different, superimposed filler/role binding representations. Conversely, the level of activation of a node contributes to the representation of each of these filler/role binding representations. There is, in general, no single representation that a unit's level of activation contributes to.

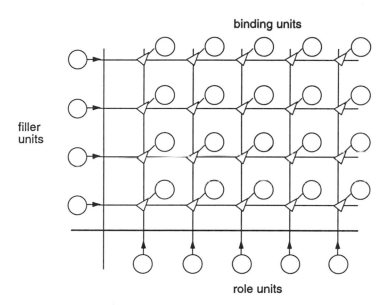

Figure 6.1: A network using multiplicative junctions to perform tensor product binding (From Smolensky 1990, 194).

Separate n-element and m-element pools can implement filler and role representations, respectively. These pools can be linked to a pool of $(n \times m)$ binding units, as in Figure 6.1.

Each binding unit is connected, via a multiplicative junction (which yields the product of two inputs), to a single filler unit and a single role unit. If a particular filler representation f and role representation r are simultaneously activated in the filler and role units, activation is passed from both pools to the binding units, and the multiplicative junctions generate the representation $f \times r$ in the binding units. Superposition can be accomplished by activating additional filler/role combinations, while a current representation remains active in the binding units.

Such a network can also 'unbind' a TP representation to recover its constituent filler or role representations. When a TP representation is actively present in the binding units, a pattern of activity in the role units corresponding to a specific role representation can function essentially as a 'query,' asking which filler (if any) occupies that role. Activity from the binding units and the role units will generate in the filler units a pattern of activity corresponding to the appropriate filler representation, thereby 'unbinding' the answer to the query. Thus, a network in which the sentence 'John loves Mary' was represented would be asked 'What is the subject?' by producing a pattern of activation in the role units corresponding to the vector representation of the role *subject*. And we would get a pattern of activity in the filler units corresponding to the vector representation of 'John.'

We have talked of tensor product *representations of* sentences, in part because this is the familiar way of speaking. In certain cases, it is appropriate to speak of the tensor product as *representing* a sentence (e.g., when the network does language processing). But the designation 'tensor product representation' means that the tensor product represents. Typically, what the network represents is not language but some other domain. In these cases, it is more appropriate to think of the tensor product representation not as representing a sentence but as *being* a sentence – a syntactically structured representation – (tokened) *in* the binding units. Thus, what is (tokened or realized) in the network is not a representation of the sentence 'John loves Mary' but, rather, the *sentence* 'John loves Mary,' which is (roughly) a representation of a certain non-linguistic state of affairs. TP 'representations,' when tokened in suitable connectionist networks, should be thought of as sententially structured representations – sentences written in the (non-classical) language of the network.[13]

Tokening a TP representation does not, in general, require tokening its syntactic constituents. Thus, the syntactic constituents of TP representations are non-classical in F&M's sense. It is here that the issue of effective syntax is joined. F&M put their complaint against Smolensky this way:

> We can now say quite succinctly what our claim against Smolensky will be: on the one hand, the cognitive architecture he endorses does not provide for representations with Classical constituents; on the other hand, he provides no suggestion as to how mental processes could be structure sensitive unless mental representations have Classical constituents; and, on the third hand (as it were) he provides no suggestion as to how minds could be systematic if mental processes aren't structure sensitive. So his reply to Fodor and Pylyshyn fails. (188)

Suppressing epistemic operators, the argument against Smolensky becomes,

(1) No classical constituents.
(2) If no classical constituents, then not structure sensitive.
(3) If not structure sensitive, then not systematic.

We agree with the first point. Constituent structure defined in terms of tensor products is not classical, and connectionist representations should not, in general, be classical. We agree in spirit with the third point. Only simple systems could be (artificially or accidentally) systematic without being structure sensitive.

Initially, claim (2) *does* look quite plausible. Godel numbers, for example, look like prime examples of representations without classical constituents. A unique Godel number can be assigned to each syntactic primitive of a language, to each well formed formula and subformula, and to each sentence in such a way that an algorithm can reconstruct any sentence from its associated Godel number and vice versa. So perhaps one might say that the (non-classical) 'constituents' of a Godel number g would be the Godel numbers of the classical constituents of the sentence numbered by g. But it seems overwhelmingly unlikely that numbers that are constituents in this sense could play a causal role in structure sensitive processing. If they could play a role at all, it would only be of a Pickwickian sort, involving first reconstructing classical sentential representations, performing structure sensitive operations on those classical representations, and then reconverting the resulting sentential representation back into Godel numbers.

Although TP representations are like Godel numbers in lacking classical constituents, it does not follow that they are relevantly like Godel numbers when it comes to susceptibility to structure sensitive processing. It is not the case that all representations are either unstructured in the way Godel numbers are, or that they possess classical constituents. There is a range of cases in between.

Consider, for example, a magnetic recording tape on which is monaurally recorded a performance of a string quartet. The tokened representation on the tape is the physical superposition of the four representations which would have been tokened had just one of the four instruments played its same sound in the absence of the other three. None of these individual lines is tokened on the tape. However, in a natural sense, each of these four non-tokened sound representations is a constituent of the actual tokened representation on the tape.[14] And these non-tokened, non-classical constituents are amenable to a form of constituent sensitive processing. In an appropriate sound reproduction system, they can produce sounds very much like those that were originally caused by the four separate instruments. And these sounds can be discerned as distinct, for example, by the human ear.

The sound recording example is, in a sense, parasitic upon the case of real sound. Sound waves – like all waves – superimpose, and yet component waves have effects as individual waves. The sound waves in a crowded room, for example, consist of the superposition of sounds produced by many voices, yet bits of individual conversations are discernible.

Wave phenomena are ubiquitous in nature, effects of non-tokened constituent waves equally ubiquitous. The wake of a boat has many effects, setting a buoy to bobbing in a certain way, knocking down a skier, and contributing to the destruction of a sand castle. But the waves in that wake exist on open water as nothing more than their contribution to the complex contortion of the surface that is the superposition of many different wave motions, including the dominant motion caused by the wind.

Holograms are a widely discussed wave phenomenon, and they offer a somewhat different example of structure sensitive processing. No separate part of a hologram represents any separate part of the scene it represents. Information about the scene is present in a fully distributed form. Nevertheless, shining a light through any large enough portion of a hologram generates a three dimensional image of the whole original scene. This effect is sensitive to the hologram's structure qua recorder of visual information, even though the encoding is distributed.

Our colleague Don Franceschetti has suggested to us a particularly clean example of the causal efficacy of component waves of a wave superposition. Suppose a square drumhead is struck simultaneously on two adjacent sides. The wave resulting from each blow will travel across the drumhead, so to speak, to strike the other side of the drum and there have the effect it would have had if the other blow had not been struck. Suppose that a toy soldier balanced on one side of the drum is knocked off by the wave emanating from the blow to the opposite side. The motion of the drumhead in the interval will be nothing more than the superposition of the two waves started at the two adjacent sides. The wave that caused the soldier's fall was not classically present.

This is just the sort of thing one wants to say about tensor product representations. The representation of John as subject of the sentence is, and is no more than, its contribution to the superposition representing the sentence as a whole.[15] The analogy with wave phenomena shows that such contributors to superpositions are not necessarily causally inert, as F&M's argument appears to assume.

There is a whole spectrum of possibilities concerning structure sensitive processing. At one end of the spectrum are sentential representations with classical constituents. At the other end are representations like Godel numbers, which very probably cannot directly subserve effective syntax at all. Tensor product representations, like the wave phenomena from which they are abstracted, lie somewhere in between. Unlike Godel numbers, they contain intrinsic information about constituency. Unlike classical representations, this information is present in distributed, not local, form.

Since sentential TP representations do contain structurally encoded information about their syntactic constituents, it is entirely possible that their structure renders them amenable to processing that is suitably sensitive to these constituents. Sound waves and light waves can have constituent- sensitive effects, even though their constituent waves are not tokened with them. Our point against F&M is that they are wrong to treat (2) as possessing overwhelmingly strong credibility. TP representations might, similarly, be capable of appropriate constituent-sensitive effects, even when their syntactic constituents are not tokened. If so, then the non-classical syntax of TP representations would qualify as effective syntax.

Can Tensor Products Provide Effective Syntax

In this section, we consider what it would take, at a minimum, to show that non-classical constituents could support the kind of constituent sensitive processing that cognition requires.[16] The first thing we want to observe about tensor product representations is that they *do* provide naturally for a certain amount of systematicity. Let us distinguish in the obvious way between *representational* systematicity and *inferential* (or, more generally, processing) systematicity. A system exhibits representational systematicity if and only if it is capable of having a representation only if it is capable of having other relevantly related representations. A system is inferentially systematic if and only if it is capable of making an inference only if it is capable of making other inferences of the same form.

Tensor product representations certainly do provide for representational systematicity. A tensor product representation of a sentence results from taking the tensor product of a vector representing a syntactic role by a vector representing the filler occupying that role and then superimposing those tensor products for each constituent of the sentence. Let *(a)* and *(b)* be representations of the same type, and let *(r)* be a role that representations of that type can occupy. Let Va, Vb, and Vr be vector representations of *(a)*, *(b)*, and *(r)*, respectively. If tensor product Vb x Vr is a representation of *(b)* in role *(r)* in a certain system, then Va x Vr will be a tensor product representation of *(a)* in role *(r)* in that system. In general, given vector representations of distinct roles and of fillers of types that can occupy the various roles, if one filler of a given type can occupy a role, then any filler of that type can occupy that role. And that is representational systematicity. Thus, tensor products *naturally and automatically* give us representational systematicity. All that is needed for representational systematicity is that complex representations be systematically related to component representations. The relationship does not have to be classical.

Furthermore, tensor products naturally provide for at least a minimum of structure sensitive processing. Take, in particular, a network that does nothing but binding and unbinding in the manner we described in Section 3. Given vector representations of filler and role, it produces a tensor product representation of that filler in that role, and it superimposes such tensor products to give representations of whole structured representations. Also, given a representation of a complex and a (query) representation of a filler (or role), it will answer with the appropriate role (filler). Such constituent extraction is certainly structure sensitive processing. And if the constituents can be extracted, one wants to say, they must *in some sense* be there.

But constituent extraction is a long way from inference. The crucial question is whether information about constituent structure is present in tensor product representations in a robust enough way to drive inference, and we think this must mean drive inference *without* extracting constituents to be tokened. If the constituents *must* be extracted for the system to make an inference, then the constituents will be (to that extent, in this system) classical in F&M's sense, and there will be a clear danger of the system being mere implementation.[17]

In order to get clearer about this issue, we will discuss a question put to us by Paul Smolensky: what would be a *minimal* connectionist system that would show that connectionist systems are capable of genuine structure sensitive inference? What we would like to see is an inference system on tensor products. A modus ponens-er (detacher) suggests itself as the simplest example. Such a system should at least be able to do something like the following: When it has a tensor product representation of a conditional and a representation of the antecedent of that conditional, it generates a representation of the consequent of that conditional without extracting the antecedent from the conditional.[18] It should at least do this for arbitrary simple conditionals not restricted to an antecedently given vocabulary for components of conditionals.

Such a system would show something significant. For it would be able to 'recognize' the identity of antecedent and free premise *without* unbinding the antecedent. However, conditionals can be arbitrarily long and complex. Assuming our only 'connective' is 'if then,' conditionals may have arbitrarily complex nested conditionals in the antecedent and consequent. Thus, a full fledged modus ponens-er should be able to deal with conditionals of arbitrary complexity.[19] There are two possible approaches one can consider.

One approach would be to try to construct a system that never unpacked the conditional (or free premise) but detached without unpacking for conditionals of any degree of complexity. This, we take it, would be quite an impressive feat, for it would involve doing something equivalent to recursively analyzing a conditional to determine its antecedent and then determining the identity of antecedent and second premise – but doing it *without* decomposing the conditional into constituents.

A second, perhaps more promising, approach would do modus ponens directly, without unpacking, only for fairly simple conditionals and would unbind the antecedents of complex conditionals to check (perhaps recursively) for identity with another premise. Such a system would be a strong demonstration of the robust presence of constituent structure in tensor product representations, for it would perform a structure sensitive task *without* unbinding in simple cases and would unbind token constituents to use in performing the *same* task in complex cases. We think this kind of thing would give the best case for the reality of constituents in tensor product representations: some structure sensitive processing without tokening constituents and, also, some processing in which constituents (fillers) are tokened in the same system for other instances of the same process.

That two sentences are conditionals and, hence, (in that respect) of the same form is encoded in their tensor product representations. For each conditional, the identity of its antecedent is encoded. A system that (sometimes) detaches without unpacking that conditional must make use of both of these kinds of encoded information. What more could you want?

We think one might, in fact, want to go one step further before admitting that real non-classical effective syntax has been demonstrated. It is a step which must be taken in any case, if any decently realistic connectionist cognitive systems are to be produced. Networks can be very fancy associative processors. Why is a modus ponens-er a structure sensitive processor and not just a fancy associator?[20]

One thing that would (or should) allay this worry would be a system that makes inferences of two different forms from the same statements, say modus ponens and modus tollens. Since this would mean introducing negations of statements, a second statement form, it would also complicate the modus ponens task. But the main thing is that if the same tensor products are used without unbinding in two structure sensitive operations, there is simply no longer any point in denying that the processing is using the structural information encoded in the tensor products. If we actually had a system that could do this kind of processing and someone were to deny that it was doing structure sensitive processing, the reasonable response would be to ignore him or her and get on about our business.

We have talked about a modus ponens (and modus tollens)-er, but, of course, that is not the only thing that would plausibly demonstrate constituent sensitive processing with non-classical constituents. The same things would be shown by systems that did, for example, analogs of syllogistic inference or analogs of choice determination on the basis of beliefs and desires.

Fodor and McLaughlin give no argument that would tend to show that it is not possible to construct connectionist systems of the kind just described. As they put what we take to be the crux of their argument, 'the constituents of complex activity vectors typically aren't "there," so if the causal consequences of tokening a complex vector are sensitive to its constituents, that's a miracle' (200). But the information – the fact – that, for example, 'John' is the subject of the sentence *is* encoded in the vector. *All* of this kind of syntactic *information* about the sentence is 'there' in the vector. If this information can play a causal role, perhaps it would not be such a miracle.

But is there any positive reason to believe tensor products can be harnessed to support the kind of processing required? Smolensky says there is. For, he says, tensor products already do these things in physics. Unfortunately, it has not been clear how to understand the physics analogy, at least not to those of us uneducated in physics. But we think there is a way of taking the analogy that does show something that is clearly pertinent to the issue, namely, that tensor products can evolve in ways that respect semantic information or semantic constraints.

The example Smolensky gives is the representation of the state of an atom in quantum theory. But vectors are used in similar ways throughout physics. Here is how the quantum story goes. The state of an atom is represented by a vector in an abstract vector space. This vector is determined as follows: the state ('spin') of an electron is represented by a vector (Vs); the orbital of the electron in the atom is represented by another vector (Vo); and the electron as situated in the atom is represented by the tensor product of these two vectors ($Vs \times Vo$). According to Smolensky, 'The atom as a whole is represented by a vector that is the sum or superposition of vectors, each of which represents a particular electron situated in its orbital. (There are also contributions of the same sort from nucleons)' (1988b, 20).[21]

The equations that determine the evolution of the atom through time apply directly to the vector representing the atom as a whole, even though the separate elements of this vector do not separately represent the component electrons, etc., of the atom. Since the equations *do* govern the (evolving) vector representation of the entire atom, it seems reasonable to say that this vector itself involves continuing reference to particular electrons, although it lacks classical constituents referring to particular electrons. It tracks them. At any time it has information about the state of each individual electron – information that can be rendered explicit by mathematically extracting separate vectors representing the states (at that time) of the separate electrons.

Suppose, then, that we had a connectionist network set up to correspond to the vector representation of an atom, with the weights set so that activation levels of nodes evolve in accordance with the equations that determine the time evolution of the atom. It seems reasonable to say that this network involves continuing reference to the components of the atom and attribution of properties to them.[22] It could, for example, be part of a larger system in which this information about components could be explicitly represented.

But the vector for the atom as a whole is decomposable in many other ways as well. Why say that reference to the components of the atom is real (F&M 198)? In particular, why say that distributed information about this possible decomposition does any *causal* work in the system? For one thing, this is a semantically interpretable decomposition. It reveals the information that the system carries about the components of the atom.

But semantics is not causality. This is why we imagined an inferencer that sometimes decomposes to explicitly token constituents as part of the inferencing process. If the system extracts and uses components in some process, those components are real for the system. Modus ponens *is*, of course, a type of decomposition task, since the derived conclusion is a constituent of the conditional premise. Other inference forms, though not simply decomposition, have conclusions that are systematically related to certain constituents of premises.

In any case, this is the degree and kind of causal efficacy one is likely to get in connectionism. Abstractly, it may not seem unreasonable to question whether it is really effective syntax. But if one had a connectionist system like the modus ponens and modus tollens-er that we imagined above, such questioning would, we hold, become pointless.

In general, the question, 'But do we have genuine effective syntax?' becomes otiose, at least when (1) there is semantically interpretable decomposition (with processing that is structure/content appropriate relative to this interpretation); (2) *some* of this processing proceeds without decomposition; and (3) some of it involves extraction of token constituents as well as combining tokens into complex representations.

But the physics system would not yet be an inferencer of the sort that we are seeking. It shows (or would show) that a connectionist system can preserve information through a complex evolution and can evolve in ways that at least respect that information. However, it is not so clear that its evolution is determined by the *form* of its representations alone, as we expect from an inferencer. And the equations for a physics network would be derived from physics. The network would be set up in accordance with antecedently given equations that apply to the physical system the network represents. Obviously, a network that is an inferencer cannot borrow in a similar way from the mathematics of its subject matter, since there are no dynamical equations governing formal inference. So it remains, we think, an open question as to whether or not connectionism can deliver the goods.

Can Connectionism *Explain* Systematicity?

Suppose there are connectionist systems of the sort that we have asked for, and that these will scale up so that there can be connectionist systems with effective syntax that are complex and general.[23] Such systems will be systematic by nature. Still, F&P have an argument against connectionism as a general theory of cognition, an argument that F&M repeat. F&M (185) take it that F&P have established, and that Smolensky does not challenge,

(S)(i) Cognitive capacities are generally systematic, both in humans and in many infrahuman organisms.
   (ii) It is nomologically necessary that this is so.

As we have seen, and as Fodor et al. repeatedly emphasize, the classical picture is ideally suited to explain (S). Classical representations have syntactic structure. They are made up of repeatable elements susceptible to combination according to certain patterns. Syntactic structure provides for systematicity. As F&M put the objection to connectionism,

> So then: it is *built into* the Classical picture that you cannot think *aRb* unless you are able to think *bRa*, but the Connectionist picture is *neutral* on whether you can think aRb even if you can't think *bRa*. But its a law of nature that you can't think *aRb* if you can't think *bRa*. So the Classical picture explains systematicity and the Connectionist picture doesn't. So the Classical picture wins (203).

It is possible to 'wire up' (as F&M say) a connectionist system so that it is possible for it to be in a representational state aRb if and only if it is possible for it to be in a representational state bRa (for any a, R, b in its representational repertoire). But it is also possible to construct networks that do not have this property. Why, then, is it, according to connectionism, that all natural cognitive systems exhibit systematicity?

This is a serious question, more serious than respondents to F&P have recognized. It cannot be answered, for example, merely by saying that cognitive systems have evolved that way – that is, networks are capable of exhibiting systematicity, and nature/evolution is capable of finding them. The question remains, why should nature (want to) find only systematic (as opposed to non-systematic) networks or perpetuate only these when she does find them?

Again, this is a serious question. But it is not a difficult one. An answer is at hand from what we have said so far. We have argued that natural, embodied cognitive systems need effective syntax to get along in the world. Any cognitive system of any complexity,[24] perhaps any worthy of the name, must employ syntactically structured representations. Only with effective syntactically structured representations can a cognitive system have the semantic richness it needs to survive. Any system with effective syntax will be largely systematic. Thus, any cognitive system will be largely systematic.

If this is correct, a connectionist explanation of systematicity is at hand, assuming a positive answer to the question of Section 5 (i.e., that there are, indeed, connectionist systems with effective syntax). Cognitive systems are, says connectionism, connectionist networks. It is a *cognitive level* law that *any* cognitive system will have effective syntax and, therefore, be systematic.

It is true that connectionism is, in a sense, neutral on systematicity. But if the tracking argument is correct, the demands of cognition are not. It is not necessary for connectionism to explain systematicity all by itself, so to speak. What is required is that there be an explanation of systematicity and that that explanation be compatible with connectionism. Otherwise connectionism would lose. But there is an explanation, and it is compatible with connectionism.

This dialectical situation led F&P to focus on systematicity rather than on effective syntax or on compositional syntax and semantics, because they felt themselves forced to argue for the need for effective syntax. But from our (H&T) point of view, the focus on systematicity itself made the matter of explaining systematicity seem more difficult than it is. There are good arguments (notably the tracking argument) that cognition has, and must have, effective syntax. These arguments do not employ systematicity as a premise. But these arguments, combined with the fact that effective syntax explains systematicity, allow an easy answer to the demand for an explanation of systematicity.

Given this, the connectionist can explain the evolution of systematic connectionist cognizers in the following way: Nature favoured successful cognizers. Successful cognizers need effective syntax, and effective syntax makes cognition systematic. So the cognizers that nature favoured were systematic cognizers.

Why Non-classical Constituents Might Yield Non-classical Processes

In Section 5 we described what we thought would be the minimum necessary to show that connectionist systems are capable of structure sensitive processing with non-classical syntax. Construction of such a system would be a convincing demonstration of the possibility of distinctively connectionist effective syntax. This is important because the possibility of effective syntax is one of the main questions concerning the viability of connectionism. Provided also that the design of this system was not task specific but looked to be capable of scaling up to something much more general (with many more structures and processes), it would serve as a *plausibility* argument concerning the possibility of a distinctively connectionist picture of cognition.

But it is important to be clear about the limited role of such a system. It would be a plausibility argument and nothing more. It would provide a significant, presently lacking, piece of evidence that an alternative, connectionist conception of cognition is possible and worth pursuing. But it would clearly *not* be a mini-version of a connectionist cognitive system. Most important, it would still be implementation in the deepest sense, for it would still be rule describable at the cognitive level and, hence, isomorphic, at that level, to a classical system. If our arguments against the classical picture (mentioned in Section 3) are correct, they would apply equally to cognition so conceived. As we argued in Section 3, a real alternative connectionist conception of cognition requires softness – the rejection of hard representation level rules.

However, we think cognitive level softness is to be expected for complex connectionist systems with non-classical syntax. It should be natural for them because of the combined effect of two factors.[25] The first is multiple realization. A given representation can be realized in many ways in the same connectionist system – in principle, in continuously many ways. Typically, a representation corresponds to a set of nodes. The representation is considered to be actively realized when a sufficient number of its nodes are sufficiently activated. But in decently complex systems, not all of these nodes need to be activated for the representation to be actively realized. Activation of different subsets of nodes can constitute active realization of the same representation.

Furthermore, for each node, typically, any level of activation above a certain minimum will count as that node being on. All these differences in activation are differences which can affect processing but which have no finer-grained cognitive level description.[26] As a result, different total activation states that receive the same cognitive level description may evolve to total activation states that receive different cognitive level descriptions.

This, we think, is the way it ought to be, because it is the way it really is with cognition. Different choices might be made by two cognizers whose 'neural wiring' is identical and whose respective total states, prior to choosing, receive the same cognitive level description. The different choices would be due to differences in the total initial sub-representational states of the two systems – that is, differences in how the total initial cognitive level description is sub-representationally realized.[27]

The second feature of connectionist systems that is likely to contribute to softness is the fact that they are well suited to multiple simultaneous soft constraint satisfaction. If you are going to buy a new car, and price is no object, then you may choose a car on the basis of your taste in automotive performance. But, in fact, most car purchases are based on many factors, which may include: price, performance (which itself is multifaceted), reliability, safety, fuel economy, comfort, size, convenience of access, availability, and dealership qualities like service, integrity, and convenience of the transaction. Each factor pushes towards one or a small number of cars. Ideally, one's choice is the car that best satisfies the largest number of considerations. It may not be possible to get what one wants in every respect. Thus, most constraints are *soft*. They can be violated when the cognitive system is doing its work properly. This sort of situation is common, not only in decision making but in, for example, belief fixation and moral judgment formation.

As the PDP volumes emphasized, connectionist systems are naturally good at multiple simultaneous constraint satisfaction. Weights are set so that if one representation (or set of representations) is the only input, the system will lead to a certain output representation. But they are also set so that if a different representation is the only input, a different output results. If the only input is performance data on the various candidate cars, a certain car would be chosen. If price data were the only input, a different car would be chosen. With a complex input involving many different representations, which would individually lead to different output representations, each tries to bring about its consequence. The several constraints simultaneously compete and conspire until the system settles into a state that best satisfies the total package of constraints. No serial processing is imposed by the system or the architecture.

Given that the representation of each of the constraints can be realized in innumerable ways, the possibility of cognitive level softness due to multiple realizability is vastly multiplied. What is necessary for a workable cognitive system is that the outcome be relevant in most cases, not that it be the same in every case that receives the same cognitive level initial description.[28] Thus, if non-classical structure sensitive processing is possible in connectionism, then, we suspect, softness may well arise naturally.[29]

Conceptually, the important point concerning implementation is softness. To be a genuine alternative to classicism, to be genuinely nonimplementational, connectionist cognitive processes must not, in general, be rule describable at the cognitive level. But, practically, the question might turn on the possibility of non-classical effective syntax, for nonclassical connectionist effective syntax looks like it might well give us the needed softness.

Conclusion

We have argued (1) that cognitive systems need effective syntax; (2) that connectionism cannot give us a new conception of cognition if it amounts to implementation of the classical picture; hence (3) that a new connectionist conception of cognition would have to differ from the classical view concerning either the nature of representation or the nature of mental processes or both; (4) that, ultimately, what really counts is the repudiation of the classical conception of mental processes as conforming to representation-level rules; (5) that, even so, non-classical connectionist representations might well be a foundation for the right sort of nonclassical mental processes; and (6) that Fodor and McLaughlin have not made a plausible case that non-classical effective syntax is unattainable. We then described the sort of task a connectionist system should perform to show that effective non-classical connectionist syntax is possible. We have argued (7) that if this is indeed possible, then (contrary to Fodor, Pylyshyn, and McLaughlin) connectionism can provide an appropriate explanation of systematicity; (8) that representation-level softness is to be expected for complex connectionist systems with non-classical syntax; and (9) that a connectionist conception of cognition that incorporates effective syntax while eschewing hard representation-level rules would be neither an implementation of the classical conception nor a reversion to associationism, and, thus, would avoid both horns of the putative dilemma posed, by Fodor and Pylyshyn, for connectionism.

Notes

1 This paper is thoroughly collaborative. Authors are listed alphabetically.

2 See, for example, Touretzky (1989), Touretzky, et al. (1989). *Artificial Intelligence* has an upcoming issue on structure in connectionist systems, and we see new papers purporting to deal connectionistically with structure almost every day.

3 We cannot, of course, show this case by case. But we think that once it is made clear what is necessary to avoid the dilemma, it is obvious that none of these systems do it.

4 On the other hand, it is important to understand that the existence of such a system would not answer F&P's charge against connectionism. If Fodor and Pylyshyn's charge is false, then it must be possible to construct connectionist systems that avoid their dilemma. But this *cannot* be done simply by constructing a connectionist system in which structure sensitive processing occurs, as will be made clear in the discussion of 'mere implementation' in Section 3.

5 We will elaborate this claim in Section 3. Smolensky, of course, also holds that mental processes are, in general, not classical. See Smolensky (1988a). The relationships between Smolensky's views on this topic and our own are too complex to go into in this paper.

6 In brief, the argument is: Real, complex cognitive systems need compositional semantics (in the reasonable sense that meanings of complex expressions must be functions of meanings of a stock of primitives). And, we hold, the only way for a complex, physical cognitive system to have compositional semantics is for it to have compositional syntax (in the sense specified).

7 We take constituent structure to be a linguistic notion. It is an abstract, functional notion. The subject of a sentence, for example, is an item that plays a certain role in determining the truth conditions and inferential relations of that sentence. This notion does not in itself imply that the subject of a sentence must be a spatial or temporal part of that sentence, nor that it must in some way be a classical constituent.

8 We distinguish the second and third claims, which are frequently not distinguished at all or, taken to be equivalent. We maintain that the second is true of cognition while the third is not.

9 With the exception of Smolensky's 'On the Proper Treatment of Connectionism' (Smolensky 1988a).

10 One reason connectionism is promising is that it is a natural implementation architecture for soft laws. More on this in the section "Why Non-Classical constituents might Yield Non-Classical Processes.

11 Smolensky (1987a, 1988b, 1990); Hinton (1988); Pollock (1988, 1989, forthcoming). Dyer (in press) and Chalmers (forthcoming) base processing on

representations like Pollock's. Van Gelder (1990) gives a nice overview of these methods.

12 There are obvious technical problems in doing this, since the vector representing 'loves Mary' as predicate must be the same dimension as that representing 'John' as subject. There are also a number of suggestions available for dealing with such problems. Pollack, for example, has been working on condensation techniques that allow arbitrarily complex recursive structure to be built into distributed representations of fixed band-width. Or one might construct constituent structure trees in such a way that the branches from a node are always of the same length. But such things clearly go well beyond the scope of this paper.

13 It is tempting to think that the language of thought might be like this, with fully distributed constituent structure and no classical constituents.

14 In conversation, Brian McLaughlin responded to this example by suggesting that representations of the lines of the individual instruments *are* tokened on the tape, because, for example, just one of these lines could be deleted by suitably modifying the tape. That would mean that representations of constituent lines of musical ensembles would count as classical. But if that is all that it takes to count as being tokened, the syntactic constituents of tensor product representations will also count as classical. Clearly, this is a suggestion that Fodor and McLaughlin should not pursue.

15 The analogy between tensor products and waves is, of course, intimate and intended and is brought out nicely by the square drumhead. The two stimulated sides are analogous to the role and filler units, the drumhead itself is analogous to the binding units. The vectorial representation of any given wave on the two dimensional surface of the drumhead will be a sum of vectors representing various (non-tokened) constituent two-dimensional waves. Each of the latter vectors, in turn, is the tensor product of two vectors respectively representing a (non-tokened) uniform sine wave along the drumhead's x-axis and y-axis.

A non-uniform wave can be mathematically characterized, through Fourier analysis, as a superposition of uniform sine waves of various frequencies, each with a specific amplitude. These constituent sine waves are not themselves physically tokened when and where the non-uniform wave is tokened. Yet non-uniform waves have numerous constituent sensitive effects that are directly responsive to specific constituent frequencies. The current in a radio or television set, for example, resonates to one specific constituent frequency of the impinging electromagnetic waves – whatever specific frequency the tuner is set to receive.

However, there is a significant *dis*analogy between wave phenomena and what we expect from a cognitive system. For the evolution of a complex wave can be analyzed as the *independent* evolution of its constituent waves. Clearly, the behaviour of a cognitive system cannot be analysable into the independent evolution of constituents, because inference and other cognitive processes depend on the interaction of constituents in distinct positions in different representations.

16 We remark that the systems (that we are aware of) that have been offered in response to F&P do not meet the conditions we shall describe.

17 There remains, of course, the possibility of what we called type 2 connectionism above: classical constituents but non-rule describable, structure sensitive processing.

18 Technical questions immediately arise, such as whether the statements in question should be represented in distinct pools of nodes or in the same pool. What is essential, we think, is that the method used not be an ad hoc solution for the specific inference form in question, but be one that generalizes to other inferences and, in principle, to systems that make a rich variety of structure dependent inferences.

19 It is necessary to say a word about the matter of arbitrary complexity. Fodor and Pylyshyn introduced the systematicity argument, essentially, as a replacement for the productivity argument because of a perception that the productivity argument begs a question against connectionism.

The productivity argument asserts that thought is productive, that is, there is no longest possible thought. For any thought a cognitive system has, there is a longer thought it could have, absent limitations of memory, mortality, etc. Thus, abstracting from such limitations, there are infinitely many possible thoughts a human being is capable of having. But human minds are finite. The only way to achieve this infinite capacity with finite means is for thoughts to be recursively structured from a finite vocabulary. Hence, constituent structure.

This has been thought to beg the question against connectionism, because it assumes the idealization of an infinitely extensible memory. But, it is thought, connectionists cannot accept this idealization, because when you add nodes (and therefore connections) to extend memory capacity, you necessarily also change content, since content is determined by weights on connections. (Our colleagues, Stan Franklin and Max Garzon, have demonstrated networks for which adding nodes does not alter content (personal communication), but never mind.) This, we think, is a classic example of classical thinking in a non- classical context. One way to extend the memory of a connectionist network is to improve resolution, so that, as smaller and smaller differences in activation at each node are discriminated in the network, processing capacity, memory, and so forth increase. Productivity is not something connectionists must deny. See Pollack (1988, 1989).

Productivity is but one of a cluster of ideas that have come under the term 'competence' in the so-called competence/performance distinction. In general, we think, contrary to what we have frequently read and heard, this distinction is as much at home in connectionism as it is in the classical paradigm.

For any given modus ponens-ing network, there will, of course, be a limit to the size of conditional from which it will infer. But the process by which it infers should, ideally, be one which permits processing of larger conditionals as the resolution of the network increases. And, as the limits of capacity are reached, we would expect degradation to be graceful.

20 One might, for example, ask this about Chalmers' (forthcoming) system that turns active sentences into the corresponding passive.

21 We have been told that this is not correct. The relevant vector representation of the atom as a whole is the sum of vectors that are *tensor products* of (roughly) vectors that represent an electron situated in an orbital. So the analogy with connectionist tensor product representation is less close than it appears, but this does not affect Smolensky's mathematical analysis of tensor product representations, nor, as far as we can see, does it affect anything we or Smolensky say about the force of the analogy.

22 Fodor and McLaughlin say: 'It's a difference between psychology and physics that whereas psychology is about the causal laws that govern tokenings of (mental) representations, physics is about the causal laws that govern (not mental representations but) atoms, electrons and the like. Since being a representation isn't a property in the domain of physical theory, the question whether mental representations have constituents has no analog in physics (200 n.).'

But that misses the point. The analogy is between connectionist networks and physical *theory* – which does contain representations – not between connectionism and physical stuff. The point is that physical theory contains (something like) representations of the sort that seem to be wanted in connectionism.

23 What we are to suppose is that such systems are at least in principle possible. It does not have to be within human capacity to construct them.

24 Note that F&M say 'many' infrahuman organisms exhibit systematicity. It is not so clear that really simple cognitive systems are systematic. If some are not, we have an explanation of this fact which the classical picture lacks. If a cognitive system gets simple enough, maybe it does not need syntax.

25 It may also be natural for connectionist syntax in which classical constituents are constructed. But it is hard to see how the second of the two factors we shall mention could be effected with classical constituents.

26 In local representation, differences in activation might be identifiable with something at the cognitive level, like intensity or degree of belief. But this is not, in general, possible for distributed representations.

In one realization of a representation, one node might be more activated than in another realization while a different node is less activated. If two different activation patterns constitute realizations of the same representation, then differences between them will have no cognitive level correlate.

There can, of course, be (a strictly limited amount of) multiple realization in classical systems. But in classical systems, multiple realization does not, and is not supposed to, affect processing.'

27 Connectionist systems are non-linear dynamical systems. (If purely linear, they face well-known limitations like those of perceptrons.) Neural systems are probably non-linear, too. So presumably both kinds of systems have chaotic attractors and also have attractor basins with fractal boundaries. When processing is chaotic (as it will be when the system commences its activity within the boundary of a chaotic attractor or gets positioned within such a boundary by its inputs), infinitesimally small differences in the realization of a total representation-level description can rapidly amplify during processing– sensitive dependence on initial conditions. And even when processing involves evolution to a point attractor (as in connectionist networks when they 'settle' to a fixed stable state), infinitesimally small differences in initial realization of a representation- level total state can locate the system on different sides of various fractal basin boundaries. Being in one attractor basin rather than another when processing commences could dramatically affect the representation level outcome of processing.

28 For present purposes, we do not need to maintain that multiple simultaneous soft constraint satisfaction (MCSSC) is itself a source of softness, only that it compounds the softness due to multiple realizability. We believe, however, that the true nature of MCSSC in human cognition does have the consequence that human cognition is soft, i.e., that it does not conform to hard representation-level rules. The basic idea is that there is no limit to possibly relevant constraints. Hence, every true generalization concerning human decision making, belief fixation, etc. contains an *ineliminable* ceteris paribus clause. The arguments for these claims are, as one might expect, rather involved. See Horgan and Tienson (1989, 1990, forthcoming).

29 To be sure, extant toy systems that do multiple constraint satisfaction do it with representations that are not syntactically structured. It is by no means obvious that multiple constraint satisfaction can be carried out with nonclassical structured representations in a way that respects structured content.

References

Chalmers, D.J. (forthcoming). Syntactic transformations on distributed representations. *Connection Science*

– Why Fodor and Pylyshyn were wrong: the simplest refutation. Manuscript, Indiana University Center for Research on Concepts and Cognition

Dyer, M.G. (in press). Symbolic neuro-engineering for natural language processing: A multilevel research approach. In J. Barnden and J. Pollack (eds.),

Advances in Connectionist and Neural Computation Theory. Norwood, NJ: Ablex Publishing Company

– (forthcoming). Connectionism versus symbolism in high-level cognition. In T. Horgan and J. Tienson (eds.), *Connectionism and the Philosophy of Mind.* Dordrecht: Kluwer Academic Publishers

Fodor, J.A. and Pylyshyn, Z.W. (1988). Connectionism and cognitive architecture: A critical analysis. *Cognition* 28: 3-71

– and McLaughlin, B.P. (1990). Connectionism and the problem of systematicity: Why Smolensky's solution doesn't work. *Cognition* 35:183-204

Hinton, G.E. (1988). Representing part-whole heirarchies in connectionist networks. *Proceedings of the Tenth Annual Conference of the Cognitive Science Society.* 48-54

Horgan, T.E. and Tienson, J.L. (1987). Settling into a new paradigm. *Southern Journal of Philosophy,* 26:97-114

– (1989). Representations without rules. *Philosophical Topics* 17:147-74

– (1990). Soft laws. *Midwest Studies in Philosophy* 15

– (forthcoming). *Connectionism and the Philosophy of Psychology.* Cambridge, MA: MIT Press/Bradford Books

Pollack, J. (1988). Recursive auto-associative memory: Devising compositional distributed representations. *Proceedings of the Tenth Annual Conference of the Cognitive Science Society*

– (1989). Implications of recursive distributed representations. In Touretzky

– (forthcoming). Recursive distributed representations. *Artificial Intelligence*

Smolensky, P. (1987a). On variable binding and the representation of symbolic structures in connectionist systems. Technical Report CU-CS-355-87. University of Colorado at Boulder

– (1987b). The constituent structure of mental states: A reply to Fodor and Pylyshyn. *Southern Journal of Philosophy* 26:137-60

– (1988a). On the proper treatment of connectionism. *Behavioral and Brain Sciences* 11:1-23.

– (1988b). Connectionism, constituency and the language of thought. Technical Report CU-CS-416-88. University of Colorado at Boulder. To appear in Loewer, B. and Rey, G. (eds.). *Meaning in mind: Fodor and his critics.* Oxford: Blackwells

– (forthcoming). Tensor product variable binding and the representation of symbolic structures in connectionist systems. *Artificial Intelligence*

Touretzky, D.S. (ed.), (1989). *Advances in Neural Information Processing I.* San Mateo, CA: Morgan Kaufmann

– Hinton, G. and Sejnowski, T (eds.), (1989). *Proceedings of the 1988 Connectionist Summer School.* San Mateo, CA: Morgan Kaufmann

Van Gelder, T. (1990). Compositionality: A connectionist variation on a classical theme. *Cognitive Science,* 14

7

Local Modelling in Phonology

John Goldsmith

Introduction

Recent work in connectionist modelling suggests the possibility of formal models of phonological representation which will offer deeper explanations of basic phonological properties than our current models allow us. The present paper is an initial exploration of certain linguistic problems from this newer perspective.[1] It is also, as I shall explain in the final section, an effort to produce a formal phonological grammar that is neither static nor derivational – a model that is not a hybrid of the two but, in fact, different from both.

Our goal in these explorations is the traditional goal in phonological work: the development of a formal model that allows for a simple and direct account of facts within a specific language, set within the framework of an approach which allows for the statement of the principles found in other languages and yet which allows for as few unobserved sorts of principles as possible. It is of some importance for us to observe that the goals we set are those of the traditional linguist, and not – at least not directly – those of other connectionist modellers, whose goals may be informed by other theoretical questions, including (but not limited to) the issues of learnability, the relevance of particular connectionist learning techniques (such as back-propagation, for example), the significance of a memory structure that is content-addressable, or the importance of prototype effects.

None of these play a central role in the present discussion, and to that extent we may recognize that the present paper may be of more interest to the linguist than to the connectionist.[2] Nonetheless, we approach one of the best studied of the higher level cognitive functions – language, and, in particular, phonology – and anything we can learn from this subject should be of general, and perhaps particular, interest to students of mental modelling.

Principles Informing Our Approach

The properties that characterize the models we will explore are the following:

(1) *Gradience:* representations consist of a set of units, each of which is assigned an activation level, a variable that can range over all values within a real interval (in most cases, the interval being all real numbers, with a practical limitation keeping them not far from the internal (-1,1)).

(2) *Categorical effects out of gradience:* continuous-valued variables may be used to model categorical effects, either by seeking maxima and minima or by use of threshold techniques. That is, a linguistic effect may be reported as reflecting a variable (e.g., stress) which takes on only a small number of values (typically two, in which case the values may be referred to as +/-). A continuous-valued variable V within the model may be reduced to a 'categorical' variable C by establishing thresholds so that a value of V above the threshold corresponds to + C, and a value below the threshold corresponds to - C. Subthreshold effects within the variable V, however, will typically continue to play an important role in a fashion which the categorical model, induced from the continuous-valued model, cannot directly simulate. More frequently, we will look not for thresholds as such, but, rather, turning points – maxima and minima – in the curves that are developed.

(3) *Local computation:* the effects with which we will be concerned will all be the result of establishing simple arithmetic relations for the activation of neighbouring units.

(4) *Homogeneity:* we will consider a number of parameters that govern the way in which units (corresponding at times to segments and at times to syllables) affect the activation level of their neighbours (our α, β, etc., below). We will assume that these parameters are uniform within a given language and may not vary from place to place within a word. This assumption has no natural grounding in current connectionist work but seems extremely natural (indeed, unavoidable) from the point of view of the linguist.

(5) *No hidden representations:* all linguistically relevant generalizations are realized within the model as connectionist effects operating simultaneously and interacting symmetrically with each other. None can be said to apply 'before' or 'after' another.

Some Specifics of Our Proposal

The central suggestions of this paper are that:

(A) First, the organizing principles of the metrical grid, which creates feet from syllables, and the organizing principle on the skeletal tier, which creates syllables from segments on that tier, are in essence the same, though they differ in the setting of particular arithmetic parameters;

(B) Second, the metrical grid and the skeletal tier should each be modelled as a linear sequence of units in which each unit is assigned a real number for an activation value and in which each unit directly affects its (left- and right-hand) neighbours;

(C) Third, the structure we observe on the metrical grid (head and non-head positions in feet) and on the skeletal tier (onset, nucleus, and coda assignment) is the result of finding peaks and troughs and of imposing thresholds on the activation values of the elements on the grid and skeleton.

The Metrical Grid

The metrical grid is a type of phonological representation designed to express naturally the properties of stress and accent systems observed in natural languages.[3] It is an object, as in Figure 7.1, that consists, first,

```
    x                 Row 2
   x  x               Row 1
  x x x  x            Row 0
  Alabama
```

Figure 7.1

of a bottom row of positions (Row 0), each of which represents (or corresponds to, or is associated with) a syllable. Above some of these Row 0 elements may be found a Row 1 element; these syllables are those that are stressed (i.e., Row 1 markings represent simple stress). Row 0 elements with no Row 1 marking over them are unstressed. A Row 2 element, in turn, may be found on top of some of the Row 1 elements (though not over any position where a Row 1 element is not found). Such syllables, which have a Row 0, 1, and 2 element above them, are taken to bear word-level primary stress and so forth: the higher the column of markings over a Row 0 element the higher the degree of its stress. While it is nowhere written in gilt letters, it is nonetheless uncontroversial to suggest that the two fundamental properties of the metrical grid are, first, its inherent avoidance of Stress Clash, and, second, its tendency towards Perfect Grid. Stress Clash refers to the congeries of ways in which stress on consecutive syllables is avoided either by blocking a rule (such as Perfect Grid or the End Rule) from applying if that would create a stress clash or by triggering a rule of stress movement or deletion in case stress clash has arisen. Perfect Grid is the name assigned (by Prince 1982) to the rule that assigns stress to alternate syllables radiating outward (left and right) from a syllable already assigned stress. These two properties are neither explained nor explainable within grid theory nor are they related to one another within grid theory. This is, we suggest, an unsatisfactory place to leave the matter.

A local network of the sort we outlined above can shed light on this problem. We may consider a model which consists of a sequence of units, each of which conceptually correspond to a Row 0 element in the familiar grid (i.e., a syllable[4]). Units whose activations are local maxima, that is, whose activation is greater than either of its neighbours', are phonologically stressed.

Each unit inhibits its two neighbours, though not in quite identical fashion. If we say generally that the activation level of the ith element is x_i, then we will say that the ith element sends an inhibitory signal of strength $\alpha.x_i$ to the preceding element (i.e., to the i-1th element), and it sends an inhibitory signal of strength $\beta.x_i$ to the element on the right (i.e., the i+1th element), as suggested in Figure 7.2; the inhibitory relations there should be understood as being established between all pairs of neighbours. This is more explicitly given in Example 7.1, where the superscript t marks time, that is, the timing of the iterative recomputations.[5]

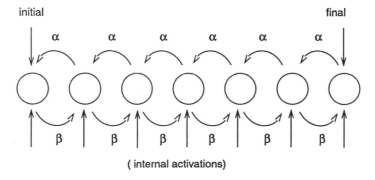

Figure 7.2: Dynamic computational network

$$x_i^{t+1} = K(i) + \alpha.x_{i+1}^t + \beta.x_{i-1}^t \qquad (1)$$

If none of the elements are activated, then the elements of the grid are all at zero level, which provides no information about stress. However, from a phonologist's point of view, the activation of a grid element is the composition of three factors:

(1) positionally-defined stress, as when, for example, the first or the penultimate syllable of a word is stressed by a general rule of the language; the amount of positional activation may be different for these two positions.

(2) the effects of Perfect Grid, i.e., the local effects of the stress of neighbouring elements; and

(3) inherent stress arising out of quantity-sensitivity, i.e., language-specific principles by which syllables with a particular internal structure are ipso facto stressed (typically, those syllables with a long vowel and often, also, those which end with a consonant) regardless of where they appear in a word.[6]

We shall not discuss the effects of quantity-sensitivity in this paper, leaving the matter to the longer treatment that it deserves. The effects of Perfect Grid may be modelled as above, with the leftward and rightward inhibitory effects indicated in Figure 7.2. In general, it is helpful to distinguish between inherent activation of an element and derived activation, where the derived activation is that produced by the effects of lateral inhibition, and inherent activation is due to the effects of positionally-defined stress or of quantity-sensitivity. Let us consider the matter of positionally-defined stress in a bit more detail.

Consider the case of a language where the first syllable is stressed. We may indicate this with a function K (mnemonically, from 'characteristic function'), defined on the indices of the grid elements, in such a fashion that $K(1)=1.0$ (i.e., the first element is activated) and $K(i)=0$ for all i other than 1.

In such a scheme, if α and β are both negative (and we assume, in this paper, that α and β are both between -1.0 and 0.0), then the positive activation of x_1 will give rise to a (negative) activation of x_2 equal to β; this, in turn, will give rise to a (positive activation) of x_3 of β^2. The negative activation of x_2 not only leads to a positive activation of x_3; it also, in turn, leads to a higher activation of x_1 through what we might call the

α=-0.2,   β=-0.7.
Syllable Number:

1	2	3	4	5
1				
1	-.70			
1.14	-.70	.49		
1.14	-.90	.49	-.34	
1.18	-.90	.70	-.34	.24
1.18	-.96	.70	-.54	.24
1.19	-.96	.78	-.54	.37
1.19	-.99	.78	-.62	.37
1.20	-.99	.82	-.62	.44
1.20	-1.00	.82	-.66	.44
1.20	-1.00	.83	-.66	.46
1.20	-1.01	.83	-.68	.46
1.20	-1.01	.84	-.68	.47
1.20	-1.01	.84	-.68	.47
1.20	-1.01	.84	-.68	.48
1.20	-1.01	.84	-.69	.48

Table 7.1

α-effect (i.e., leftward effects with a factor of α), which, in turn, leads to a cascading of effects which must then be modelled on a computer. A typical example of this is given in Table 7.1, where α = - 0.2 and β = -.7. The rows show the successive activation values of each sequential element.

This is seen graphically in Figure 7.3. The first point to notice is that the effects of Perfect Grid have been built into the local structure of this network. The α- and β-effects give rise to a pattern of alternating positive and negative numbers through local lateral inhibition of this sort, and equilibrium is quickly reached.

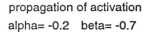

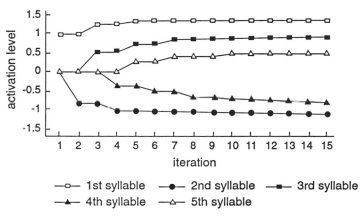

Figure 7.3: Evolution of a 5 unit system

Let us consider how Stress Clash Avoidance is also directly modelled by this system. Consider the result of placing an initial pattern of '1' unit of stress on both the first and second syllables of the word in Table 7.1 above, along with two possible settings for α and β: one where $\alpha = -0.2$, $\beta = -0.7$, and one where the settings are the opposit), i.e., where $\alpha = -0.7$, $\beta = -0.2$. The curve of the derived forms (i.e., the first and second derivatives rather than the absolute values) is what is of interest to us, and these are in Figure 7.4 and Figure 7.5.

As the final equilibrium figures show, setting one of α or β significantly higher than the other (i.e., not making them equal) leads to a situation in which, despite the inherent activation of both, only one settles into a state with an activation level close to the inherent value of 1.00. However, in both cases, only one of the elements is a local maximum and is, hence, phonologically stressed.

Indonesian

Let us now consider a recent analysis of the stress system of Indonesian offered by Cohn 1989. Cohn's analysis is placed within traditional generative terms – in particular, within the framework of lexical phonology.[7] In certain respects, her account could hardly be more at variance with the principles outlined at the beginning of this paper: the analysis relies heavily on rule ordering and on derivations in which material

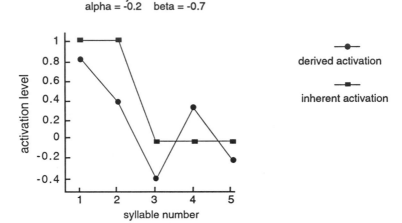

Figure 7.4: Beta-strong clash resolution

that is present at an earlier level of representation has an effect on the eventual surface form even though that material is deleted before it actually surfaces. Hers is an elegant analysis, using the resources of derivational lexical phonology in the most appropriate fashion.

Indonesian stress can be described in terms of a small number of simple principles; the facts are schematically illustrated in the bottom row of Table 7.2. Stress is applied to the penultimate syllable of a word as

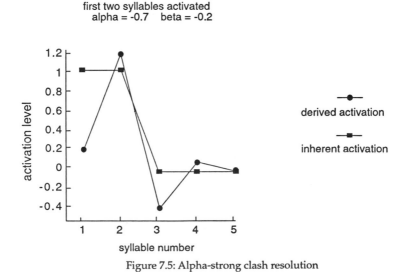

Figure 7.5: Alpha-strong clash resolution

Table 7.2: Noncyclic (monomorphemic) forms

rule	σ σ σ	σ σ σ σ	σ σ σ σ σ	σ σ σ σ σ σ
1	( )	( )	( )	( )
2	*	*	*	*
3	stress clash	*	*	*
4				*
	σ σ′ σ	σ′ σ σ′ σ	σ′ σ σ σ′ σ	σ′ σ σ′ σ σ′ σ

well as to the first syllable. If these two are adjacent (i.e., if the word has three syllables), the first syllable fails to be stressed: stress clash in this case resolves to the right-hand (penultimate) element. In addition, if the word is long enough, alternate syllables to the left of the main stressed penultimate syllable are stressed, though if this should lead to a stress on the second syllable and, hence, a clash with the first syllable, this alternating stress is suppressed. The rightmost stressed syllable is, predictably, that which receives the highest degree of stress.

These facts can be implemented in metrical grid theory, as Cohn suggests, with the ordered rules in Example 7.2. Illustrative derivations are given in Table 7.2.

(2) Indonesian (Cohn's proposal)
  (a) Final syllable is extrametrical
  (b) End Rule: Final ("Penultimate Stress')
  (c) End Rule: Initial (blocked if clash should ensue)
    'Initial Stress'
  (d) Perfect Grid (Right to Left) (blocked if clash should ensue)

Examples:

(A) bicára   'speak'
(B) bìjaksána   'wise'
(C) xàtulistíwa   'equator'
(D) òtobìográfi   'autobiography'
(E) àmerikànisási   'Americanization'

The stress system that we see in Indonesian is a clear example of the sort of system that should be modellable as well by the dynamic computational techniques discussed above. A model of the sort we have just considered, with $\alpha = -0.5$ and $\beta = 0.0$, provides precisely the right results–

Table 7.3: Monomorphemic forms

number of syllables	stress pattern	values					
3	σ σ'σ	0.20	1.0	0.0			
4	σ'σ σ'σ	0.95	-0.5	1.0	0.0		
5	σ'σ σ σ'σ	0.58	0.25	-0.5	1.0	0.0	
6	σ'σ σ'σ σ'σ	0.76	-0.13	0.25	-0.5	1.0	0.0

stress clash avoidance in the correct direction and Perfect Grid effects (i.e., alternating stress leftward from the penultimate syllable) – if we place inherent stress (our K-function) on the first and penultimate syllables: 1.0 on the penult and 0.7 on the first syllable. Needless to say, no ordering is necessary or possible. The relevant numbers are given in Table 7.3.

An especially interesting aspect of Cohn's treatment of Indonesian involves what she argues is a cyclic application of several rules, applying first to a base word to produce a derived form and then once again to a larger form 'after' a suffix is added.

The facts, as Cohn describes them, are as given in Example 7.3 for words composed of a stem plus a suffix (i.e., the case of words analyzed with two cycles), and the forms with two suffixes (analyzed with three cycles) are given in Example 7.4. The interesting cases are those where the stress is assigned in a fashion different from that found with monomorphemic forms.

(3) Two cycle case
    (A) [[σ σ'] σ
    (B) [[σ σ σ'] σ]
    (C) [[σ' σ σ σ'] σ]
    (D) [[σ' σ σ σ σ'] σ]

(4) Three cycle case
    (A) [[[σ] σ'] σ]
    (B) [[[σ' σ] σ'] σ]
    (C) [[[σ σ' σ] σ'] σ]
    (D) [[σ'σ σ' σ] σ'] σ]

A crucial case is given in Table 7.4, the case where, as Cohn shows, a monomorphemic six syllable word has a different stress pattern from a six syllable word that is composed of a five syllable base plus a suffix

Table 7.4

	σ σ σ σ σ σ
1st cycle	σ σ σ σ σ
1	( )
2	*
3	*
4	does not apply (clash avoidance)
2nd cycle	* * σ σ σ σ σ σ
1	( )
2	*
3	*
4	does not apply (clash avoidance)
output of 2nd cycle	* * * σ σ σ σ σ σ
stress clash reduction	* * σ σ σ σ σ σ
output	σ′ σ σ σ σ′ σ

added only after the base has been processed as an independent word. The derivation for the monomorphemic, noncyclic form was given above in Table 7.2; her cyclic derivational account is sketched in Table 7.4.

Cohn suggests that the missing stress on the third syllable of the bimorphemic word in Table 7.4 is due to the presence of a stress on the fourth syllable (which is the penult of the inner cycle). That 4th syllable stress is lost, however, on the second cycle, when the 5th syllable receives a stress (it now being the penultimate syllable in the word), and the 4th syllable loses its stress due to the effects of an additional stress-deleting rule that applies when stress clash arises.

Our present model derives the correct result with a good deal less machinery than Cohn's and with no intermediate hidden representations. The values generated are given in Figure 7.6a, and are, as we see, accurate predictions. These results are derived by interpreting cyclicity

surface stress

[σ′	σ	σ′	σ	σ′	σ]
0.76	-.13	0.25	-.50	1.0	0.0

monomorphemic six syllable word

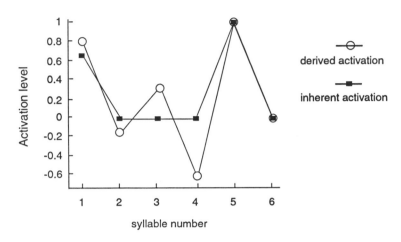

Figure 7.6a: Six syllable word

not as a derivational notion but, rather, as a statement about phonological structure.[8] Thus in a six syllable word of the sort in Figure 7.6b, the fourth syllable is the penult of the inner word (and thus receives a positional activation of 1.0), while the fifth syllable is also the penultimate syllable – of the outer word; it too receives positional activation of 1.0. Quite generally, to say that a structure is cyclic is to say that it has nested phonological word structure (i.e., structure of the form

$$[_{W2} \ [_{W1} \ xx \ ]_W \ yy \ ]_{W2}).$$

Some words quite transparently have internal word structure, such as the word *Indianaism*, for example, which plainly contains the word *Indiana*, or the compound *driftwood*, containing a sequence — *ft* — which would not be possible as a word-internal coda. Not all morphologically derived words are of this phonological form; *Buddhism*, for example, is derived from *Buddha* + *ism*, but undergoes effects occasioned by the lack of any internal word structure. In short, phonological structure and morphological structure are different; and those robust effects traditionally ascribed to cyclicity are due to nested phonological word structure.[9]

Hence if a language assigns stress to the penultimate syllable of a word, and a nested phonological structure is found, then both the 4th

surface stress

[[σ′	σ	σ′	σ	σ′]	σ]
0.64	0.13	-0.25	-.50	1.0	0.0

two 'cycles': bimorphemic, six syllables

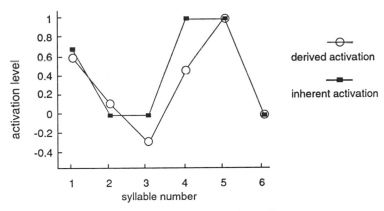

derived activation

inherent activation

Figure 7.6b: Five syllable word plus suffix

and the 5th syllables will receive inherent activation in their capacities as the penult of the internal and the external phonological word, respectively.

As we see in Figure 7.6b, as well, the activation assigned to the 4th syllable has an effect without leading to that syllable being stressed on the surface. At the same time, this result is achieved without hidden representations; it is, rather, achieved by means of a crucial character of the model – the presence of significant subthreshold difference. As we can see, the 4th syllable's activation value is strikingly different in Figure 7.6a and b; this difference is the sum total of the effects on that syllable, and this difference, in both cases, has an effect on the lack of stress on the syllable that precedes it. On the other hand, as we have seen, there are no hidden representations; the forces at work affect each other simultaneously and seek a stable resolution of their requirements.

We present in Table 7.5 and Table 7.6 the relevant calculations of all the forms.

Syllabification

The local dynamic computational models of phonological systems which are being explored in this paper were originally motivated by the study of syllabification systems.[10] In this section I will only sketch this

number of syllables	stress pattern	values					
3	σ σ' σ	0.50	1.0	0.0			
4	σ σ σ' σ	0.45	0.5	1.0	0.0		
5	σ' σ σ σ' σ	0.83	-0.25	0.5	1.0	0.0	
6	σ' σ σ σ σ' σ	0.64	0.13	-0.25	0.5	1.0	0.0

Table 7.5: Two cycle forms

number of syllables	stress pattern	values					
3	σ σ' σ	0.50	1.0	0.0			
4	σ' σ σ' σ	0.75	0.5	1.0	0.0		
5	σ σ' σ σ' σ	0.33	0.75	0.5	1.0	0.0	
6	σ' σ σ' σ σ' σ	0.89	-0.38	0.75	0.5	1.0	0.0

Table 7.6: Three cycle forms

issue in very broad strokes and will leave a detailed discussion for another place.[11]

We hypothesize that the characteristics that we have established for stress systems (i.e., for our interpretation of metrical grids) hold equally of the skeletal tier, and that the envelope – the ups and downs – of activation of the skeletal positions is interpreted linguistically as syllable structure, in precisely the same way that the ups and downs of the grid positions are interpreted (in more and less complex ways) as stress and foot structuring.

We drew a distinction above regarding inherent activation and derived activation that remains quite useful for us. When we focus on syllabification and the skeletal tier, we are soon led to the conclusion that the *inherent* activation of a segment is its (inherent) sonority, while the derived activation is a contextually determined function of its inherent sonority.

Why should this be? The answer is not hard to see. Sonority is, fundamentally, the propensity that a segment has to be the nucleus of a syllable. The most sonorous segment, *a*, has no choice; it must be the nucleus of its syllable. The least sonorous elements, the voiceless stops, have the least chance to be located in the nucleus of their respective syllables. Segments in between vary with respect to whether they will be nuclear, and the ways in which they vary involve both language-particular determinants (*l* may be syllabic in English but not in Spanish) and contextual determinants (*l* is not syllabic before a stressed syllable in the same word).

Thus we may consider the possibility that the determination of syllabification involves the same kind of contextual calculations involving inherent sonority and relative position that we considered in the preceding work. Elements with an activation above a certain threshold (call it N) will in effect play the role of the nucleus of their syllable; those below a certain threshold (call it O) are onset elements; and those with an activation level between O and N are coda elements.

```
       ---> increasing derived activation
---------------- | -------------------- | ---------------------
   onset    O        coda    N              nucleus
```

The models of lateral inhibition we have considered so far have the natural property that, in the absence of any inherent activation, they create up and down waves that change direction with each unit. In the simplest case, as we have seen, this create a situation in which the derived activations are alternating between positive and negative numbers. If we consider the trivial case where the two thresholds are both zero (O=N=0.0), then this statement amounts to the natural observation that if one could speak a spoken language without using any segments at all it would consist of sequences of onset-nucleus (... ONONONON ...): that is, the rhythmicity of syllabification follows as much from the network organization of the phonological system as it does from the choice of the segments themselves.

The Broader Picture

There is another motivation for the work that has been reported in this paper that goes beyond interest in connectionist-type modelling of phonological processes. In several recent papers (Goldsmith 1989, 1990), I have argued for a conception of phonological theory that is neither static nor derivational. Work to date on phonological theory has largely assumed – implicitly – that, much along the lines of M. Jourdan's tutor's approach, any theory that was not static in design was ipso facto derivational. The approach that I have been developing – which I call 'harmonic phonology' – posits three phonological levels (M-level, W-level, and P-level) and also posits dynamic processes on each level. Thus each level is not static; it does not consist of a single representation. However, the structural modifications that occur on each level are not just part of the wide range of effects possible within the confines of a production system (i.e., traditional generative rules); all changes serve to increase the well-formedness of a structure in a fashion that is constant across the language.

However, it is no simple task to elaborate a theory of phonological representation *cum* theory of dynamic simplification from scratch. The present research is offered as one case study – one example – of this sort. The construction of accent patterns and of syllabification is now widely regarded, correctly, as a significant portion of the phonology of any given spoken language, and the present systems are offered as an example of how a dynamic, but nonderivational, phonology may be considered as a live, interesting, and explanatory alternative to the generative conception.

Notes

1 I am grateful for very helpful discussions with Tom Bever and most especially with Gary Larson, who has made several suggestions that have substantively improved this paper; I am also grateful to members of the audience at the presentation of some of this material at the University of Rochester; Michael Tanenhaus made some suggestions that have been incorporated here. In earlier stages of this work, I also appreciated helpful comments by David Corina, Jeff Elman, Mary Hare, George Lakoff, and David Perlmutter, and, especially, Caroline Wiltshire. This paper was written in December, 1989, and revised in May, 1991. This material is based in part upon work supported by the National Science Foundation under Grant No. BNS 9000678.

2 I also presume a familiarity with both the style and content of phonological research.

3 For a detailed description of the metrical grid, the reader may consult Goldsmith 1990, Chapter 4.

4 Or perhaps a mora; see Goldsmith 1990 for discussion.

5 A brief mathematical excursus may be of interest to some readers. If we consider the effect of the network as a mathematical operator applying to the vector which represents the state of the network at any given moment t, then that operator M is built simply out of an n by n matrix, where n is the number of units. We define M as being zero everywhere except on the supradiagonal, the diagonal above the major diagonal, where it is α (i.e., $x_{i,i+1} = \alpha$), and the subdiagonal, where it is β (i.e., $x_{i,i-1} = \beta$). If we call the initial state of the system the vector $\mathbf{v}$, then after k iterations, the system is in a state defined by $\mathbf{v} + M^k(v)$, where M^k is the kth power of M.

6 See Goldsmith 1990, Chapters 3 and 4, and references there.

7 See Kiparsky 1982, and also Goldsmith 1990, Chapter 5.

8 This point is discussed in greater detail in Goldsmith 1990 and in print.

9 That phonological word structure can be nested (i.e., recursive) is no more surprising than that syntactic structure can and, in a sense, must be: we find full finite (tensed) clauses within other finite clauses, quite obviously, and hardly give the matter a moment's thought. On the other hand, just as a word can be combined with another morpheme and not retain its character as a phonological word, so too can a sentence be combined as part of a larger sentence and not maintain its independent syntactic status; in the literature, this is known as clause union.

10 I have gained much from conversations with Gary Larson, of the University of Chicago, on this topic; Larson is also developing some approaches of his own to local modelling in phonology. My thinking has also been influenced here by recent unpublished work by G.N. Clements on sonority slopes and their relation to well-formed syllabification.

11 Larson and I have several papers in progress on this point. Two early discussions have appeared: Goldsmith and Larson 1990 and Larson 1990.

References

Clements, G.N. (1990). The role of the sonority cycle in core syllabification. In John Kingston and Mary Beckman (eds.), *Between the Grammar and the Physics of Speech: Papers in Laboratory Phonology 1*. New York: Cambridge University Press

Cohn, A.C. (1989). Stress in Indonesian and bracketing paradoxes. *Natural Language and Linguistic Theory* 7:167-216

Dell, F. and Mohamed E., (1985). Syllabic consonants and syllabification in imdlawn Tashlhiyt Berber. *Journal of African Languages and Linguistics* 7:2. 105-30

Goldsmith, J. (1989). Licensing, inalterability, and harmonic rule application. In R. Graczyk, B. Music, and C. Wiltshire (eds.), *Papers from the 25th Annual Regional Meeting of the Chicago Linguistic Society* 145-56

– (1990). *Autosegmental and Metrical Phonology*. Oxford and Cambridge, MA: Basil Blackwell

– (forthcoming). Phonology as an intelligent system. To appear in D.J. Napoli and J. Kegl (eds.), *Bridges Between Psychology and Linguistics: A Swarthmore Festschrift for Lila Gleitman*. Lawrence Erlbaum 247-67

– Manuscript. Harmonic phonology. Presented at the Berkeley Workshop on Nonderivational Phonology, May 1989. To appear in *The Last Phonological Rule: Proceedings of the Workshop*

– and G. Larson. (1990). Local modelling and syllabification. In K. Deaton, M. Noske, and M. Ziolkowski (eds.),*Papers from the 26th Annual Regional Meeting of the Chicago Linguistic Society: Parasession on the Syllable in Phonetics and Phonology*

Halle, M. and J.-R. Vergnaud. (1987). *An Essay on Stress*. Cambridge: MIT Press

Kiparsky, P. (1982). Lexical phonology and morphology. In I.-S. Yang (ed.), *Linguistics in the Morning Calm*, Seoul: Hanshin. 3-91

Larson, G.(1990). Local connectionist networks and the distribution of segments in the Spanish syllable. In K. Deaton, M.Noske, and M. Ziolkowski (eds.), *Papers from the 26th Annual Regional Meeting of the Chicago Linguistic Society: Parasession on the Syllable in Phonetics and Phonology*

Liberman, M. (1979). *The Intonational System of English*. New York: Garland Press

— and A. Prince. (1977). On stress and linguistic rhythm. *Linguistic Inquiry* 8:249-336

Prince, A. (1983). Relating to the grid. *Linguistic Inquiry* 14:19-100

8

Connectionism and the Philosophy of Mental Representation

William Ramsey

Introduction

Undoubtedly one of the biggest challenges facing any physicalist account of the mind is to provide a fully naturalistic explanation of mental representation. Discussions concerning naturalized accounts of mental representation have typically focused on two central questions: (1) In virtue of what, exactly, are we justified in calling some entity or state a representation of something else, and (2) what form or structure does such a representation take in a cognitive system? In short, how do we account for the content of a representation, and how do we account for its form? Traditionally, it has been considered the business of philosophy to come up with answers to the first sort of question and the job of empirical science to answer questions of the second sort. However, it is becoming increasingly clear that the two issues are much more closely intertwined than was formerly assumed. The sorts of philosophical stories we tell about what it is for something to be a representation can place strong constraints on the sorts of accounts we give of their form and, more importantly for this essay, vice-versa.

Below, I want to consider the sort of 'How' stories that get told in connectionist research and explore the implications they might have for philosophical accounts of mental representation. My claim will be that if at least some of what connectionists have to say about the structure of representation turns out to be true, then this will have important ramifications for philosophical theories of mental states and processes.

To show all this, the essay will be organized in the following way. In PHILOSOPHICAL ACCOUNTS OF REPRESENTATION, I will present the philosophical tradition, sketching various positions taken by philosophers who have offered analyses of the notion of mental representation. I will argue that despite their philosophical origin, all of these accounts make fairly strong presuppositions about representation structure. These views will be divided into two groups, depending on whether the mental representation is thought to be of a concept or of a proposition. Subsequent divisions will then be made within both groups, and views will be classified according to the sorts of internal structure they assume representations to have. In CONNECTIONIST REPRESENTATIONS, I will turn to the connectionist account of the representation structure. In fact, there is no single account here but, instead, a collection of different representation types and styles which are not always carefully distinguished in the literature. Fortunately, we can limit our analysis to four connectionist hypotheses of representation structure that directly impinge on the philosophical views sketched in PHILOSOPHICAL ACCOUNTS OF REPRESENTATION. Finally, in PHILOSOPHICAL IMPLICATIONS OF CONNECTIONIST REPRESENTATIONS, I will explore the philosophical implications of these connectionist accounts of representation. We will see how the success of certain connectionist models will in some cases undermine and in other cases support the different stories philosophers tell about representation and higher cognitive process.

Philosophical Accounts of Representation

At first blush, it may seem a bit odd to suppose that philosophers have anything interesting to say about the form or structure of mental representations, regardless of whether they are of concepts or of propositions. After all, this seems to be an empirical matter to be decided by careful investigation in some other area of cognitive science, such as psychology or neuroscience. Nonetheless, a considerable amount of both traditional and contemporary work in the philosophy of mind and epistemology has rested on strong presuppositions about the sort of form taken by representations of concepts and propositions in the mind/brain. Consequently, philosophers now endorse a fairly diverse range of positions regarding the way information is encoded in a cognitive system. The first set of views I want to look at are those regarding the structure of mental representations of concepts.

Philosophical views on the representation of concepts

Before beginning, I should say that my focus will be on 'lexical' concepts, which are expressible in a given language with a morphologically simple (monomorphemic) predicate term, such as DOG or HOUSE.[1] These are to be distinguished from 'phrasal' concepts, which are expressible only with morphologically complex predicates, like LARGE BLUE DOG-HOUSE.[2] As we shall see in our discussion of propositions, a popular theory of the mind/brain regards lexical concepts as mental words which comprise the vocabulary of our 'language of thought.' But regardless of our theory of propositional structure, we can divide the philosophical views on the structure of concepts according to their commitment to an internal structure. Here, we need only posit two subclasses – those which require the representations of concepts to have compositional structure and those which do not.

The empiricist account of concepts

The standard empiricist picture of concept structure assumes that most lexical concepts are constructed out of more primitive, sensory-level representations, which are initially provided by experience. Empiricism takes a 'building-block' view of the structure and acquisition of basic lexical concepts such as HOUSE and GRANDMOTHER and, thus, regards them as having a rich internal structure. As Hume puts it,

> Simple perceptions or impressions and ideas are such as admit of no distinction nor separation. The complex are the contrary to these, and may be distinguished into parts. Tho' a particular color, taste, and smell are qualities all united together in this apple, 'tis easy to perceive they are not the same, but are at least distinguishable from each other[3]

Here, Hume regards the inner constituents of concepts to be primitive sense impressions. Another empiricist tradition took the inner constituents to be a set of singly necessary and jointly sufficient conditions which defined the concept's extension. This definitional view has been all but abandoned by modern empiricists, most of whom feel it has been seriously undermined by studies in cognitive psychology.[4] Rather than viewing the building blocks of concepts as necessary and sufficient conditions, most empiricists now regard them as prototypical features and properties. On this version of empiricism, we represent concepts by representing a set of common, prototypical primitive properties that are possessed by most members of the concept's extension. Hence, on this view, something qualifies as an instance of a concept if it possesses some (but not necessarily all) of the prototypical features which collectively form the representation of the concept in our mind/brain.

Given this account of concept structure, the empiricist can explain the acquisition of new lexical concepts by supposing that they are built up from primitive, sensory-level concepts or impressions. To help understand this process of joining together atomic primitives to create lexical concepts, empiricists have posited a variety of mental mechanisms, including principles of association and imagination. This account of concept structure further enables the empiricist to explain how we can create concepts of things we have not experienced, such as unicorns.

Of course, if one assumes that lexical concepts are constructed out of more primitive/sensory concepts (as does the empiricist), then one must also assume that lexical concepts can be represented in the mind/brain in a way that will support this compositional structure. In other words, the standard empiricist account of concept acquisition requires an encoding architecture sufficiently fine-grained to accommodate the internal compositional form of concepts. This means that the architecture must encode units or structures whose semantic interpretation is more primitive and atomic than the lexical concepts for which they serve as constituents. If, for example, our representation of APPLE is thought to be made up of more primitive, sensory-level parts (e.g., a certain colour and taste), then our cognitive architecture must have structures corresponding to these parts, and it must be able to hook them together in whatever manner is suitable for representing this concept. If, on the other hand, the smallest unit of semantic significance provided by the encoding architecture is no more primitive than the lexical concept itself, then, clearly, the empiricist account of concept structure and acquisition will have to be abandoned. For the empiricist, the underlying architecture must accommodate an internal, compositional structure for concepts, and it must do so in a way that is compatible with whatever assumptions empiricists make about the way various primitives are combined and interact with one another.

The nativist (or rationalist) view of concepts

For the conceptual nativist, lexical concepts like HOUSE and APPLE are not acquired or developed through learning but, instead, are 'triggered' through causal interactions with the environment.[5] In other words, non-sensory lexical concepts are thought to, in some sense, lie dormant in the cognitive system until 'awakened' by the appropriate external (or internal) stimulus. To quote Fodor, 'According to the nativist view the story that empiricists tell about sensory concepts also holds for a wide range of non-sensory lexical concepts: viz. that they are triggered but unlearned.'[6]

If this is so, then there is clearly no need for the nativist to require that representations of concepts have a composite internal structure. If one assumes that lexical concepts are simply triggered by environmental stimulus, then there is no motivation for assuming the encoding architecture must capture smaller, more primitive, semantic units. Indeed, any evidence against the claim that conceptual representations have compositional structure is, ipso facto, evidence supporting nativism.

Fodor, for example, adopts just this line of reasoning in defense of nativism, arguing that 'lexical concepts are typically unstructured, hence typically primitive, hence typically unlearned.'[7] For the conceptual nativist, then, the smallest unit of semantic significance which the architecture must accommodate is no smaller than the entire lexical concept.

While there are other philosophically relevant aspects of the issue of concept structure, its implications for the empiricist/nativist debate is the most important. As Fodor puts it, 'Roughly, what empiricists and nativists disagree about is the structure of lexical concepts.'[8] If this is so, then the success of cognitive models which put forth explicit accounts of representation structure will have enormous implications for this venerable philosophical debate. Before looking at such models, however, we must turn to the various ways philosophers have been equally committed to certain accounts of the way we represent propositions in the mind/brain.

Philosophical views on the structure of propositional representations

Before looking at the philosophical assumptions about the structure of propositional representations, it should be noted that philosophers are hardly in complete agreement over just what a proposition is.[9] Hence, when we say a given state or structure is the representation of a proposition, exactly what it is that is being represented is somewhat problematic. Moreover, as we will soon see, the account of representation structure philosophers endorse is often inspired by their views on what propositions are. But for now, it will suffice to regard a propositions as truth-conditions or states of affairs expressible by any ordinary declarative sentence of a public language, such as 'Snow is white.' A *propositional attitude* is commonly regarded as a mental state – typically a belief or desire – that is best described as an attitude towards a particular proposition which is represented in the mind/brain. The *way* in which propositions are represented in the cognitive system is the central question of this section.

While there are a number of ways one might go about categorizing philosophical views on this matter, I will opt for a classification scheme similar to the one used above for categorizing theories of concepts. This scheme, borrowed in part from Fodor,[10] divides philosophers according to the degree of compositional structure they assume propositional representations to have. Here again, the central diagnostic question used for classifying views will be, *'What is the smallest semantic unit which the encoding representational structure must accommodate?'* I will suggest that answers to this question fall into three major classes, all of which are motivated by concerns over accounting for the semantics of mental representations. My analysis will begin with what is arguably the most popular of these views – the one assuming the most fine-grained structure for propositional representations.

The quasi-linguistic picture

Undoubtedly one of the most prevailing (if not *the* most prevailing) recent accounts of mental processes is the view commonly known as the 'Language of Thought.' This position has been endorsed by authors such as Hartry Field, Jerry Fodor, Gilbert Harman, William Lycan, John Macnamara, Colin McGinn, Zenon Pylyshyn, Michael Devitt, Kim Sterelny, and countless others working in both philosophy and other areas of cognitive science.[11] While there are many variations on the theme, the basic idea is that thinking is, in many important ways, analogous to speaking.[12] That is, entertaining a proposition involves the construction of a complex thought by combining atomic mental units (often viewed as concepts) in much the same way that speech involves the construction of complex sentences out of atomic words. On this view, just as there are rules which restrict the way words can be combined to form sentences of a natural language, so, too, there are rules which guide the way concepts can be combined to form beliefs. The quasi-linguistic picture assumes that thought has a vocabulary and a syntax – just like language.

For our purposes, what needs emphasizing is just how strongly the quasi-linguistic view presupposes a certain account of representation structure. According to this picture, propositions are represented in a quasi-linguistic or sentence-like form with an *internal syntactic* structure. Just as the sentence 'Snow is white' is made up of the words 'snow,' 'is,' and 'white,' so, too, according to this view, the mental representation of the proposition that snow is white is composed of mental correlates of these words (i.e., concepts) such as SNOW and WHITE (assuming the copula itself need not be specifically represented) 'arranged' in the mind/brain in some appropriate way. And, of course, this requires propositional representations to have an internal compositional structure which reflects the syntactic and semantic structure of the proposition. Without this, the central idea behind the quasi-linguistic view – viz. to account for the content of propositional representations by appealing to a combinatorial semantics – would be lost. Hence, propositions must be represented in a way that will accommodate this internal structure. As Fodor puts it, 'LOT [Language of Thought] claims that *mental states ... typically have constituent structure.*'[13] Consequently, on this view, the atomic structural units which lend themselves to semantic evaluability must be smaller than the entire propositional representation. They must be concepts or mental words which can be conjoined in certain syntactically appropriate ways to form propositional representations. Therefore, the quasi-linguistic view requires the encoding architecture to accommodate representations more primitive (both semantically and syntactically) than propositions, and it must do this in a way that captures their syntactic role as constituents of propositions.

The monadic picture

At the next level of representational structure is a view I shall call the *'monadic'* account. Here we find those philosophers who deny that the representation of a proposition must have any sort of internal structure. Authors endorsing this position are Tyler Burge, Fred Dretske, and Brian Loar.[14] As we noted above, the quasi-linguistic picture explains the content of the representation by appealing to the content(s) of its component parts. In this way the meaning of the representation is attributable to matters concerning its *internal* make-up. And, of course, this requires the representation to *have* an internal make-up. In contrast to this, monadic theorists assume that the content of a propositional representation stems not from its inner construction but from *external* relational considerations that have nothing to do with the internal structure of the representation. For example, Loar assumes that the semantics of a representation is determined by its functional role in a rich cognitive system made up of other representational states, along with certain causal links to the world. Similarly, Dretske fixes the propositional content of a representation by appealing to its ability to indicate certain aspects of the environment, combined with its influence on certain behaviours. Hence, to account for a propositional representation's semantics, the monadic theorists appeal to the way a given representation *interacts* with other representations and features of the cognitive system.

Regarding representation structure, the important point to note is that, as far as monadic theorists are concerned, the internal structure of the representation is completely irrelevant. As Loar puts it, the monadic picture 'does not imply that the *first-order* states which realize the relevant functional roles must themselves have an internal structure that resembles the syntax of a language.'[15] And Dretske notes that it 'is not ... its *form* or its *shape*, but the fact that it stands in certain *relations*'[16] that is relevant to the representation's content. Of course, it is not necessary for the monadic theorist to deny that the representation have any sort of compositional structure or form. The crucial point, however, is that this structure is irrelevant to its serving as a representation of a proposition. Thus, a proposition that we might express with a long and complicated sentence of English could be encoded by a single, unstructured state or entity. What *does* matter for the monadic position – the sort of structural requirement it imposes – is that the encoding architecture be fine-grained enough to accommodate distinct, functionally discrete, fully distinguishable representations of separate propositions. That is, whereas the monadic view does not require constituents of propositions to be represented in any way, the propositions *themselves* must be fully represented by functionally discrete structures.

Hence, the smallest structural unit of semantic evaluability required by the monadic view need not be smaller than the entire proposition. In this way, the monadic account places a weaker constraint on cognitive architecture than the quasi-linguistic view, because it makes no demands on the internal make-up of the representation. Nonetheless, it does require an encoding architecture that possesses enough structure to represent different propositions as functionally distinct and discernible states.

Structural holism

By far the most difficult set of philosophical views on representation structure is that which I will call 'structural holism.' According to this picture, distinct propositions do not require even monadic representation. It is important to distinguish this version of holism from other forms, such as the sort of semantic holism that claims belief content stems from other functionally separate beliefs that are distinctly represented (as we saw with the monadic theory). Structural holists allow holism not just for the semantic nature of mental representation but for the structural nature as well. At times, the writings of Daniel Dennett suggest something like this, as do the writings of Robert Stalnaker and, to a lesser extent, the work of Quine and Ryle.[17] The shared intuition between these authors is that the proper way to account for the semantic properties of propositional representations is not by appealing to their internal make-up, nor by focusing upon their functional relations with one another but, rather, by appealing to certain *dispositional* states of the cognitive system. Generally, these are determined by the system's behavioural profile along with whatever environmental stimuli serve to bring about this profile. Adopting and summarizing Dennett's position, Stalnaker puts the matter succinctly:

> Belief and desire, the strategy suggests, are correlative dispositional states of
> a potentially rational agent. To desire that P is to be disposed to act in ways
> that would tend to bring it about that P in a world in which one's beliefs,

whatever they are, were true. To believe that P is to be disposed to act in ways that would tend to satisfy one's desires, whatever they are, in a world in which P (together with one's other beliefs) were true ... Beliefs have determinate content because of their presumed causal connections to the world. Beliefs are *beliefs* rather than some other representational state, because of their connection, through desire, with action.[18]

Hence, a strictly 'forward looking' dispositional account (i.e., one based strictly on what the system will do) is supplemented by an appeal to the causes of the dispositions in order to capture the content of mental representations.[19]

For present purposes, we need not worry about the various difficulties with this account, such as its unabashed parallels with philosophical behaviourism, the apparent circularity stemming from defining beliefs in terms of desires, and vice versa. In fact, structural holists have offered compelling rebuttals to many of these concerns.[20] Instead, we must concentrate on the sorts of structural demands this account makes for propositional representations. If we assume that propositional attitudes are to be captured by dispositional states, what kinds of constraints does this place on the way propositions are actually represented in the cognitive system? The answer given by most holists is that we no longer need to assume that individual propositions are represented by structurally discrete states or components of the system. For the holist, there is no one-to-one mapping from individual propositions to distinct dispositional states. Recall that a central difficulty with the behaviourist's treatment of dispositions was that, in fact, having a belief in certain situations need not lead to any one particular behaviour, since the behaviour in question will typically depend on a large number of the agents' *other* propositional attitudes. So, for example, we can assume that having the belief that dogs have tails will, in certain situations, lead to appropriate verbal behaviour *only if* we also assume that the cognizer believes that it is appropriate to speak, desires to speak truthfully, knows the proper words, and so on for a wide range of propositional attitudes. Hence, if you want to be a dispositionalist, then you need to recognize that there can be no mappings between dispositional states and individual propositional attitudes. According to the structural holist, the best one can do is to identify a given disposition with an entire set of propositional attitudes. This, in effect, removes the sort of structural constraints on the cognitive system that the quasi-linguistic and monadic theorists required for content ascriptions of propositional attitudes. If the content of a given propositional attitude is dependant upon all the other propositional attitudes taken together, then there is no need to assume a representation structure any more fine-grained than that entire set.

Indeed, structural holists often go on to argue that, in fact, propositions are not encoded by discrete structures. For example, Dennett states,

> There need not, and cannot, be a separately specifiable state of the mechanical elements for each of the myriad intentional ascriptions, and thus it will not in many cases be possible to isolate any feature of the system at any level of abstraction and say, 'This and just this is the feature in the design of this system responsible for those aspects of its behaviour in virtue of which we ascribe to it the belief that p.[21]

Dennett does not maintain that it is false, strictly speaking, to attribute propositional representations to such a system. But it is wrong to assume that propositions are represented by distinct and specifiable states which can be distinguished by appealing to the system's structural make-up. Similarly, Stalnaker suggests we need not assume that propositions are represented in the mind/brain by discrete, structurally isolable states. Instead, we can assume that they are represented by one holistic 'belief state' corresponding to a set of possible worlds. As he puts it,

> A state of knowledge or belief should not be thought of as something with propositions as components at all ... a system of beliefs need not be thought of as a list of sentence-like items. Propositions are not components but characteristics of a belief state, ways of distinguishing between the possible worlds that define a belief state.[22]

Thus, what emerges from these theorists' portrayal of propositional attitudes is a picture of mental representation that does not require individual propositions to be represented by structurally distinguishable states. As with the monadic view, this account need not deny that the encoding architecture involves *some* structure. But the salient structural divisions, components, etc., need not correspond to different propositions represented by the system. Because the structural holist relies on the organism's behavioural profile in certain environments to account for the content of its propositional representations, he places relatively weak demands on the encoding architecture. On this view, the smallest unit of semantic evaluability that the encoding structure need accommodate is the *entire* set of stored propositions.

A further dimension of representation structure

This completes my analysis of the different sorts of structural assumptions philosophers make regarding propositional representations. It is worth noting that the more popular theories among philosophers assume the finest grain of compositional structure. The more fine-grained the analysis, the greater the number of philosophers whose theories require it. Hence, that cognitive models of representation structure are more coarse-grained suggests that a considerable amount of philosophical theorizing is seriously misguided. But before looking at such cognitive models, I need to make a further distinction that is important for our understanding of both propositional and conceptual mental representations.

The structure of a given representation is just one of its many properties. Another important property – although seldom discussed in philosophical circles – is the degree to which a given representation is activated or causally implicated in the cognitive system's internal processing. For it is at least possible that we need to tell *different* structural stories of a given representation when it is in different states of activation. That is, when active, the representation may take on a different structural form than when it is inert. For example, a stored belief or concept may lack a certain degree of compositionality which it (somehow) comes to acquire when invoked during the system's processing. If the encoding system entailed something like this, then activation level must be included as an indispensable dimension of representation form, and philosophical assumptions would have to be adjusted accordingly.

To summarize this section, many philosophers make fairly strong assumptions about the structure or form assumed by mental representations of both concepts and propositions. Regarding conceptual representations, the question of internal structure is a crucial issue in the empiricism-nativism debate, with empiricists arguing that representations of concepts have a compositional form and nativists arguing that they do not. Regarding propositional representations, philosophers again disagree on the amount of compositional structure which the encoding architecture must capture. Views on this matter are typically motivated by the sort of theory put forth regarding the semantic properties of representations. Quasi-linguistic theorists endorse a compositional semantics, so they require propositional representations to have an internal structure resembling a sentence. Monadic theorists endorse a functional/inferential-role semantics and, thereby, require a relational structure between individually represented propositions. Structural holists adopt a dispositional account of semantics and, consequently, assume only a holistic encoding of information that need not admit the structural discernibility of propositions. Finally, I noted that representations might adopt different forms when in different states of activity, and that systems with this feature might cross-classify philosophical views on structure. We are now in a position to look closely at the connectionist account of representation structure – both for concepts and for propositions.

Connectionist Representations

It is important to begin by noting that, while connectionists do indeed have a good deal to say about the way propositions and concepts are represented, there is no single, unified account endorsed by all connectionists. Just as we saw that there are many philosophical stories of representation, so, too, in the connectionist paradigm, there are many variations and versions which must be properly distinguished. However, before looking at the specific details of these different styles of connectionist representation, it will be useful to elaborate a bit on their general features.

Some general aspects of connectionist representations

In some connectionist models individual units, or the joint activation of several units, are assigned a fixed content by the system's (human) designer. Here, units or activation patterns are designated to stand for certain prototypical properties of things (commonly called 'micro-features' in connectionist parlance), lexical concepts, or even full-blown propositions.[23] However, it is well known that many current connectionist networks come to acquire their ability to perform various computations through some form of learning. In many of these models, the learning process itself bestows upon certain structures a representational status. Generally, such networks have a set of input units, a set of output units, and one (or more) intermediary layer of 'hidden' units, which can be connected to other layers in a variety of ways. The acquired representations in such networks are typically 'stored' in the system's post-learning connection-weight configuration. When activated, however, many modellers believe that individual representations are manifested by patterns of activity in the hidden units. Since individual units can act in analog fashion (taking a value anywhere between zero per cent and one hundred per cent), a small number of units can produce a very large number of different activation patterns and, thus, a large number of different representations. As we shall soon see, this way of forming representations is quite unlike anything put forth in the past.

One general issue which cannot be ignored is a vexing philosophical worry about the validity of calling elements of such cognitive systems representations. That is, a question often asked about such models is, why, exactly, should anyone feel compelled to view the states or components of these networks as representations of any sort whatsoever? As we just noted, in some networks, the answer is easy: certain components or states of the network are regarded as representations of particular concepts or propositions for the same reasons we regard structures in more conventional systems as representations – namely, because we just *stipulate* it to be so. However, besides the usual worries about 'derived' and 'original' intentionality associated with this response, it is also inappropriate for connectionist models where representations are supposedly learned rather than stipulated. What is it about these latter systems that warrants the assumption that they represent anything at all?

Although this matter is seldom explicitly addressed by connectionists, I suspect their underlying motivation for calling certain features of their model representations is much in the spirit of 'indicator' stories of natural semantics, endorsed most recently by philosophers such as Dretske, Stalnaker, Stampe, and others.[24] According to these philosophers, a state's causal (or correlational) relations with aspects of the environment, perhaps in conjunction with certain of its functional properties, serve to justify our calling it a representation. Similarly, for connectionist networks where representations are learned, inner states or structures are regarded as representing concepts or propositions in virtue of their causes and the role they play in the production of the model's output. One way to think of connectionist learning is to view it as a way of modifying the system so that unusable internal states (e.g., hidden unit activation patterns) initially caused by certain inputs are abandoned and replaced with more appropriate, functionally useful states. Since these new states are brought about through learning, and acquire a function of representing the input in an appropriate way, we can (perhaps with some caution) say that such systems acquire representations which they previously lacked.

Of course, something further needs to be said about just what it is for an internal state, such as an activation pattern, to have a function of representing the system's input 'appropriately.' Providing a plausible account of this is currently the research program for a number of philosophers. While we need not dwell on this issue, it bears noting that what matters in connectionist models is not just the relationship between the activation pattern and its cause but also the similarity relationship between the activation pattern and *other* activation patterns produced by other inputs. During learning, a network will typically develop a way of organizing its representations so that different inputs come to be represented as belonging to partitioned classes or groups (which may themselves be hierarchically ordered into various subgroups). One common strategy for discovering these divisions is to do what is commonly known as a 'vector analysis' on the hidden units. If we plot the activation values of individual hidden units so that they form different dimensions in an abstract state-space, then any given pattern of simultaneous activity of all the units will correspond to a point in that space. By looking at where in this space an input's corresponding hidden unit activation is located, we can get a sense of the sort of representational taxonomy the system adopts as the result of learning. An 'appropriate' activation pattern represents the input as belonging to a class that can be exploited by the system during its various computations. As Hinton puts it, 'The search for good representations is then a search in the space of possible sets of partitions.'[25] A natural way to think of this is to suppose that the network's internal units not only represent the network's individual inputs but represent them *as* a member of some class defined by the system's learning repertoire. In this way, connectionist representations capture a notion of appropriateness in terms of their similarity relation to other representations.

Because representations of this sort develop spontaneously through learning, connectionism holds out the promise of providing cognitive models that employ representations which acquire their semantic properties naturally, not simply by stipulation.

Examples of connectionist representation

Having discussed some general issues regarding connectionist representations, we are now prepared to look at some specific examples. As noted above, if we are to understand connectionism's potential bearing on the philosophical views of representation, we must first demarcate the different accounts of the form of representation put forth by these sorts of models. Unfortunately, connectionists themselves have been less than clear on this matter, and standard distinctions – such as that between distributed and localist representation or between symbolic and sub-symbolic networks – are somewhat ambiguous and cut across important divisions.[26] A more helpful form of taxonomy classifies models in terms of (1) *what* it is that is supposedly being represented (i.e., microfeatures, concepts, propositions, or large bodies of information, such as several propositions), and (2) *how* this is being done (i.e., through individual units, activation patterns of internal units, connection weights, or series of activation patterns). We can see these distinctions captured by the diagram in Figure 8.1.

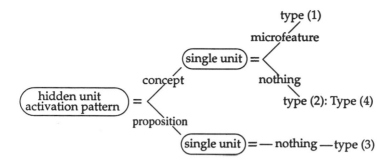

Figure 8.1: Types of Connectionist Representation

Only styles of connectionist representation that I take to have immediate philosophical significance are shown here, although many more possibilities could easily be sketched in. Thus, there are four different ways in which information can be encoded in connectionist devices that are directly relevant to philosophy.[27] To properly understand these different types of models, it will be helpful to look at each in some detail.

Type (1): activation pattern = concept; single unit = microfeature

Networks of this sort rely upon individual units to represent low-level properties and microfeatures, and overall activation patterns of several units to represent concepts. For type (1) models, individual units may have their content stipulated prior to learning or, alternatively, may acquire their content as the result of learning.[28] Either way, a given concept 'emerges' as its prototypical feature units are simultaneously excited– typically through some form of mutual activation.

A good example of a model of this sort is put forth by Rumelhart, Smolensky, McClelland, and Hinton in their 'room-schema' model.[29] In this network, individual units were taken to encode one of forty prototypical features of five different types of rooms. The connections between units were given either excitatory or inhibatory values, depending on the relative frequency with which their corresponding microfeatures are commonly correlated with one another. Thus, the feature 'sink' is positively linked with 'stove' but negatively linked with 'dresser.' By clamping on one or more individual units, the network settles into an overall activation pattern through the mutual excitation and inhibition of interacting units. Consequently, such patterns represent prototypical bedrooms, kitchens, etc. An interesting feature of this model is its ability to 'merge' features and produce hybrid concepts. For example, on one trial the units corresponding to 'bed,' 'sofa,' and 'ceiling' were clamped on. This produced a representation of a large and fancy bedroom with a fireplace.

Type (2): activation pattern = concept; single unit uninterpretable

In this sort of model, concepts are again represented by activation patterns of the network's internal units. However, for type (2) networks, individual units themselves do not admit of any semantic interpretation, even when activated. As McClelland, Rumelhart, and Hinton state, in models such as these, '[t]ypically the internal representations are distributed and it is the pattern of activity over the hidden units, not the meaning of any particular unit that is important[30] ... The units in these collections ... may have no particular meaning as individuals.'[31] For the most part, models of this sort develop their representations through learning. Since only activation patterns are taken to have representational content, nothing in the system lends itself to semantic evaluation when it is in its dormant state. In models such as these, conceptual representations are commonly revealed through vector analyses that map the similarities between different activation patterns of the network's internal units.

One example of a model of this sort has been developed by Gorman and Sejnowski.[32] Their model acquired the ability to distinguish underwater metal cylinders (mine imitations) from submerged rocks. It consisted of a three-layered network with thirty-four input units encoding echo frequencies, two output units (one for cylinders and one for rocks), and fourteen hidden units. The network was trained, using back-propagation, on a number of actual cylinder/mine echoes and actual rock echoes. After training, a vector analysis of the network's hidden units was performed, and it was discovered that their activation patterns are partitioned in quite specific ways. Prototypical cylinder echoes were clustered around one another in vector space, and prototypical rock echoes were clustered around a different and significantly distant point in vector space. This has led some to conclude that the network has developed a scheme for conceptually representing the different echo sources. For example, Paul Churchland describes this model as follows: 'The training process has generated a *similarity gradient* that culminates in two "hot spots" – two regions that represent the range of hidden-unit vector codings for a *prototypical* mine and a *prototypical* rock.'[33] If we regard such regions in vector space as representing conceptual prototypes, then activation patterns which fall within (or near to) such regions instantiate the salient concept. However, unlike the representation of concepts in type (1) models, individual units need not stand for any one particular sub-feature of that concept.

Type (3): activation pattern = proposition; single unit uninterpretable

Networks of this sort take the activation pattern of hidden units to represent not concepts but full-blown propositions. As with type (2) networks, single units in these models need not have any semantic interpretation when regarded individually. Hence, propositions are not represented in a way that provides them with an internal (semantic) structure. Instead, their form is fully determined by the ensemble of activation values of hidden units within the network.

An example of a network that lends itself to this sort of interpretation is produced by Ramsey, Stich, and Garon.[34] This network can be viewed as a question answerer trained to give 'yes' or 'no' responses to queries about certain propositions. For example, the network was trained to store and respond positively to such propositions as 'Dogs have fur' and 'Fish have scales' but negatively to propositions such as 'Dogs have scales.' After training, the network is presented with new propositions to test how well it generalizes. The important point for our purposes is that, although semantic components of propositions (such as 'Dog' and 'Fur') are explicitly encoded in the input units, they are not, in any way, retrievable from the system's internal representations. The smallest unit of semantic evaluability which can be assigned to the activated pattern of hidden units is the entire proposition. Moreover, this sort of interpretation is possible only when the system is actively processing information. When dormant, not even this coarse-grained analysis is possible, as information is stored holistically in the entire set of weights. Hence, there is no way to locate individual propositions stored in the network's architecture.

Type (4): series of activation patterns = proposition;
activation pattern = concept; single unit uninterpretable

There have been a number of recent attempts to develop connectionist networks whose representations can accommodate some form of compositional semantics without merely implementing more traditional approaches.[35] As it turns out, this is quite difficult to do, and, at the present, it is far from clear whether or not these efforts will prove successful.[36] Nonetheless, one strategy appears to hold some promise and is gradually being employed in more and more networks. The approach relies upon slight variations in activation patterns in order to capture propositional structure. In such models, semantic units are represented by activation patterns, which can then be combined in various ways to encode molecular representations. However, the way the initial atoms are hooked together, it is suggested, is syntactically unimportant – what matters is the exact value of the individual activation patterns that encode the atoms. According to this account, the syntactic role a particular atomic unit (such as a concept) plays in the representation of a larger structure (such as a proposition) is determined not by its *relation* to other atomic units but, rather, by the way it is represented by its own activity level. In this way, it is thought that slight variations in activity levels can encode syntactic or conceptual roles played by concepts in different propositions.

A nice example of a model developed along these lines is a network designed by Elman to complete partial sentences.[37] The model is a standard three-layered network, except it employs an added set of reiterative connections between the hidden units. The effect is a short-term memory, whereby the hidden units are presented not just with activation from the input units but also with their immediately preceding activation pattern. Models of this sort are particularly adept at predictive tasks, where they acquire the ability to detect patterns and regularities in the temporal series of inputs. For example, this particular model – trained on sequences of coded text – has the job of predicting new terms in the sequence. As a result of training, types of hidden-unit activation patterns come to correspond with lexical items such as nouns and verbs. The representations are highly context-sensitive and vary slightly with the input's position in a sentence. These variations are revealed by checking the position of a term's hidden unit activation pattern in state space whenever it (the term) plays a different role in a sentence. As Elman puts it, 'The location of each word in state space encodes not only the lexical identity of the word, but also the position in the sentence.'[38] Hence, insofar as activation patterns can be thought to encode lexical concepts, slight differences in the form of these conceptual representations help capture the syntactic role they play in the representation of a given proposition. The result is that the representation of individual concepts will vary in different contexts (e.g., in the complex representation of MARY LOVES JOHN, the representation of MARY is slightly different from what it is in the representation of JOHN LOVES MARY). Elman suggests that, by appealing to this variance in conceptual representation, connectionists can accommodate the apparent structure of propositional representations without adopting a 'Language of Thought' form of syntax based on the arrangement of constituents.

Philosophical Implications of
Connectionist Representations

Now that we have had a look at some of the different accounts of representation structure put forth by connectionists, we can explore the potential import of these different accounts for the various philosophical presuppositions discussed under PHILOSOPHICAL ACCOUNTS OF REPRESENTATION.

Implications of type (1) representation of concepts

As illustrated above, type (1) models represent concepts by activating an ensemble of distinct units, each of which encodes a certain prototypical property or microfeature that is constituent of that concept. Clearly, if models such as these should prove successful, then the philosophical moral to draw would be that the empiricist account of concept structure has been largely vindicated. Recall that a critical issue – indeed, *the* critical issue according to Fodor – in the debate between empiricism and nativism is the extent to which lexical concepts have internal structure:

> The empiricist bets that there will prove to be lots of interesting reductions of prima facie un-complex concepts (e.g. of de facto lexical concepts); whereas the nativist bets that ... we are not going to be able to display the internal structure of most concepts because, simply, most concepts do not have any internal structure.[39]

If type (1) connectionist models turn out to be the right story of concept structure, then it would be fair to say that the empiricist has won this bet hands down. The reason is that for networks such as these, lexical concepts such as KITCHEN are represented by structures constructed out of sub-conceptual features in much the same way assumed by empiricism and denied by nativism. If we represent our concepts in this way – by activating constituent atoms which denote lower-level features – empiricists like Hume and Locke could hardly ask for a better model to capture their views.[40] Hence, should it turn out that type (1) models provide an accurate account of the way we represent concepts, the empiricist presupposition of concept structure will be largely vindicated.

Furthermore, type (1) models whose atomic units are linked through some form of learning may provide some further insight into the actual nature of empiricist concept acquisition. By providing us with new principles of concept construction, these models may replace or justify assumptions made by past empiricists about the ways primitive concepts get hooked together to form lexical concepts. For example, if the connections are adjusted in accordance with rules of a Hebbian sort,[41] then Hume's principles of association will be closer to the mark than many have assumed.

Implications of type (2) representations of concepts

The crucial difference between type (1) representation of concepts and type (2) is that the former, but not the latter, relies on individual constituent units to encode low-level microfeatures. While type (2) concepts typically do have structural parts (i.e., several active units), these parts are semantically vacuous – not just when regarded individually but also in terms of the role they play in generating the concept. As Elman points out, 'The patterns are expressed over the entire ensemble of hidden units ... one cannot usefully look at the activity of single units; they do not even correspond to what one might call micro-features.'[42] In these models, there are no primitives which can be combined to form lexical concepts. Hence, type (2) models lack the sort of internal semantic structure which made type (1) models friendly to empiricism. If type (2) models turn out to be the correct story of concept representation, then empiricism's building-block account of concept structure and acquisition would have to be abandoned. Since the activation patterns are semantically unstructured, then, at least with regard to the structure of the representation, something more akin to the nativist notion of concepts would turn out to be the right account.

Yet, it is worth digressing a bit to note that it is far from clear that the success of these models is something advocates of conceptual nativism should hope for. For it is typically the case that models of this sort *aquire* their internal representations through one or another learning strategy. While such strategies lend themselves to a number of different interpretations, nativist notions of 'triggering' or 'activating' dormant structures seem entirely inappropriate here. Instead, the system adjusts itself in such a way that entirely new activation patterns are generated. It makes no sense to view this process as one of activating or triggering dormant states of the model.[43]

Are such networks empiricist or nativist? It seems that if we stick to traditional conceptions of these views, they are neither. Since the representations are semantically unstructured (i.e., they lack parts that can be regarded as representations of properties), traditional empiricist accounts of concept learning (which entail the conglomeration of primitive concepts of properties) are fully inappropriate. But since the network does learn new representations of concepts that are not already possessed by the system, nativist construals of concept acquisition appear to be undermined as well. One possibility is that the traditional construal of the empiricist/nativist debate is based on invalid tacit assumptions. Indeed, a further philosophical implication of models of type (2) is that they may point to areas of unexplored epistemological terrain. If models of this sort suggest that the original debate should be cast in new terms – terms that capture the salient differences between information acquired through learning and information not so acquired *in a network* – then the success of these models would require the over-hauling of important areas of traditional epistemology.[44]

Implications of type (3) representations of propositions

In type (3) networks, propositions are represented by activation patterns of hidden units, yet have no discrete form when the system is dormant. Hence, there is an important sense in which models such as these make the activity of the network a crucial element in determining the form of a given representation.[45] Since all the information eventually acquired by the network is stored holistically throughout the connection weights between individual units, the very same structures are used to preserve information about a variety of different things. As McClelland and Rumelhart put it, 'the traces of different mental states are therefore superimposed in the same set of weights.'[46] This prevents any one-to-one mapping between stored propositions and particular structures or set of structures within the system. When considered as an inert system, the smallest representational structure is the entire network, whose semantical evaluability is never more fine-grained than is the whole corpus of information on which it was trained. Consequently, the only philosophical view that such a system will support when inactive is the most coarse-grained level previously discussed: viz., structural holism. Since there are no inert structures which encode individual concepts, or even distinct propositions, neither the quasi-linguistic view nor the monadic account can be accommodated. If models of this sort turn out to be right, then philosophical accounts that require a quasi-linguistic or monadic structure encoding discrete propositions would be shown to be faulty, and holistic accounts would prove to be on the right track.

On the other hand, if we consider type (3) models when they are actively engaged in information processing, matters appear quite different. When active, one might argue that particular propositions can be identified with the different activation patterns of the system's internal units. These certainly *are* distinguishable from one another – in terms of both their 'structural' and their causal properties. Hence, if the system is active, there does seem to be a sense in which it can accommodate something like the monadic picture of propositional representation by appealing to the distinct activation states of the hidden units.

However, here again the connectionist account is not in complete accord with the philosophical picture. For the monadic picture typically assumes that propositional representations *do* have a dormant distinctiveness, that propositional representations *can* causally interact with one another, and that more than one proposition can be invoked in the processing at any given point in time. Just how these properties might be captured in type (3) connectionist models is far from clear. At the present, none of these features appear to be instantiated in models invoking this type of representation. Hence, the success of these models may provide only a very dubious victory for the monadic theorists.

While monadic theorists would be at least partially vindicated by the success of type (3) models, the quasi-linguistic account would be virtually demolished in the wake of such success. Although the hidden unit activation pattern of such networks is a structurally complex state, it does not have a *compositional semantics* of the sort required by the quasi-linguistic account. The nodes comprising the representation of the proposition lend themselves to no straightforward semantic interpretation. Hence, if models of this sort turn out to be correct, then it looks like the most popular philosophical theory of mental representation structure will have to be abandoned. There simply is nothing about the internal make-up of type (3) propositional representations that even begins to look like the sort of internal structure required by the quasi-linguistic account. Moreover, insofar as various theories of cognitive processes have been based on the assumption that information is represented in distinct, sentence-like structures, these accounts will have to be reworked or abandoned as well. For example, standard accounts of how we perform logical inference, which assume propositional representations serve as premises in deductive reasoning, could no longer assume that sub-parts of these representations (i.e., concepts) can be shared by these premises in any straightforward way. The reason is that propositional representations in type (3) models *do not have* subparts, so there are not any components which could be transitive (in any normal, syntactic sense) between premises.[47]

Finally, the 'dual-aspect' (i.e., dormant = holistic; active = monadic) of type (3) models spells trouble not just for sophisticated philosophical theories of the mind but for common-sensical theories as well. Our folk-psychology requires beliefs to be the sort of things which can have a permanent, long-standing existence. Moreover, it assumes that particular stored beliefs need not have any role to play in certain episodes of the behaviour production or inference. Yet, if the sort of holistic account of belief storage presented by type (3) models is correct, these assumptions cannot be jointly satisfied, and folk psychology will be mistaken in its presuppositions about the way stored information is invoked during processing.[48]

Implications of type (4) accounts of propositional representation

Last, but certainly not least, in our analysis of connectionist representation is the type (4) model. This type of model brings into play the idea of invoking different representations of the same concepts to capture certain structural relations. In this type of model, propositions do have individual concepts as constituent parts. However, this feature does not produce a straightforward implementation of the 'language of thought' position because of the way individual concepts are represented in such systems. In these models, the *form* of the representation of the concept itself – not its causal/functional relations with other concepts – determines its syntactic role in the proposition. In other words, we have implicitly 'stored' not one representation for a particular lexical concept but several different representations (encoded by patterns corresponding to different though nearby points in vector space), each of which accounts for a given syntactic role. Thus, we do not, on this picture, have a representation of BOY or APPLE but, rather, a cluster of representations of BOY-qua-[ ], APPLE-qua-[ ], where the bracketed blanks are filled in by the appropriate syntactic or conceptual role.

A further point worth stressing about type (4) models regards the sort of constraints they put on the system's processing elements. A common view among philosophers is that the mind is sensitive to only the syntactic (structural) properties of its representations. Some have suggested that connectionist models abandon this picture, because they 'are precluded from postulating mental processes that operate on mental representations in a way that is sensitive to their structure.'[49] If one takes 'structure' to mean the way concepts are represented, type (4) models illustrate not only that this point is false, but that it is radically false insofar as models of this sort require more sensitivity to structure than do conventional systems. The reason is that with type (4) models, only slight structural differences – slight variations in activation patterns – are relied upon to encode different syntactic roles. Moreover, the situation cannot be alleviated by making the patterns more dissimilar (by spreading their corresponding points further apart in vector space). This is because these different patterns must be treated as *semantically* alike (as standing for the same thing); otherwise the system would be incapable of performing routine inferences. (Suppose, for example, the network had two representations: (1) 'ALL A's ARE B's' and (2) 'ALL B's ARE C's' and treated the two instances of 'B' as semantically – and not just syntactically – different. In this case, the system would never draw the obvious and valid conclusion that all A's are C's.) Thus, the different patterns must be confined to a small region of vector space if they are all to represent the same thing, yet they must be distinguishable by the system if they are to represent it in different roles. The end result is that, far from ignoring the structural properties of representations, connectionist models of this type must be extremely sensitive to such features if the model is to represent appropriate propositions.

Although the details of this sort of account have yet to be fully worked out, and many authors are skeptical,[50] I will suppose for the sake of argument that something like a type (4) model can be made to work in order to explore the implications it might have for the way philosophers think about the mind. Of these implications, the most obvious is the bearing it has on associationist theories of *belief* (as opposed to concept) formation. For if the sort of account of mental processing put forth by type (4) models is successful, this theory of the mind – which has been abandoned by most philosophers and cognitive scientists – will be provided with a strategy for vindication. Associationists held that the basic principle of thought was the association of ideas and concepts, determined (in part) by the relative frequency with which the different mental units are correlated with one another. One of the most popular arguments against this view was that mere associative relations could not capture the necessary *syntactic* relations required for meaningful and coherent representation of propositions. Associations, it has been argued, do not provide any syntactic *arrangement* of the concepts which comprise a propositional representation. For example, associating one's JOHN concept with one's MARY concept and one's LOVE concept does not provide a representation of JOHN LOVES MARY any more than it provides a representation of MARY LOVES JOHN (or, for that matter, LOVES JOHN MARY). However, if what gets associated are the representations, JOHN-qua-agent, MARY-qua-patient, and LOVES-qua-relation, then it appears we no longer need any further structural organization to provide a meaningful representation of the proposition 'John loves Mary.' Insofar as the way these concepts get hooked together is no longer relevant to their syntactic role, associative principles can do all the work needed in combining concepts to form meaningful representations of propositions.[51]

Of course, one serious drawback to this approach is that while type (4) *representation* appears amenable to associationism, type (4) *processing* does not, or at least not in any obvious way. Prima facie, there does not appear to be anything like associationist relations at work among the different representations in such models, although perhaps one might focus on the similarity clustering in vector space and attempt to develop something like an associationist account based on this (for Hume, similarity was one of three principles of association). At this point, the biggest problem is that no one has a clear sense of how models of this sort can be made to scale up to full-blown inference devices that model sophisticated forms of cognition.

One final possible philosophical implication of type (4) models is worth mentioning briefly. One of the great traditions of analytic philosophy (dating back at least as far as Plato) has been that of conceptual analysis – i.e., of trying to come up with a set of necessary and sufficient conditions that capture our concept of such things as justice, virtue, truth, rationality, etc. On one (quite naturalistic) reading of this enterprise, it is an attempt to develop an account of actual cognitive structures or representations literally stored in the mind-brain. If this interpretation of conceptual analysis is correct, and if it should turn out that the type (4) representational scheme is, in fact, the one we actually use, then the traditional philosophical enterprise of conceptual analysis would appear to be deeply misguided. The reason is not simply because our concepts do not consist of necessary and sufficient conditions (as many have already argued), but, rather, because *we do not have individual concepts* of these things. If all we have in the way of conceptual representation of X (where X might be *justice* or *truth* or anything else) is always X-*QUA*-some particular role, then there seems little reason to suppose that there must be something in our heads which unites all of these other than their proximity in vector space. In other words, if the type (4) model of cognition is on target, then what we have instead are clusters comprised of related (but conceptually different) representations – some of which will be captured by certain criteria, others by contextually different criteria; some of which will be undermined by some counter-examples, others by very different counter-examples. In this picture, trying to define THE concept of something would be hopeless, primarily because there is no such thing.

Hence, type (4) accounts of representation form have important implications for traditional work in both philosophy of mind and epistemology. With respect to the former, they provide associationism with the potential means for avoiding criticisms regarding its inability to capture syntactic regularities in thought. With respect to the latter, they suggest there is reason to believe that a major program in traditional analytic philosophy – that of conceptual analysis – might be doomed or, at least, in need of serious rethinking.

Conclusion

Philosophers are leaning more heavily upon cognitive science than ever before, and one of the most important points of contact is with respect to the nature of mental representation. The goal of this essay has been to explore the implications of one type of cognitive theory of representation structure – i.e., the connectionist account – for various theories and topics in philosophy. While connectionism has already had a major impact on cognitive science, I hope to have demonstrated the different ways in which it might also motivate philosophers to rethink many of their more popular assumptions about the character of mental representation.[52]

Notes

1 I adopt the format whereby mental concepts are denoted by fully capitalized words.

2 This distinction is borrowed from Fodor (1981) and is not without its difficulties. For example, as Fodor himself notes (261), it appears to be strongly dependent upon one's particular natural language – a lexical term in one language may be, in some cases, expressed by a phrasal construction in another. Having noted such worries, I propose simply to ignore them, since my concern is with sketching the philosophical tradition – not defending it. And in this tradition, something like Fodor's distinction appears to be assumed by most authors.

3 Hume (1959), 12.

4 See, for example, Smith and Medin (1981).

5 A slippery issue in this debate concerns the differences between concept *learning*, concept *acquisition*, and concept *triggering*. Fortunately, we need not dwell on this matter here, but simply note that what *is* clear is that whatever the nativist account amounts to (whether we view it as concept triggering or some other form of acquisition), one thing it surely *will not* be is acquisition through the compounding of primitives. For further discussion of these matters, see Fodor (1981), Samet (1986), and Sterelny (1989).

6 Fodor (1981), 279.

7 Ibid, 298.

8 Ibid, 278.

9 See, for example, Cartwright (1966) and Stalnaker (1984) for discussion of different conceptions of propositions.

10 Fodor (1985).

11 Field (1978); Fodor (1975), (1981), (1987); Harman (1973); Lycan (1981), (1987); Macnamara (1986); McGinn (1982); Pylyshyn (1985). Indeed, anyone who views thought as something akin to symbol manipulation (as do many cognitive scientists) will be sympathetic to this picture. Until the advent of connectionism, the language of thought hypothesis provided a happy melding point for philosophy and cognitive modelling.

12 Perhaps one of the earliest proponents of this view was Sellars (1968). See also Harman's review of this work (1970).

13 Fodor (1987), 136.

14 Burge (1986); Dretske (1988); Loar (1981), (1982).

15 Loar (1982), 633.

16 Dretske (1988), 104.

17 See Denntt (1978), (1987); Stalnaker (1984); Quine (1960), (1970); Ryle (1949).

18 Stalnaker (1984), 15, 19.

19 To see why the supplement is needed, see Stalnaker (1984), 17-18.

20 See, for example, Stalnaker (1984), Chapter 1.

21 Dennett, (1978), 26.

22 Stalnaker (1984), 68, 71.

23 For a nice illustration of a model of this sort, see McClelland's (1981) Jets and Sharks model.

24 Dretske (1981), (1988); Fodor (1987); Stalnaker (1984); Stampe (1977).

25 Hinton (1987), 4.

26 For example, the 'distributed/localist' distinction fails to differentiate networks in which individual units have a semantic interpretation and those in which they do not. The same can said for the 'symbolic/sub-symbolic' distinction.

27 I view these distinctions as capturing very general styles of representation in connectionist networks. I do not presume there to be well-defined classes of models and admit there may be some overlapping or idiosyncratic networks which do not fit neatly under any general heading.

28 For examples of the last sort, see Hinton (1987); Gorman and Sejnowski (1988).

29 In Rumelhart and McClelland (1986b), Chapter 14.

30 In Rumelhart and McClelland (1986a), 344-6.

31 Ibid, 33.

32 Gorman and Sejnowski (1988).

33 Churchland (1989), 204.

34 Ramsey, Stich, and Garon (1990).

35 See, for example, Smolensky (1988); Hinton (1988).

36 See Fodor and McLaughlin (forthcoming) for a critique of these strategies.

37 Elman (1989).

38 Ibid, 24.

39 Fodor (1981), 283.

40 Of course, Locke or Hume would want the concept's sub-parts to be a bit more sensory/primitive than the micro-features of Hinton and Sejnowski's room schema model (i.e., I doubt if they would be happy with 'toaster' or 'floor-lamp' as primitives). But this does not affect my general point.

41 By this, I simply mean that the connection between two units is strengthened if the units' activation is correlated.

42 Elman (1989), 18.

43 I suppose someone might claim there is a sense in which potential activation patterns lie dormant in the pre-trained network. On this reading, however,

the nativist position starts looking very uninteresting – any version of nativism worth taking seriously will surely require something stronger than this.

44 See Ramsey and Stich (forthcoming) for similar points regarding linguistic nativism. See also Churchland (1989) for more on connectionism and the overhauling of orthodox epistemology.

45 The same point holds for the representation of concepts in type (2) models.

46 Rumelhart and McClelland (1986b), 176.

47 Fodor and Pylyshyn (1988) regard this point as amounting to a reductio of type (3) representations.

48 See Ramsey, Stich, and Garon (1990) for a detailed argument for this conclusion.

49 Fodor and Pylyshyn (1988), 24.

50 See, for example, Fodor and Pylyshyn (1988) Part 2, Sec. III; or Fodor and Mc-Claughlin (forthcoming). The main complaint is that this sort of representational scheme would lead to a 'grotesque explosion of primitives,' since the number of different and distinct vector points would have to be as great as the number of conceptual roles each concept could fill. This would not be too bad, except, as these authors urge, the notion of conceptual role needs to be quite rich in order to work. So, for example, one would need a distinct encoding of not just JOHN-QUA-PATIENT but also of JOHN-QUA-PATIENT-OF-HITTING, JOHN-QUA-PATIENT-OF-LOVING, JOHN-QUA-PATIENT-OF-CAREFUL-OBSERVATION, and so on for all the thoughts once can entertain about John. To see how connectionists might try to deal with these worries, see Cottrell (1985).

51 Peter Godfrey-Smith and Mike Kremer have suggested to me that this is all still very language-like if we take as our model those languages (like Latin) in which syntax is captured not by concatenation relations between words but, rather, the word's conjugation and its adjoining pronoun. If this is so, then type (4) models may still be a sort of Language of Thought account, but one that abandons traditional construals of compositionality and is compatible with associationism.

52 Much thanks to Gary Cottrell, Jeff Elman, Peter Godfrey-Smith, Mike Kremer, Kim Sterelny, and especially Steve Stich for a number of helpful comments and suggestions.

References

Burge, T. (1986). Individualism and psychology. *Philosophical Review* 95(1):3-45

Cartwright, R. (1966). Propositions. In R.J. Butler (ed.), *Analytical Philosophy*. New York: Barnes and Noble

Churchland, P.M. (1989). *A Neurocomputational Perspective: The Nature of Mind and the Structure of Science*. Cambridge, MA: Bradford/MIT Press

Cottrell, G. (1985). Connectionist parsing. In *Proceedings of the Seventh Annual Cognitive Science Society*. Erlbaum, Hillsdale, NJ, 201-11

Dennett, D. (1978). *Brainstorms*. Cambridge, MA:Bradford/MIT Press

– (1987). *The Intentional Stance*. Cambridge, MA:Bradford/MIT Press

Dretske, F. (1981). *Knowledge and the Flow of Information*. Cambridge, MA:Bradford/MIT Press

– (1988). *Explaining Behavior*. Cambridge, MA:Bradford/MIT Press

Elman, J. (1989). Structured representations and connectionist networks. CRL Technical Report 8901, University of California, San Diego

Field, H. (1978). Mental representations.*Erkenntnis*. 13(1):9-61

Fodor, J. (1975). *The Language of Thought*. Thomas Y. Crowell, New York

– (1981). *Representations*. Cambridge, MA:MIT Press

– (1985). Fodor's guide to mental representation: the intelligent auntie's vademecum. *Mind* 94(373):76-100.

– (1987). *Psychosemantics: The Problem of Meaning in the Philosophy of Mind*. Cambridge, MA:Bradford/MIT Press

– and Pylyshyn, Z. (1988). Connectionism and cognitive architecture: a critical analysis. *Cognition*. 28:3-78

– and McLaughlin, B. (forthcoming). Connectionism and the problem of systematicity; why Smolensky's solution doesn't work. To appear in *Cognition*

Gorman, R. and Sejnowski, T. (1988). Learned classification of sonar targets using a sassively parallel network. *IEEE Transactions: Acoustics, Speech and Signal Processing* 36(7):1135-40

Harman, G. (1970). Sellars' semantics. *Philosophical Review*, 89(3):404-19

– (1973).*Thought*. Princeton, NJ: Princeton University Press

Hinton, G. (1987). Learning distributed representations of concepts. *Proceedings of the Eighth Annual Meeting of the Cognitive Science Society*. Earlbaum, Hillsdale, NJ 48-54

– (1988). Representing part-whole hierarchies in connectionist networks. *Proceedings of the Tenth Annual Meeting of the Cognitive Science Society*. Earlbaum, Hillsdale, NJ 48-54

Hume, D. (1959). *A Treatise of Human Nature*. J.M. London: Dent and Sons

Loar, B. (1981). *Mind and Meaning*. Cambridge: Cambridge University Press

– (1982). Must Beliefs Be Sentences? *PSA 1982*. Proceedings of the 1982 Biennial Meeting of the Philosophy of Science Association 2, P. Asquith and T. Nickels (eds.), East Lansing, Philosophy of Science Association, 627-43

Lycan, W. (1981). Toward a homuncular theory of believing. *Cognition and Brain Theory* 4:2

Lycan, W. (1987). *Consciousness*. Cambridge, MA:Bradford/MIT Press

Macnamara, J. (1986). *A Border Dispute: The Place of Logic in Psychology*. Cambridge, MA:Bradford/MIT Press

McClelland, J. (1981). Retrieving general and specific knowledge from stored knowledge of specifics. *Proceedings of the Third Annual Conference of the*

Cognitive Science Society. Erlbaum, Hillsdale, NJ, 170-2

McGinn, C. (1982). The structure of content. In A. Woodfield (ed.), *Thought and Object.* Oxford: Oxford University Press

Pylyshyn, Z. (1984). *Computation and Cognition.* Cambridge, MA:Bradford/MIT Press

Quine, W.V. (1960). *Word and Object.* Cambridge, MA:MIT Press

— (1970). *The Web of Belief.* New York: Random House

Ramsey, W., Stich, S. and Garon, J. (1990). Connectionism, eliminativism, and the future of folk psychology. In J. Tomberlin (ed.), *Philosophical Perspectives* 4:499-533

— and Stich, S. (forthcoming). Connectionism and three levels of nativism. *Synthese*

Rumelhart, D. and McClelland, J. (1986a). *Parallel Distributed Processing: Explorations in the Microstructure of Cognition,* I, Cambridge, MA:MIT/Bradford Press

— and McClelland, J. (1986b). *Parallel Distributed Processing: Explorations in the Microstructure of Cognition,* Vol. II Cambridge, MA:MIT/Bradford Press

Ryle, G. (1949). *The Concept of Mind.* New York: Barnes and Nobel

Samet, J. (1986). Troubles with Fodor's nativism. In P. French, T. Uehling and H. Wettstein (eds.), *Midwest Studies in Philosophy X.* Minneapolis: University of Minnesota Press 575-94

Sellars, W. (1968). *Science and Metaphysics: Variations on Kantian Themes.* New York: Humanities Press

Smith, E. and Medin, D. (1981). *Categories and Concepts.* Cambridge, MA: Harvard University Press

Smolensky, P. (1988). The constituent structure of mental states: a reply to Fodor and Pylyshyn. *Southern Journal of Philosophy,* 26, Supplement, Proceedings of Sixth Annual Spindel Conference, 137-60.

Stalnaker, R. (1984). *Inquiry.* Cambridge, MA:Bradford/MIT Press

Stampe, D. (1977). Towards a causal account of meaning. In P. French, T. Uehling and H. Wettstein (eds.), *Midwest Studies in Philosophy II.* Minneapolis: University of Minnesota Press

Sterelny, K. (1989).Fodor's nativism. *Philosophical Studies* 55:119-41

9

Connectionism and the Computational Neurobiology of Curve Detection

Steven W. Zucker, Allan Dobbins, and Lee Iverson

The Dilemma of Curve Detection

One of the pillars on which modern theories of vision are based is the discovery that there exist neurons in the visual cortex with receptive fields tuned for orientation (Hubel and Wiesel 1977). Such neurons are typically interpreted as 'curve detectors,' and it is widely held that their responses are then simply fed forward to enable more abstract spatial pattern vision. Similar notions pervade other areas of vision as well, for example , motion and stereoscopic perception and can be taken to define the first paradigm in computational vision (Zucker 1986, 1991).

This feedforward view of curve detection into pattern vision is seductive in its simplicity; however, it stands at odds with much of what is otherwise known about vision and gives rise to more dilemmas than it resolves. For example, the initial measurement of orientation information is broadly tuned, which suggests the averaging necessary to counteract retinal (sensor) sampling, quantization, and noise. However, the end result of curve detection is unexpectedly precise: corners can be distinguished from arcs of high curvature, and nearby curves can be distinguished from one another to a hyperaccurate level, even though they might pass through the same receptive field.

An analogous dilemma exists for computer vision systems, even with the spectacular numerical precision of which computers are capable: quantization and noise imply smoothing, but smoothing blurs corners, endpoints, and nearby curves into confusion (Zucker 1986). At the foundation is a chicken-and-egg problem: If the retinotopic points through which a curve passes, together with the locations of discontinuities, were known, then the actual properties of the curve could be inferred by a 'fitting' or interpolation process. But initially they are not known, so any smoothing inherent in the inference process is potentially dangerous. In fact, even determining which points the curve passes through is a difficult problem (which we call the trace inference

277

problem) and may be the first segmentation task with which vision is confronted.

Two Stages of Curve Detection

We have studied the trace and curve inference problems and have discovered a computational solution involving decomposition into a first stage, during which a local and coarse description of the curve is computed, followed by a second stage, during which the global and precise properties of curves are computed. While the first of our stages has a rather similar character to the kinds of networks studied by artificial neural-network researchers, the second one does not (Figure 9.1). At a more subtle level, however, our approach differs significantly from previous ones in that no attempt is made to match curves directly against the image or even against measurements (i.e., 'curve operators') evaluated over the image. Instead we stress the organizational point that a stable, reliable, but *coarse* description should be computed as an intermediate between the image (measurements) and the global curves. A particular intermediate representation – the discrete tangent field – is proposed. It is computed by a global network that minimizes a variational form rather different from those normally proposed.

The second stage of the algorithm synthesizes the global curves through the tangent field. The novel idea behind our approach is to recover the global curve by computing a *covering* of it; that is, a set of objects whose union is equivalent to the original curve, rather than attempting to compute the global curve directly. The elements of the covering are unit-length dynamic splines, and global curves are recovered to sub-pixel accuracy.

The Model of Curve Detection

Orientation selection can be viewed as the inference of a local (low-order) description of a curve everywhere along it, and we postulate orientation selection as the goal of our first stage. In the second stage, global curves are inferred through this local description. The various stages of our process are shown in Figure 9.1 and are expanded below. Figure 9.1 illustrates the different stages of curve detection. In the first stage, a reliable, but coarse, description (tangent field) of the local structure of curves is computed, while global structure is computed in the second. This is illustrated for the small fingerprint image (Figure 9.1a); note the smooth curves and discontinuities around the 'Y' in the centre. The first stage is broken into two steps. In the first step, initial (nonlinear) measurements are performed to estimate what the local curvature

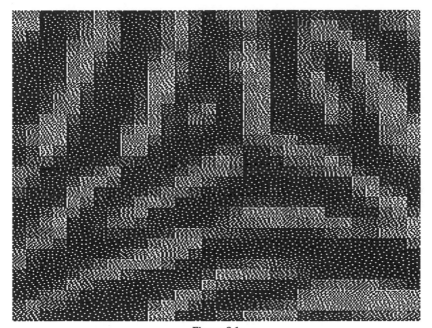

Figure 9.1a

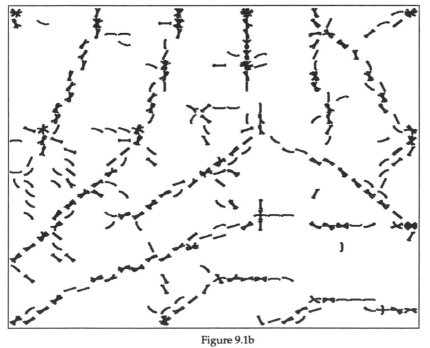

Figure 9.1b

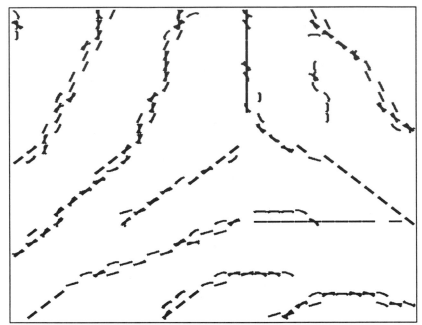

Figure 9.1c

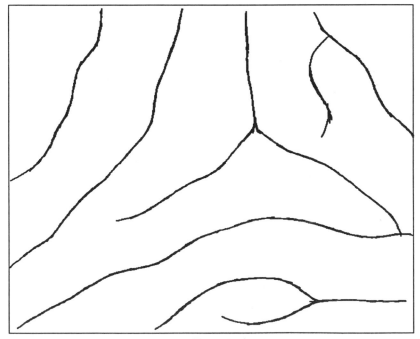

Figure 9.1d

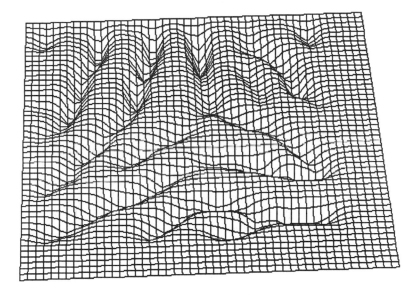

Figure 9.1e

and orientation might be (Figure 9.1b). In the second step these initial measurements are refined by a relaxation labelling process and (Figure 9.1c) shows the final tangent field after two iterations; note that most of the spurious initial responses have been eliminated. There are also two steps in the second stage, first the construction of a potential distribution from the entries in the tangent field (Figure 9.1e), and, second, the covering of the global curve by a family of short curves, or snakes (Figure 9.1d). (After Zucker et al., 1989.) We now elaborate each of these different steps.

Stage 1: inferring the tangent field

Formally, orientation selection amounts to inferring the trace of the curve, or the set of points (in the image) through which the curve passes, and its (approximate) tangent at those points. While this captures standard views of orientation selection, we extend the requirements of the first stage to include estimates of curvature at each point along a curve, except for the singular (or discontinuous) ones (Zucker 1986). For simplicity, we refer to the total of such information as the *tangent field* and note that, since the initial measurements are discrete, this will impose constraints on the (inferred) tangents, curvatures, and discontinuities (Parent and Zucker 1988).

By elaborating the tangent field to include differential-geometric information through the second order, as well as discontinuities, one can appreciate the fact that computing the tangent field is rather a more involved task than just convolving operators. So this first stage of curve detection is in turn modelled as a two step process:

(1) Step 1.1. *Initial Measurement* of the local fit at each point to estimate orientation and curvature. These estimates derive from a model of simple cell receptive fields instantiated at multiple scales and orientations at each image position. The model is nonlinear and derives from a subfield partition and then recombination which guarantees that certain structural preconditions are satisfied (Iverson and Zucker 1990). The result eliminates many of the false positive responses that plague other operators. Curvature estimates are then derived from nonlinear differences between orientation measurements at different scales, and they are described below. Overall, we propose that endstopped neurons in the visual cortex represent joint hypotheses about orientation and curvature, and that their firing rate along an (endstopped) orientation hypercolumn represents how well these hypotheses match the local image structure. However, such local measurements are inherently inaccurate (for example, broadly tuned), so we require

(2) Step 1.2. *Interpretation* into an explicit distributed representation of tangent and curvature by establishing consistency between the local measurements. There are two notions that must be developed here: (1) precisely what is meant by 'consistency'; and (2) physiologically how it might be achieved.We propose to define consistency within the theory of *relaxation labelling*, one way of formulating abstract 'neural networks' expanded below, with the connections (or compatibilities or strengths of 'synaptic interactions') derived from differential geometry. To illustrate, consider an arc of a curve, and observe that tangents to this arc must conform to certain position and orientation constraints for a given amount of curvature; we refer to such constraints geometrically as *cocircularity* (Figure 9.2a). Discretizing all continuous curves in the world that project into the columnar space of coarse (orientation, curvature) hypotheses partitions these curves into equivalence classes (Parent and Zucker 1989; Zucker and Iverson 1988). Figures 9.2b-2c illustrate compatibilities

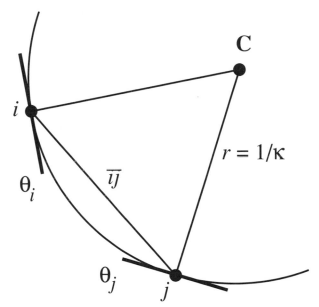

Figure 9.2a: The geometric relationships necessary for defining the compatibilities between two label pairs at nearby points $i = (x_i, y_i)$ and $j = (x_j, y_j)$.

between coarse (orientation, curvature) hypotheses at nearby positions. Eight distinct orientations and seven curvatures are represented, and three examples are shown. The magnitude of the interactions varies as well, roughly as a Gaussian superimposed on these diagrams. The values were obtained by numerically solving a six-dimensional closest point problem (Zucker et al. 1988). Physiologically, these projective fields could represent inter-columnar interactions implemented by pyramidal neurons. (After Zucker et al., 1988.)

We now expand on some of these notions; the reader is referred to the literature for more detailed, technical presentations.

Physiologically plausible curvature measurements

The problem of estimating curvature has concerned researchers in computer vision and spline approximation theory for decades (Rosenfeld and Kak 1982). The difficulty derives from the fact that, formally speaking, curvature involves second derivative functions. Given an estimate of a curve that is noisy, or even an estimate of the trace of a curve that is noisy, attempts to estimate curvature by either difference approximations or by fitting symbolically differentiated (e.g.,

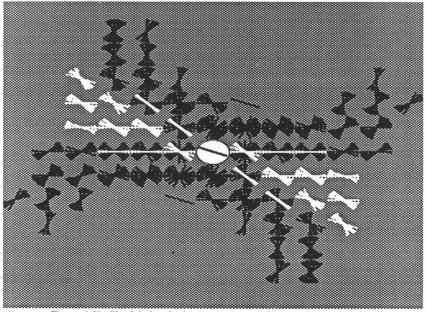

Figure 9.2b: The labels which give positive (white) and negative (black) support for a diagonal orientation with no curvature.

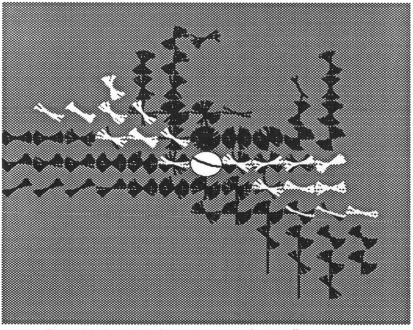

Figure 9.2c: Positive and negative support for a small curvature class.

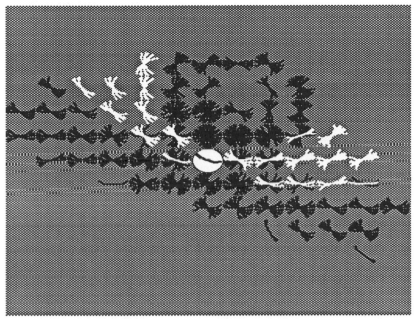

Figure 9.2d: Positive and negative support for the maximum curvature class.

polynomial) functions have not fared well. The process attempted in both cases enhances the noise and masks the curvature signal.

We have developed a very different approach to estimating curvature, based on the geometrical interpretation of curvature as 'deviation from straightness' or, technically speaking, the rate at which the curve pulls away from its tangent.

We implement the idea in a physiologically plausible way, which has led us to a novel insight regarding the function of cells in the visual cortex. The model is based on the observation that there are simple cells whose receptive field size differs as a function of cortical layer. In particular, Layer VI of cat primary visual cortex contains cells with receptive fields notably longer than those in the laminae above it (Gilbert 1977). Now, if we let R_S denote the response of a short simple cell (or, more precisely, the response of a cell with a short receptive field) and R_L denote the response of a long simple cell, with receptive fields sharing orientation preference and centred at the same retinal location, then their 'difference' is related to curvature. To illustrate, suppose the stimulus is a straight curve. Then both cells will be responding strongly, since the stimulus passes supportively through both receptive fields, and their 'difference' is zero. Curvature is zero for straight lines. Now, consider a curve with high curvature. It will stimulate the small cell to some extent, but not the large one, so their 'difference' will be large. Curvature is large.

More precisely, letting $\varphi(\cdot)$ denote a rectifying function (equal to its argument when positive and zero otherwise), the curvature response (R_K) is modelled by:

$$R_K = \varphi(c_S \cdot \varphi(R_S) - c_L \cdot \varphi(R_L))$$

where c_S and c_L are positive constants that normalize the area difference between the receptive fields. By varying the model parameters one can vary the curvature response of model instances. For example, the symmetry of the components determines the curvature sign selectivity, and the relative size and gain determine the preferred curvature and curvature tuning breadth (see Dobbins et al. 1988a, 1988b).

A rather intriguing connection emerged between this model and another common property of visual cortical neurons: end stopping, or selectivity for the length of an oriented stimulus. Selectivity for length would be signalled by a maximal response to a stimulus of a given length and a decrease in response for stimuli of different lengths. However, for such tunings to be comparable, they ought to decrease to the same level, ideally to zero or the resting level if the cells are actually signalling 'endpoints.' But this is not observed physiologically. The amount of firing drops off different amounts, usually to an intermediate value (say to 60 per cent of the maximum, or to 40 per cent). Thus it seems unlikely that these neurons are exactly detecting stimulus length or endpoints. Rather, a different interpretation is required, and one which is consistent with such broad and variable tuning characteristics

We submit that endstopped neurons are coding coarse curvature, and, in Dobbins et al. (1987) we develop a computational model for endstopping and show how it leads to quantitative predictions (now verified) about the response of endstopped simple (ES) neurons to curved stimuli. This provides the (nonlinear) operators for our initial curvature measurements.

To summarize, then, at each of a discrete number of orientations a small number of orientation selective instances of simple cells are combined to define five (say) discrete curvature classes – two on either side of the zero curvature class. The four curved classes are obtained from endstopped instances and the zero curvature estimate from a nonendstopped instance of a simple cell. Typical results above noise are shown in Figure 9.1b; although they convey a rough idea of what the curve structure is, there are both responses where there is no curve and ambiguous (multi-valued) responses where there is a single curve. We contend that no local operator can solve these problems in general, and, further, that a spatially-interactive process can. In the next subsection we sketch a computational framework within which such a process can be posed.

Orientation selection network

Given the initial measurements, we now use a relaxation labelling system to effectively impose a coarse second-order model for the curve around each putative tangent and then to select those that minimize a certain function over all responses. The result is a network that models something like the interactions between endstopped and nonendstopped simple cells in the visual cortex.

Relaxation labelling

Relaxation labelling is an inference procedure for selecting labels attached to a graph according to optimal (symmetric) or variational (asymmetric) principles. Think of nodes in the graph as image positions, phrase edges in the graph as linking nearby image positions, and the labels as indicating possible discrete (orientation, curvature) pairings. Formally, let $i = (x_i, y_i) \in I$ denote discrete coordinate positions in the image I, and let $\lambda \in \Lambda_i$ denote the set of labels at position i. The labels at each position are ordered according to the measure $p_i(\lambda)$ such that $0 \le p_i(\lambda) \le 1$ and

$$\sum_{\lambda \in \Lambda_i} p_i(\lambda) = 1$$

for all i. (Think of $p(\lambda)$ as the firing rate for the (possibly endstopped) neuron coding label $\lambda =$ (particular orientation, particular-curvature).) Compatibility functions $r_{i,j}(\lambda, \lambda')$ are defined between label λ at position i and label λ' at position j such that increasingly positive values represent stronger compatibility. It was these compatibilities that were illustrated above, and which were derived from the differential geometry of curves. The abstract network structure is obtained from the support S that label λ obtains from the labelling on it's neighbours $Neigh\ (i)$; in symbols,

$$s_i(\lambda) = \sum_{j \in Neigh(i)} \sum_{\lambda' \in \Lambda_j} r_{i,j}(\lambda, \lambda') p_j(\lambda')$$

The final labelling is selected so that it maximizes the average local support:

$$A(p) = \sum_{i \in I} S_i(\lambda) p_i(\lambda)$$

Such a labelling is said to be consistent (Hummel and Zucker 1983). An iterative, gradient ascent algorithm for achieving consistent labellings is presented in Mohammed, Hummel, and Zucker 1983 and Parent and Zucker 1985a. We now simply remark that such 'computational energy' forms have become common in neural networks and observe that Hopfield (1984) networks are a special case, as are polymatrix games, under certain conditions (Miller and Zucker 1991).

Physiological interpretation

Such relaxation interactions can be viewed physiologically as excitatory and inhibitory interactions between endstopped cells at nearby positions (adjacent hypercolumns) and can be used as follows. Since curvature is a relationship between tangents at nearby positions, two tangents should support one another if and only if they agree under a curvature hypothesis, and co-circularity provides the means to measure such support. In addition, two tangents that disagree with the curvature estimate should detract support from one another. Physiologically the relaxation interactions might be viewed as the computation implemented by pyramidal neurons as they combine information from adjacent (endstopped) orientation hypercolumns. Since only two to three iterations are required for convergence (empirically), it is natural to propose that these are accomplished by the forward- and back-projecting pyramidal neurons connecting areas V1 and V2 (Zucker et al. 1989), if not entirely by local circuits within V1.

One specific model of the physiology could be as follows: initial orientation estimates are obtained by the small (layer four) simple cells in V1; the difference required for curvature estimation can be built up from a layer six to layer four back projection, and the first iteration of the relaxation process can be implemented by a pyramidal neuron with dendritic inputs from nearby (endstopped) orientation hypercolumns. Such neurons project to V2, where a similar computation takes place; the backprojection to V1 then provides a final iteration. The tangent field is represented by those neurons whose firing rate is maintained, with tangent corresponding to preferred orientation and curvature corresponding to percentage endstopping.

Similar ideas can be applied to texture, suggesting a difference between *texture flows*, or those texture patterns with an orientation structure, and *texture fields*, for example, 'salt-and-pepper' patterns (Hel Or and Zucker 1989), and such differences may well correlate with physiological notions of 'cytochrome oxidase blobs' (Allman and Zucker 1991). The extension into three dimensions requires more sophisticated differential geometry (see Sander and Zucker 1990). Also, application to laser rangefinder imagery is very successful (Ferrie et al. 1990).

Discontinuities

One of the subtle points regarding curve detection raised at the beginning of this article is the handling of discontinuities; if too much smoothing is introduced by an interpolation (or regularization) process, then discontinuities are also smoothed over. Our network suggests a novel way to represent discontinuities in orientation (corners) as multiple tangents assigned to the same position. Mathematically this is related to the Zariski tangent space, and biologically it suggests why orientation is explicitly represented in a column of neurons rather than implicitly in terms of two orthogonal 'basis neurons.' To carry this point one step further, multiple values of curvature at a point, or two end stopped cells with different degrees of end stopping but the same orientation preference code bifurcations, as illustrated in Figure 9.1. More generally, this idea of multiply-valued representations carries over to stereo (Lappin, Norman, and Zucker 1991) and motion edges and transparency (Zucker, Iverson, and Hummel 1990).

Inferring a covering of the curve

The second stage is much more difficult to define in classic neural network terms and has typically been approached rather differently. Since the tangent is the first derivative of a curve (with respect to arc length), the global curve can be recovered as an integral through the tangent field. Such a view typically leads to sequential recovery algorithms (e.g., Kass and Witkin 1987). But these algorithms require global parameters (e.g., total length), starting points, and some amount of topological structure (i.e., which tangent point follows which); in short, they are biologically implausible. In contrast, we propose a rather different approach in which a collection of short, dynamically modifiable curves ('snakes' in computer vision; see Kass, Witkin, and Terzopoulos 1988) move in parallel.

Recovering the global curve by computing a *covering* of it; that is, a set of objects whose union is equivalent to the original curve, avoids the prerequisite global problems. Let the elements of the covering be unit-length dynamic splines, initially equivalent to the elements of the tangent field, but which then evolve according to a potential distribution constructed from the tangent field. The evolution takes two forms: (1) a migration in position to achieve smooth coverings; and (2) a 'growth' to triple their initial length.

Again, there are two conceptually distinct steps to Stage 2 of the algorithm:

(1) Step 2.1. *Constructing the Potential Distribution* from the discrete tangent field. Each entry in the tangent field actually represents a discretization of the many possible curves in the world that could project onto that particular (tangent, curvature) hypothesis. Now these pieces must be put together. Assuming the curves are continuous but not necessarily differentiable everywhere, each contribution to the potential can be modelled as a Gaussian (the Wiener measure) oriented in the direction of the tangent field entry. The full potential distribution is their pointwise sum; see Figure 9.1 e.

(2) Step 2.2. *Spline Dynamics.* The discrete entities in the tangent field are converted into unit splines initialized in the valleys of the potential distribution. They evolve according to a variational scheme that depends on spline properties (tension and rigidity) as well as the global potential (Figure 9.1e).

The potential distribution is created by adding together contributions from each element in the tangent field; see Figure 9.1e. Changing the representation from the tangent field to the potential distribution changes what is explicit and what is implicit in the representation, and local information is combined into global information. In Stage 1 there were discrete coarse entities; now there are smooth valleys that surround each of the global curves, with a separation between them. The 'jaggies' imposed by the initial image sampling have been eliminated, and interpolation to sub-pixel resolution is viable.

To recover the curves through the valleys, imagine creating, at each tangent field entry, a small spline of unit length oriented according to the tangent and curvature estimates. Figures 9.3a-d are an illustration of the splines in motion. Initially, each spline is born at a tangent field location with unit length. Then, according to the potential distribution shown in Figure 9.1e, the splines migrate in position (to find minima in the distribution) and in length, so that they overlap and fill in short gaps. At convergence, the length of each spline has tripled. (After David and Zucker 1990.)

Since each spline is born in a valley of the tangent field potential distribution, they are then permitted to migrate to both smooth out the

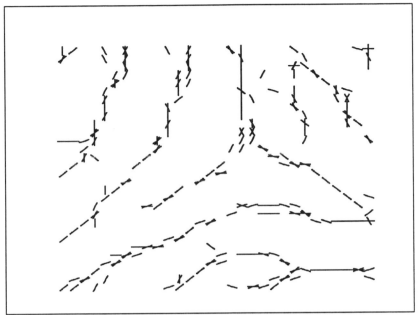

Figure 9.3a

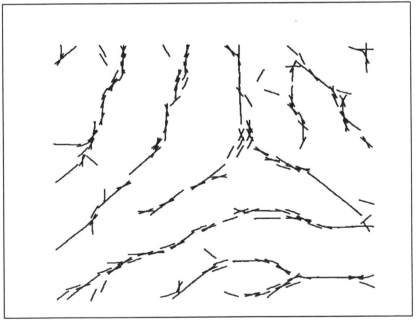

Figure 9.3b

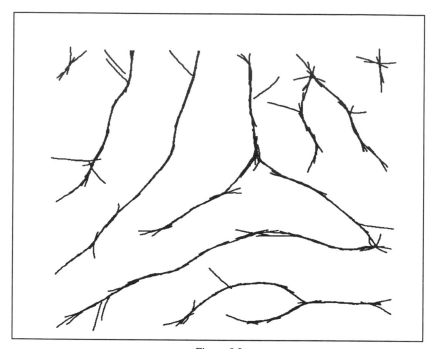

Figure 9.3c

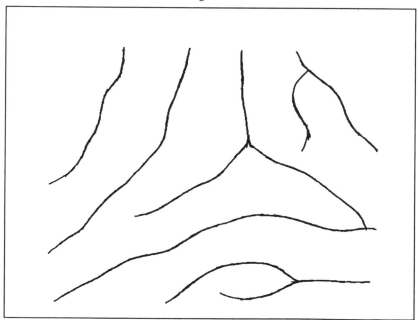

Figure 9.3d

curve and to find the true local minima. The union of these local splines is the global cover. But the splines must overlap, so that each point on every curve is covered by at least one spline. We therefore let the splines extend in length while they migrate in position, until they each reach a prescribed length. The covering is thus composed of these extensible splines which have grown in the valleys of the tangent field potential. Their specific dynamics and properties are described more fully in Zucker et al. (1988); David and Zucker (1990).

It is difficult to interpret these ideas physiologically within the classical view of neurons, in which inputs are summed and transformed into an output train of action potentials. Dendrites simply support passive diffusion of depolarization. Recently, however, a richer view of neuronal processing has emerged, with a variety of evidence pointing to active dendritic computation and dendro-dendritic interaction (Schmitt and Worden 1979). Active conductances in dendrites functionally modify the geometry, and dendro-dendritic interactions suggest that the output transformation is not uniquely mediated by the axon. Taken together, these facts imply that patterns of activity can be sustained in the dendritic arbor, and that this membrane could be the substrate of the above potential distribution computations.

The large constructed potential distributions may bear some resemblance to the large receptive fields observed in areas V4 and IT (Maunsell and Newsome 1987). While any such relationship is clearly speculative at this time, it should be noted that they have two key similarities: (1) extremely large receptive fields (potential distributions) have been created, but they maintain about the same orientation selectivity as in V1; (2) their structure can change. We have stressed how structure is controlled by upward flowing information, but it should also be modifiable by 'top-down' attentional influences as well (Maunsell and Newsome 1987; Moran and Desimone 1985). Attention could easily 'gate' the tangent field entries at the creation of the potential. Mathematically, all the information required for implementing a theory of shape also seems to be available (Kimia, Tannenbaum, and Zucker 1990; 1991).

Conclusion

Curve detection provides what might be thought of as a slice through the visual system. It begins with local operations resembling those found in receptive fields and ends with global operations resembling those required for supporting pattern recognition. We attempted to develop (1) an abstract computational model of this process to elucidate the true complexity of curve detection and (2) a computational implementation to illustrate its engineering competence. From a biological perspective, we attempted to elucidate the function of known cortical circuits, and, finally, from a neural network perspective, we attempted to illustrate a style of analysis involving constraints from both biology and computation.

Two rather different conclusions obtain. First, while much of the emphasis in neural networks and connectionism is on learning, we illustrated the power of actually deriving the structure of networks from abstract problem considerations: in our case, it led to the importance of curvature and a biologically plausible mechanism for computing it. This mechanism has provided new insight into understanding the structure of visual cortex and, in particular, has led to one of the few computational predictions that has actually been physiologically verified.

The second conclusion is more subtle in its statement. While the two stages of our curve detection algorithm seem remarkably different phenomenologically, and are even expressed in rather different mathematical terms, they share a common expression as variational forms. Perhaps this is the proper way to unify abstract problem formulations with the intricacies of neurobiology.

References

Allman, J., and Zucker, S.W. (1990). Cytochrome oxidase and functional coding in primate striate cortex: An hypothesis. *Cold Spring Harbor Symposium. Quantitative Biology* 55:979-82

David, C., and Zucker, S.W. (1990). Potentials, valleys, and dynamic global coverings. *International Journal of Computer Vision*, 5:219-38

Desimone, R., Schein, S., Moran, J., and Ungerleider, L. (1985). Contour, color, and shape analysis beyond the striate cortex. *Vision Research* 25:441-52

Dobbins, A., Zucker, S.W., and Cynader, M.S. (1987). Endstopping in the visual cortex as a substrate for calculating curvature. *Nature*, 329:438-41

–, Zucker, S.W., and Cynader, M. (1989). Endstopping and curvature.*Vision Research* 29:1371-87

Ferrie, F. P., and Lagarde, J., Whaite, P. (1989). Darboux frames, snakes, and super-quadrics: geometry from the bottom-up, *IEEE Workshop on Interpretation of 3D Scenes*, Austin, Texas, 27- 9, 170-6

–, and Lagarde, J., Whaite, P. (1990). Recovery of volumetric object descriptions from laser rangefinder images. *First European Conference on Computer Vision*, Antibes, France

Hubel, D., and Wiesel, T., Functional architecture of macaque monkey visual cortex. *Proceedings of the Royal Society* B198, 1-59

Kimia, B., Tannenbaum, A., and Zucker, S.W. (1990). Toward a computational theory of shape: An overview. *Proceedings of the first European Conference on Computer Vision*, Antibes, France, O. Faugeras (ed.), Lecture Notes in Computer Science, 427, Springer Verlag, New York

–, Tannenbaum, A., and Zucker, S.W. On the evolution of curves via a function of curvature, 1: The classical case. *Journal of Mathematical Analysis and Application*, to be published

Nelson, J.J. and Frost, B.J. (1985). Intracortical facilitation among co-oriented, co-axially aligned simple cells in cat striate cortex. *Experimental Brain Research*, 61:54-61

Hel Or, Y., and Zucker, S.W. (1989). Texture fields and texture flows: Sensitivity to differences. *Spatial Vision* 4:131-9

Hummel, R., and Zucker, S.W. (1983).On the foundations of relaxation labelling processes. *IEEE Trans. PAMI* 5:267-87

Iverson, Lee, and Zucker, S.W. (1990). Logical/linear operators for measuring orientation and curvature. Technical Report 90-6, Research Centre for Intelligent Machines, McGill University

Kass, M., Witkin, A., and Terzopoulos, D. (1988). SNAKES: active contour models. *International Journal of Computer Vision* 1:321- 32

Maunsell, J., and Newsome, W. (1987). Visual processing in monkey extrastriate cortex. *Annual Review of Neuroscience* 10:363- 401

Miller, D., and Zucker, S.W. Efficient simplex-like methods for equilibria of non-symmetric analog networks. *Neural Computation*, to be published

Moran, J., and Desimone, R. (1985). Selective attention gates visual processing in the extriastriate cortex. *Science* 229:782-4

Norman, J.F., Lappin, J., and Zucker, S.W. The discriminability of stereoscopic surface structure. *Perception*, in press

Parent, P. and Zucker, S.W. (1989). Trace inference, curvature consistency, and curve detection, *IEEE Trans. Pattern Analysis and Machine Intelligence* 11: 823-39

Rosenfeld, A., and Kak, A. (1982). *Digital Picture Processing*. New York: Academic Press

Sander, P., and Zucker, S.W. (1990) Inferring differential structure from 3-D images: smooth cross sections of fibre bundles, *IEEE Trans. Pattern Analysis and Machine Intelligence* 9:833-54

–, and Zucker, S.W. Singularities of principal direction fields from 3-D images. *IEEE Trans. Pattern Analysis and Machine Intelligence*, in press

Schmitt, F., and Worden, F. (eds.). (1979).*The Neurosciences: Fourth Study Program*. Cambridge: MIT Press

Zucker, S.W. (1986). Early vision. In S. Shapiro (ed.), *The Encyclopedia of Artificial Intelligence*. John Wiley; second edition, 1991

–, David, C., Dobbins, A., and Iverson, L. (1988). The organization of curve detection: coarse tangent fields and fine spline coverings. *Proceedings of the second International Conference on Computer Vision*, Tarpon Springs, Fla.

–, and Iverson, L. (1988). Computational networks in early vision: from orientation selection to optical flow. In Eckmiller, R., and V. D. Malsberg, (eds.), Neural Computers. New York: Springer

–, Dobbins, A., and Iverson, L. (1989). Two stages of curve detection suggest two styles of visual computation. *Neural Computation* 1:68-81

–, Iverson, L., and Hummel, R. (1990). Coherent compound motion: corners and nonrigid configurations. *Neural Computation* 2:44-57

10

PDP Learnability and Innate Knowledge of Language

David Kirsh

Introduction

It is widely assumed that PDP learnability has some bearing on questions of innateness. If a PDP network could be trained to make correct judgements of grammaticality, for instance, it seems to follow that innate knowledge of grammar is not necessary for language acquisition. The reason, quite simply, is that the learning rules used in PDP learning –whether backpropagation or related gradient descent methods–are general, *domain independent* methods. They are what AI theorists call weak methods. Hence in teaching a system to make correct judgements, we seem to have an *existence proof* that there is enough information in the stimulus to permit learning by inductive means alone. It is this idea, and the methodological implications that flow from believing it, that I wish to explore here.

The problem I have with this argument is that to discover a network that will learn successfully, designers must choose with care the network's architecture, the initial values the weights are set to, the learning rule, and the number of times the data set is to be presented to the network–this latter parameter effects the smoothness of the estimated function. If such parameters are not controlled for, successful learning is extremely improbable. In thoughtful modelling, these parameters are chosen on the basis of assumptions about the nature of the function the system is to learn. That is, on the basis of assumptions about the task and the task domain. Prima facie, then, although the learning mechanism operating on data is a general one, the success of this mechanism depends equally on a set of antecedent choices that seem to be *domain specific*.

If these assumptions are genuinely *domain specific* we ought to reject PDP learnability as proof of inductive learnability. Learning can be viewed as a controlled process of moving from an initial state of knowledge about a domain to a more advanced state. The hallmark of true *inductive* learnability is that the initial state contains zero knowledge of the domain: *all* domain knowledge is acquired through learning. To accept PDP learnability as a sound non-innatist argument, then, requires accepting that the assumptions made in designing PDP experiments are not domain specific.

The idea that assumptions are either domain specific or domain independent, and that the difference is not merely one of degree or merely in the eye of the beholder, plays an important role in discussions of language learning. It is Chomsky's belief, as well as that of many generative linguists who distinguish themselves from Chomsky, that children enter the language learning context[1] with biological constraints on the kind of grammars they will conjecture (learn). It is not an accident of particular social conditions that humans have the *type* of languages they have, nor a consequence of more general constraints on terrestrial communication. Human languages are the product of a specialized neuro-cognitive organ, whose development to full functionality is much like the prenatal development to full functionality of the liver and kidneys or the postnatal development to full functionality of flying in birds, a matter of powerful biological constraints. Change and improvement, though dependent on the environment, is strongly predetermined. The whole process is far more like a progressive tuning–the progressive specialization of a dedicated organ–than an enriching process where a more general purpose organ, largely nonspecific, is converted by powerful learning and development processes into a computational device able to correctly assign meaning to linguistic structures.

The standard view of the PDP approach is that it represents the more general cognitive approach, in which general learning mechanisms and general cognitive architectures–that is, non special purpose networks–do the learning. Instead of interpreting language learning to be a matter of specialization of an already linguistic organ, it is more natural on the PDP model to interpret it to be the product of a progressive construction of intermediate properties which simplify the language learning problem but which *might* apply to domains beyond language. Networks often succeed because they build intermediate representations–representations of properties that simplify the learning task. If these intermediate properties or representations are also found in networks learning in different domains, we have a prima facie argument that network learning of language refutes innatist views of language.

The argument must be called a prima facie argument because given the importance of what appears to be domain specific assumptions made in designing PDP experiments we may well question why we should believe that PDP language learning studies are free of domain specific constraints.The popular reason is that the PDP design assumptions required for studying language learning are no different, in principle, from the PDP design assumptions made for studying learning in other domains. Presumably, the same type of assumptions would have to be made in designing a network to learn English grammar as would have to be made if the network were to learn a function in logic, auditory perception, or motor control. They are generic assumptions. The networks are not gerrymandered or handcrafted, and the learning rule, number of repetitions, and diet are in some sense standard as well. Even if language learning requires bigger networks than do those for bird song learning, or furniture categorization, the networks are just bigger versions of the same sort. Thus, runs this argument, if, one day, a network were in fact trained to judge English grammaticality, on that day we would have strong evidence that innate knowledge of language is not a prerequisite for language acquisition. PDP learnability of language would serve as an existence proof that specific domain knowledge is not necessary for language learning.

Now if this is a sound argument certain consequences follow that are methodologically significant. First, PDP learnability would show that *poverty of the stimulus* arguments about a given domain are false. The thrust of all such arguments is that certain functions are not learnable because the available data do not contain enough structure to determine the relevant function. Accordingly, such functions are deemed unlearnable by inductive methods alone: additional domain specific knowledge is required. This is the central argument generative grammarians have offered in support of their belief that 'the child must come to the language learning task with inborn constraints about the possible form of linguistic rules'[2] or 'with a schema of some sort as to what constitutes a possible natural language'.[3]

In overthrowing poverty of the stimulus arguments, it is natural to embrace a research strategy that looks for previously unrecognized sources of linguistic information. These new sources of information may be located in the way examples are ordered in the training set, in the distribution of examples found in the set, in the frequency with which particular examples occur, or in properties of the context of usage. The methodologically salient point is that whatever the source, this extra information is available through experience. There is more structure present in the data confronting subjects than is apparent a priori. It is not surprising, then, that much PDP natural language research is devoted to uncovering the learning potential of novel sources of linguistic information.[4]

The second consequence of rejecting the need for innate knowledge of a domain is that we may substitute experiments in learnability for antecedent analysis of the domain–at least in the first stages of research. Because a function may be learned by a PDP system whether or not we already have a comprehensive theory of the function, it is not necessary to spend long hours in analysis *before* we set our net to learn it. One of the greatest differences between PDP approaches to language learning and innatist approaches is that innatists *begin* with a characterization of adult grammar and work backward to figure out how the child might arrive at this 'steady state' characterization.[5] PDP and other more purely empiricist approaches work *forward* from the existing data about children's linguistic behaviour to some characterization of adult language. It is easy to imagine, therefore, that PDP theories of the 'steady state', if such a community wide state even exists in their scheme, will be quite unlike theories of the steady state put forward in the generative tradition.

Genuine success in this methodology would mark a strong victory for *bottom up* research. At present, the best articulated and most widely admired method of cognitive research is the *top down* approach of David Marr. In this methodology formal specification and mathematical analysis take place *before* computational modelling. The prime defence of this top down style of research is an a priori argument: without antecedent analysis computational modelling can be no better than blind wandering in mechanism space. A priori, the chance of striking on a plausible biological design, one that might explain what we know of an organism's behavioural capacities, is simply too small to warrant attempting a search in design space undirected by prior formal analysis of the task. No general search techniques, no weak methods, can succeed. Against this negativism, the promise of PDP research is that if it can deliver a few striking empirical successes–cases where a plausible design has been found by using a general learning rule– we have a good reason for being optimistic that the search in mechanism space can be made tractable. The net effect might be to reset the agenda of a large, currently intransigent group of cognitive scientists.

With such weighty consequences at stake, it is worth exploring carefully what PDP learnability may teach us about innate knowledge. My main concern in what follows is with the logic of the argument: vis. that a display of PDP learnability constitutes an existence proof of inductive learnability. I will use language acquisition as my focal domain because it is an area so widely discussed. But it is incidental to the main point.

It seems to me that the heart of the anti-innateness argument requires a clear understanding of what the phrases *domain specific knowledge* and *domain independent knowledge* mean. PDP learning is meant to be an example of domain independent learning–learning that proceeds without the help of additional domain specific constraints or domain specific knowledge. If I am right, the concepts of domain specific and domain independent are too ill understood to bear the weight of the innatist non-innatist rhetoric normally associated with them. Accordingly, I doubt that the agenda of most cognitive scientists will be reset by a few PDP success stories.

The paper is divided in three. In part I, I reconsider some arguments deriving from Gold's theorem purporting to show that PDP learnability could not possibly disprove the need for innate knowledge of language. Gold showed that it is impossible to learn a context-free (or more powerful) language purely on the basis of data about grammatical sentences– a form of data that is usually called positive evidence. The learner must have access (at least tacitly) to additional information. In principle, this information could come from many sources. But, typically, the theorem is used to justify the belief that the relevant extra information is innate and is specifically about the formal structure of language. I believe this is a mistake. But many innatists see Gold's theorem as a logical obstacle to anti-innatism–PDP inspired or otherwise.

In part II, I begin exploring in greater depth some of the hidden complexities behind the notions of domain specific and domain independent knowledge. Part of the confusion enshrouding these ideas can be traced to the equally problematic notions of problem structure and task environment. I discuss some problems with these in Part III.

What Should We Learn from Gold's Theorem?

In 1967, Gold posed the problem of language learning in formal terms.[6] The field of language acquisition has never been quite the same since. Gold asked the question: under what conditions is it possible to learn the correct context free grammar of a language given a set of training instances? His most significant result was that it is impossible to learn the correct language from positive examples alone. If a blind inductive program is given an infinite sequence of positive examples, the program cannot determine a grammar for the correct context free language in any finite time. The data underdetermine the language. If learners are to induce correctly, they must have access (at least tacitly) to additional information.

The simplest source of this information is an informant who can tell the learner whether or *not* a given string is grammatical. By using these extra *negative* examples the program can eliminate grammars that are too general. If 'negative evidence' is unavailable the language may still be learned but the additional information must come from different sources.

Gold's result is thought to be relevant to *human* language learning and, therefore, to PDP research into language learning because there is a body of literature maintaining that negative evidence is not available to children.[7] Parents do not intentionally speak ungrammatically to their children, each time pointing out that this is the way *not* to speak. Nor, apparently, do they tell their children, either directly or indirectly, when the child itself is speaking ungrammatically–not in any pervasive way. They are more concerned, it seems, with the truth or appropriateness of utterances than with grammaticality per se. But then, because there is no substantial negative evidence to stop the child from choosing a grammar that generates a superset of the sentences in its mother tongue, children ought to overgeneralize wildly. They ought to be disposed to believe the grammaticality of sentences outside their language. For without additional constraints on what their mother grammar is like, children have no reason to reject sentences consistent with everything they have heard but which nonetheless lie outside their language. The psychological implication of the theorem, then, is that because children either do *not* overgeneralize wildly or are able to *recover* from overgeneralization, they must have access to additional information about their language that has nothing to do with negative information.

Gold's theorem has often been taken as supporting innatists in their belief that the extra information about language must be inborn.[8] Part of this belief is justified on the grounds that linguistic knowledge is so specific; linguistic properties seem to resemble little else. Thus, when Chomsky suggests that there are biological constraints on the kind of grammars children will conjecture he has in mind constraints on the sort of basic entities or categories–the parts of speech–children will consider trying out in rules of grammar. There may be analogues of such sub-recursive structures in other cognitive domains, but it is not obvious where. And when it comes to constraints on the way those entities or categories can be combined, transformed, or removed, it is even less clear that there are other cognitive domains (universally learnable) which have as much structure.

To take a simple example, a child is assumed to be able to detect at an early age that its linguistic community is using subject-verb-object word order. The abstract categories of subject, object, and verb are not inferred from observed regularities, it is said, they are innate. More precisely, the child is innately predisposed, at a certain stage of maturity, to represent linguistic data in structural fashion. This quite naturally simplifies the learning problem, for it allows that the input which serves as data for learning language comes in a preprocessed form. Language acquisition starts only after these abstract categories are

represented by the child. They are called *abstract* because 'their boundaries and labeling are not in general physically marked in any way;
rather, they are mental constructions.'[9]

According to innatist doctrine, language acquisition is further simpli-
fied by additional constraints that come into play when triggered by
certain discoveries. Thus, once a child notes its language has S-V-O
structure a set of triggers are fired–or parameters set–concerning related assumptions, such as that the language is not inflected.

Now because of all these constraints[10] on how children conjecture
grammars the class of learnable grammars is an immensely reduced
subset of context free grammars plus transformations. Only certain
grammars are possible *starting places*, because only certain grammars
will satisfy the framework of rules and principles and, because of additional constraints, only certain grammars are *accessible* at any point.
Universal grammar, therefore, constrains the possible trajectories of
learning as well as the space of learnable grammars.

Needless to say, one of the most unpalatable aspects of the strong innatist position is the very specificity of the framework of rules and principles. In order to combat this view and to show that stable grammars
are learnable without such specific assumptions about the nature of linguistic structures and representations, PDP oriented linguists have
sought new sources of empirical information about language.

From a PDP perspective, where might this extra information come
from? Two empirical sources are obvious candidates: observable facts
about the communicative context and spoon-feeding the child a special
diet of sentences to learn from. Let us briefly consider each in turn.

The first conjecture is the most obvious: in early phases of language
learning parents tie many of their utterances to visible circumstances. If
a child were to assume that what it hears at first relates to the structure
of the visual scene in front of it, then it has extra information about the
content of the utterance. No one of any linguistic persuasion, to my
knowledge, has seriously denied that the context of utterance supplies
valuable information to learners of a language. Ostension is an integral
part of language learning. The mystery which all admit is to explain
how the structuring process in visual understanding, or auditory understanding,[11] might effect the structuring process in language understanding, Indeed how are the two related at an abstract level?

One suggestion, by Langacker,[12] is that the child has structural schemata to help it parse visual scenes into comprehensible structures. If the
structure of visual scenes is somehow mirrored at some level in the
structure of the linguistic representations of those same scenes, then the
child has specific information about linguistic structures that goes beyond positive examples, for it has pairings of <meaning sound> or, at

any rate, additional information about the meaning of certain utterances. As attractive as this suggestion is, at this stage, convincing neuropsychological *details* of the alleged linkage between scene parsing and linguistic parsing are absent. We suspect that visual scene parsing might be related to either syntactic or semantic structure because we currently believe that almost 50 percent of the brain is devoted to visual processing; that somehow vision and speech are linked since we can say what we see; and that lesions to the visual cortex can have surprising effects on speech abilities.[13] But we have no *detailed* accounts of how a child might use information about visual context to bootstrap its way to a rough grasp of syntax for even directly referential sentences. Moreover, assuming such accounts are one day provided, they still will not serve as proof that context plus positive instances suffice for language learning unless two other conditions are proven: (1) that a child can recognize and treat as special the communicative context without having to be taught that fact using language; and (2) that no information beyond knowledge of context is required to overcome the insufficiency of positive information alone.

In the absence of a formal proof of (2), a PDP demonstration of language learning on the basis of context and positive examples would only be suggestive in establishing their sufficiency for some languages and some data sets. Aside from the need to undertake enough mathematical analysis to generalize the result to many languages and many naturally occurring data sets, there remains our initial concern that PDP learnability is not itself an existence proof of inductive learnability, because so much information is potentially hidden in the design of the PDP experiments. PDP learnability cannot establish that no language specific knowledge is required for language learning until its own design assumptions have been shown to be language independent.

The case is no better with the second possible source of extra information – distributional properties of positive examples and/or the frequency with which they are repeated. If sentences are presented in a controlled manner (simple sentences being presented before harder ones) with the choice of the next sentence to be presented determined by a teacher aiming to push the student on to the best next grammar, might it not be possible to converge on an acceptable grammar?

Perhaps spoon-feeding will work. We already know that for context free grammars a careful diet of positive examples can guarantee convergence on the correct grammar. For it has been proven that, for stochastic context free grammars, 'if the training instances are presented to the program repeatedly, with the frequency proportional to their probability of being in the language ... the program can estimate the probability of a given string by measuring its frequency of occurrence in the finite sample. In the limit, [this method of] stochastic presentation gives as much information as informant presentation of positive and negative examples: Ungrammatical strings have zero probability, and grammatical strings have positive probability.'[14] To date, however, this proof has not been generalized to harder than context free grammars (e.g., context sensitive, or unrestricted rewriting grammars).

When formal proof is absent empirical success is informative. A PDP network which learns a natural language when trained on a careful diet of positive examples will, not surprisingly, be received with considerable interest. But as with claims about structure from context, experimental demonstration of language learning can at best establish the possibility of learning certain languages in certain circumstances. It is an existence proof that there are languages and data sets that can be learned by PDP networks. The trick is to show that this result generalizes to all naturally learnable languages (or that the conditions of learning English or French are isomorphic to the structured data sets used in successful simulations), and that the assumptions built into the design and learning rule of the successful PDP system are domain independent. In short, it is necessary to show that PDP experiments in language learning do not presuppose the very assumption they wish to test: that specific knowledge of language is necessary for learning. It is time now to turn directly to the question of what domain specificity means.

What Is Domain Specific Knowledge?

In AI, the notion of domain specific knowledge became familiar with the development of expert systems where an explicit distinction was drawn between the *general* principles of reasoning built into an inference engine and the collection of problem *specific* facts, goals, and procedures that serve as input to the inference engine. In the simplest case, the inference engine is simply a box for deriving deductive conclusions. Domain knowledge might include premises such as all people are mortal and that Socrates is a person. The output would be the conclusion that Socrates is mortal. In slightly more complex cases, domain knowledge might include premises plus control knowledge to reduce the search of the logic engine, because, given a set of axioms as input, it may take an enormous amount of undirected search of theorem space to locate the sought for conclusion. In still more complex cases, the inference engine itself might be made more powerful, capable of drawing inductive or even abductive inferences. In this last case, the engine conjectures hypotheses to *explain* the input data. Language learning as portrayed in the parameter setting model can be interpreted in this light if we take as the data to be explained sentences about a language, and

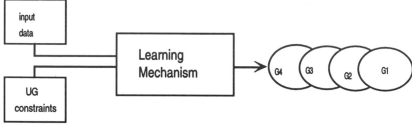

Figure 10.1.Input about the linguistic data available to children is fed into an abductive inference engine–labelled learning mechanism in this picture–along with constraints on possible hypotheses taken from the theory of Universal Grammar (UG). The job of the learning engine is to generate a grammar consistent with data and constraints. G1, G2, G3, and G4 are successive conjectures of that grammar. In reality the information present in UG may be built into the learning mechanism. But the contribution of UG is logically extractable and so is represented as a separate input.

add to that data additional inputs concerning the type and range of plausible conjectures and interparameter constraints. See Figure 10.1.

The AI distinction between domain specific and domain independent is not a rigorous one. The intuition appealed to is that a piece of information is domain specific if it is *not* useful or applicable in many different domains or many different types of problems. General strategies for deduction, induction, and abduction, then, as well as general strategies for search, sorting, and classifying normally fall on the domain independent side. On the domain dependent side, we expect to find specialized search control knowledge, metrics on goodness and so on, and factual data about the domain entities and their relations. Let us see if this intuitive idea can be tightened up.

General Cognitive Resources Versus Domain Knowledge

To begin, consider why we normally suppose there is a difference between general computational or cognitive *resources* and domain *knowledge.* Chomsky has long drawn a distinction between linguistic competence–the system of *knowledge* an agent has about the grammar of its language– and linguistic performance–the system of linguistic behaviours an agent displays. According to the doctrine, linguistic performance inevitably falls short of displaying a speaker's full competence because real agents have limited memory, calculating speed, and awareness, in short, limited general cognitive capacities.[15] It is these resource limitations, not knowledge, which explains why we find people revealing deficits in comprehending sentences with embedded clauses and the like.

Central to the competence performance distinction, then, is the idea that these performance deficits are general and have nothing to do with linguistic domains in particular. Computations have costs, and these invariably become reflected in performance. Let us look at this difference between computational resource and domain knowledge more closely.

Classically, computational resources are the primary *quantitative* features of a computation. The amount of short and long-term memory used, or the number of steps required to calculate an answer, are standard resource attributes of computations. They are measurable aspects of a process. Knowledge, by contrast, is a *qualitative* feature [16] of both a computational process and a computational system. In setting up a system to perform a given computation, knowledge of the algorithm driving the computation must be installed. If this algorithm is correct the system can be interpreted as containing knowledge of this procedure as well as knowledge of certain aspects of the problem domain it was designed to work on. This latter knowledge need not be explicitly represented anywhere in the system, and indeed is usually thought to be implicit knowledge of facts about the domain that are responsible for the algorithm's success. Knowledge of the algorithm and its success conditions tend to remain constant throughout a computation. But most of the remaining knowledge in the system is explicit and tends to change moment by moment as the computation unfolds. Thus, at the outset of a problem, a system may have explicit knowledge of the input of the particular problem instance it is to solve. For example, it may know explicitly that its current problem is to derive the cube root of 125. At the close of the computation, it explicitly knows that the answer is five.[17] The trajectory of explicit knowledge states in between is a function of both resources and algorithm.

Owing to the difference in nature between resources and knowledge, it is usually possible to distinguish limitations in processing capacity due to a shortage of *resources* from limitations due to shortages of *knowledge*. Shortages of resources, unlike shortages of knowledge, typically show up as a system tackles problem instances of larger size. For instance, a system endowed with the right (algorithmic) knowledge to calculate cube roots should be able to compute the correct answer for any sized cube. But, of course, as the size of the input number grows, there inevitably comes a point where either more memory is required or more time is needed than is available. The knowledge sufficient to compute these larger numbers has not changed; so there is no *need* to add additional knowledge, although this would help. The problem, rather, is that the system has run out of resources.

Shortages of knowledge, unlike shortages of resources, typically show up even on the smallest problems. A system that does not know how to calculate cube roots is no more likely to hit on the correct answer for a small number than a large number. Its success is *random* with respect to number size. Furthermore, the addition of knowledge, unlike the addition of resources, need not improve performance in linear or even in monotonic fashion. A system missing just one crucial piece of knowledge may perform no better than a system missing several pieces. By contrast, additions to memory or computing time characteristically improve performance monotonically.

The upshot is that changes in resources seem to have domain independent effects, either increasing or decreasing performance across domains–while changes in knowledge seem to have domain specific effects–either increasing or decreasing performance on specific problems.

This correlation becomes even more robust when we consider how a system might compensate for a loss of knowledge as compared with how it might compensate for a loss of general memory or allotted time. A reduction in memory or processing time can be accommodated on *any specific problem* simply by adding more assumptions–knowledge–about that problem's solution. As more information is made explicit about the answer set, less computation is required. This follows because, at bottom, computation is nothing more than the process of making explicit information available in an implicit form in a complete specification of the problem. For any *particular* problem, then, knowledge can compensate for resource loss. But no amount of additional computational power can make up for a knowledge poor system. If there is not enough information in a complete specification of a problem to determine an answer set, the problem is ill-posed, and no amount of cleverness in search or of additional brute computation can compensate. The answer is not implicit in the problem. Hence, resources cannot compensate for lack of domain knowledge.

Domain knowledge, on this account, is primarily about the problem to be solved: the kinds of entities that can serve as answers to problems, their range of values, and facts about the particular problem instance. This knowledge is necessary if the system is to have a clear idea of the problem. Successful systems will have additional knowledge about potentially useful algorithms and, possibly, why they succeed. If the knowledge in this algorithmic component is heuristic, it concerns methods, hints, and ideas that can reduce search. In principle, it is not essential and its loss can be compensated for simply by generating more possible answers and testing them for correctness. To do this requires knowledge of what can serve as a candidate answer and the conditions a correct answer must satisfy–that is, essential knowledge of the problem. Accordingly, it would be more precise to say that resources cannot compensate for non-heuristic knowledge loss.

We now can operationalize at least part of the intuitive notion of domain specific knowledge as follows:

> A bit of knowledge is domain specific if its loss would have an irremediable effect on task performance. No amount of additional memory or time is able to bring performance back to its prior level.

Because this definition does not cover heuristic knowledge, which is widely understood to be knowledge of domain regularities necessary for converting weak methods to strong methods, I shall call it *essential domain knowledge*.

On the assumption that this operational definition captures one important aspect of our intuitive idea of domain specifity, let us try applying it to the assumptions built into PDP experiments.

Recall the nature of the PDP design problem. Working from a more or less careful account of a problem–for example, learn phrase structure grammar from a given set of positive examples –the PDP designer must choose an appropriate network type, topology, number of hidden units, momentum factor, ordering of the data, number of trials, and so forth that s/he believes will succeed. To inform his/her choices s/he will make certain assumptions about the order, smoothness, regions of greatest interest and so on of the function the network is to learn (henceforth, the *target function*).

How are these assumptions embodied in PDP systems? The order of the target function correlates with the number of hidden units, that is, *space*; the smoothness of the function correlates with the number of times the data set is trained on[18], that is, the *time* the leaning rule is to be run; the regions of greatest interest correlate with the distribution of samples in the data set, that is, with factors external to the computation, and the choice of net type–feedforward, Boltzman, fully recurrent, and so on–correlate with the type of function (associative, predictive), that is, with the structure of the network itself. In short, at least two of the assumptions built into PDP experiments–assumptions of the order and smoothness of the target–which, on the surface, appear to be domain specific, fail to be so according to our operational definition of essential domain specificity because there is a correlation between resource and knowledge.

What, then, are we to say about the status of these assumptions? If it is true that in PDP systems one of the ways to embody knowledge about the target function is by altering the resources available for computation, for instance, by adding (memory) units, or by adding to training time, we seem obliged to regard much of the design knowledge built into networks as being domain independent.

Admittedly, there remains the possibility that this knowledge is heuristic knowledge; it is not essential domain knowledge, but, nonetheless, domain specific. However, I doubt that this can be correct. First, if choice of number of hidden units were important for efficiency only, and networks with the wrong number of units were capable of learning, (only less likely to do so on any given learning attempt), then it ought to be possible in principle to learn arbitrary functions even in networks with few units. But we know from Minsky and Papert's analysis of perceptrons [19] that this is false. Second, if the choice of the number of learning trials were merely of heuristic value, it ought to be possible to learn functions of arbitrary smoothness. Yet, as is well known, the smoothness of a function cannot be estimated reliably from noisy data. It is a desideratum which must be set. But then number of learning trials, like number of hidden units, is not merely heuristic knowledge, it is essential knowledge, for it effects the very way we understand the problem.

Should we reject our operational definition of essential domain knowledge, or should we reject the idea I have been tacitly assuming all along, that choice of hidden units and trial repetitions is domain dependent, that is, domain specific knowledge? My inclination is to drop the definition. In fields like econometrics, where statistical estimation of target functions is the stuff of life, the shape of the target (e.g. $y = ax^3 + bx^2 + cx + d$ or $y_t = ay_{t-1} + b$) is drawn from the theory of economics. The econometrician 'relies heavily on a priori knowledge [drawn from] economic theory.'[20] These assumptions are not merely heuristic; they are necessary to an adequate specification of the estimation problem. But, then, are they not as domain specific as assumptions can be? If domain specific knowledge is necessary for statistical estimation of functions in econometrics, why would it not also be necessary for PDP modelling of cognitive capacities, which is also interpreted as a mechanism for estimating functions? Let us try another tack at making more precise the intuitive notion of domain specific knowledge.

Transparency of Domain Knowledge

Why do the assumptions made in the language learning models of generative linguistics seem to be domain specific? One easy answer is that those assumptions *transparently* refer to entities, facts and regularities of languages. Parameter setting models are based on the theory of UG (universal grammar) which adverts to structural descriptions of sentences, to constraints on transformations between those essentially linguistic structures, and to entities or notions such as *bound anaphor*, which are undefined outside of language studies. Parameter setting models are transparently about language because the concepts mentioned in these language learning models cannot be readily divorced from language. One could *define* a set of mathematical structures that are isomorphic to the structures discussed in generative linguistics and so convert linguistics into a branch of mathematics that now is about formal structures rather than human languages. But these formal structures are not *motivated* by extra-linguistic considerations. They are solely motivated by the study of language. Thus, it is not an accident that there is an independent mathematical theory of tree structures, but not of phrase structures or bound anaphors. These last are too idiosyncratic. (See Figure 10.2.)

It is worth putting this argument in simpler terms. What makes a set of assumptions specific to a domain is that those assumptions are about entities and structures that are *special* to that domain. They are not general mathematical entities, such as functions or graphs, which have general application to many fields. They are highly specific and idiosyncratic–so idiosyncratic that the only natural way of talking about those entities and structures is in the terms developed in the empirical domain to which they belong. Non-generality of structure naturally leads to transparency of discourse.

Thus we have a new definition:

> Knowledge is domain specific if it transparently refers to entities and facts that are not general or generic but, rather, specialized and idiosyncratic to the domain in question.

On this account, PDP based theories of language learning, based as they are on assumptions about the form, style and size of networks

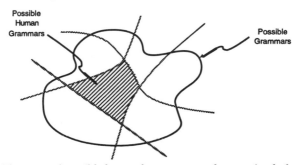

Figure 10.2: The space of possible human languages may be conceived of as a partition on unrestricted rewrite grammars. But whereas there are independent mathematical reasons for supposing there is a genuine family of functions called context free grammars, there are no such reasons motivating the family of functions called possible human grammars. The partition is idiosyncratic. If there were no such structures as natural human languages to study and describe, it is unlikely mathematicians would regard such a class as a coherent family.

needed to instantiate certain linguistic functions, the learning rule, the kind and distribution of data it will be trained on, and the number of times the data will be sent through, mention nothing that is transparently about language. Virtually the same assumptions could apply, for all we know, to auditory processing, linguistic processing, or visual processing; and the very same network and learning rule, if fed different data, could be used to learn other functions. So, prima facie, language learning networks do not contain knowledge about the linguistic domain per se; they contain knowledge about the formal properties of certain functions. Hence, PDP learning models contain no domain specific knowledge.

As reasonable as this argument may seem there is at least one good reason for not accepting it: descriptions do not have to *appear* to be about the objects they refer to in order to *actually* refer to them. Transparency of reference cannot be necessary for domain specificity.

The argument for non-transparency is familiar in philosophical circles. Descriptions may be referentially opaque. It is possible to refer to the actions of a pocket calculator as *the manipulation of numbers* rather than as the manipulation of numerals or electric currents and to the field of physics as *whatever physicists study*. The common feature of these descriptions is that they refer indirectly. They seem to be about one thing– numerals, electric current, the actions of physicists–but, in fact, refer to entities that are more directly designated by other expressions– numbers, quarks, and force fields.

But then we can grant that transparency can serve as a *sufficient* condition for knowledge being specifically about a domain yet deny that it is a necessary condition. It is entirely natural that descriptions of networks and data sets appear to be about networks and data sets, and that the assumptions going into the choice of an architecture seem to be about the order and shape of the target function–yet they nonetheless refer to assumptions about linguistic properties and structures. Transparency of reference is not necessary for domain specificity.

Evidently neither referential transparency nor the difference between competence and performance can serve as an adequate basis for determining if a given body of information is domain specific or not. I want now to consider another line of thought: information is domain specific if it is nomologically tuned to the regularity of a domain.

Law-like Attunement to Domain Regularities

Consider once again parameter setting models. Perhaps the strongest reason for regarding parameter setting models of language acquisition to be so clearly about language specific entities and facts is that every accessible parameter setting in one of these theories defines a *possible* language–a possible human grammar. Parametric space somehow mirrors linguistic space. The intuition here is that the parametric framework is perfectly *tuned* to the structure of human language. [21] This means that the assumptions that are built into a parametric model are not just about English or French or a few other natural languages–that is, *particular* examples of the language learning task. They are about any language that a human now or in the future could speak–that is, *any* example of the task. All and only possible human languages are definable as vectors in parameter space. No non-human languages are describable. (See Figure 10.3.) Thus, what makes parameter setting models seem to be about human language rather than, say, about some formal game, is that they are tuned to the possible–not merely the actual. The formalism of parametric theories is (supposed to be) perfectly adapted to language. It is related in a *lawlike* way to language because it captures what is essential to language–the constraints on possibility.

The idea here is that the way to decide whether a system has knowledge about a given domain and not about some other domain is to consider the counterfactual implications of the assumptions it embodies. There is a familiar precedent for this. The normal way of deciding whether a person has a particular concept–say, the concept of cup–is to

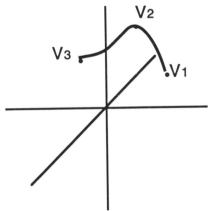

Figure 10.3: In this figure each dimension refers to a parameter. Whether some of these parameters are continuously tunable, discretely tunable, or have just two settings (on, off), and whether the total number of parameters is fixed by the time the child has bootstrapped to the parameter tuning phase, is currently a matter of dispute. As the child learns more about its mother tongue it shifts its position in parameter space. Thus each possible grammar the child entertains can be represented as a vector in parameter space. It is a further assumption of UG that there are constraints between parameter settings, so that not all vectors are possible. Only certain points are accessible. The points V1, V2, and V3 represent a sequence of grammars the child has conjectured.

see if he or she calls all cups *cups* and then to see if s/he is disposed to go on to use *cup* in the right way in the future. Shown cup-like objects s/he has never before seen, a person must classify them the way people who we agree understand the term would also classify them. That is, we assume concept owners have the right counterfactual dispositions. It is this counterfactual ability that is thought to distinguish coincidental connection from lawlike connection. It locks the concept to its referent.

We can state this condition on domain specificity as follows:

Knowledge is specific to a domain if it is connected in a law-like way to the possible entities and structures of that domain.

Although we cannot use this as an operational definition of domain specific knowledge unless we can decide when the elements of knowledge are connected to entities in a lawlike way, we can still put to use the idea that assumptions built into a computational system are domain specific or *task specific* when they are exactly tuned to the properties of the task. For instance, we can ask what conditions a network would have to satisfy to be counterfactually attuned to language in just the way parameter setting models are. If we were to discover that successful language learning networks satisfy these conditions, then we would have reason to suspect that the assumptions that go into their design are equal in size and specificity to those built into parameter setting models. If we think the one has domain knowledge built into it, we ought to believe the other has it too.

Here, then, are the conditions on a networkese version of a parameter setting model.

(1) There is a well defined family of networks N_0–the class of networks pre-tuned to the structure of human languages–that have the appropriate design to learn any human language when subjected to the same type of linguistic data as are human children.

(2) The trajectory of grammars (system of linguistic behaviours) these networks would describe as they converge on the steady state grammar mirrors that of human children. That is, when learning human languages, these networks are constrained to pass through phases or stages of behaviour that duplicate those which children pass through. Only certain grammars can be tried out in the course of learning. The learning rule, therefore, must be such that when coupled with the data set it issues in

'stable points' –regions of current best estimate of the best function fitting the data–that mimic allowable vector trajectories in parameter space. Each of these stable points represents one of the possible grammars the child is trying out. It is a grammar of a possible natural language.

If the choice of architecture, learning rule, diet, number of epoques, and the rest are as constraining to network and network trajectory as (1) and (2), I cannot see how anyone can deny that network models of language contain domain specific information, and that N_0, in particular, has as much information about language as does a parameter setting model. That would settle the question once and for all as to whether PDP networks have domain specific knowledge in them.

Once more, however, the matter is not so easily resolved. There is at least one good reason for supposing that the assumptions that go into choice of architecture, and so on, are not, in fact, this constraining. Gradient descent methods, such as backpropagation, are too sensitive to initial settings of the weight vector to expect all paths leading to stable grammars to be similar. The same network starting from slightly different intializations could describe substantially different trajectories. The same is true if we are comparing the trajectory of different networks in N_0: each will have its own idiosyncratic path from initial to final state. Moreover, gradient descent methods are weak methods; there is no provision for extra control information[22] of the sort that would overrule choice of the steepest descent. As a result, there is nothing to prevent networks from trying out weight vectors that have no counterpart in parameter space. They are not prohibited from temporarily settling on intermediate representations and subfunctions in their inductive search for the steady state grammar just because those representations or subfunctions are not linguistically 'natural'. From the network's vantage nothing is linguistically natural or unnatural. The learning rule is domain independent.

Here again is an argument for less innate domain knowledge. But note, it cannot be an argument for *no* domain knowledge. For, in the phrase 'counterpart in parameter space', we are making tacit reference to an *interpretation function* that maps vectors in weight space to expressions in another more linguistically transparent formalism. If we could agree on such a formalism, we could apply it to the initial conditions of the entire family of successful PDP language learning networks and look for invariants. Accordingly, in my opinion, the interesting question PDP studies of language learning raise is not *how much* of language is innate but *what* about language is innate.

To solve this will require agreeing on an interpretation function for language learning networks. One major source of dispute among PDP oriented linguists and generative linguists is over what the appropriate linguistically transparent formalism should be. It is fairly clear that *some such* formalism is necessary. For if there were not some way of interpreting the linguistic information in networks, there would be no way of knowing whether two different networks converge on the same grammar or on different grammars. Similarly there would be no way of knowing if there were any interesting linguistic information present in the starting state of all successful networks. It would not even be possible to derive *linguistic* generalizations from studying families of successful networks. So settling on an interpretation function is essential to PDP linguistic studies. But it also throws us right back to the question of what constitutes the domain of language–a question which some see as the defining question of the empirical field of linguistics.

Conclusion

I have been considering some of the problems undermining efforts to use PDP simulations of language learning as existence proofs that innate knowledge of language is not necessary for language learning. Virtually all parties to the dispute agree that some knowledge or some learning strategies must be innate, but there has been widespread disagreement over how domain specific that innate knowledge must be.

I tried to elucidate the notion of domain specificity by appealing to reasonable intuitions which we all have. We think that there is a genuine difference between cognitive limitations brought on by scarce cognitive resources and cognitive limitations due to insufficient knowledge. A difference, moreover, that might clarify the meaning of domain specific. But when applied to PDP style architectures, this distinction proved parochial.

I then tried linking domain specificity to referential transparency: an assumption is about a specific domain if the entities and structures it refers to are idiosyncratic–highly specialized. The more specific the entities the fewer the domains those entities could belong to. Assumptions about those entities, therefore, would have to be about a rather specific domain. This intuition, I granted, could serve as a sufficient condition for domain specific knowledge, but it was too exclusive to be a necessary condition. PDP systems might be built on more generic assumptions about functions and so forth and yet incorporate domain specific knowledge.

This led me to my final intuition that an assumption that is built into a system carries information specific to a domain if it is connected to entities in that domain in a lawlike manner. This has the virtue that some assumptions can be about non-idiosyncratic entities. But it left us grasping for a way of translating the assumptions built into a computational system into a transparent formalism. I argued that, because networks are not transparently about language, we must have an *interpretation function* to map PDP design assumptions into expressions in another, more linguistically transparent formalism–else we could not determine what entities particular system assumptions corresponded to.

The very question of linguistics is what should this formalism be. It is the hope of PDP linguists that the way to discover this formalism is by extensive PDP modelling. It is too early to say how successful this approach will be. One thing we can be certain of, though, whatever theory is eventually preferred, it will show that there is substantial information about language in the initial states of language learning networks. What I hope I have established is that this is not in itself an interesting question–the real question is what is this innate knowledge of language.

I want to close with an argument that should chasten anyone who believes that vanilla domain assumptions will suffice for PDP learnability of language and that the vaunted power of PDP systems to learn intermediate representations can do away with all but the most rudimentary assumptions about language. In my opinion it is more likely that substantial innate knowledge of language–in particular, knowledge of the constraints on intermediate representations – will have to be built into PDP language learning systems, although as yet we have no settled idea what this innate knowledge will look like and how it will play itself out in the design of networks complex enough to learn natural languages.

The Need for Constraints on Intermediate Representations

In any multilayered PDP system, part of the job of intermediate layers is to convert input into a suitable set of intermediate representations to simplify the problem enough to make it solvable. One reason PDP modelling is popular is because nets are supposed to learn *intermediate representations*. They do this by becoming attuned to regularities in the input.

What if the regularities they need to be attuned to are not in the input? Or, rather, what if so little of a regularity is present in the data that for all intents and purposes it would be totally serendipitous to strike upon it? It seems to me that such a demonstration would constitute a form of the poverty of stimulus argument.

The example I wish to discuss is illustrative only. I have no reason to suppose that it is especially analogous to the problem of language learning. But it is consistent with the theoretical nature of much of generative linguistics.

Consider, then, the problem of representation posed by the mutilated checkerboard (see Figure 10.4). The problem is a straightforward tiling question: can dominoes 1 by 2 in size be placed so as to completely cover an 8 by 8 surface with 1 by 1 regions missing from position (1 8) and (8 1)?

To solve tiling problems in general requires substantial search. But as is well known, we are able to quickly solve this particular problem by treating the surface as a square *checkerboard* missing the opposite ends of a diagonal. We can then exploit the familiar property that all tiles along a diagonal of an n by n checkerboard will be the same colour. Clipping the ends off a diagonal will therefore reduce the number of, say, black squares by 2 while leaving the number of white squares constant. Because each domino covers exactly one black and one white square there can be no pattern of tiling to completely cover diagonally mutilated boards.

There are several ways we might interpret this patterned Euclidean space but the one I prefer treats checkering as akin to a geometric construction. A legitimate geometric construction never violates the rules of geometry. It adds additional structures, which, if well chosen, alter the original problem situation by making explicit properties and constraints that were otherwise implicit. When such properties are felicitous they make discovery of the target property easier.

In checkering a board we are adding a structure to the bare statement of the tiling problem. This structure is *not* in the input, so it is not *inductively* inferable. It is a legitimate addition because the way a given space will checker, and the set of properties that follow from checkering it, is determined by the axioms of the space. But there are also an indefinite

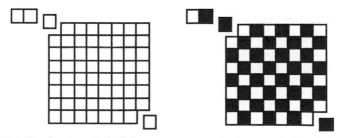

Figure 10.4: Can dominoes be laid down so as to completely cover the board above? The problem becomes trivial if we checker the board. We then note that there are two less black squares than white squares. Dominoes cover one white and one black square.

number of structures consistent with Euclidean geometry which we are not considering, because they are irrelevant to solving the current problem. Choosing the right structure to add requires insight. Accordingly, we ought to view checkering to be a *hint* or better, a *facilitating property*, that lets us discover properties of Euclidean surfaces that would otherwise be hidden.

What if the discovery of grammar requires the same felicitous addition of structure to the data of discourse? If such structure is consistent with the data but not inductively derivable from it, then inductive engines, such as PDP systems, might yet discover grammar by other more lengthy methods but miss the quick discovery that comes from operating with the right hint. This is the spirit in which I interpret Chomsky's arguments about the necessity of recoding the input of speech in structured form.

Now, prima facie, there is no reason PDP networks cannot be designed to bias recoding input in ways which lend themselves to discovery of the *best* intermediate representations. But to do so requires substantial prior analysis of the linguistic domain. The translation to networkese may be as natural as constructing a net in phases, with the global language learning problem broken down into tractable subproblems, each assigned to separate nets to learn. Or, again, perhaps the solution will involve creating low bandwidth linkages between appropriately designed subnets. If either of these cases is close to the mark, PDP theorists will have to enter the design phase with a tremendous amount of domain specific information. For in such cases PDP theorists are not just concerned with the order of a function but with its internal structure as well. That is, they must decompose the function into a set of composable parts–each with its own order and so on–and they must choose a way for the parts to interact.

Acknowledgments

This essay arose out of reflections on the Interdisciplinary Program's graduate seminar in Cognitive Science at UCSD on Language Acquisition. Special thanks to Farnell Ackernam, Marta Kutas, Marty Sereno, David Shanks, and Mark St. John for helpful conversations on this topic, and to Liz Bates for animus. Funding for this research came from NSF Grant DIR89-11462.

Notes

1 Strictly speaking, the language learning context is entered only after having solved the bootstrapping problem. See Pinker, S. (1987). The bootstrapping

problem in language acquisition. In B. MacWhinney, (ed.), *Mechanisms of Language Acquisition.* Hillsdale, NJ: Erlbaum.

2   Pinker, S. (1989). Language acquisition. In M. Posner, (ed.), *Foundations of Cognitive Science.* Cambridge, MA: MIT Press, p. 370.

3   Wexler K. and P. Cullicover. *Formal Principles of Language Acquisition.* Cambridge, MA: MIT Press, p. 4.

4   See Elman J. (1991). Incremental Learning, or the Importance of Starting Small, Proceedings of 13th Annual Conference of the Cognitive Science Society, 1991 Erlbaum, pp 443-448, for an example of PDP research dedicated to uncovering new sources of linguistic information. Elman suggests that children may suceed in simplifying their linguistic problem by searching, at first, for grammaticality in restricted word sequences. Because attention span increases over the early years, children are initially unable to attend to more than a few words of a sentence. As their memory and attention grows they are able to bootstrap to more realistic grammars providing they were successful in assigning structure to the small sequences.

5   Chomsky put the matter this way: 'we begin by determining certain properties of the attained linguistic competence, the attained steady state S_s. We ask how these properties develop on the basis of an interplay of experience and genetic endowment.' [From On Cognitive Structures and their Development, A reply to Jean Piaget'. In M. Piatelli-Palmerini (ed.), *Language Learning: A debate between Noam Chomsky and Jean Piaget.* Cambridge MA: Harvard p. 48].

6   Gold, E. (1967). Language identification in the limit. *Information and Control* 10:447-474. Gold's theorem can be established only if we are explicit about: (1) the space of possible languages, and the one which is the target; (2) the type, order and frequency of information available to the learner which is relevant to determining the correct language; (3) the learning strategy that tells the learner how to create and change its hypothesis about the target on the basis of data from the environment; and (4) a success criterion for deciding if the learner has conjectured the target. Needless to say when any one of these assumptions is made specific it may not resemble the true situation facing natural language learners.

7   Brown R., and C.Hanlon (1970). Derivational complexity and the order of acquisition in child speech. In J. R. Hayes, (ed.), *Cognition and the Development of Language.* New York: Wiley.

8   It is worth noting that Chomsky himself does not appeal uniquely to Gold's theorem. 'I have argued that we can, under an appropriate idealization, think of the language learner as being supplied with a sample of well-formed sentences and (perhaps) a sample of ill-formed sentences–namely, corrections of the learner's mistakes. No doubt much more information is available, and may be necessary for language learning, although little is known about this

matter.' (Chomsky, 'Discussion of Putnam's comments.' In op. cit. Piatelli-Palmerini p. 312.)

9 Chomsky, 'On cognitive structures and their development: a reply to Jean Piaget.' In op. cit. Piattelli-Palmerini, p. 39.

10 The Specified Subject Condition–SSC–is a more complex example which shows the type of innate constraints Chomsky has in mind that might operate on transformations. The SSC asserts, roughly, that no rule can apply to X and Y in structures of the form ...X... [...Y...]... where X and Y are noun phrases and [...Y...] is an embedded sentence or noun phrase, if the embedded phrase contains a subject distinct from Y. Under normal conditions the pairs *each of the men ... the others* and the *men ... each other* are interchangeable without substantial change of meaning. For example,

(1) Each of the men likes the other.

(2) The men like each other.

(3) Each of the men expects [John to like the others].

(4) The men expect [John to like each other].

But in some contexts this not true. Sentence (3) ought to transform to (4). But (4) is neither synonymous with (3) nor even a well-formed sentence of English. The reason the transformation is blocked is that the embedded sentence in (4) contains a subject *John* which is distinct from *each other* so that the relation between X and Y is blocked by SSC.

11 See Bregman, A. (1990). *Auditory Scene Analysis*. Cambridge MA: MIT Press.

12 See, for instance, Langacker, R. (1986). *Foundations of Cognitive Grammar.* Vol 1, Stanford CA: Stanford University Press, and Lakoff, G.(1987). *Women, Fire, and Dangerous Things*. Chicago IL: University of Chicago Press.

13 See Rubens, A. B. and A. Kertesz. (1983). The localization of lesions in transcortical aphasias. In A. Kertesz, (ed.), *Localization in Neurophysiology*. Academic Press, 245-68. Also see Sereno, M. I. (1991). Language and the Primate Brain. *Proceedings Cognitive Science Society*, Hillsdale, NJ: Erlbaum, 79-84.

14 Clarkson, K. (1982).Grammatical inference. In Cohen P. and E. Feigenbaum, eds. *The Handbook of Artificial Intelligence*. Vol. 3, p. 500.

15 A second, and in certain respects more attractive account of the competence/performance distinction, is that performance regularities are the consequence of the particular algorithm(s) driving language use and language comprehension. The same knowledge of language—competence—may be embedded in algorithms with different performance characteristics.

16 The distinction between knowledge as a qualitative property rather than a quantitative property does not mean that there cannot be more knowledge or less knowledge built into a system. It does mean, though, that we cannot measure exactly how much, using a familiar quantitative scale. This restriction applies because first knowledge is an attitude to propositions, and propositions are notoriously difficult to measure. Second, what a system is

thought to know can vary with context and, indeed, with what aspect of system behaviour we are studying.

17 For a preliminary discussion of this idea, see Kirsh D. (1990). When is information explicitly represented? In P. Hanson, (ed.), *Information, Language and Cognition*. Vancouver BC: UBC Press.

18 Both the updating rule and the momentum associated with movement in weight space can also effect smoothness.

19 Minsky M, and S. Papert, (1988). *Perceptrons*. Cambridge MA: MIT Press.

20 M. Dutta (1975). *Econometric Methods*. South Western, p. 10.

21 It is not clear that circularity can be avoided here. For if the defining feature of a humanly learnable language is that it is consistent with Universal Grammar (UG), and the meaning of UG is that it defines the space of humanly learnable languages (the innate restrictions imposed by the language organ on what languages humans might possibly learn) then it is analytically true that UG is perfectly tuned to the structure of human languages. This is one way of guaranteeing a necessary relation between UG and the domain of language.

22 This is not literally true. Most backpropagation methods allow for a *momentum* parameter whose job is precisely to slow the jerkiness of gradient descent. That is, in order to prevent taking very short steps downhill that go off in a different direction than one has been moving, an extra input is added to make smooth transitions more desirable. But the point still stands that this is not a *flexible* control method that allows backpropagation to make use of linguistic information in its moment by moment choice of how to update weight vectors.

2562

2582